THE WORLD OF
ALDUS
MANUTIUS

THE WORLD OF ALDUS MANUTIUS

BUSINESS AND SCHOLARSHIP
IN RENAISSANCE VENICE

MARTIN LOWRY

CORNELL UNIVERSITY PRESS

© Basil Blackwell 1979

All rights reserved. No part of this publication may be reproduced, stored in a retrieval system, or transmitted, in any form or by any means, electronic, mechanical photocopying, recording or otherwise, without prior permission

First published 1979 by Cornell University Press

International Standard Book Number 0-8014-1214-5
Library of Congress Catalog Card Number 78-58631

92
M3189

80090135

Set in Monotype Poliphilus and printed
in Great Britain at the Cambridge University Press.
Bound by the Kemp Hall Bindery, Oxford

LIST OF CONTENTS

	Introduction	1
	Abbreviations	5
I	Men of Business and Men of Letters	7
II	The Wandering Scholar	48
III	Barbarigo, Torresani and Manuzio	72
IV	The Chances of Business	109
V	Academic Dreams	180
VI	Authorship and Editorship	217
VII	The Great Diffusion	257
	Conclusion	300
	Bibliography	309
	Index	333

LIST OF PLATES

(Between pp. 24 and 25)

Contemporary portrait-medallion of Aldus Manutius, and his typographic mark of the Dolphin.

Aldus' pupil and patron, Alberto Pio, Prince of Capri. The date is 1512, but the artist is unknown.

Contemporary woodcut portrait of Aldus, formerly attributed to Ugo da Carpi.

The Slaughter of the Innocents, by Benedetto Bordon.

Petrarch crowned, possibly by Bordon or a pupil.

Martial crowned by the Emperor Domitian.

'I read them as I walk around on the business of the court....' Antonello da Messina's St Jerome, and Bronzino's portrait of an unknown courtier together reveal the change in reading habits that the octavo made possible, and illustrate the comments made by Thurz to Aldus in 1502.

Aldine Theocritus, illuminated by Albrecht Dürer for his friend Willibald Pirckheimer.

INTRODUCTION

To the many readers who will take justifiable exception to it, I should like to confess at the very beginning that this book came to be written by accident. Its origins reach back six or seven years, to a time when I set out, fired with the carnivorous zeal of the recently successful postgraduate, to expand my thesis into the definitive work on sixteenth-century Venetian politics, and began with what I hoped would be an exhaustive reading of all fifty-eight volumes of Sanudo's Diaries. In the event, I got about two-thirds of the way through the first volume. There I found a mention of Cardinal Grimani's purchase of the library of Pico della Mirandola. Soon, I was beginning to wonder about the broader relationship between literary activity and publishing in Venice around the turn of the fifteenth and sixteenth centuries, and to ask myself whether accepted views on the subject were really satisfactory. Still trying to pretend that I would never be able to understand the political conduct of the Venetian nobility until I had grasped what was really important to them as individuals, I set myself to examining some of the intellectual circles in which prominent members of society had made their mark. And so, like many before me, I ended by saying "Right – let's visit Aldus." I was fairly across the printer's doorstep before I realised what a terrifying task his ghost was about to set me.

The truth is that understanding the precise role of a man such as Aldus in the cultural life of his time demands a whole range of academic skills, none of which will suffice to answer the questions by itself, but every one of which claims a lifetime from those who would seek real competence within it. Aldus is remembered chiefly as a printer and publisher, so it is not surprising that much of what has been written about him is the work of experts in typography and bibliography. Here lay my first disability. As I worked through Stanley Morison's lyrical praises of his preferred Roman fount, or

Robert Proctor's Olympian proclamations on the concept of visual clarity, I soon realised that this level of technical expertise could be attained only by those who enjoyed daily contact with the books concerned as part of their professional duties. But I also began to feel an uneasy suspicion that these great bibliographers had their heads far above the clouds, in a world of unchanging and unchallengeable aesthetic truths, and that their encyclopedic knowledge of the exterior of a book was sometimes matched by their ignorance of its contents, and even of the circumstances that brought it as far as the press. In any case, granting that Aldus is remembered chiefly as a maker of books, can he be understood simply as such? He shares with his contemporary, William Caxton, the distinction of having done very well in a quite different walk of life before turning to publishing, and he had no obvious economic or environmental reasons for doing so. So we must turn to other influences, intellectual or idealistic, to explain his career, and sure enough, much of the most stimulating research devoted to his life over the last two decades has been the work of intellectual historians or classical philologists. It soon became clear to me, too, that Aldus was a man of profound convictions, the most profound of all being his dedication to Greek antiquity and its revival. But was I competent to judge him on these terms? I can at least claim to have been well trained as an undergraduate classic, but I stopped far short of the hair-trigger sensitivity required of a textual critic and I have no more than a basic teaching acquaintance with the complex intellectual history of the later Quattrocento. And here again, I found myself wondering whether the intellectual historians and classicists were not working, like the bibliographers, in their own world of eternal verities, and missing the more mundane but also more pressing details of how a fifteenth-century publishing house was run and what made it successful. So I was driven back, finally, to the resources which I did have at my disposal – a reasonable knowledge of the Venetian history of the period and a sometimes rather twisted fascination for the private quirks and foibles of the men who made that history. If I could not interpret Aldus' life and career from empyrean heights of intellectual or aesthetic truth, perhaps I could approach him instead through the grimey and ink-spattered world captured so brilliantly by one of his own friends. This book is an attempt to understand Aldus at what I can only call "ground level": if it neglects higher disciplines in the process, then I can only ask my readers to be indulgent.

Even before my path was clear, there was no lack of friends to urge me forward, and I hope that all will now accept both my thanks and their due measure of responsibility. Several generations of students have listened patiently to lectures into which Venetian printing has been dragged on the slightest pretext: their interest has encouraged me, and their questions have directed my enquiries. The University of Warwick itself has thoughtfully dispatched me to Venice every year, besides providing me with the two sabbatical terms needed to bring my research to a conclusion, and the British Academy generously provided me with funds to spend a good deal of this time abroad. Obviously, my preparation has involved many visits to many different libraries, and while my thanks are due to all the staff who helped me, I must make special mention of the John Rylands Library of Manchester, the Universitätsbibliothek of Basel, the Estense of Modena, the Marciana of Venice, and the London Library, which always seems able to provide what cannot be found elsewhere. My main ally and advisor has been that guru of all visitors to the British Library, Dr Dennis Rhodes, who having for some reason declined to write the book himself has fed me a constant stream of information vital to it and been my final court of appeal on all points of doubt. Ruari McLean directed the early stages of writing: and since he first became aware of it, Sir Basil Blackwell has taken a kindly interest in the project and encouraged me in every way possible. He, Professors Denys Hay and Elizabeth Eisenstein, Michael Mallett and Robert Finlay, have all read various stages of the draft and combed out countless errors. Nigel Wilson has done everything in his power to put a sheen back on my sadly tarnished classical scholarship. Numerous friends and colleagues have helped more than they or I now realise by providing references, translating passages, or simply by throwing a chance suggestion across a coffee-table. I have even dragged Volker Berghahn on several occasions into the unlikely role of research assistant in Greek textual criticism. But at least I hope that Jaynie Anderson, Jonathan Alexander, Humfrey and Susie Butters, Stanley Chojnacki, Cecil Clough, Henry Cohn, Desmond Costa, Conor Fahy, Paul Grendler, Michael Knapton, Reiny Mueller, Marilyn Perry, Chris Read, Rick Ruggiero, and Donald Russell will understand that I am grateful to them, even if they do not quite remember why. Finally, my wife and family have submitted patiently to the vagaries of a husband and father in academic birth-pangs, and calmly accepted the shade of Aldus to their hearth and home. I will not go so far as to say that this book would never have been written without them: it would in fact have been written a good deal sooner. But it would have been a very different book, and a great deal duller.

Martin Lowry   *Langley, Stratford-on-Avon, 27–28 February 1978*

ABBREVIATIONS

The following abbreviations are used for the most frequently cited reference works, collections of documents, and periodical series:

ARIV = *Atti del reale istituto veneto di scienze, lettere e arti.*
Allen = *Opus Epistolarum Desiderii Erasmi*, ed. P. S. and H. M. Allen, 12 vols, Oxford, 1906–1958.
ASI = *Archivio storico italiano.*
ASL = *Archivio storico lombardo.*
A.S.V. = Archivio di stato, Venezia.
AV = *Archivio veneto.*
Baschet = A. Baschet, *Aldo Manuzio, Lettres et Documents, 1495–1515*, Venice, 1867.
Bernoni = D. Bernoni *Dei Torresani, Blado e Ragazzoni, celebri stampatori a Venezia e Roma nel XV e XVI secolo*, reprinted Farnborough, 1968.
BJRL = *Bulletin of the John Rylands University Library of Manchester.*
BMC = *Catalogue of Books Printed in the Fifteenth Century Now in the British Museum*, 9 vols., 1909–1949.
BP = B. Botfield, *Praefationes et Epistolae Editionibus Principibus Auctorum Veterum Praepositae*, Cambridge, 1861.
Burger = K. Burger, *The Printers and Publishers of the Fifteenth Century: Index to the Supplement of Hain's Repertorium Bibliographicum*, London, 1902.
CAM = P. de Nolhac, ed., "Les Correspondants d'Alde Manuce: Materiaux Nouveaux d'Histoire Littéraire, 1483–1515," *Studi e documenti di storia e di diritto*, Anno VIII, 1887, and IX, 1888. (References are to the number of the letter cited, as this selection has been separately reprinted and page numbers vary.)
CSV = C. Castellani, *La stampa in Venezia dalla sua origine alla morte di Aldo Manuzio Seniore*, new edition, 1973.
DBI = *Dizionario biografico degli italiani*, Rome, 1960–.

Ec. HR = *Economic History Review*.
FD = R. Fulin, "Documenti per servire alla storia della tipografia veneziana," *Archivio veneto*, XXIII, 1882, pp. 82–212, 390–405.
GJB = *Gutenberg Jahrbuch*.
GSLI = *Giornale storico della letteratura italiana*.
Hain = L. Hain, *Repertorium Bibliographicum ad Annum MD*, Stuttgart, 1826–38.
IMU = *Italia medioevale e umanistica*.
LBF = *La Bibliofilia*.
OAME = G. Orlandi, *Aldo Manuzio, editore*, 2 vols., Milan, 1976. (References in Roman figures are to the number of each preface, as the division of text and commentary between volumes means that both often carry important material. References to particular passages are given in arabic numerals.)
Panzer = G. Panzer, *Annales Typographici ab Artis Inventae Origine ad Annum 1500*, Vol. III, Nuremberg, 1795, VIII, 1800.
RAIA = A. Renouard, *Annales de l'Imprimerie des Alde*, 3 vols, Paris, 1825.
R.I.S. = Rerum Italicarum Scriptores.
RSI = *Rivista storica italiana*.
Schück = J. Schück, *Aldus Manutius und seine Zeitgenossen in Italien und Deutschland*, Berlin 1962.
SDP = A. Sartori, "Documenti padovani sull'arte della stampa nel secolo XV," in *Libri e stampatori in Padova*, Miscellanea di studi storici in onore di mon. G. Bellini, Padua, 1959, pp. 112–228.
Valla = J. Heiberg, ed., "Beiträge zu Georg Vallas und seiner Bibliothek," *Zentralblatt für Bibliothekswesen*, XVI, 1896, pp. 54–103.
ZFB = *Zentralblatt für Bibliothekswesen*.

I
MEN OF BUSINESS
AND MEN OF LETTERS

On 18 September 1469 a German resident named John of Speyer was granted a five-year monopoly over the craft of printing, which he had recently pioneered in the Republic of Venice. Petitions of the sort which John had presented were very common: they punctuate the records of all the main bodies in the Venetian state, cover every subject from improved windmills to experiments with poison-gas, and were normally treated with the same polite and sympathetic encouragement which John received.[1] Few came to anything. In this case, the thirty or so members of the College who voted on the privilege must have had much else on their minds: war with the newly established Ottoman power in the Aegean; the manoeuvring of their Italian neighbours, who regarded Venice with profound suspicion after her rapid expansion onto the mainland during the first half of the fifteenth century; above all, the preservation of the lucrative Eastern trade which Venice had effectively monopolised since her defeat of Genoa in 1381 and which by now had made her the most prosperous and most envied commercial centre in Europe.[2] John's petition can hardly have been more than a small item of extra business, and there was little to show that, within a few years, the craft which he represented would transform the life of the city more radically than the Sultan would ever do. John himself died within a few months of gaining the monopoly. His work was continued by his brother Windelin, but the privilege died with the original holder and competitors were soon thrusting themselves forward. The disgruntled scribe who complained in 1473 or 1474 that the city was "stuffed with books" appears to have been perfectly right. Since the beginning of the decade 176 different editions had been published:[3] by the end of the same decade the figure would be 593; by the end of the century roughly 150 Venetian presses had turned out over 4,000 editions, representing nearly twice the known

production of the city's nearest rival, Paris, between a seventh and an eighth of the total output of Europe's presses during the period, and, at a very rough guess, twenty books to each individual member of the Venetian population.[4] Not surprisingly, two of the largest-known and fastest-growing private libraries of the age belonged to Venetian citizens, the diarist Marin Sanudo and Cardinal Domenico Grimani.[5] The look of the city itself was affected, for the printers rapidly took over the parishes of San Zulian and San Paternian as their particular quarter, and by the early 1490s rank upon rank of bookstalls tempted the passer-by as he walked from the Rialto down the Merceria towards San Marco.[6] Venice may not have been even the first city in Italy to establish a printing industry:[7] but the amazing expansion of that industry, once established, leaves no doubt that Venice was the first city in the world to feel the full impact of printing, and to experience the most important revolution in human communications between the development of letter-symbols some time in the fourth millennium before Christ and the emergence of electronic mass-media in our own age. Any study of the intellectual, social or economic life of Venice during the later fifteenth century must take account of this fact, and do something to explain it. Why, and how, did the press expand so rapidly? How did established intellectual circles react? How was society affected?

The lure of imagined wealth, and the apparent ease of achieving it will do much to explain the activity of the press in Venice, where the glitter of gold was more inviting than anywhere in fifteenth-century Europe. First, everyone was convinced that printers were rich. "Richissimo", wrote Sanudo of Nicholas Jenson, the most celebrated publisher in Venice during the 1470s. Erasmus credited Andrea Torresani with 1,000 ducats net profit each year, and an overall fortune of 100,000. As late as the 1530s a Basel printer, Thomas Platter, stated his motives with a disarming naïveté which must have been anticipated many times in a less experienced age: "But when I saw how Hervagius and the other printers had a good business, and with little work made a good profit, I thought, 'I should like to become a printer'."[8]

Next, and perhaps more important, there was nothing to stop those who felt this way from trying their luck, for the printing industry had grown up too quickly for the regulations which normally controlled medieval crafts to grow with it. Becoming a printer, wrote Erasmus acidly, was a great deal easier than becoming a baker.[9] This freedom of access probably does much to explain the bewildering variety of people who were involved in printing, and the very different fortunes which their trade brought them. The names of two noblemen, Andrea Badoer and Francesco Viaro, stand on Venetian copyrights of the 1490s.[10] Jenson, once a metallurgist at the French mint, died in 1480 as a papal count palatine and the head of an international company.[11] At the other end of the scale we find Nicholas of Harlem financing his operations in Padua from the largesse of a certain lady, whose jewellery he attempts to redeem from the local Jewish pawnbrokers, or Gerard of Lisa, a Fleming who sinks into debt-ridden obscurity during the 1490s after some thirty years as teacher, choirmaster, ecclesiastical tax-collector and, incidentally, printer.[12] For the truth is that the "boom" of the fifteenth-century press in Venice, like many similar surges of industrial activity, was a mad scramble in which numerous competitors trampled one another underfoot for a vision of prosperity that few attained, since it existed largely in their own minds. The real wealth even of those successful few hardly matched its reputation. Jenson's will disposed of approximately 4,000 ducats, a respectable fortune, certainly, but nothing alongside the hundreds of thousands left by Venice's merchant-noblemen, and a mere tenth of the sum made by one spice-dealer out of one year's shortage.[13] Jenson was probably less typical than Gerard of Lisa. Rather more than 100 printing-companies have been identified in Venice up to 1490: twenty-three were still active during the following decade; only ten survived the century.[14] Some were so small and short-lived that the only surviving traces of their existence are two or three unattributed, and often undated, editions. Court-humanists and dilettanti might rhapsodise about the "divine art", just as later historians have written airily of the Venetian presses' enjoying a "sweeping triumph": the printer, better informed, complained of the "treacherous rage and rivalry which are usual in this miserable trade". He knew that he was operating in a transient, hazardous and ruthless world.[15]

The first, and for many also the final, obstacle was expenditure on capital equipment. It is a mistake even to try reckoning the sum involved in absolute terms, since the different stages of production were not identified in the early days as integral parts of a single process, and the wide variety of aspiring printers had an almost equally wide measure of choice in the size of their investment. What never varied was the need to tie up money over a long period in an unpredictable and highly competitive market.

Oddly enough, the least problematic item appears to have been the press itself. Whether or not the story that Gutenberg was inspired by a wine-press is true, it is a simple matter of fact that the screw-press, set between two upright beams, had been known in Europe since the first century A.D., and was used to produce not only wine but cheese, linen and paper as well. It is possible that some of these presses could even have been adapted for printing: it is certain that the technology would have presented no especial difficulties.[16] As early as 1474 we find Peter the Baker of Padua selling "one press for printing letters, wooden, fully equipped" among a job-lot of bric-a-brac which also included a lute (with case) and a moth-eaten fox-fur. The price asked was 100 lire, or just over sixteen ducats.[17] It is an interesting comment on the ready availability and comparative cheapness of this vital piece of equipment.

Buying or preparing a type-fount was a quite different matter, since the skills involved were much more specialised and some of the processes quite new. The man best qualified to help will have been the trained metal-worker, and it is not surprising that goldsmiths figure largely in documents on early printing, whether they are producing books themselves or assisting those who do in the preliminary stages. To the metallurgist, the filing of a letter-form in relief onto the end of a hard steel punch will have been a familiar task from his experience with hall-marks, or with the preparation of coins and seals. Sinking the punch into a wedge of copper to form a "matrix" for each letter was simply a new form of the old operation. Fitting each matrix into a mould with adjustable sides and pouring in the correct alloy of lead, tin and antimony to form type-sorts of varying width and identical height, were all new processes, but they could be readily derived from existing workshop techniques.[18]

If the tradition that Jenson had been trained in the French royal mint is correct, this could explain a great deal about his success, his influence, and the size of his investment. In his will, he valued the contents of his workshop at the very high figure of 500 ducats, specifically excluding the steel punches which he bequeathed separately to one of his partners.[19] Whether he had also used them to strike matrices for re-sale to other printers is not clear, but in Andrea Torresani's claim to have worked with Jenson's types, and in the fact that some thirty founts similar to his in design can be traced in various Italian centres, there is the strongest suggestion that this was the case.[20] Jenson must stand as our most striking example of the pioneer-printer in full control of the means of production, and the value of his plant shows the scale of the investment that might be needed to secure that control.

We do not know how many printers tried to carry out every stage of type-cutting and founding for themselves, but even before 1500 it cannot have been a very large proportion. Only a minority possessed the technical skills: fewer still could afford the time for design and experiment, which, as we shall see in Aldus' case, might take literally years. Subcontracting began very early. Gutenberg himself paid out 100 gulden to the goldsmith Dunne, and in 1475 one of Jenson's partners, Johan Rauchfass, directed Francesco da Bologna to copy two of the Frenchman's Gothic founts, probably by striking matrices from his punches.[21] Over the first century of printing, the designing and cutting of punches was gradually becoming a specialised service-industry which reached full development around 1540, with the emergence of the Frenchman Claude Garamond as supplier of type to most of the prominent presses of Europe. How far this development had advanced during the fifteenth century is an almost complete mystery. A certain Hans Frank of Strassbourg was described as "a cutter of letters" as early as 1476, and by the end of the century similar phrases, now apparently signifying a distinct profession, were being applied to a number of individuals like Rynman of Augsburg or Corvus of Venice.[22] But the capitalist printer, the ambitious goldsmith, and the amateur engraver, are still inextricably confused. For the aspiring printer, the confusion could only breed difficulty. If he was investing in his own punches, he must buy specialised equipment and a great deal of time. If, like most, he was restricting himself to matrices or even to finished types, he must still buy the metals and the skills required to fashion them. The lucky few with cash in hand would have to make a substantial investment: the small artisan would probably be forced to borrow on the security of future production. And even when he had his two basic pieces of equipment, a press and type-founts, he might still be many months from producing anything.

The largest items of recurrent expenditure were paper and labour, which appear to have accounted for roughly equal sections of the fifteenth-century printer's budget. Paper-prices varied enormously: the smooth "carta reale" cost five times as much as the cheapest grade which could be bought for only 2 soldi per quire, and by 1500 the demands of the market were becoming so voracious that the manufacturers were able to afford a general reduction of charges.[23] But the manufacturers themselves were established capitalists, sometimes holding a monopoly of the supply to an entire area. As small a press-run as 300 breviaries could demand forty ducats worth of paper which, once again, the printer might have to raise on the security of future production: so it was easy for the paper-supplier to turn creditor as well, to issue paper ream by ream as work was completed, and secure complete control over a press if it ran into difficulty.[24] From the other side the master-printer might be threatened at any moment by trouble with his own workers. Labour was not scarce, and a large force was not needed. The earliest illustrations show three men – compositor, inker and "torculator" or operator – at work on each press, so a small company could be run by a nucleus of less than half a dozen all told, and the master who employed twenty or thirty men on six to eight presses was in business on a substantial scale. Only the compositors needed any special training, and to judge by the remarks of contemporary satirists, there seems to have been no lack of unemployed domestic servants and penniless students to fill each and any one of the necessary posts.[25] But though readily available, labour was also surprisingly expensive. The three ducats per month which a compositor earned in Padua during 1475 was precisely the sum which the Venetian government offered in 1492 to a skilled hydraulic engineer, and it does not appear to have been the highest wage a compositor could demand.[26] So far as I can judge from a glance through the surviving records of the Signori di notte, Venetian printing workers do not appear to have been more active or riotous than other occupational groups, but their skills and their feeling of teamwork do seem to have given them a sense of identity which could erupt quickly in the overcharged atmosphere of a workshop that was also a home.[27] For apart from hiring them, the master-printer was normally also responsible for housing and feeding his workmen: this meant finding anything between five and fifty ducats per year in rent, and facing the constant problem of fluctuating food-prices. It is not surprising that disputes were frequent, or that they often took the form of domestic squabbles that make modern labour-relations look staid and sober in comparison. We have record of a group of compositors in Padua staging a walk-out because their beds had not been made. They were sacked.[28]

Labour and capital equipment presented demands which every printer had to face, but there were still numerous incidental items on the budget which, though less regular and liable to affect different men in different degrees, all added to the already formidable list. The soft type-metal soon wore out and needed replacing, so supplies of lead, tin and antimony had to be kept at hand. Ink had to be provided. The small operator might beg or borrow other printed texts for copy, or scratch out a living as a jobbing-printer, but the more ambitious would obtain access to manuscripts, hire professional scholars to edit them, and possibly proof-readers to check the results. Hire or purchase of a manuscript might involve almost any sum. Scholarly editors might settle for prestige and a lump-sum, but a proof-reader could claim a wage of four to six ducats per month.[29] When the Venetian printer Paganinis stated in 1492 that his edition of Nicholas of Lyra's commentary on the Bible would cost him a total of 4,000 ducats to produce, he was presenting a case for special treatment: so was Aldus, when he set the monthly expenses of his organisation at 200 ducats. Such round figures, produced in such circumstances, excite a good deal of suspicion. But we shall see in a later chapter that Aldus' statement of his "cash-flow situation" was more than mere rhetoric.[30]

The difficulties of marketing were if anything worse than those of production. It has been said many times that no sharp line divided the world of the manuscript from the world of the printed book: scribes such as Zacharias Callierges readily became printers, and if printing did not bring sufficient returns, became scribes again.[31] But, though cases like this can be used to show that one generation of book-producers was not immediately ruined by the arrival of the next, they also imply a slow readjustment of the market which brought problems of its own for the printer. He had to sell quickly, and in quantity, to cover the overheads we have just described. But what titles should he select? How many copies should he print? Where should he sell them, and what sort of competition ought he to expect from other printers? The world of the scribe, with its precise gearing of supply to demand, gave no help with these new questions, which could only be answered by equally new and often harsh experience. In the early 1470s an uncontrolled enthusiasm for the classical revival, probably inspired by the professional scholars who advised the printers, deluged the Italian market with more editions of the Latin classics than it could possibly absorb and left the printers with nothing but unsold copies to face their creditors. The Venetian industry reeled, its output declining by sixty-five per cent in 1473.[32] In Rome Sweynheim and Pannartz, who claimed to have printed no less than 20,475 copies of their various editions, appealed to the Pope through their editor Gianandrea de Bussi, who reported that the workshop was "full of printed sheets, empty of necessities".[33] But even a timely grant of benefices did not save the partnership. Clearly, a great deal was learned from the shock. The surviving printers consolidated their credit-structures, sought to exploit special fields as their own, and avoided unnecessary competition with one another. The development of international book-fairs at Frankfurt and Lyons provided more detailed information about production in different centres and business methods became more refined and subtle.[34] Unfortunately, subtlety can take many forms. Some of the petitions for copyright presented to the Venetian government during the 1490s conjure up pictures of a sinister underground at work within the industry: its agents sniff out any new and important work which is in preparation, bribe some disaffected worker, and secure a copy; secret presses mass-produce the stolen text; a cheap version appears on the market before the original, and the poor printer who has invested his money and expertise in the project is left destitute.[35] Accounts such as this are probably over-dramatised: fierce competition in a business which is too young to recognise or implement rules of fair trading may easily have seemed like conspiracy. But the problem of plagiarism troubled Aldus continually, and will play a considerable part in this study.

Time was probably a worse enemy to the printer than the industrial spy. He had not only to distribute a sufficient number of books over a large enough area, but also to realise the profits from their sale quickly enough to cover his investment. The actual process of distribution was by no means as primitive as is sometimes supposed. The pedlar with his donkey has become very popular among later historians, and he definitely played some part at the lower end of the market, distributing woodcuts of a local saint on his feast-day or printed sheets of the latest blood-curdling romance. But the more substantial book, printed or in manuscript, was valuable merchandise to be handled by merchants who knew their business. There is a particularly interesting case in the Florentine Gerolamo Strozzi, who in 1474 received from his clients in London a request for some vernacular translations of the Florentine Histories of Bruni and Poggio. Since he already dealt in books, Strozzi had manuscripts by the following June. But his business-interests took him to Venice and there, for unknown reasons, he decided on a far more ambitious investment. The two Florentine Histories were handed over to the printer Jacques le Rouge, and an edition of Landino's Italian translation of Pliny's *Natural Histories* was ordered from Nicholas Jenson. By the summer of 1476 the original order had grown to more than 1,500 volumes, which were being distributed by Strozzi's agents in Rome, Siena, Pisa and Naples, or transported to customers in Bruges and London aboard the state-owned galleys of the Venetian Republic.[36] This extraordinarily detailed story not only illustrates the easy transition between manuscript and printed book, but shows how both could be distributed by the relatively sophisticated methods of international trade. It is worth recording that during the same period Jenson had 500 ducats worth of stock in Pavia alone, agents in most of the main centres of Italy, and a mysterious English contact named William Tose to manage his affairs north of the Alps. And when we read of salaried agents circulating in university-towns with books for sale, or professors recommending still unpublished editions in their lectures, we appear to be moving into a high-geared world of advance publicity and pyramid salesmanship.[37]

But for the printer's or publisher's position to be secure, the quickening of supply had to be matched at every stage of the trading-cycle, and this readjustment took time: in fact the recorded reaction of both retailers and buyers casts a good deal of doubt on the notion that printing had to be invented in order for the supply of books to meet the demand. In 1476, the year of Strozzi's bold experiment, one bookshop in his native Florence stocked only two printed texts, and Strozzi himself left some very explicit instructions for his agent when business took him abroad again in 1477: "...you must dig the spurs into them [the booksellers] and drag the cash out of their hands. Make them enter all copies you give them in the account-book, in their own hand-writing."[38] In 1482 a retailer in Siena simply returned his unsold copies to Strozzi, and a year later the price of the books had to be reduced.

If we turn from this comparatively well-organised company to one of its more primitive contemporaries, the press run by the Ripoli convent in Florence, we find a comic-opera world in which books are bought piecemeal, on the security of silver spoons or tablecloths.[39] It is clear that many buyers were loath to abandon the leisurely habits of the manuscript-market: and since the printers tried to persuade their customers that printed books were every bit as good as manuscripts, this is not altogether surprising. Even in Venice, where demand must have quickened more rapidly than elsewhere, the surviving accounts of the bookseller Francesco da Madiis reveal dizzy changes in the pattern of sales. Between 17 May 1484 and 23 January 1487–8 Francesco disposed of more than 12,000 volumes: but the number sold in any one month varied between a mere sixty in October 1485 and 535 in May 1487, while the takings in cash might stand anywhere between thirteen ducats and 210. The market was still utterly unpredictable, and the problems it imposed on the small producer, relying on credit, need not be emphasised further. "Even when copies are complete", lamented Bernardino Stagnino in 1496, "they cannot be sold quickly."[40] In sales, as in capital expenditure, the fifteenth-century printer was poised on the edge of a precipice.

To face their difficulties, printers naturally sought to spread the risks out amongst themselves or other interested parties, and an almost infinite variety of contracts, one frequently overlapping another, emerged from such dealings. Some were no more than short-term expedients to cover the cost of one or two editions: Gerolamo Strozzi, for example, had no long-standing concern with printing, but he bought paper to the value of 731 ducats for the texts in which he had an interest and presumably paid Jenson and le Rouge for the necessary time and labour. Then as now, an aspiring author might be expected to shoulder the expense of publishing his own work. Within their limits, agreements of this kind seem to have been popular, especially for risky or prestigious publications: they brought in capital from outside the industry, and above all, they brought in lump-sums which would cover the costs of paper and labour without an anxious wait to see how sales would go.[41] But printers also banded together to pursue more distant aims. From 1507 we have the text of a contract which is particularly important because it illustrates the activity of a Venetian syndicate during the same period as Aldus. The de Tortis brothers, Zorzi Arrivabene, Lucantonio Giunti and Amadeo Scotto set out a joint plan for five years of business and specified the works to be published. Expenses and profits were to be divided into four equal shares: Giunti and Scotto, who in this instance provided only financial backing and were not involved in the actual printing, held one share each; Arrivabene and the de Tortis brothers, who offered four presses and took responsibility for the supply of paper, held the third share jointly: another partner had to be found for the fourth. The printed sheets would be stored in a warehouse whose rent would be paid collectively and to which each of the partners would have a key. Any decisions affecting prices, or the number of copies to be printed, were

MEN OF BUSINESS AND MEN OF LETTERS 17

to be taken by majority vote.[42] The entire spirit of this document is one of co-operative enterprise.

But others show the business in a rather different light. In 1478 Leonardus of Ratisbon and Nicholas of Frankfurt, both resident in Venice, entered an agreement to produce 930 copies of the Bible over the following nine months. Since Nicholas undertook to provide both the paper and 243 ducats expenses, Leonardus, who handled the actual press-work, must have been well protected against the immediate problems of cash-flow: but he could draw the money only in instalments, as each batch of printed sheets was delivered, and he was barred from taking other work in hand. The craftsman, in fact, was bound hand and foot to the financier.[43] During the same year the French typographer, Peter Maufer, signed a new contract with a Paduan gentleman named Bartolomeo Valdezocco who was commissioning a large edition of the *Digestum Novum*. The two men had been associated in an earlier agreement rather similar to that between Leonardus of Ratisbon and his sponsor, and Maufer had ended with debts of 225 ducats to Valdezocco, who took formal possession of the entire workshop in settlement. The new contract made the situation cruelly explicit:"Item, in the printing of the aforesaid work the lord Bartolomeus is to be the superior party and the principal author: he shall collect...all quires of the aforesaid work as they are printed, day by day, until the entire work is completed. Master Peter is to be his servant."[44]

The normal processes of jungle law meant that the risks of printing tended to favour those best equipped to survive them: in other words, those with capital, contacts, and experience. The need for capital investment soon created a special kind of entrepreneur. Convenience demands that we call these men "publishers", though the term is in fact anachronistic since they formed no special group socially or occupationally, and their interest in the business of publication varied greatly. Johan Rauchfass, a Frankfurt merchant whose multifarious activities earned him the title "Big John", may have regarded even his shares in the company of Nicholas Jenson as little more than an exotic item in his portfolio.[45] But Lucantonio Giunti, whom we met in the contract of 1507, and his associates of the Scotto family, clearly operated as professional underwriters, since they formed contracts with several different printers over a considerable number of years. They also printed editions on their own account. Andrea Torresani was active as a printer, bookseller and underwriter for more than a decade before he formed a partnership with Aldus, and he continued to print independently of Aldus for twelve years afterwards.[46] There is a good deal to suggest that these printer/booksellers, who were able to delegate the immediate problems of production to their dependents and sniff the wind of international demand through their commercial contacts, were also the quickest to profit from the invention of printing. By the end of his life Jenson was concerned almost entirely with sales. Giunti more than doubled his company's capital base between 1491 and 1499, and had almost doubled it again by 1509.[47] Beyond question is the fact that, from the first decade of its existence, the Venetian printing industry was acquiring a thoroughly capitalistic structure, and that control of that structure was passing into the hands of merchants or printer/booksellers of the kind we have just described. According to Victor Scholderer's calculations, rather more than fifty presses turned out some 600 editions up to the end of 1481: of those editions, 260 – forty-three per cent – were the work of two companies, those of Nicholas Jenson and John of Cologne; their numerous rivals averaged only seven editions each, and the nearest rival to the output of the two giants was – significantly – an assorted group of seventy unattributed relics. There is, as he commented, "a sharp contrast between the few successful men at the top and the crowd of transient and financially embarrassed phantoms down below".[48]

We do not have sufficient evidence to state bluntly that capital and long credit were the main ingredients of success for the early printer. But the fortunes of Jenson and John of Cologne provide, at the very least, powerful confirmation of money's tendency to gravitate towards money. Jenson was backed from an unknown date by two Frankfurt merchants, "Big John" Rauchfass and Peter Uglheimer, who became a considerable book-collector in his own right. All we know of the scope of this triangular partnership is that Uglheimer's shares in it were ultimately liquidated by the payment of 1,000 ducats in gold to his heirs.[49] John of Cologne's company was a messier and more sprawling affair. He and an associate named Manthen salvaged the remains of Windelin of Speyer's company after the over-production crisis of 1473, and an astonishing lady named Madonna Paola, daughter of the painter Antonello da Messina and widow of Venice's first typographer John of Speyer, brought her personal talents to bear on the problem of cementing and diversifying the new company's interests. She first moved in with Manthen, though without apparently marrying him:[50] she then, at an unknown date, married another printer, Rinaldus of Nijmegen, who was promptly drawn into the syndicate; finally, in 1477, she married off her daughter Hironima to a prosperous bookseller named Gaspar of Dinslaken, who gained a handsome dowry of 3,000 ducats – well above the limits permitted in Venice at the time – and was also immediately made a partner.[51] Throughout the central and later 1470s, the two combines fenced cautiously, Jenson concentrating on legal texts, John and his partners on commentaries: both were obviously anxious to avoid choking the market with duplicated editions, as had happened in 1472–3. But in 1478 an even worse threat, plague, convulsed the Venetian industry yet again. Exactly half of the twenty-two active companies either suspended business or left the city, and the two main rivals, who had naturally been among those strong enough to survive this new shock, appear to have decided that there was more to be gained by joining forces. On 29 May 1480 a protocol brought into being the five-year syndicate of Nicholas Jenson, John of Cologne, and Company: a partnership to which John made an initial contribution of nearly 5,000 ducats worth of books, which was able to turn out some twenty folio editions in the next twelve months, and which exercised such an absolute domination of the Venetian industry that it became known simply as "The Company". The two main partners died almost immediately afterwards, and evidence of "The Company's" overt activity vanishes from the end of 1481.[52] An influx of new names gives the Venetian book-world of the 1480s a more dispersed and confusing character. But far into the age of Aldus, we find hints of an underlying and mighty influence from the past: Hironima, daughter of Madonna Paola and widow of Gaspar von Dinslaken since the late 1470s, still held stocks valued at 660 ducats in 1511, and was owed a further 207 ducats in gold by Lucantonio Giunti.[53] Even more important, perhaps, was the power of "The Company" as a golden image of success, beckoning the next generation to imitate, and prosper.

For as we move from the examination of Venetian printing as such to consider the relationship between the presses and the public, the tactics pursued by Jenson and John of Cologne provide important confirmation of a more general point which has been made about the Venetian editors: they were cautious and conservative, favouring established circles of readers and doing little to encourage the growth of a more popular market.[54] We can prove this observation up to a point from the statistical analysis of editions, but this is a hazardous method. I suspect that far more chap-books and pamphlets than we realise may have disappeared without trace. But we can partly cross-check the statistics from evidence about demand and reading-habits – wills, bookshop and library inventories, the remarks of contemporaries in diaries, manuscripts, or prefaces to printed editions – and the signs still form a consistent pattern. The "new reader" – the man in the street, lacking a formal education – was not an important feature of the Venetian literary world. The printers tended to play follow-my-leader not only with established academic trends but with one another, and by the early 1490s they were beginning to operate in predictable and rather well-worn grooves.

In spite of the crisis of 1472–3, the demand for classical texts remained enormous. Scholderer's figures for the period up to 1481 – 206 editions out of a total of 600 – are distorted by the prodigious output of 1471–2, and both Jenson and John of Cologne clearly followed a much more cautious policy after 1475. But as the century progressed, trial and error produced a list of ever-popular authors – Virgil, Horace, the elegiac poets, the satirists, prose-writers such as Valerius Maximus, Livy, and above all Cicero – and editions followed one another with monotonous regularity. Philippus Pincius reprinted Virgil four times during the 1490s alone, and various works of Cicero account for ten per cent of his total output during that decade. Tacuinus specialised almost exclusively in Latin classics. The sales recorded by Francesco da Madiis suggest that roughly twenty per cent of his turnover in any one month consisted of classical texts, and while this proves that the local market was strong, it must also leave us with the suspicion that a considerable proportion of the total output was intended for export.[55] A good deal of the demand in Venice itself clearly derived from the city's active population of public and private teachers, to whose busy world we shall return in a later chapter. Jenson's text of Diogenes Laertius was edited by Benedetto Brugnolo, the head of the School of San Marco, at the request of two pupils, Lorenzo Zorzi and Jacobo Badoer: in 1478 Giorgio Merula published as a commentary on Cicero's *Oratio pro Ligario* the series of public lectures he had recently delivered; several petitions for the monopoly of particular editions contain references to the interest of students.[56] But it is also clear that demand extended far beyond the schools. In the dedication to his commentaries on Martial, Merula wrote of Marc-antonio Morosini's asking for guidance on that author's poems, and taking Calderinis' commentary to read during his time as governor of Cremona. On several occasions Francesco da Madiis sold virtually complete libraries of classics, and few even of his specialist customers, who came for legal or theological texts, left the shop without taking some Latin literature to leaven the academic lump. We cannot tell whether any of the surviving volumes, often finely bound, illuminated, and carrying the arms of noble families, once belonged to these now nameless purchasers: but we can be certain that the fashionable taste for antiquity was spreading rapidly through the upper echelons of Venetian society.[57]

Though Venice lagged behind other European centres in the production of theological and liturgical works, there is a good deal to suggest that editions of this type formed a vital part of her printers' output, and, before 1500, probably the majority of her booksellers' stocks. In 1572 a papal observer commented: "They [the printers] have been used to relying on these little service-books for their livelihood."[58] At first sight this would seem hardly applicable to an earlier period. Even a printer like Simon Bevilaqua, who produced five missals during the 1490s, turned out a great deal more classical literature during the same period and can hardly be said to have relied on liturgical editions. On the other hand Francesco da Madiis' turnover of theological works, devotional literature, and service-books was truly colossal: it accounted for roughly half his total sales in any one month, doubling the proportion of any other type of material. There are two possible explanations of what seems a paradox: first, it seems likely that a good deal of theological work was brought into Venice from other centres; second, editions of this kind brought problems and advantages of their own, which are well illustrated in a series of directives issued during 1495 by the Patriarch of Aquileia, Nicolo Donato. In an attempt to standardise religious practice throughout his sprawling ecclesiastical domain, Donato commissioned 500 copies of a *Missale secundum rubricam Aquileiensem* for compulsory circulation to all beneficed clergy. The price was set at the very high figure of twenty-three lire - more than three and a half ducats - for a bound volume.[59] Though in this case the work was to be carried out in Augsburg, it is easy to see how the printer who secured such a commission could forget the problems of cash-flow and pour copies into what was effectively a captive market. Wide variations in local practice served to increase the printers' opportunity, and even on the open bookstall, liturgical texts seem to have sold easily and in bulk. On 7 January 1487-8 Francesco da Madiis disposed of 50 psalters in a single batch.[60]

If Venetian printers seem on the face of it to have produced a relatively small proportion of theological and liturgical material, we should remember that the number of editions by itself is no sure guide to the popularity and economic importance of the books concerned. It is clear that the service-book of the fifteenth and sixteenth centuries enjoyed many of the commercial advantages associated with a first-rate text-book in the twentieth: many had to buy it as part of their professional duties, many more might want to do so for personal reasons.

But in commercial value, in prestige, and in sheer bulk all other fields of Venetian publication were eclipsed by the Law. It was a costly and rather exclusive market, into which a printer might have to earn his way by several years of successful activity and careful cultivation of the necessary contacts: some of the most active publishers of the 1480s and 1490s – Arrivabene, Benalius and the de Gregoriis brothers – worked with classical texts for up to five years before moving on to Law, while Tacuinus and Aldus himself avoided it entirely. The reasons for both caution and ambition appear clearly in da Madiis' accounts. The actual number of legal texts he sold never approached the figures achieved repeatedly by classical or devotional literature, and he sometimes sold none at all for several months on end. But when a customer arrived, he bought in quantity and he paid in ducats. During the lean month of September 1485 when takings were down to thirty-nine and a half ducats, nearly a third of the total came from a single sale of seven law-books for twelve and a half ducats.[61] Every fat legal folio that Francesco passed over the counter cost at least a ducat. For the printers, the results of this situation are obvious enough. A legal text represented a large investment in terms of paper, time, and labour, and a novice would generally be unable to face the high risks involved: but for an established man who could sound out the market accurately the profits might be sure and large. Law apparently made the fortunes of both Jenson and John of Cologne, accounting for twenty-nine per cent of the Frenchman's output and forty-eight per cent of the German's: they set an example of success which the next generation found irresistible, for fifty-one per cent of Arrivabene's editions and fifty-three per cent of Torresani's, were also legal. This is one area of Venetian publication where we can be quite specific about the causes of prosperity and expansion. The Venetian industry was perfectly placed to supply the nearby universities of Padua, Bologna, Pavia and Ferrara, all of which were increasing their numbers during the relative political calm of the later Quattrocento, while none had its needs fully met by the local presses.⁶² Cooperation between Padua and the Venetian printers was very close indeed, since the university town was barely twenty miles away, ruled by Venice, and much frequented by its citizens and subjects. Alessandro de Nevo, Pietro Fossano and other academic lawyers edited and corrected texts: when Benalius approached the government in 1494 to seek protection of his edition of Alessandro Tartagni, the request was backed in writing by the rector of the law-school and a number of lecturers; and almost every petition concerning a legal text contains reference to the advantages which students may expect to derive from it.⁶³ There is also a good deal to suggest that professional lawyers, who needed a wide range of reference-works and were accustomed to treating books as necessary equipment rather than aesthetic objects, adjusted to print rather more quickly than those fastidious spirits whose values were dictated by their own visions of classical antiquity. Jacopo Zen, canon-lawyer and cardinal-bishop of Padua, died in 1481 when the presses had been operating in Venice for just over a decade. But when his library was inventoried a year later more than forty per cent of it – 149 volumes out of 361 – was composed of printed texts. So long as he had the books, the Cardinal seems to have had few inhibitions about how they were produced.⁶⁴

The importance of the academic market can be demonstrated yet again, if less forcefully, from philosophical, scientific and medical texts. One of the busiest printers of the 1490s, Bonetus Locatellus, chose to avoid the Law entirely and concentrate on classics, theology, and philosophy, the latter accounting for over half his total production up to 1500. Even an experienced legal publisher like Torresani thought this field a worthwhile alternative, and brought out a burst of Aristotelian commentaries during the early years of the sixteenth century. Pomponazzi's lectures in philosophy could generate as much excitement, publicity, and consequently business as could Jason de Mayno's in Law.⁶⁵ There is no need to labour the argument further: the evidence for direct academic co-operation is similar, and the point to be derived from it is identical. According to all available statistics of production and purchase, the flood of reading matter which poured from the presses after 1470 was aimed at the upper levels of society. It was the established sections of the reading public – priests, teachers in school and university, lawyers, doctors, students, secretaries and clerks – who felt its first impact.

But how were such people affected and how did they react? Though there was an immense range of individual opinions, all can be placed somewhere between committed acclamation and absolute rejection. The mass of cheaper books and the standardisation of material might mean an increasing number of readers, a general spread of enlightenment, a better society, and a surer way to God: or they might mean the debasement and dilution of learning that had once been pure and precious, the spread only of confusion, obscenity and heresy among simple people who would consequently be led straight to damnation. It was a division of ideals which in many ways anticipates the cultural and educational debates of the present day: certainly, the sense of hostility to the press could not be better summed up than by the modern slogan, "More means Worse". But in practice the division was much less clear-cut than one might expect. Few intellectuals were bold or decisive enough to commit themselves wholeheartedly to either position, for there was no traditional thought to give them guidance and the situation was changing so rapidly that many shifted ground uneasily or moved from one extreme to the other. In Venice, where change was most rapid, opinions were naturally very confused: and in seeking to unravel them, the historian is not helped by the easy assumption that, since scholars such as Merula and Sabellico worked for the Venetian press, they were wholly committed to the idea of printing.[66]

The most enthusiastic statement on behalf of the early press comes not from Venice, but from Rome and from Gianandrea de Bussi, Bishop of Aleria and editor for the first typographers in Italy, Sweynheim and Pannartz. Introducing him here is therefore something of a digression: but it can be justified, first, by the clarity of his opinions, second, by the faint possibility that they may have reached the young Aldus Manutius.[67] Whether Gianandrea's views were quite as altruistic as he implied is a debatable point, which I shall not labour here. What matters is that his prefaces and dedications set out a programme which was logically consistent, broadly related to certain current educational theories, and circulated between 1468 and 1472, during the earliest stages of Italian printing and in time to serve as a statement of principle for those who came afterwards. Gianandrea's background had given him a profound sense of the importance of literacy and the duty of spreading it. From around 1440 he had studied at Mantua under Vittorino da Feltre, a philanthropist who overspent the budget allowed him by filling his school with penniless

Contemporary portrait-medallion of Aldus Manutius, and his typographic mark of the Dolphin. From the Museo Civico, Vicenza.

Aldus' pupil and patron, Alberto Pio, Prince of Carpi. The date is 1512, but the artist is unknown. From the National Gallery, London.

Contemporary wood-cut portrait of Aldus, formerly attributed to Ugo da Carpi. From the Kupferstichkabinet, Berlin.

The Slaughter of the Innocents, by Benedetto Bordon. From the British Library, Additional manuscript 15815, f. 11v.

Petrarch crowned, possibly by Bordon or a pupil. From the British Library, C.4.a.5.

Martial crowned by the Emperor Domitian. From the British Library, C.4.d.11.

'I read them as I walk around on the business of the court....' Antonello da Messina's St. Jerome, and Bronzino's portrait of an unknown courtier (shown on the opposite page), together reveal the change in reading habits that the octavo made possible, and illustrate the comments made by Thurz to Aldus in 1502. From the National Gallery, London, and the Metropolitan Museum of Art, New York.

Bronzino's portrait of an unknown courtier.

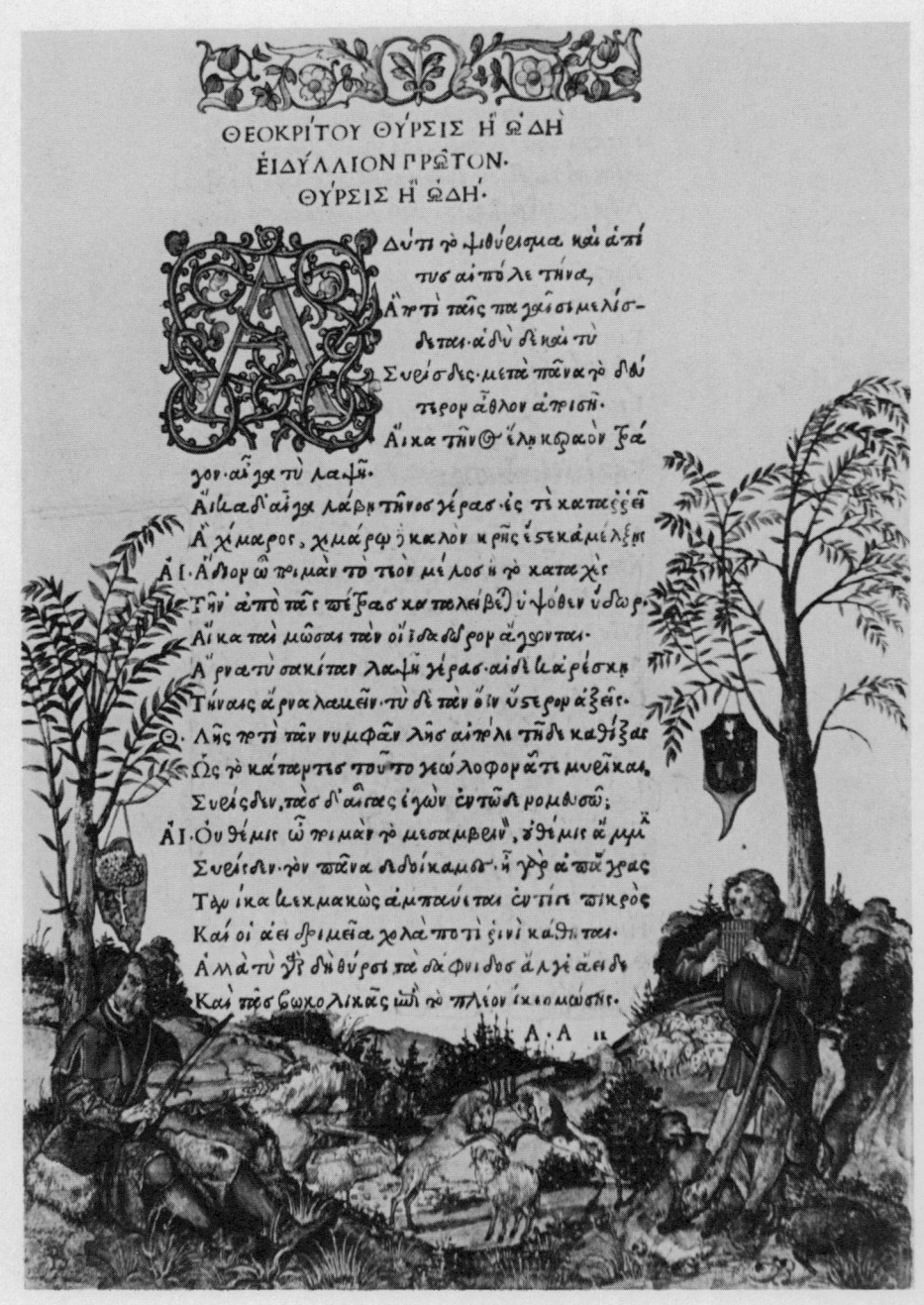

Aldine Theocritus, illuminated by Albrecht Dürer for his friend Willibald Pirckheimer.

waifs, and had on one more than one occasion to be helped out by his understanding patron Gianfrancesco Gonzaga.[68] For a while, de Bussi taught on his own account in Genoa. Then he was exposed to the still more dynamic influence of Cardinal Nicholas of Cues, whose secretary he became in 1458. One of the most adventurous and speculative minds of the century, Cusanus owed his early education to a religious group known as the Brethren of the Common Life, whose wide visions of religious and educational reform included both the improvement of living conditions for students and the large-scale copying of manuscripts in their own communities.[60] We know from one of de Bussi's first prefaces, the dedication of St Jerome's *Letters* to Pope Paul II, that Cusanus had been keenly interested in bringing the art of printing to Italy, and there is a strong possibility that de Bussi saw his work for the press as a means of translating the liberal ideals of Cusanus and Vittorino into reality. The image of the "poor scholar" was constantly on his mind, and soon swelled into a vast army of new readers, eager for knowledge. Books, he wrote in the same dedication, and with a bold neglect of reality, now cost a bare fifth of the price that would have been asked only a few years ago: even "the poorest" were forming their own libraries. His words, and his activity, naturally exposed him to some bitter criticism: the "boorishness, envy and greed" of those who refused to lend him manuscripts and the snobbish venom of the contemporary who called his prefaces "a sewer running past the altar". But his vision of universal enlightenment enabled him to brush such attacks aside, and he would probably have answered the more serious modern critics who have pointed to his ill-informed and over-hasty editorship in much the same way.[70] Hidden manuscripts, however excellent, are not read. Printed texts, however makeshift, will "spread through the whole world in an abundant flood", bringing some copies inevitably into the hands of scholars with superior manuscripts, who will make the necessary corrections, and carry the gradual process of purification and enlightenment one stage further. To Gianandrea, quantity and diffusion provided the answer to all difficulties: "This is my aim, this is my one great desire – that all men of the Latin world may become more learned, and that I may be among them."[71] The crisis of 1472–3, whose effect on the Venetian industry we have already seen, must have shown him that this noble ideal was not going to be realised as quickly as he had hoped. The partnership collapsed, and de Bussi retired without further comment to the calm and security of the Vatican library. But he had shown the strength of his conviction by editing twenty-four texts in four years.[72]

Appropriately, Gianandrea's opposite number came from Venice. His name was Filippo di Strata, and one of his poems informs us that he was Pavian by birth, a Dominican friar by vocation, a resident in the convent of San Cipriano in Murano, and a master of theology. He was probably not a professional copyist, for he clearly had other means of support and the surviving manuscripts which he wrote cover a long period of time and are very diverse in character: there is a version of the *Fiori di virtù*; a number of sermons and extracts from patristic commentaries; some love poems, apparently commissioned by friends; an elegy against the use of the organ in church; and the various personal compositions which are our main interest. One of these, a ponderous Latin address to Doge Nicolo Marcello, must have been written between August 1473 and December 1474. Another, which refers to Aldus as a celebrated printer, must have been written after 1495, and several references to the French invaders also prove that Fra Filippo was still active at the end of the century.[73] He was therefore an observer and critic of the Venetian press throughout the period of its early expansion, and his virulent hostility to it gives him a special place in this study.

At the root of Fra Filippo's feelings lay a deep dislike of printers as people, his various descriptions of them revealing an interesting fusion of snobbery and nationalism. They were vagabonds, idlers, dismissed servants: they were ignorant, but at the same time ambitious; they would snore away the hours in a drunken stupor, but they would still be dreaming of their profits; they were German interlopers, driving honest Italian scribes out of work. He would have no objections, wrote Fra Filippo, if men like these would stay where they belonged, squabbling and singing in alleys or cheap taverns and selling their sordid wares to their sordid equals: but they were trying to rise above themselves, and in doing so were threatening the whole fabric of society. First, they were vulgarising intellectual life. The city was so full of books that it was hardly possible to walk down a street without finding armfuls of them thrust at you, "like cats in a bag," for two or three coppers. The texts were hopelessly inaccurate, since they had been prepared by ignorant oafs and then never corrected: but they still drove valuable manuscripts out of the market, and tempted uneducated fools to give themselves the airs of learned doctors.

>   Now folk who don't know 'talian
>   Will teach you to speak Tullian.[74]

A second and graver danger lay in the threat to morals. Books were now so cheap that children could afford them and the crafty printers, seeing their opportunity, produced volumes of pagan mythology and lascivious Roman love-poetry to titillate the erotic fantasies of the young. Finally and worst of all, religion was in imminent peril. Vernacular translations of the scriptures dimmed the beauty and twisted the subtle meaning of the Latin: now that cheap printed versions, prepared by unqualified profiteers, were circulating throughout society, simple people were bound to be led astray towards heresy, damnation and hell. Let the Doge be warned that printing was a whore: or rather it was worse than a whore, since it deserved to be banned from Venice by law.[75]

Fra Filippo is a caricature of the reactionary: at one point he actually says that the world has got along perfectly well for six thousand years without printing, and has no need to change now. When we set his words against their background of surging expansion in press activity, it is easy to treat him with pity or ridicule as the last survivor of a doomed generation, screaming in the faces of a solid phalanx of noblemen, intellectuals, and artisans who march shoulder to shoulder towards enlightenment and a better life. But he cannot be brushed aside so easily. His attitudes were consistent and, as we shall see, based on a better appreciation of facts than de Bussi's. It is interesting enough to find that, even when printing had been established in Venice for nearly thirty years, Aldus could still be warned that he was building a higher wall on the same weak foundations, and would have further to fall.[76] When we find that Fra Filippo addressed himself to a doge, a member of the powerful Council of Ten, and a number of other nobles, it becomes apparent that he was not without friends, and the fact that sixty members of the Senate out of 159 voted against a printer's petition in 1492 suggests that some opposition to the press may have lingered on for a surprising length of time. Fra Filippo was by no means alone in his fears: no one else made the same points so coherently or with such virulence, but even scholars who worked continuously with the press repeated one or other of his objections to it.[77]

A degree of personal dislike for the printer was almost universal among intellectuals. Sebastian Brant used many of the same terms of abuse as Fra Filippo in giving both masters and workers a prominent place in his *Ship of Fools,* and the general charges of rowdiness, greed and incompetence, which were already abroad in the 1470s, had hardly changed when Erasmus prepared the Venetian edition of the *Adagia* with Aldus in 1508. But the argument from silence is if anything more significant. Giorgio Merula, the public lecturer whom we have already mentioned, worked intermittently throughout the 1470s with a number of Venetian printers, including Windelin of Speyer, Jenson, and John of Cologne: but apart from a generally worded tribute to Jenson, he has nothing to say about printers as people, and even in the preface to a printed edition, does not hesitate to question whether the new craft is a help or a hindrance to scholarship.[78] Marcantonio Sabellico, one of Merula's successors, provides an even more striking example. According to contemporary opinion, he owed his appointment to a substantial popular history of Venice, which he composed in fifteen months and on which he obtained the first known author's copyright in 1486.[79] He worked closely with a number of presses during the later 1480s and 1490s, and probably deserves the title usually reserved for Erasmus – that of being the first writer to make a career from the new medium. Naturally, his twelve books of letters abound in references to the press, which range from the broadest judgements down to details of marketing technique. But printers themselves are mentioned only as tiresome tradesmen, whose demands come at difficult moments and whose work is invariably slipshod.[80] For a while this barrier of mutual incomprehension may have been kept up by national, local and linguistic differences. For the first decade of its existence, the Venetian industry was dominated largely by German immigrants, and Merula could not forget, even when he was working for John of Cologne and still wholly enthusiastic about printing, that the invention had come from "that once rugged and brutish land of Germany".[81] When Italian printers began to push themselves forward after 1480, they still came from outlying towns, and often kept their local origins before the public eye – Philippus Pincius of Mantua, Bernardinus Benalius of Bergamo, and Andrea Torresani of Asola. Differences of dialect were still strong, traditions of local prejudice even stronger: it must have been perilously easy for the sophisticated and metropolitan Venetians to treat the newcomers as boorish, grasping and provincial.[82] Until the age of Aldus, there is little sign of anything more than a business relationship between printers and scholars. Though the bookseller might perhaps have aspired to the respectability of international trade, the printer, with his grubby ground-floor workshop and his drunken assistants, was on the face of it a small artisan. In 1493 Matteo of Pavia was cited for assaulting and killing a deaf-mute in the Fondaco de' Tedeschi: in 1499 "Morgante, a printer of books", was accused of a similar attack on a common prostitute. It was a world for which the intellectual had been schooled by the urban violence of the previous century to feel nothing more than a mixture of horror and contempt.[83]

To some extent, complaint about the printers' debasement of intellectual life must have been derived from the premise that printers were low characters already. But the idea was based on observed fact as well as prejudice, and could gain ground with remarkable speed. Merula edited Cicero's *De Finibus* for John of Cologne in 1471, and his dedication of the work to Ludovico Foscarini uses language very similar to that of Gianandrea de Bussi: man has always wielded Promethean skills, but the invention of printing surpasses any previous achievement; the rarest works are now ready to hand and anyone can savour their wisdom. But only a year later Merula was much cooler, when he edited the *Scriptores Rei Rusticae* with Jenson. He still clung to de Bussi's hope of purifying the Latin language by saturating the learned world with books, but he was gravely concerned about the more immediate consequences of the process: "matters which in happier times were remote, secret and barely known even to the wise are now bandied around in alleyways by the vilest people, in the vulgar tongue".[84] The resemblance of his repulsion to Fra Filippo's is obvious.

There are signs of a rather similar shift of ground in the comments of another editor, Hironimo Squarciafico. In 1477 he wrote enthusiastically of persuading John of Cologne to publish all the Latin classics, just as he had published all the commentators on Civil and Canon Law: but in 1481 he imagined an argument in the Elysian Fields between the great authors of the past, some pressing the benefits of the new art, others complaining that "printing had fallen into the hands of unlettered men, who corrupted almost everything".[85] Sabellico raised the same problems in the dialogue *De Latinae linguae Reparatione*, which he published in 1493, and, as we shall see in due course, he was most reluctant to give a direct answer to his own question. The issue was still open when Erasmus visited Venice in 1507: and in 1515 the Venetian government felt bound to intervene, for it gave the new librarian of the Marciana the additional duty of revising all literary texts published in the city. Constant protestations in colophons that the work concerned has been printed "accuratissime" hint obliquely at the printers' awareness of the hostility felt against them.[86]

There are two points involved here, one academic and philological, the other relating to society at large. First, de Bussi's hopes for a sober exchange of information about the Latin classics worked out in a very different way. The science of textual criticism was not even into its infancy. Poliziano's *Miscellanea*, which appeared in 1489, offered some important guidelines, but there were no clear ideas on the relative antiquity of various scripts, the merits of different manuscripts, or the means and the necessity of establishing connections between them. The availability of the manuscripts themselves was a matter of chance, for many owners were reluctant to let valuable property out of their hands. Another risk lay in the fashionable cult for eloquence: it tempted editors to score points off each other by daring conjectures, on the basis of their own assumed knowledge of what the Latin text ought to have said, and distracted them from a careful examination of the authorities. Conjecture was in any case a much faster way of working, and the printers, desperate to get books sold and their investments recovered at the earliest possible moment, badgered their collaborators for a finished copy or simply published what they had, regardless of its quality.[87] The results were inevitable. Editions of the classics were prepared at breakneck speed, generally from a very narrow selection of recent manuscripts, often from a single copy or an earlier printed edition peppered with a few conjectures or variant readings selected at random from whatever manuscript happened to be available. Once copies reached the market, the process of vulgarisation took another and possibly more dangerous turn. Classical texts were widely used in schools, and the pupils, accustomed for generations to listening and memorising while their teacher read and commented on an ancient author, were delighted with this opportunity to follow and to think for themselves. They noted their lecturer's emendations in the margins of their own texts: they made suggestions of their own; they were only too ready to pass a copy on to the printers and pocket a few ducats and a little academic prestige for themselves. Poliziano, Sabellico and Giorgio Valla all complained of their ideas being poached in this way, and Codrus Urceus of Bologna framed one of his satirical monologues round "a sleek young man with a ready tongue and a good store of learning", who was making a considerable name for himself by working as a sort of literary shark within the University. Unquestionably, the later fifteenth century saw a "classroom revolution". The teachers and lecturers were pleased, but at the same time disconcerted because they could not control a process which indirectly challenged their own authority and which threatened to turn their cautious reconstruction of correct Latin usage into a babel of confusion and dissent. They blamed their pupils for irresponsibility, and the printers for greed: modern critics have in their turn blamed their fifteenth-century colleagues for lack of intellectual discernment.[88] In fact, the hard economic necessity which we mentioned earlier may have been the most potent factor of all.

The social dimensions of "vulgarisation" are easier to explain because the attitudes involved are less abstract, less intricate, and much longer-lived. The fears of Fra Filippo or Merula found a more curt expression in Squarciafico's words – "abundance of books makes men less studious" – and they still find their way to the surface in criticisms of modern electronic culture, with its "Invitation to a Candy-Floss World". Fundamentally, the position taken is as follows: true learning demands profound knowledge, acquired through long application; superficiality is dangerous in itself because it can mislead, and dangerous socially because it can undermine the position of those who are properly qualified to answer the questions concerned. Nowadays, these objections tend to fasten onto the colour supplement, the paperback synopsis, or the overstated documentary film: in the fifteenth century, they fastened onto equivalents – the abridgement, the commentary, the paraphrased version of a major author's work. This is a field of early publication which has received relatively little attention from bibliographers, and which is difficult to define, quantify, and consequently to assess. But the hostility towards it can be easily illustrated from a single successful title, Jacobo Filippo Foresti's *Supplementum Chronicarum*, a compilation of world-history which was first printed by Bernardinus Benalius in 1483 and ran triumphantly through nine Latin editions and a vernacular translation, including various supplements to the original supplement, during the next thirty years. Though he was a member of the Augustinian order, Foresti welcomed printing with none of the mystical fervour of de Bussi, but as a short cut to self-improvement. Why, he asked in his introduction, should older men be preferred to their juniors, now that it was possible for young men, by diligent study, to acquire the same knowledge and experience? His own work offered them the ideal text. It covered all civilizations:

it spanned the period from the Creation until 1483, and was regularly brought up to date. He proudly claimed to have summarised the contents of both the Old and New Testaments, the works of Josephus, Herodotus, Diogenes Laertius, Plutarch, Valerius Maximus, Livy, Pliny, Strabo, Solinus, Suetonius, Aelian, Julius Capitolinus, Aulus Gellius, Justin, Orosius, Eutropius, Polycrates, Paul the Lombard, Jerome, Augustine, Gregory, Eusebius, Isodore of Seville, Bede, Gratian, Leonardo Bruni, Flavio Biondo, and Platina, to say nothing of Virgil and Ovid. Here indeed is the ancestor of the "Readers' Digest" mentality. It is easy to imagine how such boasts must have seared the nerves of those who had spent a lifetime in the patient study of their preferred authors, and disturbed the more reactionary sections of Venetian society, which set the highest premium on age, respectability and experience.[89] Here too was a manual for Fra Filippo di Strata's self-styled doctors, with their vulgar display of superficial learning. But when one glances through Foresti's brisk narrative of contemporary events, his portraits of celebrated intellectuals and his observations on the arts, one cannot help feeling that his readers must, in their way, have been better informed people than Merula or Filippo di Strata.[90]

If intellectual uneasiness about the press was fairly widespread, and based on observation as well as mere prejudice, moral and religious anxieties had no particular connection to the press at all: the arrival of printing simply sharpened fears which were already centuries old. Plato had pointed to the dangerous effects of love-poetry in the early books of the Republic. The idea passed into Christian tradition through Basil of Caesarea, and a sharp controversy between Giovanni Dominici and the circle of the Florentine chancellor, Coluccio Salutati, had drawn renewed attention to the issue only a generation before the invention of printing.[91] When Fra Filippo complained of "tender youths and delicate maidens" panting over their texts of Ovid and Tibullus, he was using a commonplace: but he was using it to illustrate what must have been one of the more striking developments of his own time – the wide availability of books to the young. On his facts, Fra Filippo was perfectly correct. Ovid ranks with Virgil as the most popular poet of the fifteenth century, and the large stocks held by Hironima von Dinslaken, or the fact that Bevilacqua reprinted the *Metamorphoses* three times during the 1490s alone, underline Venetian tastes emphatically enough.[82] But neither was Fra Filippo alone in his anxieties. Baptista Mantuanus published his

Contra Poetas impudice loquentes Carmen, a sharp attack on all lascivious or pagan verse, in 1489, and his prestige gave the work considerable circulation. In 1497 the Patriarch of Venice, Tomaso Donà, was horrified to discover that Giovanni Rubeo and Lucantonio Giunti were preparing an edition of the *Metamorphoses* which was not only in the vernacular, and therefore liable to be more widely read, but illustrated with woodcuts of the various transformations and feats of erotic athleticism described in the text. The publishers were ordered, on pain of excommunication, to remove the pictures of "naked women, phallic deities, and other unclean objects".[93] Two years later a scholar from Camerinum named Macarius Mutius published in Venice a short hexametric poem entitled *De Triumpho Christi*, which served mainly as a vehicle for two prose essays, the first attacking the indecency of pagan poetry, again with particular reference to the perilous *Metamorphoses*, the second suggesting more suitable, Christianised themes.

It is most unlikely that these well-intentioned citizens achieved a great deal. The tides of popular taste were running too strongly, and enthusiasts could always take refuge in the excuse that mythology contained deep and subtle lessons.[94] An even more reliable defence lay in the purely physical difficulties of imposing effective censorship on what was fast becoming a mass-medium. Somebody worked through at least a portion of Rubeo's illustrated *Metamorphoses*, discreetly inking out the erogenous zones: but the epigrammatist who warned another outraged friar that it would now be easier to emasculate the readers than the books was the real prophet of the 1490s.[95] What must not be overlooked is the existence, even in an ebullient and high-living society like Renaissance Venice, of a ground-swell of moral sensitivity which in times of crisis could break out with surprising force and produce repression, sumptuary legislation, even victimisation. When this occurred, the press was liable to to feel its effect immediately.

Objections to the reading of the Scriptures and of popular devotional literature in the vernacular probably derived mainly from the fears engendered by the heresies of the late fourteenth and early fifteenth centuries. Here again, printing only gave wider scope to an already open issue. But the problems are slightly more subtle, since the critics of the press for the first time become concerned with the ordinary reader rather than the upstart, and we must attempt to analyse different strata in the reading public. Fra Filippo's onslaught upon Italian Bibles was, yet again, based on an accurate appreciation of the facts.

Venice led Italy in the production of such books: eleven editions had appeared by 1500, three of them being underwritten by the funds of that dangerous populariser, Lucantonio Giunti.[96] But this version was most certainly not turned out by an "unproven person", as Fra Filippo contended, and it is at least very unlikely that many copies found their way into the hands of "simple and ignorant people". The translator was Nicolo Malermi, Venetian abbot of San Michele di Lermo, and the Bibles, like the classical texts or legal commentaries we have already discussed, were well produced folio volumes obviously intended for a moneyed and literate clientele. Here, too, the established sections of the reading public were the first to feel the benefits of printing. But the hunger for religious information was felt at every level of society. We catch a hint of it in the anonymous preface to a short work entitled *Luctus Christianorum ex Passione Christi*, printed by Jenson during 1471 in a small quarto form which would have been well within the reach of the less wealthy buyer.

Dearly beloved, I have been pressed for many months now by your warm and most earnest requests to translate into ordinary language (vulgar stilo) the common points of all four Gospels, adding to them in the form of a meditation a few modest and appropriate words such as might, perhaps, have been uttered at the time both by our Lord Jesus and by every other person who took part in the events of the Passion.

It is hard to believe that this gentle, devoted pastor – evidently a parish priest of a kind hardly believed to exist in the fifteenth century – misled any of his flock with the simple narration which followed. But this kind of free composition by an individual on a sacred theme could easily, and not always unjustly, provoke accusations of making the Scriptures "ugly and confused", or perverting their meaning. Turning to the contemporary *Fioretti della Bibbia*, which was also published as a small quarto,[97] we find an astounding tissue of fantasies: a series of metaphysical propositions on omnipotence, which would hardly have pleased a theologian or enlightened a humble seeker after knowledge; a smattering of recognisable stories from the apocryphal tradition; and a great variety of what one can only think were half-remembered gleanings from the schoolroom combined with fragments from old sermons. Herod, we learn, had two sons named Aristotle and Alexander, the first being renowned for his wisdom, the second for his strength. Christ had two teachers, the first of whom he drove distracted, while the second, Socrates, he finally converted. Much of this, as

Fra Filippo seems to imply, may have been the silt of unnumbered generations of story-telling at street corners and by tavern fire-sides: in that form it was not dangerous, because it was still subject to infinite variation, it was not widespread, and it was not noticeable. But once such stories found their way into print, they lost this fluid quality and began to acquire the mysterious potency which surrounds the written word. Ecclesiastical authorities could no longer ignore their existence.

Venice reacted more slowly than her neighbour imperial Germany, where the University of Cologne was granted a general supervision over publication as early as 1479, and from 1485 the Archbishop of Mainz launched a fairly consistent campaign to prevent the translation of "learned texts into incorrect and vulgar German", their distribution to the "common people", and the consequent "misunderstandings".[98] But in 1491 the Bishop of Treviso and papal legate, Nicolo Franco, warned against the diffusion of certain works "tainted with heresy", and attempted to subject future editions to the approval of the local bishop or his vicar:[99] and in 1494 the Venetian Senate gave a clear sign of its willingness to act by ordering the confiscation and burning of all copies of a scurrilous pamphlet published by a renegade Franciscan in Verona.[100] Finally, in 1510, the patriarch Antonio Contarini made a more comprehensive if rather simplistic effort to call the Venetian printers to heel. He expressed pained regret at the number of uncorrected religious works which had appeared, and at the confusions which they might have spread in "the hearts of the simple". The printers were urged in future to submit all works of a religious nature to his approval, and to avoid any texts, in Latin or Italian, which alluded to "the lewdness of women, or of anything else".[101] Contarini's decree was one part of the surge of moral revulsion which swept Venice after the disasters of 1509, and like the other episodes of that crusade, was probably soon forgotten. But it still provides some confirmation of the point from which we began: the fears of Fra Filippo di Strata about the press, and the language that he used, were fairly common currency in Venice at the time.

Fra Filippo seems to have been alone only in his consistency, in his unremitting hatred of the printers and everything they represented. For if any general conclusion emerges from this analysis, it must be that intellectuals were thrown into complete disarray by the arrival of a medium which they did not understand and soon found themselves unable to control. The tension is perhaps most obvious among the clergy. It has been reckoned that some two fifths of the entire output of Europe's presses during the fifteenth century were made up of the works of Franciscan and Dominican authors, and even this comparatively limited study has already shown examples of an interest among clerics which bears no resemblance to the reactionary obscurantism denounced by the humanists of Erasmus' generation. De Bussi was a bishop, Sweynheim and Pannartz were both in minor orders. The abbot of Lermo and the author of *Luctus Christianorum* worked through the night to bring knowledge to the faithful. The Patriarch of Aquileia happily contemplated the uniformity in the divine service which his 500 new missals would bring, and the bumptious Augustinian Filippo Foresti offered instant edification to his readers. But the bishop of Treviso and the two Patriarchs of Venice who wrung their hands over the spread of moral corruption and heresy, or the Dominican Filippo di Strata who consigned the printers and all they stood for to perdition, must, at their various levels in the hierarchy, have been men of an education and outlook basically similar to those of the enthusiasts. Secular intellectuals seem to have been hardly surer of their position. There is the same polarisation of eagerness and outrage: the Ferrarese court-humanist Ludovico Carbone on the one side, the disgruntled Vespasiano de' Bisticci on the other.[102] But these men knew little about the press. The most informed opinion seems to be represented by the embarrassment, the shifts of position, and the enormous silences of Venetian editors such as Merula or Squarciafico. These uncertainties find their most intriguing expression in the dialogue of Sabellico which we have already mentioned in passing. But we must now analyse them in greater detail as our best available reflection of views about printing in Venice immediately before the developments with which this study is mainly concerned.

Sabellico wrote and published *De Latinae Linguae Reparatione* in 1493, when Aldus Manutius had been in Venice for at least three years and was seeking support for his own plans.[103] The two overlapping scenes which the dialogue describes – a walk through Venice's bookselling quarter and a discussion between friends under the portico of the ducal palace – may have been partly or wholly fictitious. But they were common enough experiences. All the main participants in the discussion were alive at the time, and all were in Sabellico's circle of acquaintances. They included the humanist Battista Guarino, Aldus' teacher in Ferrara: the head of the Venetian School of San Marco, Benedetto Brugnolo; and a number of patrician intellectuals such as Daniel Renier, and Gerolamo Donato, who later took an interest in Aldus' activities. Clearly, the writer could not make characters like these express views which they did not hold, and the dialogue must represent a carefully staged reproduction of many similar encounters whose opinions it must to some extent reflect. Sabellico opens with one of those descriptive passages in which he excelled, and which in this case one can only wish he had extended. A Venetian named Sararisius sets out one morning with his guest, Juliarius, to walk along the Merceria from the Fondaco dei Tedeschi towards San Marco. But their route is lined with bookstalls: Sararisius soon has to leave his friend and go about his own affairs. When he returns some hours later, Juliarius has hardly moved and stands surrounded by his purchases. He is finally coaxed into walking on towards the Piazza, where the two companions are joined by Sabellico himself, and discussion turns to the morning's experiences. Does he feel, Sabellico asks Juliarius, that the flood of new writings has purified or enriched the Latin language? Up to this point the writer has given us a superbly vivid picture of literate society in the process of transition, and of the intellectual excitement that was driving it forward: the new question seems to promise some more searching examination. But none is forthcoming. Sabellico is persuaded to tackle the problem himself, and he does so by recalling a conversation with Battista Guarino during the recent visit of Alfonso d'Este. It is hardly more than a biographical outline of the previous century and a half of classical scholarship, which pays eloquent tribute to the achievements of Barzizza, Bruni and Lorenzo Valla but makes no direct attempt to answer the question in hand. Only at the very end is Guarino made to observe, in much the same terms as Squarciafico, that commentaries and abridgements of the ancient authors may encourage intellectual idleness in readers who would be better employed in studying the original texts. All of these were now readily available.[104]

It is the manner, rather than the matter of this dialogue that deserves our attention. As has already been said, the author owed a substantial part of his success to the Venetian press, and his opening lines show how clearly he knew the world of books. He was well known as a popular writer. His notes on Pliny and Valerius Maximus, his paraphrase of Suetonius, his *Enneades* of world history, and his *Exempla* of heroic lives, of which Hironima von Dinslaken stocked forty copies, all prove that he played a great part in the diffusion of commentaries and abridgements whose value he is suddenly found calling into question. Obviously, he felt the need to justify himself. He attempted to do so not by appealing, as de Bussi had done, to the spread of literacy, but by identifying himself with the dreams of the humanist past – the recovery and purification of correct Latin usage. Petrarch, Poggio and Valla filled his mind: there is not a word of John and Windelin of Speyer, of Jenson, or Torresani. It is a striking comment on the uneasiness of intellectuals about the press, and on the yawning gulf that still separated the men of letters from the men of business.

Though we cannot hope to take the temperature of opinion at all accurately at such a distance and with such uncertain evidence, there are some reasons for believing that dissatisfaction with the world of publishing and speculation about its future were beginning to spread in Venice during the early 1490s. Sabellico's ambiguous position is significant enough. "The Frenchman, Jenson, was long famed among the Venetians.... After him, barbarity invaded a noble art",[105] complained another contemporary. In technical terms, the decline can be appreciated simply by setting one of Jenson's texts alongside any of those turned out by his immediate successors, even reputable typographers like Tacuinus or Philippus Pincius, who stayed in business for many years. The Frenchman's bold Roman type was widely copied, but inferior cutting or casting always made the result less precise: and instead of the evenly spaced lines of text, the reader is faced by a page jumbled with commentary which is often packed on fifty or sixty lines at a time, with dislocated half-lines and syllables jostling one another for any available space.[106] But the problem went far deeper than the printed page. Jenson and John of Cologne had set a pattern which their followers found difficult to abandon because of its proven success, and the intellectuals, whirled along by the functioning of a medium which they did not understand and often deplored, gave no clear guidance. So the legal commentaries and classical texts followed one another in a sequence which must, after ten or a dozen years, have been wearing a tired and monotonous look. There was a need not only for new techniques, but for new ideas, and for a firm lead. Sure enough, during the 1490s, the new ideas came. There were experiments with the printing of maps, of oriental languages, and of music.[107] But the first and most important development was the arrival of a scholar with an established reputation in the intellectual world, who had become convinced of the value of printing and was determined to give it a new direction. His background, and his personality broke through the barriers of prejudice and incomprehension, setting the men of business and the men of

facit. Primum igitur legum diuinaeq; lator ita cucta deo patere oftedit: ut nihil agi nihil excogitari poffit quod eu lateat: deinde caeteros omes hoies falfo multitudinem deorum introducere docuit: quu ipfi multo praeftatiores fint q̄ dii fui quos uenerātur: quoq; fimulacra lapidea uel lignea tanq̄ imagines eorum qui ad uitam fibi non nihil contulerunt adorant fenfum ipfi habentes ea quae infenfata penitus funt. Cur aūt oīo quafi dii a gentibus coluntur illi qui ad ufum humanae uitae aliqd inuenerunt: quum non fecerint neq; produxerint ipfi quicquam: fed meliorem eorū quae funt ufum excogitarit: aut cur hodie quoq; multi non adorantur: quum antiquioribus ad inueniēdum excogitandumq; multa fagaciores acutioresq; fint? Nam de Aegyptiis quide nefcio qd dicere oporteat: baeluas enim & ferpētes & uiuos & mortuos uenerant. Haec igitur ifpiciēs diuinus ille uir moenibus ferreis & iuiolabili uallo a caeteris gētibus fepare nos uoluit: quo pacto facilius corpore atq; aīo īmaculatos lōgeq; ab huiufcemodi falfis opinioībus remotos fore uide- bat: ut folū uerū deum praeter caeteras gentes adorantes illi folūmodo inhaereamus. Vnde factum eft ut a nōnullis aegyptiorum facerdotibus qui difciplinam noftram altius cōfiderarunt dei homines gens noftra fit appellata: quod nemini nifi deū uerū colat accidere poteft. Nec id iniuria: reliquis enim cibo potui ueftituiq; inhiantibus noftri omībus iftis contemptis per totam uitam de omnipotētia dei cogitant. Ne igit' conuerfatione atq; confuetudine aliorum corrupti ad īpietatē eorum deferamur: cibi & potus tactus & auditus atque uifionis purificatione legali nos a caeteris feparauit. Cuncta enim ab una potentia oīpotentis dei gubernata naturali ratiōe fimilia funt: q̄uis fingula a q̄bus abftine- mus & quibus utimur profundam habeant rationem: quorum uṇum aut alterum exempli gratia ponam: ne putes temere de rebus tam p̄uis a Moyfe fuiffe cōfcriptum: fed omnia uideas ad probitatem hoīum & iuftitiae pfectionem fancte ptinere. Volucres eīm omnes qbus utimur domefticae mūdaeq; funt tritico aut leguminibus cōnutritae: ut colūbae turtures perdices anferes caeteraeq; huiufmodi: quae uero prohibitae fūt

Jenson's Roman Type

Tacuinus' Roman Type

letters onto a common path. "Aldus", wrote the poet who lamented the decline of printing,

> Saves our times from the stain of disgrace.

NOTES

1 FD p. 99, Doc. 1. CSV pp. 69–70. For an odder case compare M. E. Mallett, *Mercenaries and their Masters*, London, 1974, p. 204.
2 F. C. Lane, *Venice, a Maritime Republic*, Johns Hopkins, 1973, pp. 225–238.
3 V. Scholderer, "Printing at Venice to the end of 1481", reprinted from *The Library*, V 1924, pp. 129–152, in *Fifty Essays in Fifteenth- and Sixteenth-Century Bibliography*, ed. D. E. Rhodes, Amsterdam, 1966, pp. 74–89. See esp. the chart on p. 88.
4 Figures up to 1480 are reasonably secure: afterwards, the number of unidentified presses grows (see Scholderer, *op. cit.*, and H. Brown, *The Venetian Printing Press*, London, 1891, pp. 28f. Venetian editions until 1500 were numbered at 3754 by J. Lenhart, *Pre-reformation Printed Books*, New York, 1935, p. 76, the figure for Paris being 2,254. Scholderer raises the Venetian total to *c.* 4,500 ("Printers and Readers in Italy in the Fifteenth Century", *Proceedings of the British Academy*, XXXV, 1949, pp. 28–30) but in view of the frequent references in diaries to speeches or sermons which were printed but have not survived, I am inclined to think that the real figure may be higher.
5 Sanudo's library grew from around 500 volumes in 1502 to 6,500 by the 1530s: see OAME XLIII and K. Wagner, "Sulla sorte di alcuni manoscritti appartenuti a Marin Sanudo", LBF LXXIII, 1971, pp. 247–262. Grimani's library numbered 15,000 volumes in 1523: Lowry, "Two Great Venetian Libraries in the Age of Aldus Manutius", BJRL 57, 1974, No. 1, pp. 128–166. On the exceptional level of these totals see L. Febvre, H.-J. Martin, *L'Apparition du Livre*, Paris, 1958, pp. 397–400.
6 M.-A. Sabellico, *De Latinae Linguae Reparatione*, in *Opera Omnia*, Vol. IV, Basel, 1560, p. 321.
7 Brown, *Venetian Press*, pp. 1–10. If John of Speyer was the first printer in Venice the city ranks third in Italy behind Rome and Subiaco. The earlier date 1461 carried by Jenson's *Decor Puellarum* is probably not authentic.
8 P. Munroe, ed., *Thomas Platter and the Educational Renaissance of the Sixteenth Century*, New York, 1904, p. 195. On Torresani see below, Ch. III, passim: and on Jenson's reputation, Brown, *Venetian Press*, p. 12.
9 M. M. Philips, *The Adages of Erasmus – a Study with Translations*, Cambridge, 1964, p. 182. For general comment, R. Hirsch, *Printing, Selling and Reading, 1450–1550*, Wiesbaden, 1967, pp. 17f.
10 A.S.V., Senato, Deliberazioni Terra, Registro XI, f. 60r (Badoer): FD p. 107, No. 14 (Viaro – "nobilis noster").
11 CSV pp. 24–5.

12 SDP pp. 143–4, Doc. XX. Scholderer, "A Fleming in Venetia: Gerardus of Lisa, printer, bookseller, schoolmaster and musician", *The Library*, Fourth Series, X, 1930, pp. 253–73.
13 CSV pp. 85–92.
14 Figures from Hirsch, *Printing*...., pp. 42f.
15 FD p. 132, No. 77. Compare BP p. 132 (Carbone to Borso d'Este).
16 J. Moran, *Printing Presses*, London, 1973, p. 19. On the possibility of adapting existing presses, R. Deacon, *A Biography of William Caxton*, London, 1976, pp. 97–9.
17 SDP pp. 124–5. At this date 1 ducat was worth 6.4 lire.
18 H. Carter, *A View of Early Typography up to about 1600*, Oxford, 1969, pp. 5–8, 102–5.
19 CSV p. 88. There is a measure of doubt about Jenson's background: see L. Gerulaitis, *Printing and Publishing in Fifteenth-Century Venice*, London, 1976, p. 22, n. 12.
20 Carter, *Typography*, p. 71. For Torresani's link with Jenson, see below, Ch. III, n. 25.
21 Carter, *Typography*, p. 103. On Francesco da Bologna, see below, Ch. III, n. 66.
22 Carter, *Typography*, loc. cit., and pp. 84f, on Garamond.
23 SDP, p. 103, quotes a document of 1503 reducing prices by one third. On the general theme see Febvre-Martin, *op. cit.*, p. 168.
24 W. Pettas, "The Cost of printing a Florentine incunable", LBF LXXV, 1973, pp. 67–85. For a case of the supplier as creditor see SDP XXIV.
25 S. Brant, *The Ship of Fools*, trans. E. Zeydel, New York, 1962, p. 125. See also below, n. 71. For illustrations of early presses see Moran, *op. cit.*
26 SDP Doc. VII: A. S. V. Senato, Terra, Rg. XI, f. 122r. See also Hirsch, *Printing*..., pp. 36–9, on the variation in wage-levels.
27 A.S.V., Signori di Notte, Notizie di crimini, 1472–1507, reveals a few assaults involving printers but nothing like the organised agitation traced by N. Z. Davis, "A Trades-Union in Sixteenth-Century France", Ec. HR 19, 1966, pp. 48–69.
28 G. Mardersteig, "La singolare cronaca della nascita di un incunabolo", IMU VIII, 1965, pp. 251–2.
29 E. Motta, "Demetrio Calcondila, editore", ASL 20, 1893, pp. 163–5 (purchase of manuscript for 1499 edition of Suda for 25 ducats: proof-reader to receive 5 ducats per month). Compare SDP p. 125, Doc. VI (payment of 10 ducats to editor Vernia).
30 FD, pp. 104–5, Doc. 9, pp. 149–50, Doc. 126. See below, Ch. III, nn. 103–10.
31 E.g. Hirsch, *Printing*..., pp. 27–30: C. Buhler, *The Fifteenth-Century Book*, Philadelphia, 1960, pp. 15–40. On Callierges see below, Ch. IV, nn. 61, 69.
32 Scholderer, "Printing at Venice...", pp. 132–3 in *The Library*: "Printers and Readers...", pp. 28–30.
33 BP pp. 64–7: see Scholderer, "The Petition of Sweynheim and Pannartz to Sixtus IV", *The Library*, Third Series, VI, 1915, pp. 186–90, reprinted in *Fifty Essays*..., pp. 72–3.
34 Hirsch, *Printing*..., pp. 62–3.

35 FD pp. 121-2, Docs. 44 and 47.
36 E. de Roover, "Per la storia dell'arte della stampa in Italia: come furone stampati a Venezia tre dei primi libri in volgare", LBF, LV, 1953, pp. 107-15.
37 G. d'Adda, *Indagini storiche, artistiche e bibliografiche sulla libreria Viscontea-Sforzesca del Castello di Pavia*, Vol. I, Milan, 1875, pp. 137-8. SDP p. 159, Doc. XXXVI (Tose): p. 152, Doc. XXVIII (agents in universities).
38 De Roover, *op. cit.*, pp. 116-17. Compare G. Martini, "La bottega di un cartolaio fiorentino della seconda metà del Quattrocento", LBF LVIII (Supp.), 1956, p. 21.
39 P. Bologna, "La stamperia fiorentina del monastero di S. Jacopo di Ripoli e le sue edizioni", GSLI XX, 1892, pp. 366-8.
40 Biblioteca Marciana, Venezia, Ms. italiani, Cl. XI, 45 (7439). On this manuscript see Gerulaitis, *Printing...*, p. 3. For Stagnino's complaint see FD p. 126, Doc. 58.
41 De Roover, *op. cit.*, p. 110. A glance through Panzer or Hain reveals the number of editions produced "by the labour of...(printer's name) and at the expense of... (backer's name)".
42 FD pp. 401-5 (Supplementary piece).
43 FD pp. 100-1, Doc. 2.
44 SDP p. 157, Doc. XXXIII. See also Docs. XXVII and XXXII, and Mardersteig, *op. cit.* under n. 23, for a discussion of the relationship.
45 SDP pp. 160-4 (mention of Rauchfass in several contracts): B. Cecchetti, "Stampatori e libri stampati nel secolo XV – testamento di Niccolo Jenson e di altri tipografi in Venezia", AV XXXIII, 1888, p. 458 (translated extract of R.'s will).
46 P. Camerini, *Annali dei Giunti*, Vol. I, Florence, 1962, pp. 21f: C. Volpati, "Gli Scotti di Monza, tipografi-editori in Venezia", ASL 59, 1932, pp. 365-382.
47 Camerini, *op. cit.*, Vol. I, p. 22. 4,500 Florins (1491) had become 11,302 by 1499.
48 "Printing at Venice...", pp. 146-7 (in *The Library*).
49 E. Motta, "Pamfilo Castaldi, Antonio Planella, Pietro Ugleimer ed il Vescovo d'Aleria", RSI I, 1884, p. 260. Jenson's will (see n. 16, above) left his type-punches to Uglheimer.
50 K. Haebler, "Das Testament des Johann Manthen von Gerresheim", LBF XXVI, 1924, pp. 1-9. "Domina Paola, relicta ser Iohannis de Speier, quae de presenti habitat mecum..." received a legacy of 225 ducats.
51 On the structure see Scholderer, "Printing at Venice...", pp. 134f (*The Library*) and for the source-material G. Ludwig, "Contratti fra lo stampador Zuan di Colonia ed i suoi soci e inventario di una parte del loro magazzino", *Miscellanea di storia veneta, R. Dep. veneta di storia patria*, Seconda serie, Tom. VIII, 1902, pp. 45f. A thorough review of all the evidence is now available in Gerulaitis, *Printing...*, pp. 20-30.
52 Information from Scholderer and Ludwig (see especially the will of Hironima, pp. 60-2). For use of the term "La Compagnia", cf. Brown, *Venetian Press*, p. 38.
53 Ludwig, *op. cit.*, pp. 65-85. For possible influence on Aldus see below, Ch. III, nn. 66, 96-7.

54 Hirsch, *Printing...*, pp. 149–51.
55 Statistics from Scholderer, "Printing in Venice...": BMC v; Burger III; Panzer VIII.
56 FD pp. 127, 151, Docs. 63,134. Merulae, *Annotationes in Ligarianam Ciceronis*, Venetiis per Gabrielem Petri, 1478.
57 Georgii Merulae, *Adversus Domitii commentarios in Martialem*, Venetiis per Gabrielem Petri, 1478. Da Madiis, cod. cit. f. 34v. On surviving copies see D. Fava, "Libri membranacei stampati in Italia nel Quattrocento", GJB 1937, pp. 55–84.
58 Quoted in P. Grendler, *The Roman Inquisition and the Venetian Press*, Princeton, 1977, p. 177, n. 42.
58 V. Joppi, "Dei libri liturgici a stampa della Chiesa d'Aquileia", AV XXXI, 1887, pp. 259–267.
60 Cod. cit. f. 112r.
61 *Ib.*, f. 27v.
62 Statistics from Burger, Bernoni. On the universities see C. Piana, *Ricerche sulle università di Bologna e di Parma nel secolo XV*, Florence, 1963: P. Vaccari, *Storia dell'università di Ferrara, 1391–1950*, Bologna, 1950; on Padua see below, Ch. V, nn. 44–9. On local presses see C. Buhler, *The University and the Press in Fifteenth-Century Bologna*, Indiana, 1958 and V. Scholderer, "Printing at Ferrara in the Fifteenth Century", in *Fifty Essays...*, pp. 91–5.
63 FD p. 110, Doc. 20: see also Docs. 4, 16 etc.
64 E. Govi, "La biblioteca di Jacopo Zen", *Bolletino dell'istituto di patologia del libro*, Anno X, fasc. i–iv, 1951, pp. 34–118.
65 Burger, and Bernoni, pp. 269f. On the Paduan philosophy school see E. Gilson, "L'affaire de l'immortalité de l'âme à Venise au début du XVIe siècle", in *Umanesimo europeo e umanesimo veneziano*, Venice, 1963, pp. 31–61. SDP p. 125, Doc. VI, for a case of an academic philosopher working for the press.
66 F. Gabotto and A. Badini Confaloniere, *Vita di Giorgio Merula*, Alessandria, 1893, pp. 38–66.
67 See above, under n. 29, for reference to De Bussi, and Ch. II, nn. 6f, for his possible affect on Aldus. For a full study and bibliography see DBI 15, Rome, 1972: and for some critical discussion E. J. Kenney, "The Character of Humanist Philology", in R. Bolgar, ed., *Classical Influences on European Culture*, Cambridge, 1971, pp. 123–4, further developed in *The Classical Text*, Berkeley, 1974, pp. 12f.
68 See the Lives of Vittorino by Platina and Francesco da Castiglione in E. Garin, *Il pensiero pedagogico dell'umanesimo*, Florence, 1958, pp. 540, 678.
69 The most recent and comprehensive study is R. Post's *The Modern Devotion – Confrontation with Reformation and Humanism*, Leyden, 1967.
70 BP pp. 98–9 (Lucan): *Praefatio in S. Hieronymi Epistolas*, Sweynheim and Pannartz, 1468. For comment DBI p. 569, Kenney, *The Classical Text, loc. cit.* De Bussi's texts were based on inferior manuscripts even when better copies were available, and on at least one occasion he simply reprinted an earlier text.
71 BP p. 81 (Aulus Gellius).

MEN OF BUSINESS AND MEN OF LETTERS

72 *Ib.*, pp. 64–5 (list of editions in preface to Nicholas of Lyra's Commentary). See also DBI p. 568. De Bussi did not edit the texts of the Subiaco period.

73 The most important texts are Biblioteca Marciana, Venezia, Ms. italiani Cl. II, 133 (4846) (personal information): Cl. I, 72 (5054) (Vernacular poem against printing and Latin address to doge Marcello). For further information and references to other manuscripts see A. Segarizzi, "Un calligrafo milanese", *Ateneo veneto*, XXXII, i, 1909, pp. 63–77: F. Novati, "Ancora di Fra Filippo di Strata: un domenicano nemico degli stampatori", *Il libro e la stampa*, v, N.S. fasc. iv, 1911, pp. 117–28. Segarizzi quotes the vernacular poem against the press in full, but makes little use of the address to Marcello.

74 The vernacular poem of the 1490s (Cl. I, 72 (5054) f. 1r) gives the most vivid account of social realities. Cl. II, 133 (4846) ff. 41r–42r, contains a poem which demands the immediate return of a number of books: Fra Filippo was afraid that one "Gaspar", who had borrowed them, was about to sell the manuscripts to the press and ruin their value.

75 "Est virgo hec penna: meretrix est stampificata." The address to doge Marcello, though more formal, makes most of the same points as the Italian poem.

76 Segarizzi, *op. cit.*, p. 71.

77 II, 133 (4846) f. lv, contains an address to Zuane Capello, a member of the Ten. I, 71 (4832) contains a number of welcomes to new bishops, local administrators, etc., of a very conventional nature. FD p. 105, Doc. 9, for the numbers voting in the Senate.

78 BP pp. 145–8 (*Scriptores Rei Rusticae*). On his editions see A. Zeno, *Dissertazioni Vossiane*, Vol. II, Venice, 1753, 62f.

79 A. Pertusi, "Gli inizi della storiografia umanistica nel Quattrocento", in *La storiografia veneziana fino al secolo XVI*, Florence, 1970, pp. 319f. FD p. 102, No. 3, for his copyright.

80 *Opera Omnia*, Vol. IV, p. 358. "Vix dici potest, quantum illorum incuria vel ignavia potius verae lectioni ademerit."

81 Georgius Merula, *In Ciceronis Libros De Finibus Bonorum et Malorum*, Venetiis, 1471, Ioanne ex Colonia Agrippinensi sumptum ministrante impressum. See also below.

82 On this type of local prejudice see F. Braudel, *Le Mediterranée e le Monde Mediterranéen à l'Epoque de Philippe II*, Paris, 1966, Vol. I, pp. 39–42.

83 A.S.V., Signori di notte, Notizie di Crimini 1472–1507, ff. 60r, 74v. See G. Brucker, "The Ciompi *Revolution*", in *Florentine Studies*, ed. N. Rubinstein, London, 1968, pp. 314–56.

84 BP p. 147.

85 Asconii *Commentarii in Orationes Ciceronis*, Manthen and John of Cologne, 1477, f. 183r. For the argument of the great authors see L. A. Shepherd, "A Fifteenth-Century Humanist, Francesco Filelfo", *The Library*, Fourth Series, XVI, 1936, p. 25.

86 For the text of Andrea Navagero's appointment see P. Papinio, "Nuove notizie intorno ad Andrea Navagero e Daniele Barbaro", AV III, 1872, p. 256. "... le piui

incorrecte stampe vadino per il mondo sonno quelle escono e qui, non senza infamia de la città." For some remarks on the claims of colophons and a very different interpretation of them see D. Marzi, "I tipografi tedeschi in Italia durante il secolo XV", *Festschrift der Stadt Mainz zur Gutenbergfeier im Jahre 1900*, pp. 423-4.

87 Ovidii *Metamorphoses cum integris ac emendatissimis Raphaelis Regii commentariis*, Bevilacqua, 1493, f. 167v. Regius warned readers that this was the correct version of his commentary, which had been published in the previous year in an incomplete version, without his permission.

88 Codri Urcei Sermo Primus, in *Opera Omnia*, Platonides, Bologna, 1502 (unpaginated). For comment see Kenney, *The Classical Text*, pp. 3f, and below, Ch. V, nn. 35-8.

89 On this aspect of Venetian social attitudes see D. S. Chambers, *The Imperial Age of Venice*, London, 1970, pp. 82-4.

90 Eg. 1486 edition, f. 282v (Gutenberg and the press), ff. 291v-292v (Bellini's mission to paint the Sultan's portrait): 1513 edition, ff. 328v-329v (Account of the discovery of America). Filippo's introduction, which is not carried by the later editions, can be found on ff. 30r-v, of the 1486 text.

91 On the dispute over Florentine classicism, and the intellectual background, see the first chapter of G. Holmes, *The Florentine Enlightenment*, London, 1969.

92 On the popularity of Ovid, see Febvre-Martin, *op. cit.*, p. 386. On Bevilacqua, Burger, pp. 347-8. Ludwig, *op. cit.*, p. 76, shows that Gaspar's widow stocked 49 copies of the *Fasti* in 1511.

93 A. Niero, "Decreti pretridentini di due patriarchi di Venezia su stampa di libri", *Rivista di storia della chiesa in Italia*, XIV, 1960, pp. 450-2.

94 Daphne's transformation into a laurel showed that the girl who defended her virginity to the death was rewarded with an evergreen crown of chastity: Regius, in the edition of *Metamorphoses* cited under n. 87.

95 *Cantalycii Epigrammatum Liber*, Matteo Capcasa, Venice, 1493. "In praedicatorem iubentem comburi ovidianas artes."

96 Hain, Nos. 3148-3157. See K. Forster, "Vernacular Scriptures in Italy", in *The Cambridge History of the Bible*, Vol. II, Cambridge, 1969, pp. 453-465.

97 The version examined was that of Giorgio di Rusconi, printed in Venice during 1503.

98 R. Hirsch, "Pre-Reformation Censorship of Printed Books", *The Library Chronicle*, XXI, No. 1, 1955, pp. 100-5.

99 G. Putnam, *The Censorship of the Church of Rome and its Influence on the Production and Distribution of Literature*, Vol. I, London, 1906, p. 79.

100 A.S.V., Senato, Terra, Rg. XII, ff. 54v-55r.

101 Niero, "Decreti pretridentini...", p. 452.

102 BP p. 132: C. Buhler, *The Fifteenth-Century Book*, Philadelphia, 1960, pp. 20-24, 50.

103 Sabellici, *Opera Omnia*, Vol. IV, pp. 320-32. On Aldus' early years in Venice see below, Ch. V, nn. 50-3.

104 *Ib.*, p. 332: compare the remark "Abundance of books makes men less studious",

which Squarciafico attributed to the ghosts in the Elysian Fields. See the article cited under n. 85, above.
105 Museo Correr, Venezia, Fondo Cicogna, Ms. 949, No. 56: Hieronimi Bononii Tarvisini Promiscuorum septimus libellus.
106 Brown, *Venetian Press*, pp. 34–5. My observations here are based on Tacuinus' text of Ovid's *Fasti* (1496), but they can be multiplied at will.
107 FD p. 153, Docs. 81, 82 (petitions for copyright on music and oriental languages). The petition of Andrea Badoer cited above under n. 10 refers to the printing of navigational charts.

II

THE WANDERING SCHOLAR

How far is it possible to trace the currents within this maelstrom of interests and opinions which led Aldus Manutius to become the scholar who turned printer? The question is as important as it is puzzling: Aldus made his crucial decision when he was forty, and comfortably established in the career of a professional teacher, so we must explain first why the decision was made at all. But we have virtually no information about these forty years. Even the biographer's usual stepping stones, a date of birth and the influence of a family, are denied to us, for Aldus' son and grandson disagreed over the year of his birth and we know nothing of his family except the names of three sisters for whom he assumed responsibility.[1] We can only approach the first half of Aldus' life by fitting the few established facts as closely as possible into a cultural framework. And the facts give us at least one promising line of investigation: Aldus must have been aware of printing from almost the first moment of its arrival in Italy.

He was born at Bassiano, near Rome, a year or so on either side of 1450, and his early education was naturally acquired in Rome. We learn this from two very oblique references in his later dedications: the first, in the Theocritus of 1495, recalls the Latin lessons of Gaspare da Verona; the second, in the Statius of 1502, mentions a lecture of Domizio Calderini which the writer had heard "at Rome, when I was a boy".[2] The mention of Calderini is useful chiefly as a chronological guide. This aggressive Veronese philologist had arrived in Rome around 1467 and over the next eight years established a reputation which for a while stood very high, even though it was soon eclipsed by Calderini's early death in 1478, and by the rising fame of Poliziano and Ermolao Barbaro. He began his career as an apostolic secretary: but in 1470 he was hired by the university and lectured with conspicuous success on a number of Latin authors. In 1472 he accompanied Cardinal Bessarion to France, and later attempted to inflate his own reputation by claiming to have discovered the lost *Elegantiae* of Asconius and the works of a previously unknown Latin grammarian called Marius Rusticus. Both claims were in fact pure fabrication. But by recalling the lecture in which he had heard of them, Aldus at least shows that he was still studying in Rome during the mid-1470s, after Calderini's return from France. It is hard to squeeze much more than this superficial information from the facts. Calderini was clearly a man who recognised the potential of the press for keeping himself in the public eye: he edited Quintilian, and published commentaries on Juvenal, Martial, Statius' *Silvae*, Ovid's *Sappho* and *Ibis*, and some of the poems of Propertius before his early death, leaving a number of other works to appear posthumously. But Aldus says only that he "heard" his lectures: so, according to contemporary accounts, did most of the intellectuals in Rome. There is no proof of any closer connection which might have contributed to Aldus' views on the press.[3]

Gaspare da Verona presents problems of a different order. He belonged to an earlier generation, having known Guarino Veronese, studied under the future Pope Nicholas V, and corresponded with Ambrogio Traversari. A footloose and rather thrusting character, he had at one time been attached to the Porcari family and visited France and England with them, but by the early 1440s he had acquired a solid respectability and took advantage of his connections at the papal court to settle permanently in Rome. At first he ran a small private school which was attended mainly by the "nipoti" of higher clerics, including Roderigo Borgia: but during the later 1450s he was named professor of rhetoric at the Sapienza, without apparently being obliged to abandon his prestigious assignment at the papal palace. Aldus presumably studied under him at the Sapienza, and he may have done so at almost any time between 1460 and 1473, when Gaspare withdrew to Viterbo. To judge from his *Regulae Grammaticales* his commentary on Juvenal, and from the respectful if not effusive tributes of ex-pupils such as Sabellico and Cantalycio, Gaspare was a thoroughly competent but hardly inspiring teacher who worked along the lines set out by the elder Guarino. There is nothing to suggest that his personality fired Aldus or anyone else.[4] But when, probably during 1467, Gaspare composed his laudatory biography of the reigning Pope, Paul II, he made a crucial note of one minor incident:

About this time certain young Germans arrived in Rome and in a single month produced the works of Lactatius Firminianus On the Creation of Man, On the Anger of God, and Against the Gentiles. They made 200 such books every month. It would be most difficult to give an account of their craft, which was the invention of great genius, if many did not know the whole truth.

They also printed (finxerunt) Augustine's *City of God*, Cicero's *On the Orator*, and his *Letters to his brother Quintus*, all of which they sold at a low price. They are intending to produce other books in the same way."[5]

The precision with which Gaspare recorded the first publications of Sweynheim and Pannartz, including those from the Subiaco period, leaves no doubt that he was immediately aware of the impact of printing and keenly interested in its future development. It is impossible to believe that this interest was not communicated in some form to his pupils, and there is an overwhelming temptation to find the first vital influence on Aldus' career in the school of Gaspare da Verona.

Sure enough, Aldus' work shows slight but unmistakeable traces of the first Roman editions, and his ideals of a society enlightened by the press bear some resemblance to the dreams of Gianandrea de Bussi. The Aldine text of Bessarion's *In Calumniatorem Platonis* was based, by the editor's own admission, on that published by Sweynheim and Pannartz in 1469.[6] In the dedication to one of his earliest editions, the Theocritus of 1495, Aldus used and elaborated an argument which could have been borrowed from de Bussi: unknown manuscripts, he claimed, are never corrected, but at least some copies of a printed text will find their way into learned hands and so knowledge will be shared, and the author's work restored to its original purity. He cited the recent discussions of Quintilian and Pliny to prove his point.[7] When Aldus appeals to the good of all mankind, or speaks of supplying the books which will restore all fields of knowledge to their ancient splendour, or looks up from his books in the din of the print-shop to tell Erasmus that he is studying, the reader naturally recalls de Bussi's hopes of taking part in a universal enlightenment.[8]

But there are grave difficulties in treating any single aspect of Aldus' experience in Rome as a decisive influence on his future career. He refers to Sweynheim's text of *In Calumniatorem Platonis* only to call it a shoddy piece of work, and he never mentions de Bussi's name at all. If the idealism of de Bussi, or the comments of Gaspare da Verona on the possible development of printing, had made a really deep impact, then it is hard to understand why Aldus waited for twenty years before applying the lessons he had learned. When he did so, he chose to concentrate on Greek literature: in Rome, as he states explicitly, he had studied only Latin. Both on an intellectual and a personal level, Aldus seems in fact to have neglected his Roman background so completely that it is hard to treat his attitude as a simple matter of coincidence or oversight. As has been said, the mentions of Gaspare and Calderini are very terse, and partly intended to express a debt to another city and another man: Verona and Battista Guarino rather than Gaspare and Rome. The contrast with Aldus' usual expressions of respect is almost pointed. His intellectual rejection of Roman scholarship is obvious. Pomponio Leto and his school valued exhaustive commentaries on the works of individual Roman authors: Aldus emphasised Greek, and printed plain texts. His small, unelaborated, octavo editions of Juvenal, Martial, Statius and Ovid owe nothing to the copious observations of Calderini on these authors.[9] Aldus' rejection appears to have gone further than questions of scholarship. When he arrived in Venice around 1490, one of those best placed to assist him was Marcantonio Sabellico, whose experience of the publishing world has been discussed in the previous chapter and who, as librarian of the Marciana, was in charge of the richest collection of Greek manuscripts in the Western world. He was a fellow-Roman, and a pupil of both Gaspare da Verona and Calderini. A connection would have been obvious, and highly advantageous. But the only evidence we have that contact was made lies in the request of another scholar to Aldus, who is asked to pay respects to Sabellico. Rather than cultivating his influential senior, Aldus made a life-long friend of his main rival Giambattista Egnazio, who in his *Racemationes* of 1502 sharply attacked Sabellico's scholarship, and his attempts to undermine Egnazio's own popularity.[10] We can only speculate about the reasons for Aldus' apparent hostility to the Roman school. A sincerely pious Christian, he may have been disturbed by the more bizarre antiquarian posturings of Pomponio Leto and his circle, and by the suspicions of paganism or conspiracy which had fastened onto them in 1468.[11] But this could hardly have affected his feelings about Gaspare or de Bussi. Whatever the reasons, it is clearly most unsafe to attach any decisive importance to Aldus' period of study in Rome. The early view of printing, and the visionary hopes of de Bussi, may have fallen on fertile soil. If so, they sank very deep, and many years of different experience would be needed before they could germinate.

In the same, vital dedication of his edition of Theocritus to Battista Guarino Aldus shows that he had studied Greek under that distinguished teacher in Ferrara. The exact dates are again uncertain, and they were very probably discontinuous. To have heard Calderini's higher flights of imagination, Aldus must still have been in Rome around the mid-1470s: while a document from the archives of Carpi, dated 8 March 1480, grants him citizenship of that town, naming him tutor to the princes Alberto and Lionello Pio and a resident for some time.[12] Obviously, Aldus studied in Ferrara during the later 1470s. But in a letter of 1485 he states explicitly that he left Ferrara only in 1482, and much later he claims to have taught there himself.[13] Even though they apparently conflict, these references build up a picture which, against the academic background of the times, is perfectly consistent. It was common enough for scholars of mature years to support their own studies from the patronage of their more fortunate fellows, whether by tuition within the university or intermittent teaching outside it. Exactly how or when Aldus secured his post at Carpi is not clear: it seems most likely that he was recommended by the famous uncle of the two princes, Giovanni Pico della Mirandola, who was also studying in Ferrara during this period. A sober and gentle character, approaching the age of thirty and with a good background of Latin scholarship, Aldus must have been an obvious choice.[14] He probably passed frequently between Ferrara and Carpi not only during the 1470s but again after 1484, when peace between Venice and the Estensi made conditions possible again and Alberto Pio went to study at Ferrara in his own right. The scattered references show that Aldus was now fully launched on the career of a professional man of letters, clinging to the fringe of the academic world and taking the opportunities that came his way.

To such a man, Ferrara must have offered good prospects during the 1470s and 1480s. Though the university could not rival Bologna or Padua in numbers or prestige, it had made steady progress during the fifteenth century thanks to the interest and protection of the ruling Este family. By the 1450s and 1460s an average of thirty or more degrees was being awarded every year, and since nearly forty per cent of those known to have graduated came from the transalpine countries, there was a definite air of cosmopolitanism.[15] The university also had its particular areas of excellence: Niccolo Leoniceno's research on the text of Pliny's *Natural Histories* made the medical faculty the focus of considerable interest and controversy during the later years of the century.[16] An even more lasting reputation was enjoyed by the grammar school of Guarino Veronese, which was closely linked to both the university and the Este court by Guarino's dual position as court tutor and Professor of Rhetoric. Until 1460 the school was a major international centre which attracted scholars from all over Europe, five from England alone: the elder Guarino's death removed the unique quality of the teacher who had studied Greek in Byzantium and taken part in the first heroic quests for lost manuscripts, but Battista maintained much of the impetus by carefully codifying and continuing his father's work. His *De Ordine Docendi et Studendi*, perhaps the most elaborate of the humanistic educational treatises, sets out a precise scheme of grammatical instruction, insists on the interdependence of Latin and Greek, and recommends translation between the two languages as a means of learning both thoroughly.[17]

The direct impact of Guarino's methods and the subtle influence of the Ferrarese cultural environment upon Aldus' outlook are so obvious that they provide a striking contrast to the uncertainties which surround his view of Rome. In his last will, he named three Ferrarese executors including the duchess Lucretia Borgia: in his first, he suggested that his young wife should seek another partner in Ferrara if he failed to return from his imminent journey: and one of his earliest publications, the text of Theocritus and Hesiod which we have already mentioned on several occasions, was dedicated to Battista Guarino with the words: "Here, most illustrious master, is the Theogonia of Hesiod, which you ask me to provide for the public instruction of your pupils."[18] Co-operation between the press and the intellectual could hardly go further. How far we should trace Aldus' conviction that Greek held the key to excellence in every field of learning back to the teaching of Battista seems a great deal less certain. There were other Hellenists within the university – Leoniceno, Codrus Urceus, and Giorgio Valla, for example –[19] and there is some evidence to suggest that, even if Aldus learned the rudiments of Greek from Guarino, he received some more important instruction outside the main stream of academic life. His association with the family of Pico della Mirandola has already been mentioned, and it is now time to estimate the precise nature and effect of that relationship.

On 28 October 1485 Aldus wrote to offer his friendship and service to Angelo Poliziano. The aim – common enough at the time – was plainly to gather some reflected glory by linking his name to that of the great philologist whose letters were passed frequently from hand to hand: the tone was therefore obsequious, and the form was a brief account of how Aldus' regard for Poliziano had originated and increased. When the Venetians attacked Ferrara three years earlier, Aldus wrote, he had sought refuge with Pico in Mirandola and had been shown by his "great friend" Manuel Adramyttenus a Greek letter written by Poliziano. The purity of the Attic style had impressed him greatly. Shortly afterwards, Manuel had set out for Pavia in Pico's company and died there, but Pico had passed through Carpi on his return and shown Aldus a copy of Poliziano's *Silvae*, which had swelled his admiration yet further. Aldus could now restrain himself no longer: he asked only to be included among Poliziano's friends, and treated as one of his domestic servants.[20]

Though this letter is full of information, and presents a vivid picture of the mobile academic life of the time, there is plainly a great deal which it leaves unsaid and which is very difficult to reconstruct now. First there are the uncertainties which surround the life of the mysterious Adramyttenus. We know that he was a Cretan who studied under Michael Apostolis for seven years during the 1460s and 1470s, and subsequently quarrelled violently with his old teacher as a result of his friendship with another Manuel who led him into dissipated, Westernised ways. The two reprobates seem to have set out from Crete to seek their fortune some time during the mid-1470s, and it was possibly this expedition which led Adramyttenus eventually to Mirandola: Aldus' expressions – 'a great friend', and 'devoted to me' – suggest that he had known Manuel for some time and profited considerably from his teaching. But all we know of Adramyttenus during the later 1470s is that he acted, as did so many Cretans, as a professional scribe: there is little to show what his intellectual attainments were, or where he exercised them before he was drawn into Pico's circle.[21] Next, what sort of "circle" was this? Aldus' remarks about the favour shown by Pico to literary men may be no more than the polite inanities of humanist language, but scattered evidence in other letters does suggest that Pico made a considerable effort during the early 1480s to turn Mirandola into a centre of scholarly patronage. On 20 July 1482 he addressed a breathless invitation to Leoniceno, whom he had failed to find in Florence and now sought in Bologna:[22]

You must have forgotten this little town of mine, or despised it. You seem, Nicholas, to mistrust either my good will or my resources, which are indeed far smaller than your services to me. But they are greater than you believe. I shall be delighted if you will tell me what your plans are, and most delighted of all if you will deign to make my house yours and take your ease here while others are caught up in the business of war. I send you the rest of John the Grammarian, which I have at last found after many days of search. I am yours, and I expect you. Farewell.... Please take care, as you love me, to have a list made of all the books in the library of Saint Dominic's, and to send it or bring it yourself. Again, farewell. I have built a villa outside the town, and it is pleasant enough considering the nature of the site. I have written a long poem about it: you will like the villa and you may quite like the poem as well. Farewell again.

The tone is that of a charming and slightly overzealous youth trying to cut a figure in the literary world. Pico was not simply opening his court as a refuge for the displaced scholars of embattled Ferrara: he was trying to tempt distinguished intellectuals to his side from a considerable distance, and he seems to have scored some success. We have too little information even to guess whether or not this was an attempt to establish some kind of academy on the pattern of those in Florence and Rome, and Pico himself stayed in one place for such short periods that there can hardly have been any continuity. But there was clearly some formal academic discussion, and some sense of cameraderie among the inmates. A jovial letter from Pico to Poliziano, probably written during 1483, describes the reception given to the Florentine's *Enchiridion Epicteti,* stressing the excitement with which the Latin text was read through, "even though there were some in the assembly, who knew Greek", and the wholesale conversion of the company to the Stoic philosophy as a result of the translator's skill.[23] Aldus' own story of reading Poliziano's Greek letter with Adramyttenus offers a hint that he had learned a good deal of his Greek in this kind of half-social, half-intellectual gathering at Pico's villa. His friendship with Adramyttenus was obviously close. Giambattista Scita – one of those mentioned by Poliziano in the letter quoted above – wrote to Aldus in 1483 about the progress that Pico ("our prince") was making at Pavia, and remained in touch when his old colleague began work as a printer. Leoniceno became one of Aldus' most active helpers, both as a corrector of texts and a contributor of original material. Such activity as there was probably did not survive the turbulent years of Pico's wandering from Florence to Paris, thence to Rome, but at least between 1482 and 1484, the activity was real enough.[24]

A lively imagination could derive endless consequences from Aldus' experiences during these years in Ferrara, Carpi and Mirandola: later in life, when he dreamed of founding an academy of his own, was he remembering hours of animated discussion with like-minded friends at Pico's pleasant villa? Perhaps: but there is no point in pretending that we have the evidence to prove it. All we can do is place Aldus more accurately in his intellectual background. It is too easily implied that he was a passing acquaintance and minor protégé of Pico's, hardly able to do more than admire the count from a distance.²⁵ But the evidence suggests that Pico was trying actively to form his own intellectual circle, and Aldus' presence must argue either that he already enjoyed at least a fair reputation as a scholar, or that he was well known to Pico, or both. His letter to Poliziano, with its eager commendation of Hellenism, entirely follows the tone of those directed by Pico to Poliziano during the same period. "I will imitate you", wrote the count, "in justifying yourself to the Greeks on the ground that you are a Latin, and to the Latins because you are studying Greek".²⁶ In the single surviving letter that passed between them, Pico urged Aldus to press ahead with his philosophical research, but never to take his eyes from the final revelation.²⁷ Aldus was an associate as well as a client, and was whirled along in the currents of Pico's quest for universal knowledge.

These hints are expressed far more forcefully in the only other surviving pieces written by Aldus during the 1480s, which are preserved in a short pamphlet variously known as *Musarum Panegyris* or *Epistola ad Catherinam Piam,* according to the different components. These include some trite Latin elegiacs written to encourage Aldus' young pupils, Alberto and Lionello Pio, and a longer justification of his educational aims directed to the princes' mother. Only four copies survive, and the presswork, contained on eight quarto-sized leaves, has been attributed on typographic grounds to Baptista de Tortis of Venice. The date of publication must fall between March 1487, since Pietro Barozzi is named as Bishop of Padua, and March 1491, since Ermolao Barbaro could hardly have been called "the glory of the Venetian senate" after his acceptance of the Patriarchate of Aquileia and consequent banishment. The actual composition is probably earlier: the lumbering elegiacs definitely belong to the school-room, and a declaration of educational aims would have come far more naturally from Aldus during the early 1480s than at the end of the decade, when his mind must already have been turning to printing. Possibly he touched up and published some early drafts as a form of self-advertisement when he arrived in Venice around 1489, for there is evidence that he acted as a teacher in the early 1490s, and the link with a princely family would have been an excellent selling-point.²⁸ Juggling dates in any case hardly affects the overall relevance of the assorted pieces: they amount to a broad statement of Aldus' intellectual standing as he wished it to be known, both to his patrons and to a wider audience, and the statement itself follows naturally from the correspondence with Poliziano. In the elegiacs, the princes are urged to "read the Greek books, those divine volumes, along with the Romans..."[29] and immediately after the preliminary courtesies of his letter to Catherina, Aldus asks: "How can one who does not know Greek imitate the Greek authors, who are the most advanced in every field of learning and from whom, as is known, everything that is worthy of praise has passed into the Latin tongue?"[30] Cicero, Horace and Quintilian are cited to prove both the charms of Greek literature and its absolute necessity as an aid to true Latin scholarship. True to the humanist principle of instruction by example, Aldus then proceeds to the examples set by learned princes: Philip, Alexander and Julius Caesar lead on to the contemporary Federigo da Montefeltro, and so to the arts of peace and virtues of Pico, Pietro Barozzi and Ermolao Barbaro, "a most famous knight, a most learned lawyer, a most celebrated philosopher, profoundly skilled in the Greek and Roman languages". There is no evidence to prove that Aldus actually met Barbaro, who must have left Venice on his ill-starred embassy to Rome very soon after Aldus' arrival, if not before: but the special praise reserved for his universal knowledge, and the insistence on an educational system which provided for a thorough grasp of Greek, show that Aldus was now a complete convert to the exhaustive programme of Poliziano, Pico and Barbaro. The values of the ancient world must be recreated by an all-pervading scholarship which recognised no boundaries of language or discipline.[31]

It is vital to remember, and almost impossible to express, the absolute faith which these men placed in their philological skills, and the soaring hopes which they erected over its narrow foundation. Poliziano corresponded with Leoniceno about the texts of Pliny and Dioscurides: but he addressed him as the new Asclepius, whose knowledge would rescue his generation from disease and death. If rightly understood, there was nothing which the word, that supreme expression of the rational faculty which separated man from beast, might not accomplish.[32] Pico's dream of reconciling all faiths in a single ultimate mystery rested on the same conviction. No doubt Aldus, the client and intellectual shield-bearer of the great men, had seen the same visions and dreamed the same dreams. But this still leaves the crucial question of his life unanswered: why did he decide to become a printer? There is little sign that Pico, Poliziano or Barbaro held any very strong views on the new art. Pico wrote to Aldus in 1491, when his old friend must already have been in Venice pressing ahead with his plans, and he sent a Homer which may well have had a place in those plans: but the subject of printing was not mentioned. Poliziano clearly understood many of the implications of printing for the author and his reputation, but his anxieties seem to have centred on seeing that the right text was printed rather than that the maximum number of people read it.[33] Barbaro's attitude was thoroughly conservative. In the dedication of his *Paraphrase of Themistius*, written in 1480, he had commended Plato's advocacy of a rigid censorship of all material to be circulated in private or in public, observing that here was the way to control the flood of books which, in his own time, was being composed by rogues and read by fools.[34] These great scholars might write of human dignity, the human word as the rational expression of that dignity, and ancient literature as the highest expression of the human word: but there is little to show that they had found a place for the press in their scheme of things. However much we emphasise the idealism of Aldus' letter to Catherina Pia, or stress its dependence on the ideas of Pico and Barbaro, the fact remains that it does not once mention printing. There is nothing to suggest that it is more than a piece of educational publicity. Finally, we should remember that neither Ferrara, where Aldus had pursued his formal studies, nor Florence, the main source of inspiration for Hellenic scholarship, had become a major centre of press activity by 1490.[35]

If his intellectual contact with the great humanists of the 1480s gives no obvious explanation of Aldus' decision to become a printer, his social links with them and their peers make the entry into a ruthlessly speculative field even more difficult to understand. For a contemporary who had assessed his position during the later 1480s would surely have reckoned that Aldus' ship was now riding safely and comfortably in port. He was approaching forty, an age at which men of the time began to feel the creaking of their joints and the blurring of their eyes.[36] His career had been thoroughly respectable, if unspectacular. He had acquired the attention of his superiors, the respect of his peers, and – most important of all – patronage which offered as much security as a second-rank man of letters could hope to enjoy.

It is somewhat less than just that Alberto Pio should now be remembered chiefly as the pupil of Aldus, a young man who perhaps took himself and the world rather too seriously, a bitter opponent of Erasmus, and a tragic casualty of repeated foreign intervention in Italy.[37] His absolute commitment to literature and the arts is difficult to appreciate outside his native Emilia, and a casual observer might wonder how he had time for such interests. During the 1490s, his early manhood was taken up in a vicious feud with his cousin Giberto for the possession of Carpi: in July 1497 his house was sacked and he was forced to take refuge in Ferrara.[38] Yet even as a refugee, Alberto was able to maintain a considerable household, to spend nearly fifty florins in five months on the purchase and decoration of books, and to employ Musurus as Greek tutor and librarian.[39] In 1500 a new Ferrarese initiative followed by the providential death of his cousin meant that Alberto could return home in comparative safety: so he celebrated the occasion by spending 800 gold crowns on the library of the deceased Giorgio Valla, and set immediately about transforming the city of Carpi.[40] He resided there for only seven years. But during that time the Cathedral was reconstructed on the new, Bramantesque, design, the Palazzo rebuilt and frescoed by Bernardino Loschi, and a sweeping classical arcade extended along the opposite side of the piazza.[41] So anxious was Alberto to establish Carpi as a centre of all the liberal arts that he eventually invited the typographer Benedetto Dolcibello de Manzi, a native of the place who had already been prosecuted for violating Aldus' Greek copyright, and immediately violated another by printing Latin texts in cursive.[42] But Aldus seems to have held his old pupil politely at arm's length. He thanked him for constant support: he gratefully mentioned offers of estates, complete authority over an entire town, even the chance to found an academy; but he would not settle in Carpi.[43] In the context of 1497, when Alberto was an exile and Aldus was bound to his investors, the discreet refusal is not too surprising. But when we read in Aldus' earliest preface "Though I could lead a quiet and peaceful life, I have chosen one full of toil and trouble",[44] then recall the type of patronage which was certainly available to him, we are brought directly back to the original problem. Aldus did not need to become a printer.

So we must shift the emphasis of the enquiry, and look for personal motives which could have inspired the decision. Lack of evidence makes the search exceedingly hazardous, and at first sight deepens the mystery: for such information as we have suggests that Aldus was a rather retiring man who did not pursue literary fame in the aggressive fashion adopted by many of his contemporaries, and was even slightly embarrassed at times by the reputation that printing brought him. His prefaces may stress the pains taken over a text, and exaggerate the excellence of the version produced.[45] But he wrote little else, and in his first will left instructions for his executors to destroy certain small grammatical works which the sensitive author did not consider sufficiently polished for publication.[46] He knew of the savage academic controversies of the time, approved them as a stimulus to the purification of classical texts, and lived surrounded by their main participants: but he took no part himself.[47] Two of the leading humanists of the university of Padua, Giovanni Calfurnio and Raphael Regius, exchanged insults throughout the later 1480s. Aldus remained on good terms with both.[48] He showed no inclination to join his friend Egnazio's attack on Sabellico. And when several of his associates became rivals for one of Venice's public lectureships, he avoided taking sides. Finally, we have the evidence of Aldus' plain texts of the classics to reinforce the point made both by the scarcity of information about his personality, and by the quality of what little there is: the press was not seen as a means of self-advertisement, and the ancient authors could be left to speak for themselves.[49]

At first sight, there is some case for seeing Aldus as a committed and discerning antiquarian, a man cast in the same mould as his idol Poliziano, and one who spent a good part of his life collecting precious skills and information which he eventually felt the need to communicate. Erasmus' discussion of the proverb "Hasten slowly" centred on the dolphin and anchor depicted on a Roman coin which Aldus had shown him, and though what we know of the printer's busy life does not suggest that he had time or money to indulge a taste for antique-collecting, he certainly lived in a world of dedicated antiquarians. Pietro Bembo, who is supposed to have given him the coin in question, spent his life expanding an already considerable family collection. Several of Aldus' associates were avid students of Latin epigraphy, and as we shall see in due course, his own choice of type-founts reflects what was probably an interest he shared with many friends.[50] But there is more information about his personal library. In the same passage, Erasmus called it "a treasure-house", and a similar claim was made in the later sixteenth century, when Aldus' grandson began to speak of selling the books. In 1580 the Mantuan ambassador reported from Venice: "I have spoken this morning with Master Aldo Manuccio, who, according to rumour, has one of the most beautiful libraries which a scholar could desire, even if he were also a prince."[51]

But in the event, the rumours proved to stem from the owner himself, and to be no more than the sales talk of a man in serious financial difficulties. The younger Aldus was counting on his family library as a capital asset, and anxious to inflate its value at any cost. Eventually, no sale was arranged: the books were appropriated by the Holy See after the owner's death in 1597 in part-settlement of his debts, and the inventories made for the Vatican library show that even Erasmus' estimate was probably overgenerous.[52] We have no means of knowing how many of the 343 manuscripts and 1,564 printed texts had been in the possession of Aldus the elder, unless the printed editions are dated after his death. But this hardly matters. Even in 1600, as a contemporary commented, there was little "to make one's month water", and there was certainly nothing among the manuscripts which could have formed the basis for a major programme of publication in both the ancient languages.[53] A few Greek items – a Lycophron copied by Arsenios Apostolios, and a selection of letters – might possibly have been used, and can be identified with reasonable precision. But they do not even carry Aldus' signature, let alone any sign of comment or conjecture on the text.[54] The great part of the manuscript collection was a commonplace bundle of Latin classics, local chronicles, devotional works, anthologies, and commentaries. The younger Aldus did succeed in passing off one printed text, an early edition of Ovid's *Metamorphoses,* to the Roman bibliophile Fulvio Orsini as a genuine specimen of his grandfather's preparatory work, and the book carries Orsini's proud heading "Ovidii Metamorphoseos cum emendationibus Aldi". The buyer may, or may not have been the victim of a confidence trick. Once again, it hardly matters. For what Orsini termed "emendations" are no more than explanations or paraphrases, with the occasional correction of an obvious printing error: nowhere is there any sign of a keen editorial brain criticising a clumsy first effort, bringing superior textual and linguistic knowledge to bear, and sharpening its wits for a shrewder cut at the same problems.[55] Even when he had been printing for some years, Aldus was no textual critic, and it was certainly not expertise in this field which led him to printing.[56]

There is one trait in Aldus' character of which we can be absolutely sure and which, though it cannot by itself explain why he began printing, may shed some light on the working of his mind and on the principle which ruled him. He was fascinated by language: not by language as the expression of man's rational faculty, though he would no doubt have paid lip-service to that fashionable idea, but by language in itself, as a pattern of sounds with music in its rhythms and riches in its variety. Perhaps as a result of this, perhaps because of the many years he had spent in the school-room, he was almost morbidly sensitive about grammatical accuracy and correct pronunciation. Erasmus joked light-heartedly about this: in the *Praise of Folly*, written just after his departure from Italy, he showed how the Goddess sustained the grammarians in their wild rejoicings over a new inscription and their furious quarrels over a disputed case-ending. No trouble was too much in the fight to settle these imaginery issues: Aldus alone had written five grammars.[57] The quip was not maliciously intended, and Aldus would probably not have been displeased by it. Only a year later he was writing that he had never yet produced a book that satisfied him, and would gladly redeem every error he had made for a gold piece.[58] And Erasmus' joke was true in spirit, if not yet in fact. Aldus published his Latin Grammar for the first time in 1493, mentioning a Greek Grammar, grammatical exercises, and various shorter works which he hoped would soon follow. The Latin Grammar was re-issued in 1501, 1508 and 1514, with additions, alterations in layout, the change of a word here or there: the Greek Grammar was still unpublished at the time of its author's death, and was seen through the press by his friend Musurus; all but one of the others seem to have perished, as Aldus wished.[59] We can only agree with Erasmus, that Aldus was meticulous to a fault. But in a publisher, it might prove to be a good fault.

The Grammars also reveal the more positive side of the author's attitude to language. In the introduction to the 1501 edition, Aldus revealed his deep dissatisfaction with the standard work, the twelfth-century *Doctrinale* of Alexander of Villedieu: the style was so appalling, the labour of committing to memory the 2,000-line poetic exposition of Latin grammar so daunting, that many pupils came to regard the whole process of learning with horror and even those who survived the ordeal forgot what they had learned immediately, since they could not relate it to anything; far more could be gained if some of the time spent in learning by heart was devoted to reading Cicero or Virgil, who would provide models of proper Latin style.[60] These objections reveal Aldus' fundamental position. Villedieu's *Doctrinale* tended to treat the rules of Latin grammar as the dictates of some Divine Reason, existing by logical necessity rather than evolving through constant use. Little was said of exceptions or anomalies: examples were generally invented, and authorities rarely cited. To Aldus, such an approach to language was repugnant, first because it neglected the essential mobility of words, second because it took no account of the classics, third because the divorce of grammar from its origins and from literature made the subject educationally stultifying. His own Grammar was not, in fact, a great success. It was re-issued some fifteen times before 1568, but it certainly never supplanted the despised *Doctrinale,* which ran triumphantly through 279 editions during the fifteenth and sixteenth centuries.[61] Aldus' Grammar is rarely mentioned in the correspondence of his friends, and I suspect that even its limited success was due more to the prestige of its author than to the intrinsic merits of the work. It is not very original. In the 1514 edition, Aldus claimed to have "followed the ancient Greek and Latin grammarians": this meant, in effect, that he had adopted the three-part scheme laid down by Donatus' fourth-century Grammar, devoting one section to nouns, pronouns and declension, a second to verbs and conjugation, and a third to syntax.[62] In spite of the protest against too much learning by rote, the material was still laid out in a "question and answer" format which would compel the bemused ten-year-olds to intone the complex definitions back to their teacher. Even Alexander of Villedieu's use of poetic rhythms as a mnemonic device was preserved in Aldus' lists of nouns arranged in hexameters.[63] But the signs of a fundamentally different approach to language are still apparent. Aldus' lists of nouns are lists of exceptions, which decline only in the singular or the plural: he was abreast of his English contemporary, John Holt, in providing explanations of Latin moods and tenses in the vernacular; and he stated his principles firmly in the opening definition: "What is Grammar? An art and a profession based on reason, usage and authorities."[64] Linguistic rules were at least being given a life of their own.

Aldus' twin convictions – of the dynamism of language and the predominance of classical authority – appear even more clearly in his shorter works than in his full-length Grammar. To his earliest edition, the Greek Grammar of Constantine Lascaris, he appended a few pages of his own "On Greek letters, diphthongs, and how they have come down to us", laying careful stress on correct pronunciation and on the differences or similarities of the Latin and Greek forms.[65] He offered a comparative index of Greek and Latin proper names to readers of his text of Ovid's *Metamorphoses,* again inviting them to watch the parallel but distinct development of the two languages.[66] Problems of correct usage, whether in speech or writing, wholly obsessed him. Even in his "Brief introduction to the Hebrew language" (of which he can hardly have known more than the barest rudiments) he gave careful instructions on the pronunciation of palatal, dental and labial phonemes.[67] The widespread tendency to shorten Latin and Greek diphthongs into long vowels troubled him deeply. He reacted against it in a short essay – presumably one of the "fragments" which should have been destroyed – argued that both vowel-sounds ought to be given their proper length and value, and appealed to the authority of Terence and Eustathius.[68] He printed accusative plurals in -eis in his first text of Virgil, justifying his choice from Priscian.[69] Whenever we find Aldus at work on a project of his own, rather than the editing of a text, he seems crouched in an attitude of intense concentration over some minute problem of linguistic usage. His text of Caesar contained a long list of the place-names of ancient Gaul and their modern French equivalents.[70] His edition of the Roman agricultural writers concluded with a detailed exposition of Palladius' system of days, and a table showing how to calculate the exact length of a Roman hour during each month of the year.[71] Even the growing interest in lyric metres which becomes apparent in the short appendix attached to Prudentius in 1501, or in the new book added to the Latin Grammar in 1508, may have derived from the same profound philological curiosity.[72] By 1509 Aldus was able to correct his manuscripts of Horace on the basis of a thorough metrical knowledge.[73]

This concern with microscopic questions of language and antiquity could easily have developed into the crabbed, sterile pedantry which, we may note, is commonly associated with bachelor schoolmasters of advancing years. Aldus managed to avoid the danger. Possibly his temperament helped him: as we have seen, he did not enjoy controversy and he was not basically a crabbed or pedantic person. There is no questioning his respect for classical authority. Occasionally, he annexed short "Lives" to his editions, and they are little more than extended lists of citations from the author concerned. The personality of Aldus encroaches only to add a cross-reference or a counter-argument from some other authority: Suetonius or Pliny on the reasons for Ovid's exile, Symmachus and Ambrose on the dating of Prudentius' works.[74] In his own writings preferred quotations and classical catch-phrases – "You would need an Oedipus to guess that" or "the spear of Achilles" or "faithful Achates[75] – flow from the end of his pen with a facility which shows how deeply the ancient authors had penetrated into his mind. But Aldus' intellectual attitude to the classics was never pedantic. To him, they formed only one part of a broader linguistic picture: the most elaborate and interesting part, certainly, but still only a part, and one which had no exclusive claims to a scholar's attention. In 1501 he defended his text of Petrarch with as much vehemence as he had lavished on his Virgilian readings, and at far greater length: it was absurd, he told his critics, to latinise Tuscan forms by writing "vulgari" for "volgari" or "Canzona" for "canzone" because any Tuscan knew that his dialect did not follow Latin forms in every case. His manuscripts showed that "canzone" was good enough for Petrarch.[76] The message is exactly that of "Greek letters and diphthongs, and how they come down to us", of the index of Greek and Latin names in the *Metamorphoses*, and of the list of Latin and French place-names: languages have lives of their own, they are constantly changing, and they all deserve attention. As early as 1496, Aldus had compared the varieties of Italian local usage to the rich tapestry of the Greek literary dialects, and his comments on that occasion sum up his attitude perfectly: "Sometimes I cannot help laughing at this change in the form of words."[77] All language was interesting and amusing.

There can be little doubt that when Aldus gave his contemporaries the texts of Horace and Homer, Sophocles and Sannazaro, Dante and Dioscurides, he was giving them the authorities to follow and appreciate a phenomenon which fascinated him – the phenomenon of language, its changes, and its correct use. It is not in fact possible to treat Aldus' publications simply as the expression of his humanist ideals: we shall see in the next chapter that his programme was capable of exciting commercial interest, and was carried out in what for the times was a thoroughly businesslike fashion. But, since we lack any clear evidence of economic need or intellectual pressure, the case for regarding Aldus' original decision to become a printer as the result of personal conviction is very strong indeed. This seems to have been his own version of the story, so far as he gave one. In 1501, he addressed his Latin Grammar to the teachers whom he hoped would use it, and gave them a portentous reminder of the responsibilities they carried for the good and evil in the world: they formed the characters of boys who would go on to become laywers and philosophers, rulers and princes, bishops and even popes; they must not bore, or brutalise, their pupils but lead them, through the study of the best authors, to a knowledge of good literature and upright conduct.[78] A splendidly phrased homily, no doubt, but not very startling in itself. The notion that reading directly frames character had passed very early into the Western educational tradition from Plato and St. Basil, and been widely discussed by the liberal theorists of fifteenth-century Italy: it will almost certainly have reached Aldus through Battista Guarino.[79] But Aldus took the reasoning one stage further. In 1495 he attached a sort of declaration of intent to his edition of Lascaris' Greek Grammar, re-printing it in all subsequent issues of that work and of his own Latin Grammar: "I have decided to spend all my life in the service of my fellow-men. God is my witness, I desire nothing more than to do something for them, as my past life shows, wherever it has been spent, and as I hope my future life will show still more...."[80]

Though it is expressed in the sugary rhetoric of the times, this passage does reveal a consistent process of reasoning. Literary education improves character. The more good literature is made available, the more characters will be improved. To Aldus, printing was not a break in his activity as an educator, but a continuation of it into a new dimension. We have no means of knowing how or when he came to this conclusion: six years of teaching must certainly have affected him; so, perhaps, did the examples of Pico, Poliziano and Barbaro, though it is hard to be sure. All we can know for certain is that by the end of the 1480s, Aldus had formed his conviction and was ready to put it into practice.

NOTES

1 Aldus' son Paulus put the date in 1452 by saying that his father died "in his sixty-third year" (1515). The younger Aldus pushed the date back to 1449 by referring to 1597 as "the hundred and forty-seventh year after the birth of my grandfather". For citations see E. Pastorello, "Di Aldo Pio Manuzio – testimonianze e documenti", LBF LXVII, 1965, p. 165. An even earlier date, 1447, is suggested by A. Zeno and D. M. Manni, *Vita di Aldo Pio Manuzio insigne restauratore delle lettere greche e latine* Venice, 1759, p. 2. Pastorello argues for the latest possible date, as this would explain Aldus' calling himself a "boy" when he heard Calderini.

Aldus made provision for three sisters named Julia, Petrucia and Benevenuta, in his first two, but not in his last will: CSV pp. 92–9.

The recent attempt of L. Gerulaitis to provide Aldus with a pedigree seems to me ingenious rather than enlightening: "The Ancestry of Aldus Manutius", *Renaissance News*, XIX, No. 1, 1966, pp. 1–12.

2 OAME V, XXXIX.

3 Information from R. Weiss, "In memoriam Domitii Calderini", IMU III, 1960, pp. 309–20: C. Dionisotti, "Calderini, Poliziano e altri", *ib.*, XI, 1968, pp. 151–85; J. Dunston, "Studies in Domizio Calderini", *ib.*, same number, pp. 71–150.

4 G. Zippel, introduction to *Le vite di Paolo II di Gaspare da Verona e Michele Canensi*, R.I.S. Tom. III, pars xvi, Città di Castello, 1904. D. S. Chambers, "Studium Urbis and Gabella Urbis: the University of Rome in the Fifteenth Century", in *Cultural Aspects of the Italian Renaissance*: essays presented to P. O. Kristeller, ed. C. Clough, Manchester, 1976, pp. 68–87.
5 R.I.S. vol. cit., p. 57, with Zippel's notes.
6 OAME L, B (Vol. I, p. 78): "multa correximus, quae perperam Romae impressa fuerant."
7 *Ib.*, v. Compare De Bussi's preface to St. Jerome, Rome, 1468: "Adde quod quicquid ingeniorum olim fuit, latebatque paene in pulvere et tineis propter immensos labores ac nimium describentium precia, sub tuo principatu coeptum est scaturire et per omnem orbem uberrimo fonte diffluere." See also BP pp. 98–9.
8 OAME I, B, XI: compare BP p. 81 (preface to Aulus Gellius).
9 C. Dionisotti, "Aldo Manuzio umanista", in *Umanesimo europeo e umanesimo veneziano*, Venice, 1963, pp. 213–43. Chambers' article, cited under n. 4, above, reveals the instability of papal patronage and the uneven functioning of the university.
10 Schuck, Doc. v, p. 119. On the dispute with Egnazio see below, Ch. V, nn. 11, 19.
11 On the activities of what has been called a "heathen and republican secret society" see L. von Pastor, *History of the Popes*, Vol. IV, London, 1923, pp. 37–79. Though never censorious, Aldus was clearly suspicious of poets such as Lucretius: see Dionisotti, *op. cit.*, p. 233.
12 OAME v. The document from Carpi, and a tax-return of the same year, are now lost: they have been reconstructed from eighteenth-century descriptions by Pastorello, "Testimonianze de documenti...", p. 166.
13 See below, n. 20. Also OAME LXXIII.
14 CAM I. The letter, dated 5 November 1483, calls Aldus "Cato", apparently in jocular allusion to the Roman censor. The term "our prince", applied to Pico, also suggests a close relationship.
15 For a convenient guide to the development of the university and for further bibliography see the recent study of W. Gundersheimer, *Ferrara – the Style of a Renaissance Despotism*, Princeton, 1973, pp. 59–65, 162–3. The almost day-to-day involvement of Duke Ercole in university matters comes out clearly in the *Diario Ferrarese* of Bernardino Zambotti (R.I.S. Tom. XXIV, pars vii, Bologna, 1937).
16 D. Vitaliani, *Della vita e delle opere di Niccolo Leoniceno vicentino*, Verona, 1892: A. Castiglioni, "The School of Ferrara and the Controversy on Pliny", in *Science, Medicine and History: Essays on the Evolution of Scientific Thought and Medical Practice Written in Honour of Charles Singer*, ed. E. Underwood, Vol. I, Oxford, 1953, pp. 269–79.
17 R. Sabbadini, *La scuola e gli studi di Guarino Veronese*, Catania, 1896. For the text of *De Ordine*, as well as various speeches in Guarino's honour, see E. Garin, *Il pensiero pedagogico dell'umanesimo*, Florence, 1958, pp. 434f. Grey, Fleming, Free, Gunthorpe and Tiptoft are named by Ludovico Carbone among his pupils, p. 477.
18 OAME v (Vol. I, p. 9). See references to Aldus' wills under n. 1.

19 See under n. 16, above, on Leoniceno. Valla's presence is noted by G. Bertoni, *La biblioteca Estense e la cultura ferrarese ai tempi del duca Ercole I, 1471–1505*, Turin, 1903, p. 113, but I have found no definite evidence of it. See below, Ch. V, nn. 12f. The presence of Urceus, and his subsequent interest in Aldus' career, are beyond question: C. Malagola, *Della vita e delle opere di Antonio Urceo, detto Codro*, Bologna, 1878, pp. 150f.

20 For the correct text of this letter see L. Dorez, "Alde Manuce et Ange Politien", *Révue des Bibliothèques*, Ann. VI, 1896, pp. 319–21. For Poliziano's reply, pp. 321–3. Hostilities between Venice and Ferrara lasted from 2 May 1482 until 8 August 1484: S. Romanin, *Storia documentata di Venezia*, Vol. IV, Venice, 1973 ed., pp. 97–117.

21 Information from H. Noiret, *Lettres Inédites de Michel Apostolis, Bibliothèque des Écoles Françaises d'Athènes et de Rome*, Paris, 1889: pp. 29–30 contain an account of the known facts about Adramyttenus, and name him as the scribe of Bibliothèque Nationale, Paris, Ms. Graecus, 1761 and Biblioteca Apostolica Vaticana, Ms. Palatinus 115.

22 Ioannis Pici Mirandulae, *Opera Omnia*, Basel, 1557, pp. 363–4.

23 Politiani, *Opera Omnia*, Aldus, 1498, unpaginated: Epistolarum Lib. I, Nos. 4 and 5 (Poliziano's letter and Pico's reply). For the dating see E. Garin, "Ricerche su Giovanni Pico della Mirandola – l'epistolario", in *La cultura filosofica del Rinascimento italiano*, Florence, 1961, p. 258.

24 For Scita's letter see reference under n. 14, above. His involvement in the printing-company was much less active than Leoniceno's, but perhaps shows in the epigramme he contributed to *Hypnerotomachia Polifili* in 1499. An exhaustive bibliography of Pico's career is not necessary, but a useful introduction is now available in the English translation of some of Garin's essays: see *Portraits from the Quattrocento*, New York/London, 1972, pp. 190–221.

25 Compare for example the passing reference of A. Firmin-Didot, *Alde Manuce et l'Hellénisme à Venise*, Paris, 1875, pp. 6–7.

26 Politiani, *Opera Omnia*, Ep. Lib. I, No. 8.

27 Pici, *Opera Omnia*, p. 359.

28 The text is now readily available in Orlandi's appendices: Vol. I, pp. 157–164. The problems of composition and dating can only be solved by assuming that some reworking was done: see C. F. Buhler, "The First Aldine", *Papers of the Bibliographical Society of America*, XLII, 1948, pp. 3–14, and "Aldus' Paraenesis to his Pupil, Lionello Pio", *The Library*, Fifth Series, XVII, 1962, pp. 240–2. See also Buhler's *Early Books and Manuscripts*, New York, 1973, where his scattered bibliographical essays are collected. For evidence of Aldus' teaching activity see below, Ch. V, n. 53.

29 OAME, Vol. I, p. 160.

30 *Ib.*, p. 161.

31 *Ib.*, pp. 163–4. I do not think that Aldus' words can be used to prove that he actually met Barbaro, but the point is unimportant since it is clear that he belonged to the

same intellectual circle and accepted the same values. See V. Branca, "Ermolao Barbaro and late Quattrocento Venetian Humanism", in *Renaissance Venice,* ed. J. R. Hale, London, 1973, pp. 218-43.
32 Politiani, *Opera Omnia,* Ep. Lib. II, Nos. 6, 7. For full discussion of the intellectual positions involved, cf. Branca's article, cited in previous note.
33 See above, n. 27, for Pico's letter. Some of the polemics concerning his 900 theses were printed, but this may not have been of his choosing: R. Marcel, "Pic et la France", in *L'opera e il pensiero di Giovanni Pico della Mirandola,* Florence, 1965, pp. 205-30. On Poliziano's attitude see *Opera Omnia,* Ep. Lib. IV, No. 13 (request to Andrea Magnanimo of Bologna to be sure that correct texts are printed).
34 *Ib.,* Ep. Lib. XII, No. 44.
35 R. Ridolfi, *La stampa in Firenze nel secolo XV,* Florence, 1957: V. Scholderer, "Printing in Ferrara in the Fifteenth Century", in *Fifty Essays...,* pp. 91-5.
36 C. Gilbert, "When did a Man in the Renaissance Grow Old?", *Studies in the Renaissance* XIV, 1967, pp. 7-32.
37 M. Gilmore, "Erasmus and Alberto Pio, Prince of Carpi", in *Action and Conviction in Early Modern Europe,* Essays in Memory of E. H. Harbison, ed. T. Rabb and J. Seigel, Princeton, 1969, pp. 299-318.
38 P. Guaitoli, "Memorie sulla vita d'Alberto Pio III", *Memorie storiche e documenti sulla città e sull'antico principato di Carpi,* I, Carpi, 1877, pp. 135-41.
39 A. Morselli, "Intorno a una lista di libraro ferrarese", in his collection of material "Notizie e documenti sulla vita di Alberto Pio", *Ib.,* XI, 1931, pp. 135-52. The document records the sale of over 200 volumes to Alberto between August 1499 and February 1500. On Musurus' position see D. Geanakoplos, *Greek Scholars in Venice,* Harvard, 1962, pp. 125-8.
40 On the pacification imposed by Ferrara see Guaitoli, *op. cit.,* pp. 150-4. On the purchase of Valla's library, D. Fava, *La Biblioteca Estense nel suo sviluppo storico,* Modena, 1925, p. 152.
41 On the building programme see Morselli, "Alberto e la corte di Carpi", *Memorie storiche...,* Vol. cit., pp. 153-83.
42 Fava, *op. cit.,* pp. 150-2, and "L'introduzione del corsivo nella tipografia e l'opera di Benedetto Dolcibello", *Internationale Vereinigung für Dokumentation, Dreimonatliche Berichte,* Haag, IX, fasc. i, 1942, pp. 2-7. Dolcibello printed two folio volumes of commentary on Scottus in April and May, 1506. On his infringement of Aldus' Greek copyright see below, Ch. IV, nn. 64-6.
43 Dedication of Aristotle and Theophrastus, in OAME VIII.
44 *Ib.,* I B.
45 See below, Ch. IV, n. 178. But Aldus did claim credit where none was due in his edition of Craston's Lexicon: RAIA pp. 13-14.
46 CSV p. 95.
47 OAME V.
48 Raphaelis Regii *De quibusdam Quintiliani locis cum quodam Calfurnio Dialogus,* Venetiis, Guliemus Tridentinus, 1490. The issue was one of those noted by Aldus in the

passage cited above. OAME XL, XLII, show him addressing dedications to both of the antagonists.

49 See Ch. V, below, nn. 11, 19. On the tacit "declaration" made by Aldus' plain texts see Dionisotti, *op. cit.* under n. 9, above.

50 M. M. Philips, *The Adages of Erasmus* pp. 174–5. See Ch. IV, below nn. 78 f., on Aldus' types.

51 A. Bertolotti, "Varietà archivistiche e bibliografiche", *Il Bibliofilo*, Anno VII, 1886, p. 181.

52 J. Bignami-Odier, *La Bibliothèque Vaticane de Sixte IV a Pie XI*, Studi e Testi, No. 272, Città del Vaticano, 1973, p. 81.

53 Biblioteca Apostolica Vaticana, Ms. Latini No. 7121, ff. 51r–59r: Biblioteca Ambrosiana, Milan, Cod. J. 100 inf.

The comment is that of Fulvio Orsini in 1590: P. de Nolhac, *La Bibliothèque de Fulvio Orsini*, Paris, 1887, p. 245: "...non vedo cosa da far venire l'acqua alla bocca."

54 Bibl. Ap. Vat., Ms. Graeci Nos. 1467 (Epistolographi), 1471 (Lycophron).

55 Ib., Incunabulum III, 16 (= 1135). See Nolhac, *Fulvio Orsini*, pp. 243–4: it is not clear that the writing is that of Aldus.

56 Kenney, *The Classical Text*, p. 18. See below, Ch. VI, passim.

57 Ch. 49. There is now a readily available English edition, ed. A. H. T. Levi, London, 1971. The work was first published in 1511.

58 OAME LXXVIII.

59 The "Rudimenta Grammatices" of 1501 was not divided into books, and the introductory material on letter and syllable-forms was fairly brief. In the next edition a new section on metres was added, and the whole work was divided into four books: the introductory sections were completely replanned, and a number of word-forms changed (eg. "Quaestiones" replaced "Interrogationes"). On the Greek Grammar see RAIA p. 73.

60 OAME XXV.

61 Space does not allow an exhaustive bibliography on the *Doctrinale*: for a clear introduction, and the source of my own remarks, see R. Bolgar, *The Classical Heritage and its Beneficiaries*, London/New York, 1964 ed., pp. 208–10, with notes. My estimate of the number of editions of Aldus' Grammar is derived from the British Museum Catalogue.

62 A comparison of Aldus' Grammar with the *Ars Minor* of Donatus soon reveals the exact similarity of structure. Since Donatus was still widely used, Aldus' failure to attract much attention is not very surprising.

63 *Rudimenta Grammatices*, 1501, f. c iv.

64 Ib., f. a vi r. On Holt see N. Orme, *English Schools in the Middle Ages*, London, 1973, pp. 28–9.

65 RAIA, p. 1. This section was also appended to the 1512 edition of Lascaris' Grammar, and the 1501 edition of Aldus' Latin Grammar.

66 Ovidii *Metamorphoseon libri quindecim*, 1502, ff. a iii r–f iiii r.

67 Appended to the *Rudimenta Grammatices* in 1501, and to all subsequent editions of Aldus' Grammar. RAIA pp. 31, 69.
68 *De vitiata vocalium ac diphthongorum prolatione*. It seems likely that Erasmus had secured a copy of this work, since it was published along with his *De recta Latini Graecique Sermonis Pronunciatione* in Basel during 1528.
69 OAME XXVII C.
70 *Ib.* LXXIV B. See also Vol. I, p. 191.
71 *Ib.* LXXXIII B.
72 Printed in Orlandi's appendix, Vol. I, pp. 167-9. On the addition to the Latin Grammar cf. n. 59, above.
73 *Adnotationes in Horatium*, in Orlandi's appendix, Vol. I, pp. 172-90.
74 Ovidii *Metamorphoseon* libri, f. g i r-v. "Aurelii Prudentii Vita per Aldum Romanum", in *Poetae Christiani Veteres*, Vol. I, 1501, f. 4 r.
75 OAME V: XVII B: LXXXVI. Orlandi's commentary provides an exhaustive guide to Aldus' classical citations, and a glance at any of the prefaces will reveal the extent of the printer's debt to his preferred authors.
76 *Ib.*, XXX.
77 *Ib.*, VI (Thesaurus Cornucopiae). On the comparison between vernacular and Greek dialect usage see C. Dionisotti, *Gli umanisti e il volgare fra Quattro-e Cinquecento*, Florence, 1968, pp. 1-14.
78 OAME XXV.
79 E. Garin, *L'educazione in Europa*, Bari, 1957, pp. 137-59.
80 OAME I.

III

BARBARIGO, TORRESANI AND MANUZIO

Since I undertook this wearisome business of printing – it is more than six years now – I can swear to you that I have had not an hour of unbroken rest.

In August 1496 Aldus addressed readers of his newly printed *Scriptores Grammatici Graeci*[1] with rhetorical, but not the less grim determination as he wrestled with the problems of his publishing company and apparently dated them from his first arrival in Venice in 1489 or 1490. But the earliest dateable productions of the Aldine press belong to 1494 or 1495, so it follows that nearly five of the six years mentioned by Aldus must have been taken up by preliminary negotiations.[2] This is hardly surprising. Both economically and technically, the preparation of a Greek type fount was a serious problem, and we have contemporary evidence to show that Zacharias Callierges needed five or six years to find a satisfactory solution.[3] There is a certain amount of information about Aldus' activity as a scholar between 1490 and 1495. But these years leave some grave difficulties in the way of understanding his career as a printer. Unless we can reconstruct some notion of the commercial organisation which he established, of the advantages which it gave him and the pressures that it put upon him, we shall be judging his entire cultural achievement in a vacuum. We should be approaching it without even a clear idea of his motives for coming to Venice in the first place.

It has been the custom to fuse these questions into one and then envelop them in a single aromatic whiff of rhetoric. Aldus' motives, achievement, and success pose no particular problems because they form an inseparable part of a much larger whole, the "total cultural experience" of High Renaissance Venice. The city, it is said, had a large colony of Greek exiles who could advise, copy, and correct proofs: it had an unrivalled collection of Greek manuscripts in the personal library which Cardinal Bessarion had bequeathed to the

Republic in 1468; it had a commercial aristocracy with the money for patronage and the taste for classical literature; it had a flourishing printing industry.[4] Aldus fitted so naturally into this historical jigsaw that no one troubled to ask what he had to complain about in 1496, or why he was exploring the chances of leaving Venice as early as 1499.[5]

Reflected across five centuries by the patriotic enthusiasm of her mythographers, the cultural role played by Venice from around 1490 seems an inevitable consequence of her own position and the political developments of the time. It does not follow that this was equally the case in 1490. At almost exactly this time a student at Padua named Gerolamo Amaseo, who would in due course become an associate of Aldus, found himself in the grip of a passion to study Greek. He turned to his friends for advice. His elder brother, blank-faced, asked "Why learn Greek?" Leonicus Tomaeus, soon to become Padua's official teacher of the language, cautiously advised him to stay: Milan was a possibility, but Demetrius Chalcondylas taught the rudiments unwillingly, and at a price. Two Tuscan visitors, Carlo Antenori and Scipio Fortiguerra, were far more decisive, and urged him to set out immediately for Florence. So Amaseo departed on one of those scholarly wanderings which were the fashion of the age. He took the boat down the Brenta to Venice, slept out under the colonnade of the ducal palace, then continued up the Po to Ferrara where he was forced to leave his coat in the clutches of the local pawnbrokers. Filippo Beroaldo put him up in Bologna, and he was able to finish the journey on foot. Towards the end of April 1493, he wrote a full account and explanation of his actions to his brother, mentioning his kindly reception by Poliziano, the progress of his studies under Varino Camerte, and the vital services which were being rendered to Greek culture by Janus Lascaris, both as librarian to the Medici and as editor of the printed texts which were now appearing in increasing numbers. He ascribed to Florence almost all the advantages which subsequent historians have lavished upon Venice, where not one of his advisors, all of whom later swam into Aldus' orbit, had ever recommended him to go.[6]

Patrician patronage, the use of libraries, and the migration of Greek scholars are all major subjects, which can hardly be dismissed in a paragraph or on the strength of a single letter. We shall turn to them in their due place. But Amaseo's evidence is a valuable caution against the perils of historical foreshortening, and a reminder that, though Venice already possessed a vigorous local tradition and connections with a great university, she could still not by herself match the international prestige of the established centres as a haven for more advanced philological studies. A closer look at the relevant biographies will show that in 1490 the most distinguished Greek scholars, including almost all of those on whose help Aldus would later rely, were still in Florence and likely to remain there for the foreseeable future. No one could have known that in two years the Magnificent Lorenzo would be dead and that in two more Piero, who continued his father's patronage, would be swept away by revolution. Chalcondylas remained as professor of Greek until an offer from Milan tempted him away in 1491.[7] Lascaris filled a number of functions before departing for France at some unknown time after the middle of the decade. He was librarian of the Medici private collection; he did some teaching alongside Chalcondylas, amongst his more able pupils being two of the first Aldine editors, Marcus Musurus and Arsenios Apostolis; and he took an interest in the designing of types and the editing of texts for the press of Lorenzo di Alopa.[8] At precisely the same moment the concentric circle of Italian-born Hellenists which centred on Poliziano and Ficino was at the summit of its activity and prestige.[9] If Aldus had been concerned principally with hopes of patronage and scholarly cooperation, it is hard to understand why he turned in 1490 towards Venice rather than Florence, where the opportunities were more promising and where his own chances would have been greatly strengthened by his past connections with Pico and Poliziano. It is true that in 1490 the Venetian senate was throwing out conscience-stricken hints that it might soon carry out the terms of Bessarion's will by making his library fully accessible to the public: but any dreams which had grown from these proposals must soon have been shaken by the Signoria's refusal to admit Poliziano to the library during June of the following year.[10] All the evidence suggests that we should shift the emphasis of Aldus' plans for his move to Venice towards solidly commercial and technical considerations. As a centre of trade, it offered chances of finding the expert designers and the capital investment which he would need. Also, while Florence already had a Greek press and Milan had seen a number of experiments, Venice was still virtually an open field. Here again, we must beware of the perils of foreshortening. The Alopa press collapsed so quickly that we now think of it chiefly as a notable precursor to the Aldine enterprise. But in the 1490s Codrus Urceus spoke of the two companies in the same sentence, as associates or competitors.[11]

Apart from the tendency to fuse him into a larger cultural phenomenon, there is an important, if negative, argument which might excuse us from deeper examination of Aldus' commercial background. This is the view that his organisation was backed by his old pupil Alberto Pio and, as the beneficiary of princely patronage, must have been insulated against all but the direst economic misfortune.[12] In a limited sense, this is probably the case, but it is very hard to say precisely where the limits lie. Aldus referred twice to the help he had received from Alberto's "resources", using unfortunately the word "opes" which can signify resources in a financial sense or support of a more general kind.[13] Since the same passages mention an offer of Alberto's to invest Aldus with the lordship of one of his towns, since we know that Aldus did own land in his patron's principality, and since it is clear that Alberto remained devoted to his tutor even beyond the grave, there is every likelihood that financial support was available.[14] But the legal documents to which we shall turn in a moment show beyond any question that Alberto Pio had no commercial interest in the company. There are two possible explanations of this apparent paradox, both of which may be true. The first is that Alberto's financial assistance was of a purely personal nature, aimed at giving Aldus some stake in the company without involving his own sponsor. The second is that Alberto provided funds only to underwrite the edition of Aristotle's works. On the whole, I think the second solution is more probable, since Alberto received the dedication of every volume and it was the regular practice of the time to seek influential backers for ambitious publications. The printing of Aristotle was a colossal enterprise which may well have needed help of this kind. But whichever explanation we adopt, the conclusion is the same. Alberto Pio had nothing to do with the business organisation of the company, and Aldus must have arrived in Venice with little but his ideals. Before he could even buy the technical skill he needed to cast a Greek fount, he had to have firm financial backing.

At least he had come to Venice at a suitable moment for seeking investment. Argument from the general to the particular is more than usually hazardous in a field as little known as the fifteenth-century Venetian economy, but all contemporary accounts seem to reflect a willingness in both the individual and the community to spend money on enjoyment and display. Palaces were being built everywhere. Stone bridges were replacing the makeshift wooden affairs which had spanned the canals for centuries. When the Scuola di

San Marco was gutted by fire in 1485, private subscriptions and public contributions rapidly raised the funds to replace it with the magnificent structure which now forms the entry to the Hospital of San Giovanni e Polo. The diarist Malipiero watched with mixed feelings as endless construction and decoration went on in the ducal palace, and as the Torre del Orologio was begun simply "to show that the city is not without money".[15] Pamphlets exuded an air of confidence and self-congratulation as they invited the throngs of visitors and pilgrims to inspect these glories: and the visitors, often envious but always admiring, paid tribute in their turn to the expansive opulence of Venetian life.[16] As we shall see, Aldus was able to fit into that life without difficulty and at the highest level, through his impressive connections with men like Pico and Poliziano, and through the introduction which these connections gave him to a number of prominent families in Venice itself.[17] The publication of the *Epistola ad Catherinam Piam* declared his respectability and his ideals to anyone who cared to read it.[18] We can at least say with absolute certainty that Aldus was in touch with one of his future partners by 9 March 1493, for on that day the first edition of his *Institutiones Grammaticae Latinae* was published by Andrea Torresani of Asola.[19]

Because of his long business association with Aldus, we have a great deal more personal information about Andrea than about most printers of the time, though it must be admitted that we know very little to his credit. His treatment by posterity was settled finally and devastatingly in 1531, when Erasmus, who had been attacked by several Italians for alleged ingratitude to Aldus and gluttony during his stay at Torresani's house in 1508, dipped his pen in acid for a reply. The result was his dramatic dialogue *Opulentia Sordida* ("How to be rich without showing it"), in which he maintained that there had been nothing to eat in the Torresani household anyway, and that the Italians owed as much to him as he to them. The scene is set with the return of "Gilbert" (Erasmus) from "Synodium" (Venice), and his meeting with an old friend who comments on his wan appearance. Gilbert explains this by the rigorous pattern of life and work in the home he has known for the past few months, the workshop owned by "Antronius" (Andrea Torresani), and run by his son-in-law "Orthrogonus" (Aldus).[20] It must be said that this was not an attack principally on Aldus. Orthrogonus is in fact a minor figure in the dialogue: industrious, basically sympathetic, he is still portrayed as being entirely under the control of his partner and father-in-law, to whom he defers on every question. This is a description of Aldus' position in the company which should be borne in mind when we turn to the surviving legal documents. The real target of Erasmus' wit was Antronius, the very embodiment of the tight-fisted arriviste. He economises on fuel by grubbing up sodden roots for the fire: he economises on food by serving such dainties as shellfish from the public latrines, minestra made with ancient cheese-rinds or decomposing tripe, and sour wine diluted with water; his guests are racked by kidney-stone and his neglected sons go to the bad while Antronius piles another thousand ducats each year onto his massive fortune. This portrait of Andrea Torresani is of course sharply biased by personal factors, not all of which are discernible now.[21] But its general outline, and some of its details, are almost alarmingly consistent with other versions. As early as 1505 Aldus' friends were sniping at Andrea for his meanness.[22] In 1517 Baptista Egnazio, a close personal friend of the now deceased Aldus and one of his leading editors, wrote that Andrea was utterly indifferent to anything except his own profit, and worthless as an academic publisher.[23] Erasmus' taunt about the low life of the Torresani family may not have been true in 1508: but in 1523 Andrea's son Federigo was fined a total of 1,200 ducats for cheating at cards, and banished from Venice for four years.[24] Andrea's own career definitely suggests that he was a cautious and pragmatic man of business who built up his own position by methodical steps and did not speculate rashly. He came from Asola in the territory of Mantua – hence the name "L'Asolano" which he sometimes used – , arrived in Venice at some unspecifiable moment in the mid-1470s, and apparently studied the art of printing under Nicholas Jenson. Since he was born in 1451 we can perhaps assume that this was the planned decision of a mature man to make his name in publishing. Andrea bought types from Jenson when the Frenchman retired. In 1479 we find him in partnership with two other printers to produce a Breviary:[25] in 1483 he is described as a bookseller in a contract which appoints him agent for the Paduan company of Ercole de Busca and Bartolomeo Valdizocco, so it is clear that he soon extended the range of his operation beyond mere printing.[26] By 1490 Andrea was thoroughly entrenched in the Venetian book world as a printer in his own right, as a dealer, and as an underwriter of other projects. Besides his large venture with Aldus, he embarked during that decade on short-term partnerships with four other printers.[27]

Overall, Torresani's publications were supremely conservative. Of the 160 editions catalogued between 1476 and his eventual merger with Aldus in 1508, more than half consist of the weighty legal texts and commentaries which, as already suggested, found ready buyers both in the Paduan law-school and among the numerous practising lawyers. The other half divides between philosophical texts and commentaries – also aimed obviously at the academic market in Padua –, the ever-saleable breviaries and a very small seasoning of classics and contemporaries including writers such as Cicero, Livy and Sabellico who were all among the bookseller's stock in trade.[28] There is no doubt that Andrea was following in the footsteps of his successful forebears Jenson and John of Cologne, directing a carefully selected range of specialised works at reasonably predictable groups of buyers who both needed them and could afford them. He may have inherited a number of Jenson's contacts, as well as his types and techniques: it is significant that the designer who cut Aldus' founts, and the merchant who distributed many of his books to Germany, may both once have been in the orbit of the Frenchman's great syndicate.[29]

There is nothing here which further crosschecks any of Erasmus' remarks. But the general impression of close-grained business acumen round which he built his dialogue definitely fits the image projected by Torresani's career. Cautious, successful and well connected in the trade, he was a splendid partner for an outsider such as Aldus.

But what made Andrea Torresani accept such a partner as Aldus? Justified or not, the humanists' hostile view of Andrea merely repeats a question which his own publications ask just as emphatically. For more than a decade, he had followed the conservative path of established business methods, and they had served him very well. Why should he choose to back this visionary idealist, whose declared plan of enlightening Europe through the study of Greek literature and philosophy must necessarily involve a leap in the dark through experiment with an almost unknown field of publication? We know too little about Andrea's personal designs to give any definite answer. But we may perhaps suggest that Aldus' ideals, however sincerely held, had a commercial side or were at least capable of being given a commercial interpretation.

When he was paying tribute to Lascaris' work for the Florentine press, Amaseo drew some significant conclusions:[30] "...there is no doubt that more [Greek] books will soon be published, since Italy is daily becoming more inflamed with interest in Greek literature."

By the early 1490s there were a number of signs that Hellenic studies, which had long been concentrated within intensely active but rather unstable cells, were beginning to gain more general prestige and academic recognition. Once the tendency became well marked, the printers would be tempted to follow it. The strength of the Florentine circle, already noted, is in any case so well known as to need no further emphasis. Chalcondylas' departure for Milan in 1491 seems to have had little effect upon it.[31] In Bologna, Aldus' friend Codrus Urceus was doing solid work between about 1480 and his violent death in 1500, offering lectures on Aristophanes, Homer, Theocritus and Hesiod.[32] The situation in the Veneto itself is harder to assess. Information is not lacking, but it is not always easy to interpret and it suggests some sharp contrasts. Under the influence of Cardinal Bessarion, a Chair of Greek was established at Padua for Chalcondylas in 1463, and he seems to have lectured with some success until tempted away to Florence exactly ten years later. No official replacement was made, and we enter one of those periods of uncertainty.

Probably private interest kept some momentum going: the presence of the great Ermolao Barbaro definitely produced a small focus of activity during the mid-1480s, and it seems clear from Leonico Tomeo's advice to Amaseo that some informal instruction in Greek was still available on the fringe of the university curriculum in 1493.[33] Some of this may well have stemmed from Leonico himself, for in 1497 he was recognised by the Venetian Senate, in response to considerable demand from the students, as Padua's first lecturer on the Greek text of Aristotle.[34] It is clear that even in the intervals between official appointments, we have to reckon with an undercurrent of interest in Greek studies which eventually became strong enough to make itself felt from below, without relying on the influential sponsorship of some exalted figure like Bessarion. In Venice, we find a rather similar pattern of private pressure and public uncertainty. By rights, the bequest of Cardinal Bessarion's library in 1468 ought to have given Hellenism a real impetus, but the Venetian government's failure to make any proper arrangements for the handling of the books seems to have deprived scholars of the immediate benefit they should have derived.[35] More was probably achieved by the appointment in 1485 of Giorgio Valla, an expert in Greek writings on the natural sciences, to one of the public lectureships.[36] But here again, individual effort seems to have been the most important factor. Barbaro's mighty influence exerted itself in Venice, too, in a series of lectures on the text of Aristotle which he delivered during the winter of 1484 at his own house, and which attracted a degree of interest that disconcerted Barbaro himself.[37] From about 1490 we are confronted by a force which is at once more permanent and more puzzling – a footloose and irrepressibly cheerful Franciscan named Urbano Valeriani who decided to open a private school of Greek in Venice and is said to have achieved a substantial success. The funeral oration which is our only source on this point may not be the most reliable witness. But Fra Urbano had just returned from a tour of the Eastern Mediterranean which had taken him to the most important sites on the Greek mainland, throughout the Aegean islands, across Asia Minor to the Holy Land and Egypt, then ultimately to Sicily where he twice visited the crater of Mount Etna. It was indeed a remarkable journey for those times and it is not hard to believe that he was a fascinating person, and well equipped to expound the poems of Homer which were his chief love.[38]

When speaking of Greek studies in the immediate context of Aldus' programme, we should think on a variety of different levels. The personality of Chrysoloras, the teaching of Guarino, and the munificence of Bessarion are all long-term factors which we can understand and applaud now, but it is hard to see Andrea Torresani's being particularly impressed by them in 1490. He will have needed convincing that the taste for Greek was growing day by day in his own vicinity. And the evidence was there.

The development of printing in Greek up to the time of Aldus in some ways resembles the contemporary development of Hellenic studies: isolated experiments are followed by a period of more concerted effort. It is accurate enough to say that only a dozen or so books had been printed entirely in Greek before 1494, so long as we remember that the titles involved represent twenty-seven separate editions, and that Jenson had been able to add the Greek passages to his edition of Aulus Gellius in a fine, rounded type, with all accents and breathings in place, as early as 1472.[39] There was no lack of interest, and the basic problems had been solved in a variety of ways. The point is that no one had thought it worthwhile, or been able, to establish Greek typography on a commercial level. The early attempts were lonely, small-scale affairs: a *Batrachomyomachia,* probably produced by Tommaso Ferrando of Brescia around 1473, and now surviving in a single copy;[40] Reno da Vicenza's text of Chrysoloras' *Erotemata;*

the Milanese first edition of Constantine Lascaris' Grammar, printed with type designed by a certain Demetrius in early 1476. During the next decade activity showed signs of quickening. In Milan, Bonus Accursius took charge of Demetrius' types and by the end of 1481 had produced seven editions, including Aesop's *Fables,* a Psalter, parts of Hesiod and Theocritus, two issues of Craston's Greek Lexicon, and another of Lascaris' Grammar. Some time in 1487 or 1488 Chalcondylas invited Demetrius from Milan to Florence to help with the printing of the first edition of Homer, and their success in obtaining financial support from Bernardo and Neri di Tanai de' Neri, two prominent members of the Medicean circle, suggests that this was a more solidly based operation.[41] But isolated and tentative experiments with a limited range of titles remained the rule. Chrysoloras' *Erotemata* went through three more issues, one in Parma at the very beginning of the 1480s, two in Vicenza between 1490 and 1491: in this case the typographer was Leonardus of Basel, who also reprinted Lascaris' grammatical works. Giovanni Craston's *Lexicon* was twice reproduced, on both occasions by Dionysius Bertochus in Venice or Vicenza: and in 1486 two Cretans named Laonicus and Alexandros printed the *Batrachomyomachia* and the Psalms in a type so archaic and complicated that even Robert Proctor gave up the attempt to unravel it after counting 1,223 different sorts.[42] But by the early 1490s the tempo was definitely changing. Chalcondylas' move to Milan brought a revival in the use of Demetrius' types to print a first edition of Isocrates and three smaller, grammatical works, though the operation seems to have been on a fairly limited scale.[43] The same cannot be said of the press established in Florence by Lorenzo di Alopa, with the help of Janus Lascaris. In the two years between 1494 and 1496 they produced ten editions and experimented with three different types, including an uncial which has been universally admired by modern critics for its boldness and clarity. Their output covered the Planudian Anthology, selections from Euripides' tragedies and Callimachus' poems, Lucian's dialogues and the *Argonautica* of Apollonius Rhodius: it was, in fact, the first attempt to venture beyond introductory linguistic works into the wider field of Greek literature. When we consider that in Venice itself two other companies besides that of Aldus must have been experimenting with Greek founts by the mid-1490s, the growing interest in this branch of typography becomes obvious.[44]

If we now superimpose the two broad patterns of the academic and publishing worlds upon one another, it becomes possible to make some plausible guesses at the thought which lay behind the association of Aldus and his partners. Torresani had based much of his success on law and philosophy, both of them academic or semi-academic fields. We must imagine his being approached by Aldus, a professional scholar of his own age, with a solid reputation and a range of social contacts which a small-town artisan like Andrea may frankly have coveted. The scheme he proposed was certainly daring: but he could point to the enthusiasm of his noble acquaintances, the vague rumblings from Padua (of which Andrea himself may well have been aware), the crowds attending Giorgio Valla's lectures or Fra Urbano's classes, and perhaps most threateningly of all, to growing interest in Greek typography in Florence and Milan. Aldus definitely believed, as did Amaseo, in a growing popular demand for Greek texts.[45] He may have succeeded in persuading the more commercially minded Torresani that there was a golden opportunity of "scooping" another academic market, which was still almost open, but might not remain so for much longer. If this was the case, both men were making a grave miscalculation. But they were also constructing an organisation strong and flexible enough to survive in circumstances which would probably have sent any one of their predecessors reeling after one or two publications.

It must be confessed that even with the aid of this flight of imagination, the relationship between Aldus and his partners remains extremely blurred. The notarial act of 1542 which finally dissolved the contract between them dated the original contract to 1495: according to the "Venetian style", that means some time after 1 March, and it is hard to believe that a legal document was mistaken on a point which could have affected its own validity.[46] But Aldus' edition of the Greek Grammar of Constantine Lascaris carries the date "1494, on the last day of February", and many experts place the undated Musaeus and *Galaeomyomachia* even earlier. We have also to reckon with the quotation which begins this chapter – Aldus' own claim that he had been at work for more than six years in August 1496.[47]

This is a conflict of evidence which only guesswork can resolve. There appear to me to be two main possibilities: either we can say that before 1495 Aldus was experimenting independently, possibly with capital provided by Alberto Pio, and that Andrea Torresani remained in the wings as an interested spectator until his prospective partner had shown that his scheme was feasible; or we can assume that some preliminary contract between Aldus and Torresani preceded the full partnership of 1495, and that the earliest publications must be treated as experimental pieces. The second solution seems marginally more probable, since there are some signs that Aldus received technical advice from Torresani from an early stage, and it seems doubtful if he could have made much progress as an independent operator. This kind of precautionary or provisional agreement was not unknown in the publishing world, and it seems appropriate to a scheme as ambitious as the one which Aldus proposed.[48] But this is mere surmise. Our one fixed point is a vague and retrospective reference to the establishment in 1495 of

a company for the printing of books between the late lord Pierfrancesco Barbarigo, son of the most Serene Prince, on the one side, and the late lord Andrea Torresani, bookseller, with the late lord Aldus de Manutiis, a Roman, also taking a certain part....[49]

In spite of the tantalising uncertainties, the discovery and publication of this notarial act allow us to draw together many threads of evidence which had long been dangling loosely. To scholars of the ninteenth century, even the formal business-partnership of Aldus and Andrea seemed to begin only in 1508.[50] The association of doge Marco Barbarigo's son with their company was a matter of gossip, and not very respectable gossip, since it formed the merest anecdote in a rambling and at times almost paranoid letter written more than forty years after the event by a little known antiquarian named Zuane Bembo. Speaking admiringly of his friend Santo Barbarigo, Zuane added in passing that Santo's father had "helped Aldus with several thousand ducats". Though two copies of the letter were known, and both had been published, not much credence could be attached to the story.[51] But early this century Mario Brunetti searched through the records of the Procuratori di San Marco, Venetian officials who dealt with the implementation of wills, and discovered a file relating to Pierfrancesco Barbarigo, the father of Bembo's friend Santo. Amongst other items, it contained the agreement of the Barbarigo, Torresani, and Manutius heirs to realise the capital value of the now inactive company by liquidating its surviving stocks. There were also parts of an account book which revealed something of the day-to-day workings of that company, though not its overall financial state. These two inserts were enough to prove that the company of Aldus Manutius was a far more potent organisation than had ever been suspected: not only had Torresani been involved from the very beginning, but the anecdote of

Zuane Bembo was proven beyond even its own face value. Pierfrancesco Barbarigo was not merely a sympathiser who helped Aldus out on one occasion, but a shareholder who put the weight of his capital and the influence of his ducal family name behind the company from its very beginning.

We should be impressed, but not nonplussed, by this involvement of a very highly placed Venetian aristocrat in a printing company. Though there is little evidence to suggest that the governing class interested themselves in the new discovery to the extent of getting their own hands inky in the workshop, a number of applications for copyright do carry the names of noblemen, and in the generation after Aldus two patricians, Bragadin and Giustiniani, would lead Venice in the publication of Hebrew texts.[52] There was probably more indirect than direct interest. We know, for example, that the immensely powerful Corner family held a monopoly on the manufacture of paper in Padua, and that by 1503 the trade was becoming so profitable that they were able to cut their prices by a third.[53] A thorough search of notarial records, or of the Procurators' files, might well reveal similar investments. There is no doubt that Pierfrancesco and his family were directly involved: but, apart from the casual reminiscence of Zuane Bembo, they are never mentioned in the correspondence of Aldus and his friends, never received a dedication, and cannot therefore have been very frequent visitors to the workshop. Whether their high connections were of any practical use to the printers we have no means of telling. Numerous petitions for copyright were lodged during the 1490s and 1500s, so contacts in official position must have had their uses. Pierfrancesco Barbarigo's father Marco had been doge for less than one year in 1485, but was immediately succeeded by his uncle, Agostino, who exercised an unseemly degree of power until his death in 1501. Pierfrancesco himself rose to become a member of the Senate, but died in 1499. None of the heirs who succeeded to his interest in the printing enterprise achieved any political prominence, and after 1501 the family as a whole was in very bad odour because of the corruption of which the late doge stood convicted.[54] Association with the Barbarigo, if it did convey any hidden advantages, may have been a double-edged weapon.

Readers of Erasmus' *Adagia,* or Aldus' own prefaces, were almost bound to think of the printing company as an embattled citadel of enlightened scholarship struggling to hold its own in a hostile world:[55] in fact it was a powerful organisation underwritten by one of the most

successful publishers of the age and the nephew of the titular head of
the Venetian state. But this discovery, though removing many uncertainties, leaves us to face a question of far graver implications – how
far did Aldus really control the organisation? There can be little
doubt that the basic initiative was his. Barbarigo and his family were
interested only in their dividends, and Torresani did not have the
academic skills to direct a programme which, as we shall see, lost its
momentum and prestige soon after Aldus' death. By the same argument
most of the administration – the hiring of compositors who could
work with Greek type, the selection of material and the preparation
of editions – must have come under Aldus' control. Odd entries in
the Barbarigo account book bear this out. In April 1499, for example,
we find Aldus simply buying paper and charging the company: in
1478 Peter Maufer, printer in Padua, had been obliged by contract
to draw paper as he needed it from his financial backer Bartolomeo
Valdizocco.[56] But the Barbarigo documents, though never quite
specific, also reveal something of the background against which Aldus
was working. The annulment of 1542 plainly spoke of the company
as the foundation of Andrea Torresani and Pierfrancesco Barbarigo,
with Aldus only "taking a certain part, as is said...". The extent of
that part is never stated, but it cannot have been large. All payments
made by the company to its shareholders and recorded in the account
book are divided squarely down the middle, one half going to the
Barbarigo estate and the other to Torresani, to whose name Aldus' is
usually linked.[57] The explanation is probably as follows: the working-
capital, and the profits of the company, were divided into two equal
shares, of which one was controlled completely by the Barbarigo
estate while the other was held jointly by Torresani and Aldus. This
is roughly the arrangement which prevails in the contract of 1507
between the de Tortis brothers, Lucantonio Giunti, Amadeo Scotto,
and Zorzi Arrivabene: the underwriters, Giunti and Scotto, control
one complete "share" each, while the printers themselves, Arrivabene
and the de Tortis brothers, hold one jointly. The proportion of Aldus'
share to Torresani's, and the total sum of capital staked in the company,
are fundamentals which the documentary sources simply do not
reveal. But we do know that when Aldus and Andrea formally
unified their property and assets in 1506, four-fifths of the total was
Andrea's,[58] so it seems at least possible that Aldus' holding in the
company was of the same order: one fifth of Andrea's half-share, and
one tenth of the total. This argument is of course conjectural: but

the wording of the documentary sources hardly allow us to assume that Aldus' holding was larger than twenty-five per cent at the most.

This makes it difficult to believe that Aldus ever had the decisive word on business policy, and there are a number of signs, long incomprehensible or unnoticed, which suggest that he had constantly to defer to his richer partners. In 1499 he wrote in friendly terms to the Florentine secretary Adriano Marcelli, sending a Greek Book of Hours and a Nicander as gifts, and apologising that the other books which Adriano had bought could not be offered at a reduced price "because they were a joint venture with certain others".[59] At the end of 1501 Janus Lascaris openly reproached Aldus with what he termed a "desertion of Greece for Italy", urging him to press ahead with his original programme:[60] and the letter of 1505 in which John Cuno reported that Torresani was blocking further publication in Greek, offers some explanation of Lascaris' words.[61] During the same year Isabella d'Este wrote in decidedly supercilious terms to inform Aldus that she was returning the four vellum copies he had sent, as they were worth barely half the sum asked and she understood that his partners would accept no less.[62] In the light of the legal documents, the scenario of Erasmus' dialogue *Opulentia Sordida* also becomes far easier to understand. As long as Aldus was regarded as the dominant force in the printing company, readers were bound to find both an attack on him personally and an inconsistency with Erasmus' admiration for his work in the *Adagia*. When we realise Aldus' true situation, the dialogue becomes at the worst a shift in approach, at the best a compliment to Aldus for his behaviour under such conditions.[63]

Unfortunately, this revised view of Aldus' relationship with his partners leads to difficulties which reach far beyond the organisation of the company. The old view, that saw a dedicated humanist sponsored by a dedicated humanist and prince, could also see the programme of publication as the pure expression of humanist ideals. But Aldus was not nearly as free an agent as used to be supposed. We are now bound to examine his printed editions not simply as parts of a great whole, but individually, and in a more critical spirit.

Having sketched the organisation of the company, we must now turn to its technical development, especially to the origin of the famous Aldine types. Logically, this is of course a separate issue, but the separation is artificial. For the earliest editions to have appeared in 1494 or 1495, experiments must have been in hand during the first few years of the decade, alongside the commerical negotiations: and without the powerful business structure which eventually emerged, the casting of such a variety of types would have been wholly impossible. The type-fount was always the most expensive item in a printer's capital equipment, and a Greek fount posed particular problems. First there was the question of finding a craftsman competent to design it: then there was the matter of the language itself. Greek uses "oxytone" or "perispomenon" accents on all words except enclitics, and "rough" or "smooth" breathing-symbols over all initial vowels. These symbols had either to be designed and cast along with the appropriate letter-form, in every possible combination, or cast as entirely separate type-sorts which could then be set in place by the compositor above the letter they were to accent. The first solution vastly multiplied the number of types needed, and consequently the expense incurred: Victor Scholderer calculates that the font used by Laonicus and Alexandros in Venice during the mid-1480s must have contained over 1,400 separate letter forms. The second made the compositor's task much slower, and meant a wider spacing of lines to leave room for the accents: the books therefore took longer to produce, needed more paper, and were naturally more expensive. All contemporary evidence, implicit or explicit, points to the formidable difficulties of working in Greek. Of Aldus' predecessors and immediate contemporaries, only Accursius and Lascaris were able to afford the luxury of experiment with a variety of designs. Several sets of type passed from hand to hand. As late as 1542 a fine Greek fount cut on the orders of Cardinal Cervini to print the rarer works in the Vatican library had to be abandoned, because it was simply too expensive to use.[64] But Aldus planned to print not only in Latin and Greek, but from an early stage of his career in Hebrew as well.

He faced his difficulties with the aid of a faceless genius named Francesco da Bologna, arguably the most important single figure in the establishment of the Aldine company but now so utterly obscured by time that both his name and identity must remain in doubt. He was once thought to have been a goldsmith called Raibolini, but the goldsmith died in 1517 and the type-cutter was still extremely active a year later.[65] A more probable candidate can be found in the "Franciscus Griffus de Bononia incisor litterarum stampae" mentioned by a Perugian notarial act of 1512. But his origins are still very vague. I should like to believe that he is identical with the "Franciscus de Bononia quondam Caesaris aurifex" whom Rauchfass directed in

1475 to copy two of Jenson's Gothic types, for this would provide a connection with Jenson, through Jenson to Torresani and Aldus, and would link the most celebrated Venetian printing-houses closely to one another.[66] But though it is just possible to believe that a man who had been goldsmith to the Emperor before 1475 was still active as a printer more than forty years later, this cannot be treated as more than hypothesis. Nor can we feel any more certain that Griffo designed the Roman types used by the de Gregoriis brothers to print the *Decameron* in 1492, a translation of Herodotus in 1494, and Ketham's *Fasciculus Medicinae* in 1495: it is a conjecture that rests on esthetic judgements only.[67] We have, in fact, only three fixed points from which we can investigate Francesco's connection with Venetian printing. The first is the three-line tribute added by Aldus to the first text he printed in the italic cursive, the Virgil of 1501.[68] The second is the claim made two years later by Gerolamo Soncino of Fano, that he had just secured the services of the expert who had cut all Aldus' types and deserved the real credit for their invention and design.[69] The third is the repetition of that claim by Francesco himself in an edition of Petrarch's *Canzonieri* which he published on his own in 1516. The strains of independent action seem to have been too much for him: shortly afterwards he brained his son-in-law with an iron bar – perhaps an incomplete type punch – faced a murder-charge in Bologna with unknown results, and sank into an obscurity from which the most searching efforts of scholarship have still failed to rouse him.[70]

The style of the various types which Francesco cut for Aldus will be considered separately, as an aspect of the company's commercial history and its appeal to the taste of its readers. For the moment, we are concerned to reconstruct what we can of the professional relationship between the main characters involved: and it is clear from the start that this was an important, an intense, and at the end a turbulent affair. Soncino states explicitly that Griffo was "a most excellent cutter of Latin, Greek and Hebrew letters, a man whose genius finds no equal in this craft" so it is clear that we are dealing with a specialist, working exclusively for the press, not with an ambitious jeweller or coppersmith bent on acquiring new skills. Yet again we see Aldus searching out and securing the best available advice and expertise. Precisely when he contacted Griffo we have no means of knowing. If he did indeed cut all Aldus' types – and the terzain in Virgil confirms that claim implicitly at least until 1501 – then Griffo must have begun to experiment with the first Greek designs very early in the 1490s, some years before the publishing company came into formal existence. On the breaking of the link we can be more specific. Aldus' last distinct type was the small Greek cursive introduced for the Sophocles of August 1502: if Griffo designed and cut these punches, then equipped Soncino with a Latin italic fount in time to produce an edition by the following 7 July, the signs are that he must have left Venice late in 1502. This reckoning brings us significantly close to 14 November 1502, when Aldus was granted a comprehensive monopoly over all Greek publication, and all Latin printing in italic, within the Venetian dominions. The connection between Aldus and Griffo therefore lasted for ten or twelve years at the most, and for only seven of these was the publishing company in production. But these years had a crucial effect on its development. During this period, Aldus commissioned and used twelve type-founts in three different languages: six rounded or "Roman" Latin types, and the famous italic; four Greek cursives, similar to each other in basic conception, but different in detail; and one Hebrew fount, which, though never applied to the ambitious projects planned for it, was used sporadically throughout Aldus' lifetime.[71] When we speak of Aldine typography, we are speaking of Griffo's workmanship. After 1502, individual sorts were no doubt replaced by castings from the same matrices, for this was a normal printer's chore, and a set of cursive capitals was commissioned towards the end of Aldus' life. But no new designs were introduced. There is the strongest contrast between the heady expansion of capital investment up to 1502 and the straightforward use of existing resources which followed. Experiment ended with Griffo's departure.

From Soncino's direct charges that Aldus and others had usurped the credit for inventions made by Griffo, we must assume that a violent outburst of professional jealousy cut this fruitful relationship short. There is indeed a complete contradiction between Aldus' claims in his petitions for privilege to have "discovered two new methods" to improve printing in Greek, or to have "devised a new kind of letter called cursive" and the counter-claims advanced by Soncino and Griffo himself. By 1514 the Giunti of Florence were also stoutly proclaiming that they had been the first to print in the now popular italic type.[72] Where there was so much contemporary disagreement, it is almost impossible to decide where the right lies, and the fact is that the means for deciding such issues had not yet come into being. One of the innovations in Greek typography mentioned in Aldus' petition was as system of "kerning" accents into the top of each vowel-sort as it was required, and so avoiding the problems discussed earlier. This looks like the device of an expert caster, and should probably be attributed to Griffo.[73] But the other new methods under dispute, the Greek and Latin cursive styles, are a quite different matter. Before type-styles became standardised, it was normal for the printer to copy or have copied onto punches a manuscript-model which would be acceptable to the reading-public that he hoped to reach: so Jenson followed a humanistic, "Roman" pattern for his students of classical literature, Caxton an ornate Gothic for his Anglo-Burgundian readers of courtly romance. Aldus' Greek and Latin cursives followed the most sophisticated academic tastes of the time so exactly that a lively argument has raged over the scribal models he used, and at least one critic has attributed the pattern for the Greek cursive founts to Aldus himself. That Griffo both designed and cut the types, as he claimed, is most unlikely. In any case, who deserved the real credit for this complex operation – the scribe, the type-cutter, or the intermediary? The clumsy system of press-privileges sought only to protect the interests of the investor, and that always meant the printer or publisher, who was obliged to bear the costs both of the metal and of the labour required to work it. So when Aldus tried to protect his company's huge investment with a privilege that outlawed all imitation of his Greek and italic styles, he was effectively, though perhaps unintentionally, preventing Griffo from selling his most original and fashionable designs to other printers. It is not surprising that they quarrelled.[74]

On matters such as this, where personal interests seemed to be interrupting his cloudy ambitions, Aldus was capable of showing an extraordinary insensitivity, even though he did not indulge in that refined academic malevolence which delighted many of his contemporaries. But the vital link with Francesco Griffo was less a casualty of some personal clash than of the fast-changing commercial situation. The pioneering age of Gutenberg and Jenson, when one man could direct every stage of the printing-process on the strength of his own skills, was fading into the past. The more regulated world of Garamond and Plantin, with a limited number of recognised and expert type-cutters supplying the needs of an established industry, still lay in the future. Aldus and Griffo fell between. It is interesting to notice that at no stage does Aldus appear to have assumed immediate responsibility for the production of his own types: in his first will, he made a grateful bequest to the daughters of Jacomo the Hungarian, his caster of letters, and in his last, he directed his executors to place a commission for a fount of cursive capitals with Julio Campagnolo.[75] In these small deals, we can follow the changes which were creeping into the industry as it reached maturity. In Aldus himself, we see the printer edging gradually away from purely technical questions towards the wider issues of organisation and public relations. In Campagnolo, we find one of the last of the heroic amateurs, a socialite "wunderkind" equally renowned as painter, sculptor, poet, singer, or calligrapher, well known and accepted both in Paduan intellectual circles and at the courts of Mantua or Ferrara, a man to whom cutting a set of punches probably meant no more than a small financial bonus and a favour done for a friend. But in Jacomo, we have a professional "intagliator di lettere" resident in Venice for forty years: and when, in 1513, he developed a new technique of printing muscial scores, he immediately protected his inventions with a privilege which declared his own special status and perhaps did something to protect him from the fate of Francesco Griffo.[76] When men of such wildly different background and commitment as these last two were doing the same job, and when the concept of a specialised service-industry had yet to emerge, it was almost inevitable that a man like Griffo would get hurt. Aldus' treatment of him may not have been admirable or generous, but it was not necessarily vindictive.

Finally, we cannot neglect the opportunities which the flood of investment from Torresani and Barbarigo must have offered Griffo, or the light which the scale of that investment sheds on the power of their company. The documents do not, unfortunately, permit us to suggest even an approximate figure. But when we find that in 1541 Claude Garamond was paid 225 Livres Tournois for cutting Robert Estienne's Greek Royal types, and remind ourselves that this figure represents approximately one third of the pension paid annually to Leonardo da Vinci, the scale of Aldus' capital outlay at least falls into some kind of perspective. Two of his designs – the Greek and Latin cursives – were wholly new: a third – the Hebrew fount – demanded the most specialised skills and could draw only on the narrowest range of precedents. In monetary terms, this must surely be reckoned in thousands, rather than hundreds of ducats. It would have been hard for Griffo to find a more prolific paymaster.[77] And when we recall that in the late 1490s the companies of Demetrius Chalcondylas, Zacharias

Callierges, and Gabriel of Brasichella were starting to print with one fount each and with disaster only months ahead, we can take the measure of the commercial juggernaut which Aldus and his colleagues had set in motion.

Thus far we have been concerned with the overall pattern of the mechanism, and with the large wheels that set it into motion: what can we reconstruct of the more mundane, day-to-day functioning of the company, and of the smaller cogs which kept it moving? Disappointingly little: the Barbarigo account book gives only occasional glimmers of light, which have constantly to be supplemented by chance comments in letters, and the overall effect is of brightly-lit but not very interesting tableaux rather than a continually developing scene.

After finding investors and overcoming the basic problems of technique, Aldus' next concern must have been a place of business. He discovered what he needed in the S. Polo area of Venice, near the church of Sant' Agostin: it was some distance from the parishes of San Zulian and San Paternian, where the booksellers were thoroughly entrenched by the 1490s, but still fairly convenient for the main business-centre at the Rialto, or for Andrea Torresani's shop which stood close by the bridge "at the sign of the Tower".[78] Two inscriptions now dignify No. 2311 as Aldus' house and workshop. The dignity may or may not be deserved: we are faced by an unpretentious fifteenth-century Gothic building, which looks appropriate and more or less fits the most exact address we have – "on the square of Sant' Agostin, beside the baker's";[79] but it is useless to pretend that the argument rests on more than a process of elimination, for there are no tax-records for this period and we do not know how Aldus found his premises, how much he had to pay for them, or even whether he occupied the whole building. The custom of the times was for a man needing a workshop to rent space on the ground-floor of some larger structure, often a nobleman's palace, and a small printer might pay as little as six or seven ducats rent per year.[80] But Aldus probably needed a fairly large establishment. Writing of his visit to Venice in 1508, Erasmus spoke of a household of some thirty people, including workmen, servants, the family and eight or nine guests:[81] this of course refers to the years after Aldus' marriage to Maria Torresani, when the numbers of the now combined families who lived together at the Torresani home in San Paternian will have been somewhat greater; but the press had been far more active at the beginning of the century,

Death in an early bookshop. The close proximity of printing and selling should be noted.

so the workmen and the visitors may well have been more numerous while the company was still based in Sant' Agostino. Since the master-printer was normally responsible for housing and feeding his staff, we should almost certainly think of Aldus' original base as a substantial complex, with work-space below and living accommodation above: one of those combined "botteghe e case" whose rents, generally ranging from forty to sixty ducats per year, occur frequently on the tax-returns of city landlords.[82] As far as we can reconstruct them, the conditions reflect a now almost incredible mixture of the sweat-shop, the boarding house, and the research institute. In 1508 Erasmus sat in one corner of the printing-room, writing the *Adagia* from memory and handing his text sheet by sheet to the compositors, too busy, by his own account, to scratch his ears. In another corner sat Aldus, quietly reading over the proofs and countering all pleas that they had been checked already with the words "I'm studying". Between them the types rattled in the hands of the compositors, and ink was daubed over anything that happened to be in the way, until far into the night, while the Dutchman's stomach, unused to this pressure of work on short commons, rumbled in ever increasing protest.[83] Finally, the company would disperse according to a social hierarchy that abruptly reasserted itself: the guests, the family and the intellectuals upstairs to their Spartan meal and their avid discussion, the workmen to their separate dinner and thereafter, perhaps, to the livelier pleasures of the city. The constant flow of visitors, and the bewildering range of activities seem to have been constant factors. In 1498 the Englishman William Latimer wrote in urgent and somewhat embarrassed tones from Padua, asking Aldus to return a bed whose owner, having apparently first loaned it to Latimer, now wanted it back. During 1504, when the programme of printing was being pushed ahead with far greater force than in 1508, the German John Cuno claimed later to have studied under Aldus – one wonders under what conditions.[84] In many ways the scene resembles some timeless student world rather than the centre of a business organisation. But the strange fusion of spontaneity and prejudice, of personalities and of activities was being re-enacted all around, and although Aldus' workshop was a remarkable place even in its own times, it will not have seemed in Renaissance Venice the bizarre union of opposites which it appears today. Aldus' immediate neighbourhood, indeed the whole of Venice, was one vast mixture, in which the distinctions of rank still held sway. Directly opposite the workshop stood a palace owned by the Pisani family: the great houses of the da Molin, Donà and Bernardo were all within a minute's walk; just across Campo San Giacomo lived the amazing Marin Sanudo, who in the later 1490s must have been beginning work on his fifty-eight volume diary and his library of 6,500 books.[85] Members of these patrician families would in due course show the keenest interest, and a degree of pride, in the rising fame of their neighbour. But so, apparently, did Aldus' humbler "compatres", Antonio, Petro da Cafa, and Marco da Capodistria, the tailor.[86]

Somewhat surprisingly, this constantly shared activity seems to have given Aldus very little understanding of or goodwill towards the men who actually worked his presses. They must have been fairly numerous: Erasmus' figures are clearly not exact, but if we work on the basis of a household of thirty, eliminate eight or nine guests, and allow for servants and the family, we have still to reckon with fifteen workmen or more. They will have been sufficient to operate between four and six presses: ingenious critics of Aldus' text of Pliny have estimated that in 1508 there were, indeed, four presses at work, and though there was plainly room for a good deal of variation, that appears to have been an average number.[87] Both in composition and in number, the workforce also must have varied greatly. Twice the Aldine press closed down for more than a year, and the staff will presumably have been dismissed, and continuity lost: in any case press-operators seem to have shown constant readiness to walk out, or transfer their allegiance, and the renegade with an advance copy to sell to some rival concern is almost as common a figure in petitions for copyright as the rowdy, drunken printer is in contemporary satire.[88] But even allowing for all this, the total lack of information about either the persons or the methods employed in the Aldine workshop is a little surprising. It is hard to believe that compositors who could work competently in Greek were wholly dispensable, especially to a man who valued accuracy as Aldus did. Possibly some of the explanation lies in his own attitude. In 1501 he referred openly in a preface to what he termed "the conspiracies of my damned runaway slaves," and two years later, in his complaint about the activities of the Lyon press-pirates, he offered some further explanation. "Four times now my hired men and workers have conspired against me in my own house, led on by that mother of all evils, Greed: but with the help of God I so smashed them that they all thoroughly regret their treachery."

These are strong words, and one cannot help longing for more details. If Erasmus was anywhere near right when he said that the workers never had more than half-an-hour throughout the day to spend on their meals, it is not surprising that there was some discontent.[89] Apparently Aldus judged all work by his own pitiless standards, and it sounds as if the strikers learned that Venice was not the place to cross a master whose principal partner was the doge's nephew.

Only two of the humbler members of the company are even known by name, and they appear to have been domestic servants rather than press-operators. The first, Hilarius of Parma, received a mention in Aldus' first will and seems to have been a man worthy of some trust since we find him away from Venice and in the company of Paolo Bombasio as late as 1509.[90] Of the other, Federigo da Ceresara, we know rather more, since he has the dubious distinction of having provoked an international incident. In itself, the story has little significance, but it has an amusing side, and it does shed some oblique light on the reputation of the early printers among their critics and the difficulties with which they often had to contend. Federigo was apparently a distant relation of Aldus, and came from a community in the territory of Mantua. At some unknown moment he had killed his brother in a violent quarrel. His plea of self-defence had been accepted by the regular authorities, but the tightly knit community divided into factions and when Federigo visited his home-town during the summer of 1504, he was promptly seized by his late brother's partisans. There is some indication of the political leverage that Aldus could now exert in the fact that he went straight to the papal nuncio and the imperial ambassador in Venice, persuaded them to write in the strongest terms to Federigo Gonzaga, and secured his servant's release.[91] But the blood-feud had not been quenched, and the drama was by no means finished. Two years later Aldus was returning from an extensive search for manuscripts, and passed through the Mantuan town of Casa Romana accompanied by Federigo, who had naturally grown rather jumpy and was riding with his head muffled to avoid recognition. A cavalry patrol approached them, and Federigo's nerve cracked. He set spurs to his horse, managed to reach the frontier – this was often a matter of yards in the patchwork of the North Italian principalities – and left his astonished master to be flung into prison on suspicion of robbery.[92] A week of frantic diplomacy followed, while Aldus languished in a "loathesome and stinking" cell, trying to explain the tangled situation to his jailor by word of mouth, and to the Marquis of Mantua by letter. Finally, a deputation led by the French ambassador rode out from Mantua to free him ceremonially, touching apologies and compliments were exchanged on all sides, and the curious incident closed as inconsequentially as it had begun.[93] An ominous silence settles over Federigo's career in the Aldine company from this moment. But there is an interesting contrast between the pains which Aldus would take, and the tolerance he would show for this tiresome relative, and the apparently total indifference with which he regarded his hired workers. Pointless though it may seem, Federigo's story serves to reinforce one of Erasmus' views of the company – the extent to which it depended on family solidarity.

Moving away from the centre of production to examine means of distribution we seem at first to have more chance of reaching solid ground, since there are a number of promising trails: but they all peter out before the general direction is revealed. The act of annulment shows that the company rented warehouse space in the Ca' Foscari, and this hints at another useful connection in high places, since Francesco Foscari was not only an extremely powerful politician but one who admitted that his influence could be bought.[94] From the warehouse, the books were ferried up the Grand Canal to several outlets, and their progress can be followed from the Barbarigo account book. A great many naturally went to Andrea Torresani's shop at the sign of the Tower: he drew 520 ducats worth in the two and a half years between March 1502 and August 1504, but unfortunately this is not a very helpful figure since it reveals neither the turnover of Torresani's shop nor the total number of dispatches made from the company's store.[95] Several other booksellers are mentioned – Piero Benzoni, a German named Peter Piner who seems to have bought in quantity from Torresani, and possibly Tadio Contarini. But only one – Jordan von Dinslaken – is more than a name. Jordan bought books in such numbers – 101 copies of Perotti's *Cornucopia* on 20 November 1501, another 106 early in the following year – that he seems almost certain to be the merchant whom Aldus and Reuchlin criticised in 1502 for "buying many books at the same time" and so forcing the price in Germany even below the Venetian level.[96] His name alone looks back to a great past, and forward to a sinister future. Almost certainly he was a relation or connection of the Gaspar von Dinslaken who was a partner in the great company of Jenson and John of Cologne during the 1480s, and whose widow Hironima was still alive in 1511.[97] He seems also to have been the first Venetian bookseller to be denounced for selling Lutheran works: in August 1520, some of his stocks were confiscated, though Sanudo, who records the incident, slyly adds that he had one of the prohibited books in his study.[98] Jordan von Dinslaken was evidently a man who knew his business thoroughly and was not scrupulous about his means of pursuing it. His involvement, alongside that of a number of other booksellers, shows that Aldus had a wide network of trade contacts besides the individual academic friends who, as we shall see, often publicised and distributed his editions for him. The probability that a good deal of the Northern traffic was handled by the mighty house of Fugger is simply another link in the powerful commercial system which was a feature of the Aldine company from its beginning.[99]

One further detail revealed by the Barbarigo account book must be mentioned at this point, although its real importance can be shown only when we follow Aldus' policy and fortunes year by year. Payments made by the booksellers to the company were channelled through the bank of Mafio Agostini. In 1495 this arrangement was a technicality. In 1499 it may have assured the future of Aldus and his partners.[100]

Once its shareholders have been examined, its workers discussed, and its contacts reviewed, one salient fact should be clear about the enterprise of Barbarigo, Torresani and Manutius: the evidence concerning it is circumstantial only. We have no figures which enable us to judge its size and profitability, and only one imprecise estimate of its liabilities in Aldus' plea to the Senate in 1502, when he claimed to have overheads of around 200 ducats monthly.[101] Like any figure submitted to the government of an Italian city state, this total must be suspect. But since we know at least what it implies, and since we can do something to cross-check it from Erasmus' information and documented wage-levels, this estimate offers the best chance of drawing the scattered fragments of evidence about Aldus' company into some sort of pattern. We have a useful point of comparison in the tax-declaration returned in 1537 by Nicolo Bernardo, Procurator, one of the most powerful political figures in Venice, and, incidentally, an ex-neighbour of Aldus, since he lived in the huge Palazzo Bernardo which still stands between Sant' Agostino and Campo San Polo. He reckoned his income from property in the city and a small estate near Mestre at 239 ducats per year.[102]

It has already been said that Erasmus' account of the Torresani household in 1508 indicates a workforce of around fifteen. Allowing three men per press – a compositor, an operator or "torculator", and an inker – we can construct our model upon a basis of five press-crews, remembering that this figure is almost certainly too low for the busy years at the beginning of the century. We have no exactly contemporary information about wage-rates, but Paduan documents of the 1470s suggest 2.5–4.5 ducats per month for the compositors, 2–3 ducats for the operators, and around 2 ducats for the relatively unskilled inkers.[103] If we apply these figures at their median level to the Aldine model, we emerge with a wages-bill of 15–18 ducats per month for compositors, 12–15 for operators, and 10 for inkers. The total cannot have been much less than 40 ducats per month and may well have been nearer 60, since the actual numbers involved were probably higher and there is also a chance that compositors who could work in Greek earned a higher wage. We can now extend this calculation by applying to it one of the accepted axioms of early printing: that the cost of labour and the cost of paper were roughly equivalent.[104] This will bring the reckoning of Aldus' monthly expenditure close to 100 ducats with only two items taken into account. Some of the others can be quantified fairly accurately: we know, for example, that Chalcondylas and his partners set aside 5 ducats per month as the salary of their proof-reader in 1499. Aldus appears to have paid at the same, or a slightly higher rate, and since he used more presses and had more learned contacts, he may have had to foot a bill three or four times that size.[105] We happen also to know that in 1482 it cost 4 ducats per month to hire an illuminator. The surviving copies which Aldus printed on vellum for special customers show not only that he employed such a man, but suggest that the craftsman concerned was the Paduan master Benedetto Bordone, whose time will not have been bought cheaply.[106] Francesco Griffo may have commanded a fee of up to 9 ducats per month, besides the costly materials he needed.[107] The purchase of manuscripts, the payment of scribes to make copies and of scholars to edit them, must also have made heavy demands on Aldus' budget, though the amounts involved must have varied, and come round irregularly: a 60 ducats guarantee had to be staked on the proper treatment of three volumes of the works of St Catherine of Siena;[108] Erasmus is known to have earned 20 ducats for his various services, Fra Giocondo 10 for his work on the *Scriptores Rei Rusticae*.[109] And beyond all this came the constant problems of rent and food-bills. We cannot, at any stage during Aldus' career, make a precise estimate of his liabilities, and it is unlikely that the demands on him were consistent. But the separate items we have reviewed suggest that his estimate of 200 ducats per month was not ludicrous, and we can crosscheck it from another direction by using Aldus' assertion that in 1503 he was producing 1,000 copies per month. The price of almost all the octavo editions printed around this time was 1.5 lire mocenighe per copy. Each month's work, or each edition, was therefore costed at around 1500 lire, or 234 ducats.[110] It may indeed have taken the landed income of a powerful nobleman for an entire year to keep the printshop active for a month, and the profits cannot have been very great for a partner who controlled only a small percentage of the capital.

One has only to glance at the comprehensive accounts which have been written of great banking houses or of tiny and short-lived printing companies to appreciate the pitiful inadequacy of the information which we have been able to produce about Aldus' partnership with Andrea Torresani and Pierfrancesco Barbarigo.[111] The preponderance of intellectual evidence over economic is complete. This has made it possible and tempting to speak of an "Aldine circle" or "Academy", as if Aldus had been simply a humanist who turned printer, and was enabled by the patronage of like-minded princes and noblemen to translate his own ideals into a coherent programme of publication. Such a view does Aldus himself much less than justice. His company was not a club for literary dilettanti, but a business organisation: not an organisation like any other, since it was far stronger than most, but still a company which had to make its way in the dangerous and savagely competitive world described in the first chapter. Aldus may have been the mind which stirred the matter: but he had bills to pay and shareholders to satisfy, and we have seen what kind of pressure such people could exert. Whatever their intellectual significance, Aldine publications had to have a marketable value if the partnership was to stay in business, and Aldus had, perforce, to become a man of business as well as the man of letters which he already was. His achievement must be judged not only as the expression of an ideal, but as an exercise in maintaining a delicate balance between the tensions and pressures which were at work upon him.

NOTES

1 OAME VI A.
2 Though the precise dating of the Aldine Musaeus and *Galaeomyomachia* is disputed, there is no documentary proof that the press went into production before early 1495:

Lascaris' Greek Grammar is dated February 1494, but the alphabet printed at the end is marked March 1495, so it is clear that the "Venetian style" of changing years at the beginning of March is being used. See R. Christie, "The Chronology of the Early Aldines", in *Selected Essays*, London, 1902, pp. 200–3.

3 BP p. 226.
4 See Firmin-Didot, Brown, Geanakoplos, Branca, "Ermolao Barbaro...". Also A. Renaudet, *Érasme et l'Italie*, Geneva, 1954, pp. 76–7, 80–9.
5 See below, Ch. V, nn. 90f.
6 G. Pozzi, "Da Padova a Firenze nel 1493", IMU IX, 1966, pp. 192–201.
7 D. Geanakoplos, "The Discourse of Demetrius Chalcondylas on the Inauguration of Greek Studies at the University of Padua, in 1463", *Studies in the Renaissance* XXI, 1974, esp. pp. 122–3. For a full biography G. Cammelli, *Demetrio Calcondila*, Florence, 1954.
8 B. Knös, *Un Ambassadeur de'Hellénisme: Janus Lascaris*, Paris/Uppsala, 1945. (Full biography): E. Piccolomini, "Delle condizioni e delle vicende della libreria Medicea privata dal 1494 al 1508", ASI Ser. iii, XIX, 1873, pp. 101–29, K. Müller, "Neue mittheilungen über Janos Laskaris und die Mediceische Bibliothek", ZFB I, 1884, pp. 333–413 (on his activities as a librarian and collector): Pozzi, *op. cit.*, p. 194, and Ch. IV, below (interest in the press): Geanakoplos, *Greek Scholars*, pp. 113–14 (on his teaching).
9 The number of foreigners studying in Florence seems to have become very high at this time: see *Reuchlins Briefwechsel* (L. Geiger) Tübingen, 1875, p. 29: G. Parks, *The English Traveller in Italy*, Rome, 1954, pp. 457f.
10 Poliziano, *Prose vulgari inedite e poesie latine e greche edite e inedite a cura di I. del Lungo*, Florence, 1867, pp. 79–80.
11 Codri Urcei, *Opera Omnia*, Platonides, Bologna, f. Di r. "...doctos et multae probitatis viros, Lascarim Florentiae, Aldum Venetiis..."
12 Firmin-Didot, *Alde Manuce*, pp. 45–7.
13 OAME III B, VIII (Vol. I, pp. 6, 15).
14 *Lettere di Paolo Manuzio*, ed. G. Renouard, Paris, 1834, pp. 335–7. (Letter from Lionello Pio, 23 September 1498.)
15 *Annali veneti*, in ASI 7, pt. ii, 1844, pp. 675, 683, 699. For background, see S. Romanin, *Storia documentata di Venezia*, new ed., 1973, Vol. IV, pp. 339–70.
16 E.g. Sabellico's *De venetae urbis situ* (1492) and Sanudo's *Cronacetta* (1493). The impression made on the French ambassador Commynes in 1495 is well known: *Mémoires*, ed. J. Calmette, Vol. III, Paris, 1965, pp. 106–39.
17 Below, Ch. V, nn. 50–2.
18 Above, Ch. II, n. 28.
19 C. Scaccia Scarafoni, "La più antica edizione della grammatica latina di Aldo Manuzio finora sconosciuta ai bibliografi", in *Miscellanea bibliografica in memoria di Don Tommaso Accurti*, Rome, 1947, pp. 193–203.
20 C. R. Thompson, *The Colloquies of Erasmus*, Chicago, 1965, pp. 488–99.
21 On the wider problems of this dialogue see Thompson's introductory notes and the

comments of M. M. Philips, *The Adages of Erasmus*, pp. 62-9: for still fuller coverage Renaudet, *Érasme et l'Italie*, pp. 80-9, M. Dazzi, *Aldo Manuzio e il dialogo veneziano di Erasmo*, Vicenza, 1969. Dazzi shows how personal quarrels with Alberto Pio and Aleander combined with Erasmus' wider disagreement with the Italians over the imitation of Cicero to produce a general rejection of all things Italian in which Aldus became involved by association only.

22 *Willibald Pirckheimers Briefwechsel*, ed. E. Reicke, Vol. I, Munich, 1940, Ep. 86, pp. 280-2, 21 December 1505.

23 Allen, II, pp. 587-9, No. 588.

24 C. F. Buhler, "Some Documents Concerning the Torresani and the Aldine Press", *The Library*, 4th Series, XXV, 1945, pp. 111-21.

25 Background from Bernoni. Torresani's dependence on Jenson can be inferred from the colophon to his edition of Panormita's commentaries on *Decretals* Bks. IV and V: "Exactum est hoc opus inclytis instrumentis formosisque litterarum characteribus quondam in hac arte Magistri Nicolai Jenson Gallici... Venetiis MCCCCLXXXII tertio Nonas Februarias." Quoted in CSV p. 26.

26 SDP p. 198, Doc. LXVIII.

27 BMC V, 1924, p. xxvi. The other printers involved were de Choris, de Luere, Hamman, and Locatellus.

28 My reckoning, based on Bernoni's list of editions, is roughly as follows: Law, 53%; Philosophy, 14%; Liturgical works, 13% Classics, 9%; Theology, 7·5%; others, 3%.

29 See below, nn. 66, 96.

30 Pozzi, *op. cit.* under n. 6, above, p. 194.

31 Cf. note 7, above, for Chalcondylas' appointment in Milan, and 9 for the unbroken vitality of Florentine Hellenism and intellectual life.

32 C. Malagola, *Della vita e delle opere di Antonio Urceo, detto Codro*, Bologna, 1878, pp. 172-3. His appointment was made official only in 1482, but he had been teaching privately before that date. For the subjects he covered cf. his introductory *Sermones*, printed in the edition of his *Opera Omnia*, cit. under n. 11, above.

33 Barbaro, *Epistolae, Orationes et Carmina*, ed. V. Branca, Florence, 1943, Vol. I, p. 56, Ep. xl, 24 June 1484. "Cupierunt hic boni quidam juvenes ut poetas eis Graecos temporibus successivis meis praelegerem."

34 A.S.V., Senato, Deliberazioni Terra, R. XII, f. 201r, 21 April 1497. Reference is made to the "instantia omnium illorum scolarium".

35 See Ch. VI, below.

36 A. Segarizzi, "Cenni sulle scuole pubbliche a Venezia nel secolo XV e sul primo maestro d'esse", ARIV LXXV, pt. ii, 1915-16, p. 651. See also below, Ch. V.

37 *Epistolae*, Vol. I, p. 78, Ep. lxi.

38 A. Castrifrancanus, *Oratio habita in funere Urbani Bellunensis*, Venice, 1524: G. Bustico, "Due umanisti veneti – Urbano Bolzanio e Piero Valeriani", *Civiltà Moderna*, IV, 1932, pp. 86-103.

39 The very curt account which follows is based primarily on R. Proctor, *The Printing*

of Greek in the Fifteenth Century, Oxford, 1900: pp. 49–51 give a table of early editions, identifying dates and types where possible. V. Scholderer's *Greek Printing Types, 1465–1927*, pp. 1–6, is also extremely useful, and stresses the speed with which the basic problems were solved. Reference has been made to E. Legrand, *Bibliographie Hellénique ou description raisonnée des ouvrages publiés en Grec par des Grecs au XVe et XVIe Siècles*, Vol. I, Paris, 1885, pp. 5f, though the list of works is not exhaustive.

40 John Rylands University Library of Manchester, No. 3325. Proctor, *op. cit.*, p. 83, considers this the earliest complete Greek work in print, since the interlinear Latin translation is in a type used by Ferrando, and the only definite date which can be attached to his name is 1473.

41 Legrand, *op. cit.*, pp. 9–15. My colleague Michael Mallett tells me that Bernardo and Neri were the middle sons of an important political figure, and that two of their brothers were resident as merchants in Venice during the 1490s.

42 Proctor, *op. cit.*, pp. 73–7. Geanakoplos, *Greek Scholars*, p. 59, gives a facsimile of the type.

43 The documents quoted by Motta in "Demetrio Calcondila, editore", ASL 20, 1893, pp. 163f, show that in 1499 only a single press was used.

44 There is no detailed documentary study of the Lascaris/Alopa press. Reference can be made to the relevant sections of Legrand, *op. cit.*, pp. 20f, and to Proctor, *op. cit.*, pp. 78–82. On the wider background see the references under n. 8, above. In his introduction to *Etymologicum Magnum* (1499) Zacharias Calliergies claimed to be in the sixth year of his experiments, so he must have begun work in 1494. The same is presumably true of Gabriel of Brasichella's organisation. See below, Ch. IV, nn. 63–6.

45 Dedication to Vol. I of Aristotle, OAME IIIB (Vol. I, p. 6).

46 Pastorello, "Testimonianze e documenti...", p. 214, Doc. XI.

47 See the citations under nn. 1, 2.

48 A Parisian contract of 1528 may be relevant: "et après ce qu'ilz auront faict et parachevé de imprimer le premier livre...s'ilz veoyent que lad. association ne leur feust bonne, se pourront séparer et deppartir l'un avec l'autre..." Text in E. Coyecque, "Inventaire sommaire d'un minutier Parisien", *Bulletin de la Société de l'Histoire de Paris et de l'Île de France*, 21, 1894, p. 156.

49 Pastorello, *loc. cit.* under n. 46, above. Original in A.S.V. Procuratori di S. Marco, Supra, Rg. 203, ff. 70v–72r.

50 Firmin-Didot, *Alde Manuce*, pp. 304f. Confusion about the financial background persisted long after the discovery of the relevant documents, which Brunetti never published. His thesis, submitted in 1907, remains in the hands of his family. See M. Ferrigni, *Aldo Manuzio*, Milan, 1925, pp. 188–9; E. Robertson, "Aldus Manutius, the Scholar-printer, 1450–1515", BJRL XXXIII, 1950, p. 67; M. Dazzi, "Aldo Manuzio", LBF LII, 1950, p. 130.

51 Extracts from an incomplete seventeenth-century copy (Biblioteca Marciana, Venezia Ms. Latini Cl. XIV, 235 (4714) were published by G. Morelli in his *Dissertazioni*

intorno ad alcuni viaggiatori eruditi veneziani poco noti, Venice, 1803, pp. 14-30. The autograph was later discovered in Munich Stätsbibliothek, Ms. Latinus 10801, and published in *Sitzungsberichte der Bayerischen Akademie der Wissenschaften,* I, 1861, pp. 584-609, by Theodore Mommsen.

52 See Ch. I, above, n. 10. J. Bloch "Venetian printers of Hebrew books" *Bulletin of The New York Public Library* 36, 1932, pp. 71-92.

53 SDP pp. 133-4.

54 M. Barbaro, Genealogie delle famiglie patrizie veneziane, Ms. in Archivio di stato, Venezia, Vol. I, p. 172. Pierfrancesco himself had no legitimate children, so his investment passed in the first instance to his brothers, then to their heirs whose names stand on the annulment of 1542 (Pastorello, "Testimonianze e documenti...", *loc. cit.*). Sanudo, IV, cols. 100-200, reports violent reaction against the late doge and his family for corruption after Agostino's death in 1501, adding that the sons were obliged to pay 7,600 ducats in retrospective fines (v, cols. 87-8).

55 Cf. M. M. Philips, *op. cit.* under n. 21, above, pp. 171-209. Erasmus drew a comparison between Aldus' efforts and the Labours of Hercules. For Aldus' own attitude cf. n. 1, above.

56 Compare Pastorello, "Testimonianze e documenti...", Doc. I, p. 189 with SDP, Doc. XXXIII, p. 156.

57 Pastorello, "Testimonianze e documenti...", Doc. I, p. 190 (entries f, g), p. 192 (entries x, z). For the wording of the contract cf. n. 49, above.

58 The full text of the Giunti/Scoto/Arrivabene/de Tortis contract can be found in FD pp. 401-5. The original deed uniting Aldus' property with Torresani's does not survive, but reference is made to it in the act of annulment (Pastorello, "Testimonianze e documenti...", Doc. III, p. 195) and in Aldus' last will (CSV p. 97).

59 Schuck, Doc. X, pp. 126-7.

60 CAM 24.

61 See reference under n. 22, above.

62 Quoted in GSLI VI, 1885, p. 276, n. 4. "M. Aldo. Li quattro volumi de libri in carta membrana che ne haveti mandati al juditio di ogniuno sono cari dil doppio che non valeno: havemoli restituiti al messo vostro, il qual non ha negato esser il vero, ma scusatovi che li compagni vostri non ni voleno mancho."

63 On this issue see above, n. 21.

64 Proctor, *op. cit.,* pp. 49-51. A. Tinto, "The History of a Sixteenth-Century Greek Type", *The Library,* Ser. v, XXV, No. 4, December, 1970, pp. 285-93: W. Pettas, "Niklaos Sophianos and Greek Printing in Rome", *Ib.,* XXIX, No. 2, June, 1974, pp. 206-13.

65 Raibolini was suggested by A. Panizzi, *Chi era Francesco da Bologna?* London, 1858, but conclusively rejected by Mardersteig, "Aldo Manuzio e i caratteri di Francesco Griffo da Bologna", in *Studi di bibliografia e storia in onore di T. de Marinis,* Vol. III, Verona, 1964, p. 121.

66 Both documents printed by P. Arnauldet, "Graveurs de Charactères et Typographes de l'Italie du Nord", *Bulletin de la Société Nationale des Antiquaires de France,* 7e ser. 4,

1903, pp. 288–95. See also Mardersteig, "...nascita di un incunabolo", pp. 253–4.
67 Suggested by Mardersteig, "Aldo Manuzio...", p. 118. For facsimiles of the types see C. Castellani, *Early Venetian Printing Illustrated*, Venice/London/New York, 1895, pp. 105, 108–9.
68 IN GRAMMATOGLYPTAE LAUDEM.
Qui Graiis dedit Aldus, en Latinis
Dat nunc grammata scalpta daedaleis
Francisci manibus Bononiensis. RAIA, p. 27.
69 G. Manzoni, *Annali tipografici dei Soncino,* Bologna, 1886, pt. ii, pp. 26–8.
70 Mardersteig, "Aldo Manuzio...", pp. 121, 144. The attack on his son-in-law occurred in May 1518, and by October 1519 Francesco was called "the late...".
71 Count based on Mardersteig, *op. cit.*: for details of the Hebrew fount and Aldus' use of it see Bloch, *op. cit.* under n. 52, above; A. Marx, "Aldus and the first use of Hebrew Type in Venice", *Papers of the Bibliographical Society of America*, 13, 1919, No. 1, pp. 64–7. Aldus had some Hebrew characters as early as 1498 (*Hypnerotomachia Polifili,* f. b8 r–v, h8 r, *Politiani Opera,* f. c5 v, h8 r–v), and in July 1501 sent Conrad Celtis some sheets of a projected trilingual Bible (*Briefwechsel des Konrad Celtis,* ed. H. Rupprich, Munich, 1934, p. 516: possible relic in Bibliothèque Nationale, Paris, Mss Graecus 3064). An "Introductio perbrevis ad Hebraicam Linguam" was issued in 1501, 1508 and 1514.
For a more general introduction to Hebrew typography see E. Howe, "An Introduction to Hebrew Typography", *Signature,* 5, 1937, pp. 12–29.
72 Compare Manzoni, *loc. cit.*, with CSV pp. 72, 77. For details of the Giunti claim see the reference in Ch. IV, n. 145.
73 V. Scholderer, *Greek Printing Types,* pp. 6–7.
74 On the general background see Carter, *Typography,* pp. 45f. For the debate over Aldus' designs see E. Quaranta, "Osservazioni intorno ai caratteri greci di Aldo Manuzio", LBF LV, ii, 1953, pp. 123–30, and below, Ch. IV. Text of Aldus' comprehensive privilege in CSV pp. 78–9.
75 CSV pp. 93, 99. On the theme of rapid professionalisation among typecutters after 1500 see Carter, *Typography,* pp. 93–116, esp. 107–8 on Aldus and Griffo.
76 DBI 17 (Campagnolo): FD p. 178, No. 189 (Jacomo the Hungarian). See also K. Haebler, "Schriftguss und Schriftenhandel in der Fruhdruckzeit", ZFB 41, 1924, p. 99.
77 A. Sorbelli, "Il mago che scolpi i caratteri di Aldo Manuzio – Francesco Griffo da Bologna", GJB 1933, pp. 117–23. On the cost of Estienne's types, E. Armstrong, *Robert Estienne, Royal Printer,* Cambridge, 1954, p. 52, and on Francis I's pension to Leonardo, D. Seward, *Prince of the Renaissance,* London, 1973, p. 88.
78 The siting of the Venetian book-world is described by Sabellico in *De Latinae Linguae Reparatione*: on the position of Torresani's shop see CAM 88.
79 The usual address was "a sancto Agostino" (CAM 33, 34) which is too vague to help. Legrand, *Bibliographie Hellénique,* Vol. II, p. 298, prints the undated letter

80   from Callierges to Gregoropoulos which gives the more exact location. This has been used (CSV pp. 54–6, notes) to question the identity of the accepted site, on the grounds that the palazzo is not "on" the campo. But the wording is so unspecific that I doubt if it can bear the weight of a definite decision.

80   A.S.V., Savii sopra le Decime in Rialto, Condizioni della città, 1514, Busta 81 – S. Zulian: Jacomo Bianco receives 6 ducats per year from "Francesco stampador": Andrea Surian receives 7 ducats per year from "Jacomo stampador".

81   *Opulentia Sordida,* in Thompson, *op. cit.,* pp. 492–4.

82   This estimate is based on a general view of records of the Savii sopra le Decime, which are fragmentary at this date. CSV p. 56, n. quotes a tax-return showing that Torresani paid 60 ducats per year rent: no exact reference is given and I have been unable to trace this return among the 1514 records. But the amount is similar to that paid by other well-to-do craftsmen and non-nobles.

83   Description based on *Opulentia Sordida* and the extract from *Apologia adversus Rhapsodias Calumniosarum Querimoniarum Alberti Pii* (1531) quoted by M. M. Philips, *op. cit.,* pp. 67–8. Erasmus' observations on the difference between Northern and Mediterranean diet are born out by Braudel, *La Mediterranée,* Vol. II, p. 217.

84   CAM No. 87. The date – Sunday, 4 November – is cunningly pinned to 1498 by P. Allen, "Linacre and Latimer in Italy", *English Historical Review,* XVIII, 1903, pp. 514–17. References to Cuno may be found in Chs. V–VII, below, *passim.*

85   For the position of these palaces see G. Lorenzetti, *Venice and its Lagoon,* Rome, 1961, pp. 580–620. On Sanudo's library, K. Wagner, "Sulla sorte di alcuni codici manoscritti appartenuti a Marin Sanudo", and "Altre notizie sulla sorte dei libri di Marin Sanudo", LBF LXXIII, 1971, pp. 247–62, LXXIV, 1972, pp. 185–90.

86   First will, in CSV p. 93.

87   For the estimate of overall numbers cf. n. 81, above. My calculation is based round the estimate of three men (compositor, inker, operator) per press, which is normal in early woodcuts. An effort was made by G. P. Winship to reconstruct the method of work from certain patterns of errors in the text of Pliny: "The Aldine Pliny of 1508", *The Library,* Fourth Series, VI, 1925, pp. 358–69. But quite different conclusions can be drawn from the same facts: A. E. Case, "More about the Aldine Pliny of 1508", *Ib.,* Fourth Series, XVI, pp. 173–87. The Giunti/Scoto/Arrivabene/de Tortis syndicate operated with four presses (cf. n. 58, above), as did Froben, when working at relatively low pressure. C. Heckethorn, *The Printers of Basle in the XV and XVI centuries – their Biographies, printed Books, and Devices,* London, 1897, p. 88.

88   Compare Ch. I, nn. 25, 35.

89   OAME Vol. I, pp. 34, 170. For Erasmus' comments, *Opulentia Sordida,* ed. cit., p. 497.

90   CSV p. 93. CAM 76 (mission with Bombasio).

91   Since these letters are unpublished and to the best of my knowledge unnoticed, it is worth quoting the text of the more informative version.

      "Ep. Tyburtinus Legatus Apostolicus...Federigo Gonzaga. Ex. me Dme, Dne mi singular. me comm.s. Multa sunt quibus vehementer amamus Aldum Manutium sed praecipue quia Romanus est atque ob insignes eius virtutes et doctrinam iam ubique terrarum celebrem, patriae meae Romanae summo est honori et gloriae. Ei est familiaris et affinis carissimus quidam Phedericus Ceyesarensis subditus Ex. tiae vostrae pro quo, cum exularet a propria ob homicidium quod in sui defensionem coactusque perpetraverat, veniam ab EX.v. intercedente eius conjuge Illustrissima Isabella impetravit, abhinc circiter menses decem. Qua remissione confisus iste Phedericus securus visebat Ceyesarem, ac in toto Dominio vostro. Nunc a quibusdam instantibus qui eum oderunt vel ob eius bona iam impetrata vel aliam ob causam coniectus est in carcerem iussu Vr. Exc." (The usual formalities follow)....

The imperial ambassador's version adds that Federigo had killed his "proprium fratrem" and calls him Aldus' "consanguineum" or blood-relation. This seems odd in view of their widely different origins, and the nuncio's version "affinis" or in-law would be more natural, since Andrea Torresani came from the Mantuan area. But Aldus did not marry into Torresani's family until 1505. There is plainly some confusion, as the ambassador's version linguistically contradicts the legate's, and Aldus does not mention the relationship at all. Since the imperial ambassador's letter casts some light on Aldus' ties with Maximilian, it will be quoted later. See Ch. V, n. 92. Originals in Archivio di stato, Mantova, Carteggio Estero, Carteggio ad inviati, Busta 1440, bb. 13, 25 and 28 July 1504.

92 Baschet, pp. 27f. This description of the incident is given by Aldus himself in Doc. XIV, p. 30, 18 July 1506.
93 *Ib.*, Docs. XV, XVI, 20 and 25 July (Renewed appeals from Aldus), XVII (Apology and explanation from the Marquis). In his dedication to the works of Horace (March 1509) Aldus thanked the French official Jeffroy Charles for his kindness on this occasion and described his arrival "omni equitatu tuo comitante, necnon et aliis quibusdam ex Mantuanis nobilibus...". OAME Vol. I, p. 101.
94 Pastorello, "Testimonianze e documenti...", Doc. XI, p. 214. The Foscari tax-return of 1514 mentions a total income of 150 ducats from rents on the palazzo and its "magazzini", but does not specify the components. (A.S.V., Savii sopra le Decime in Rialto, B. 56.) In 1508 Francesco was implicated in an electioneering scandal, and admitted to having bought votes "come la terra usava di fare" (Sanudo, VII, col. 606). But this did not prevent his being elected Savio Grande on 1 July 1509.
95 Pastorello, "Testimonianze e documenti...", Doc. I, pp. 191-2.
96 For the various names and Jordan's purchases see Pastorello, *loc. cit.* Tadio Contarini is not specifically identified as a bookseller, but he seems to be handling unusually large consignments for a private customer. For Aldus' complaint about block-purchases cf. Reuchlin, *Briefwechsel, ed. cit.*, p. 79, No. lxxxv, 24 December 1502.
97 See Ch. I, nn. 47-50 for references to this syndicate.
98 *Diarii*, Vol. XXIX, col. 135.
99 The Fugger connection is suggested by their function as intermediaries between Aldus and his German friends Henry Urbanus and Georg Burkhard (Spalatinus). Schuck, Doc. XIII, pp. 132-3 (1505), XVI, p. 136 (1514).

100 Pastorello, "Testimonianze e documenti...", Doc. 1, passim.
101 CSV pp. 76–7.
102 A.S.V., Savii sopra le Decime in Rialto, Condizione della citta – S. Polo: Rg. 366, cc. 40v–41r. Nicolo was among the nobles most frequently elected to the vital post of Savio Grande between 1520 and 1550. (A.S.V., Segretario alle voci, Senato, Rg. 1.)
103 Figures derived from Mardersteig, "...nascita di un incunabolo", pp. 258–9: R. Hirsch, *Printing*, pp. 36–9. Hirsch sets the figures somewhat higher, but since there was no guild control, wages probably varied considerably.
104 Hirsch, *op. cit.*, pp. 39–40. L. Febvre, H.-J. Martin, *L'Apparition du Livre*, pp. 168–72. For more detailed documentation, W. Pettas, "The Cost of Printing a Florentine Incunable", pp. 67–85. The compositors in this case were paid 4 florins per month, and the costs were: paper, 40 florins; labour, 47 florins.
105 Motta, "Demetrio Calcondila", p. 163. Arsenios Apostolios felt that the two months of correcting he had done were worth more than the 10.5 ducats which Aldus was allowing him. Geanakoplos, *Greek Scholars*, p. 175.
106 SDP p. 191. On Bordone, see G. Mariani-Canova, *La miniatura veneta del rinascimento*, Venice/Milan, 1969, pp. 122–30. Also n. 47 to the following chapter.
107 Hirsch, *loc. cit.* under n. 103, above.
108 Facsimile of contract with Antonio Condulmer in Castellani, *Early Venetian Printing Illustrated*, p. 32.
109 CAM 86 (Fra Giocondo): Allen. I, No. 212, p. 443.
110 See the introduction to Euripides (OAME XLVI) for the figure of 1,000 copies per month. For the prices see P. S. Leicht, "I prezzi delle edizioni aldine del' 500", *Il libro e la stampa*, Anno. VI, Fasc. iii, 1912, pp. 74–84. A ducat at this period was worth approximately 6.4 lire mocenighe.
111 E.g. R. de Roover, *The Rise and Decline of the Medici Bank, 1397–1494*, New York, 1966. P. Bologna, "La stamperia fiorentina del monastero di S. Jacopo di Ripoli e le sue edizioni". GSLI. The article of W. Pettas cited under n. 104 gives a more complete picture of the economics of early printing than can be derived from all the evidence about Aldus' company.

IV

THE CHANCES OF BUSINESS

Aldus came to Venice with a strong sense of purpose. Five years of preparation brought him to a position where he could enjoy some freedom to translate his ideals into reality: but he was never free from the obligation of showing his partners that those ideals were also commercially practicable. How far did he succeed in combining, and in attaining, these two aims? Across four and a half centuries, his achievement looks so triumphant as to need no further justification: around 130 editions in twenty years; some thirty first editions of the Greek literary and philosophical texts in whose value Aldus so passionately believed; a number of unquestionably successful popular works, such as Bembo's *Asolani* and Erasmus' *Adagia*; and two experiments in book-production – the octavo-sized volume and the italic script – which were immediately and almost universally adopted in contemporary Europe.[1] But it is by no means clear that this record represented either commercial success or the expression of Aldus' ideals. Some of his most celebrated publications, including the notoriously controversial *Hypnerotomachia Polifili*, were financed by outside enthusiasts and may have meant little more to Aldus than the fee he received for printing them. We can also be certain that what Aldus planned during the 1490s and what he eventually published were very different things. As early as 1497 he was promising an edition of Plato which did not appear for nearly two decades, and another of Galen which was printed only after his death.[2] For years he dreamed vainly of producing a Bible in all three of the ancient languages. The true scenario for Aldus' work was the maelstrom described by Erasmus, and implied by the printer himself during one of his rare moments of self-revelation: suddenly finding two spare sheets in his text of Lascaris' Greek Grammar, he added a hasty note of apology to his readers and a number of corrections to the text as it had appeared so far, pleading that he lacked a moment to snatch a bite of food, to relieve himself, or to wipe the drop off the end of his nose.³ Though the business of publishing was making great strides, and though Aldus was leading the way, he still lived in a world of stops and starts, of frantic improvisation, and of desperate last-minute expedients. It is misleading even to treat his career as a unit, since it was frequently interrupted and divides into at least four fairly well defined phases, each with its own features and its own problems. The first, lasting roughly from 1495 to 1501, is a time of preparation and consolidation, marked chiefly by the development of different types and by a heavy concentration on Greek material. The next three years are a period of exuberant fulfilment, producing most of the achievements for which Aldus is now remembered: the large octavo edition as a medium for literary texts; the italic type; a range of publication which covers every contemporary field of interest in classical and Italian vernacular literature; and the apparent attempt to harness intellectual activity to the service of the press. Then, at a moment which is hard to pinpoint precisely, signs of difficulty appear. Publications decline in number during 1504 and 1505, then cease altogether. A brief flutter of activity between 1507 and 1509 is immortalised by Erasmus, but cut off by the ruinous wars of Venice with the League of Cambrai: there are even some signs that Aldus intended to abandon printing entirely. Finally, after an interval of more than three years, work starts again and continues beyond Aldus' death in 1515. Superficially, there is a return to the rhythm of 1501–3, but in fact policy is far more cautious. At the end of his life Aldus was a crushed and disillusioned man, tragically unable to see the successes that are so obvious to us today.

To attempt any explanation of these various bursts of activity and changes of direction, we must steer a middle course between the long view of Aldus' work, which tends to hide his more immediate problems from our vision, and a minute bibliographical examination of single editions, which is in any case hardly necessary. To provide some guidelines, I have simplified and subdivided the bibliographical data into a form designed to give fairly rapid, tabular pictures of the different phases of Aldus' career, and to help us set his actual production against his promises and plans on the one hand, and against the wider commercial background on the other. An analysis of the earlier Aldine editions on this basis can be found in Table I. From the standpoint of Aldus' own hopes and ideals, one general feature becomes quickly obvious: the dominance of Greek over all other material. This is in fact far greater than the comparatively even balance of printed volumes reveals. The number of leaves printed in Greek totals 4,212, more than double the 1807 printed in Latin. The five volumes of Aristotle alone cover 1,792 large folio leaves, excluding introductory material: this almost equals the total output of Latin in number, and far exceeds it in overall quantity since most of the Latin texts were published in fairly small quartos.

But the strength of Hellenism can be traced beyond mere statistics, for several of the Latin editions seem also to have been intended by Aldus as satellites to his Greek programme. The edition of Iamblichus which he published in 1497 was a full series of short works by various Neoplatonist writers, translated and revised personally by the Florentine philosopher Marsiglio Ficino, and clearly considered by Aldus as a part of the scheme which he proclaimed in the same year: that of printing "all the works of the divine Plato, and all the surviving commentaries upon him".[4] A substantial part of the astronomical writings printed in 1499 consisted of Latin versions of the Greek originals of Aratus, Theon and Proclus.[5] Even the Lucretius of 1500 was dedicated to Alberto Pio as an exposition of the Greek philosophy of Epicurus, not as a work of Latin literature.[6] When discussing his programme in prefaces and dedications, Aldus was constantly stressing Greek texts: and when he applied for copyright protection in 1496 and 1498, he mentioned only Greek editions.[7]

Turning now towards the Greek editions themselves, we find a selection which is overwhelmingly academic, not only in the wider sense of the word but in the context of contemporary interests within the northern Italian universities and schools. Pride of place must naturally go to the five volumes of Aristotle's works. They form the culmination of a considerable amount of editorial work on related texts, including a six-volume version of Averroes' commentaries edited by the Paduan lecturer Niccoletto Vernia and printed by Andrea Torresani during 1483 and 1484, and a variety of the more recent translations of Aristotle produced by Bernardino da Tridino and the de Gregoriis brothers between 1489 and 1496.[8] It is also significant that the Aldine text was printed over the period 1495–8, which exactly straddles the time of agitation for lectures on the Greek originals of Aristotle within the university of Padua, and Leonico Tomeo's official appointment in 1497.[9] In the dedication of the second volume, Aldus paid tribute to the help of "the learned men in Venice and Padua", naming some of them: the Englishman

Table I. Aldine Publications, 1494–1500

Year	Greek	Latin	Italian
1494?	(Musaeus 10f 4°... (Galaeomyomachia 10f 4°)	12f 4°)	
1495	Lascaris, Grammar 166f 4° Gaza, Grammar 198f **fol.**		
	Theocritus etc. 140f fol.	Bembo, De Aetna 30f 4°	
	Aristotle I 234f fol.		
1496	Grammatici Veteres 270f fol.	(Benedetti, Diaria 68f 4°)	
1497	Aristotle II 268f fol. Aristotle III 475f fol. Aristotle IV 517f fol. Valeriani, Grammar 212f 4°...		
	Dictionarium 243f fol.	Iamblichus 184f fol. Epiphyllides 54f 4° De conversione propositionum 72f 4° Quaestio Averrois 32f 4° De Gradibus medicinarum 55f 4° De Morbo Gallico 29f 4° (De Tiro seu Vipera 8f 4°)	
	Horae Virginis 112f 16° (Psalterium 15of 4°)		

Table I (cont.)

Year	Greek	Latin	Italian
1498	Aristotle V 316f fol.		
	Aristophanes 339f fol.		
		Politiani Opera 452f fol.	
		Reuchlin Oratio 12f 4°	
		Catalogus 1f fol.	
1499	Epistolographi Graeci 266f 137f 4°		
		Perotti, Cornucopia 321f fol.	
	Aratus, Theon, Proclus...Astronomici Veteres 376f fol.		
	Dioscurides, Nicander 167f fol.		
		(Amasei Poema* 12f 4°)	
			Hypnerotomachia Polifili 234f fol.
1500		Lucretius 101f 4°	
			Epistole de Sancta Catherina 412f fol.

This table has been compiled from RAIA, supplemented where appropriate by BMC v. The figures following the titles represent respectively the number of leaves in the text concerned and the size of the volume. Undated editions are bracketted. Benedetti's *Diaria de Bello Carolino* can in fact be dated securely by his application for copyright on 26 June 1496 (text in FD, p. 123, No. 50). Both this and Leoniceno's *De Tiro* have long been recognised as Aldines on typographic grounds, though neither book carries his name. Cf. RAIA pp. 259, 260.

* Hieronymi Amasei Utinensis Bononia oriundi poetae et philosophi poema ad Accursium Mainerium Avenionensem Iureconsultum clarissimum et Ludovici Christianissimi Gallorum Regis apud Venetos Oratorem facundissimum. 1499 die XX Septembris. This is not listed by Renouard, but the type is that of *Polifilo*. British Library IA 24497 and Bibliothèque Nationale, Vélins 2110, are the only known copies.

Thomas Linacre, whose personal copies are still in the library of his Oxford College, and form the only complete surviving series of the Aldine Aristotle printed on vellum;[10] Francesco Caballi, a doctor who practised in Venice but whose influence in Padua is shown by his frequent attendance at degree examinations;[11] also two prominent scholars from the university of Ferrara, Niccolo Leoniceno and Lorenzo Maioli.

If the volumes of Aristotle were university texts, most of the other Greek works which Aldus printed at this stage can be regarded as steps towards this exalted intellectual level. There is a large amount of what we can call basic linguistic material: three modern Grammars, including that of Urbano Valeriani whose Greek instruction was enjoying a great success in Venice and whom Aldus himself persuaded to write what was to become one of the most favoured Grammars of the following century;[12] a selection of earlier grammatical writings; and the Dictionary of Giovanni Craston.[13]

The seasoning of literary works is largely composed of recommended introductions to Greek language and style, some of them dedicated to contemporary teachers on the express understanding that they will be used in the classroom. The most interesting of these is the edition of Theocritus, Hesiod and selections from the Greek gnomic poets. Relatively short, containing a wide variety of linguistic forms, and packed with mythological or moralising passages, these works were obvious favourites for the educationalist, had been strongly recommended by Battista Guarino, and had already received a certain amount of attention from Aldus' predecessors. It was Guarino who suggested them to Aldus, and the dedication was addressed to him. In the same spirit the plays of Aristophanes were commended in an introduction by Musurus as the perfect guide to conversational Attic Greek and were dedicated by Aldus to another educator, Daniele Clari of Ragusa.[14] The only apparent outsider among the Greek literary editions of this period is found in the combined works of Dioscurides and Nicander, two comparatively late and difficult writers on pharmacology who could hardly have offered much enlightenment to the student looking for introductory material. But even this volume fits the overall pattern: for the writings were printed by Aldus as a contribution to one of the sharpest academic controversies of the time, the interpretation of Pliny's *Natural Histories*, and the central figure in this controversy was his personal friend and editor, Niccolo Leoniceno.[15] This entire sector of Aldus' publications has a strongly programmatical character, and such evidence as we have suggests that the books found a market chiefly amongst the students for whom they were obviously intended. Ficino's translations from the Neo-platonic commentators appeared during December 1497. In less than a month Aldus received a letter from no less a person than the epic poet Ludovico Ariosto, who explained that Sebastiano da Aquila's lectures on the *Timaeus* had been attracting a keen interest in Latin translations of Platonic works amongst the students of Ferrara, that Alberto Pio's copy of the new edition had been coveted by all, and that any further copies would be sure of a ready sale.[16] The coincidence between the printer's ideals and the requirements of his market would appear at first sight to have been perfect.

But two vague and slightly threatening features lurk, almost indistinguishable in the background of this bright picture. First, it seems certain that Aldus was not progressing nearly as fast as he had originally hoped. We have already seen some signs of this in the unfulfilled promises of his introductions, and there is further proof in his second application for copyright, which was presented to the senate on 6 December 1498. The document lays stress on plans for the publication of medical works, names a number of literary and philosophical texts – the Suda, Demosthenes, Hermogenes, Plutarch, Dioscurides, Stephanus, and the commentators on Aristotle – then peters out with the ominous words "Let no more be written." Only Stephanus and Dioscurides had appeared within the next four years.[17] Second, these Greek texts were exceedingly expensive. This follows naturally from what has already been said about the difficulty and cost of working with Greek types, but Aldus has such a reputation as a publisher of cheap editions that it is as well to establish the point beyond doubt by comparing the prices quoted in the catalogue which he brought out in 1498 with those charged by his predecessor Francesco da Madiis during the 1480s. The five volumes of the Aldine text of Aristotle ranged from 1.5 to 3 ducats each, or 11 ducats for the complete set. The comedies of Aristophanes cost 2.5 ducats, Craston's Dictionary and Gaza's Grammar 1 ducat, the Idylls of Theocritus 8 marcelli – the equivalent of about two thirds of a ducat. The smaller Grammars of Lascaris and Valeriani cost 4 marcelli.[18] In some of these cases we can make a more or less direct comparison. Francesco da Madiis stocked "large Greek Dictionaries" at 3 lire mocenighe or less than half a ducat, "Erotemata Graeca" at 10 soldi or 1 marcello, and a selection of Hesiod and Theocritus at 1 lira 5 soldi or slightly over 2 marcelli. In all probability these will have been the early Milanese editions of Bonus Accursius, and it can be seen at once that the prices asked were barely more than half those of the Aldine equivalents, and sometimes even lower.[19]

For counterparts to the Aldine Aristotle we must search among the most ambitious publications of the time, such as de' Paganini's edition of Nicholas of Lyra's Biblical commentary: in a special petition to the Senate the printer set the total cost of the enterprise at 4,000 ducats, and 6 ducats as the price of each four-volume set.[20] Even a personal friend of Aldus, the Bolognese Hellenist Codrus Urceus, complained in 1498 that he could have bought ten fine Latin manuscripts for the sum he had paid for his volumes of Aristotle: and when we read of Alvise Capello's walking into Francesco da Madiis' shop, paying just over 2 ducats, and walking out with a dozen different books, we are bound to feel that Urceus had some justification for what he said.[21] No doubt it was an excellent idea to satisfy the most advanced academic tastes: but how many students had the resources of Ariosto or Alberto Pio?

Though they form nothing resembling the coherent pattern of the Greek editions, the Latin texts which Aldus published in this period shed an interesting light on the different levels of the early printer's work, and on the variety of forces that worked upon him. We have already mentioned the subordination of several Latin works to the Greek programme: several more were clearly personal favours whose main purpose must have been to thank the editors of the Greek texts for their trouble. In 1497 Aldus published two short works by his Aristotelian collaborator, Lorenzo Maioli – *De Gradibus Medicinarum* and *Epiphyllides in Dialecticis*: in an introduction to the last work he explained that he had originally refused to print so crude a piece and had only given way to his friend's earnest plea that pupils were clamouring for the book.[22] Maioli had a certain moral hold over him.

Two short pieces by Niccolo Leoniceno – *De Morbo Gallico* and *De Tiro seu Vipera* – must have been printed at almost exactly the same time and in part for the same reasons, though both concerned questions of pressing intellectual and medical interest.[23] Bembo's *De Aetna*, famed for the Roman type named after it, and Alessandro Benedetti's *Diaria de Bello Carolino* both belong in the same general category. Bembo's little book described some experiences of his own during a trip to Sicily to study Greek, and among the souvenirs which he brought back was a valuable manuscript of Constantine Lascaris' Greek Grammar Aldus used it for his first dated edition, and we shall discuss it in detail later.²⁴ Benedetti was a fashionable Venetian doctor who had served with the army during the campaign against the French in 1495, and now sought literary fame by producing a personal account which he peppered liberally with compliments to influential noblemen. He bore the costs of the edition, and Aldus did not add his own name. But correspondence reveals that Benedetti was a close friend of Giorgio Valla, the public lecturer through whose good offices Aldus made his own entrance into Venetian high society. It was worth obliging such a man.²⁵ In odd contrast to the coherently planned Greek editions, these Latin texts should serve to remind us that Aldus had his supporters, as well as his ideals to satisfy.

Two short and now exceedingly rare works, the speech of Reuchlin and the prophetic poem of Amaseo, form a special group which in a later age would have been the province of a newspaper office rather than a publishing firm. The customs of the time expected any distinguished visitor to deliver, and be welcomed by, a highly formalised address which could then be printed and circulated as a small pamphlet to stress the justice of this particular mission, or the solidarity of some new alliance. The distinguished German scholar Reuchlin had been to Rome during the summer of 1498 as the representative of his patron, the Elector Palatine, in a dispute with the Abbey of Wissemburg, and he apparently had a few copies of his speech to the papal authorities printed while he was on his way home. They would prove how carefully he had executed his commission. Accursius Mayner, to whom Amaseo's Latin poem was addressed, arrived in Venice during the summer of 1499 to finalise a delicate re-alignment which was to bring the Republic into the field with the French Crown against the neighbouring Sforza Duchy of Milan. As ambassador, he struck up a friendship with Aldus, and the poet Amaseo offered him a turgid hexametric vision of the future greatness of French and Venetian arms. Such occasional pieces may be considered ancestors of the propaganda leaflet: and appropriately, the Bibliothèque Nationale still has a magnificent copy printed on vellum and blazoned with the lilies of France, the Lion of St Mark, and the Keys of the Papacy. No doubt Mayner had it sent home to impress King Louis. But in spite of their temporary importance, pamphlets like these were ephemera in the truest sense: they were flimsy, they were probably printed in small numbers only, and it is not surprising that they are now among the rarest Aldine editions.²⁶

Poliziano's *Opera* must be considered separately, for their publication has a complex history which illustrates the force of sheer chance, as well as personal taste. It has been usual to regard the edition as part of some "grand design" of humanist publication: apart from Aldus' admiration for Poliziano as the embodiment of that perfect philological skill to which he himself aspired, we might notice that the book was printed as a large folio, costing 1.4 ducats and demanding typographic experiments such as the first use of Hebrew letters.[27] In fact, Aldus was probably uninvolved in and unaware of the preliminary preparations. Since the early 1490s a number of Poliziano's individual works had been published in Bologna by Platon Benedetti with the help of an ambitious young scholar called Alessandro Sarti, who inserted complimentary but entirely spurious references to himself into Poliziano's letters and appears to have been a typical press-shark. At some time which cannot be pinpointed Sarti was drawn into the orbit of a slightly more respectable attempt to organise Poliziano's papers: this centred on Florence, was carried out by a younger member of the Medicean circle named Pietro Ricci and sponsored by Gianfrancesco Pico della Mirandola, nephew and intellectual heir of Aldus' first patron. So when the prospective publisher Benedetti died in August 1497 the entire project dropped suddenly and unexpectedly in Aldus' lap. It must be said that having found it there, the printer took every means of giving the edition that eventually appeared a personal and programmatic touch, incorporating the letter in which he had declared his own faith in Poliziano's bilingual approach and probably using his contact with the Barbaro family to acquire a number of letters which may not have been available to the Florentine editors. But the text is a monument to commerical improvisation as well as humanist principle.[28]

During this first period of his printing career, Aldus published only two editions in Italian, both appearing within a single year. But one of these books, the *Hypnerotomachia Polifili,* has generated more controversy than the rest of Aldus' publications combined. Whole books have in their turn been devoted to it, and learned studies beyond counting have left its problems still unsettled. Who wrote it? Why did he play hide-and-seek with his readers? Who was the illustrator, where did he get his ideas, and how wide an effect did they have on the art of the time? What part did Aldus play in the whole scheme?[29] Where much is uncertain and space is limited, the razor must be applied: this is a study of Aldus, and we shall confront only the questions which relate immediately to him. The issue of authorship I believe to have been settled at least beyond reasonable doubt. The identity of the illustrator seems to me to present problems which are insoluble without further documentary evidence, and in the meantime are best left to art-historians competent to deal with them. Aldus' part I believe, however unfashionably, to have been fairly slight: great enough to provide illustrations of the tensions and embarrassments into which a printer could run, but quite insufficient to allow any argument about his own views on Italian literature.

The first link in the chain of events, though apparently irrelevant, is at least securely documented. On 10 May 1498 the Senate resigned itself to the fact that there was plague in the city. The proveditori sopra la sanità took prompt measures to prevent large gatherings, and the outbreak was contained with merciful speed.[30] But one of its victims was Aldus. He cannot have been desperately ill, since work was going ahead in the print-shop by June, but the horror of death cut deeply into his sensitive and religious temperament, inducing him to vow that he would become a priest if he recovered. Having done so, he promptly appealed to Rome for a dispensation on the grounds that he was very poor and his trade was his only means of support: a somewhat disingenuous plea, one feels, since he was not really poor, he had other means of support in his teaching skills, and he must have been perfectly well aware that his colleague Bonetus Locatellus had been both priest and printer for many years. Alexander VI issued the dispensation, but suggested to the Patriarch that Aldus should be turned towards "other works of charity".[31] Besides his own conscience, Aldus was now subject to definite moral obligations, possibly even checks, since the Patriarch Tomaso Donà had recently been taking an interest in improper publications, and the influential canon-lawyer Cardinal Felino Sandeis of Lucca had noted in his copy of the Aldine Iamblichus that there was "much in this book which a Christian should not read". He had read it himself with great absorption, but that was not the point.[32]

The required dispensation came through on 11 August 1498, and it cannot have been long afterwards that Aldus received one of those visitors whom he came to dread in later life: a literary dilettante with a manuscript which he wished to have published. In this case the man concerned was Leonardo Crasso, a well connected Veronese gentleman whose brother was an officer in the Venetian army and who had just secured his own doctorate of Law on the way to becoming an Apostolic protonotary.[33] The work he had to offer was an amorous romance in two distinct but loosely associated versions. The second – shorter, relatively simple alongside its companion, and almost certainly written earlier – kept at least some hold on a recognisable world. The heroine Polia is made to tell of her native city Treviso, her family the Lelli, and of the origins of Polifilo's love for her. She is stricken by the plague, vows to preserve her chastity, recovers, and rebuffs the advances of Polifilo, who collapses as though dead. Polia flees from the scene in horror, and is warned of the enormity of her actions by a series of symbolic visions and dreams. She returns to Polifilo, who revives in her embrace, and the lovers' dialogue carries the text to its still fairly distant ending. The narrative is set in Treviso, and dated at its conclusion to 1 May 1467. But the more elaborate version, which appears first in the existing text, cuts these slender links with reality. Polifilo is led on basically the same journey from pain to joy through a fantastic archaeological dream-world of pyramids and obelisks, ruined temples and crumbling altars, amongst which Polia is revealed as a nymph who leads her lover to ultimate enlightenment beside the fountain of Venus.[34] It must be emphasised that the work bears not the slightest resemblance to the racy novels of the Trecento. This was a linguistic and literary debauch, choked with recondite imagery, erudite periphrases, and exotic verbiage: a work so bizarre that many critics have felt a certain uneasiness at Aldus' agreeing to print it. He is reputed, after all, to have been a man of good taste, and his handling of Maioli and Celtis shows that he was quite capable of saying "No" to a work he considered unsuitable.[35] But I doubt if Aldus was inclined, or able, to feel such scruples in this case. For all its weird form, *Polifilo* contained much to interest him. The linguistic experiments must have intrigued a man who had pointed, only two years earlier, to the analogy between the rich pattern of Greek literary dialects and the variations in Italian local usage.[36] Aldus, along with all his close friends, was passionately involved in the study of the antique remains described. He may have felt challenged by the technical difficulties of printing and illustrating such a work. He may even have been mildly titillated by a story which set the same value as he had done on a vow taken during dangerous illness. And though the "high fantasies" contained in the book may be utterly alien to our own empirically minded age, they were acceptable to Rabelais and were thought worthy of Sir Philip Sidney's circle by an anonymous English translator.[37] But all such aesthetic considerations probably weighed less than the stern dictates of business and public relations: Crasso's brother Francesco was an associate of the influential doctor Benedetti, whose account of the French invasion Aldus had published two years before, and who could exert a strong leverage through his own friendship with Giorgio Valla. *Polifilo* almost certainly arrived at the print-shop with the backing of literary friends whom Aldus neither dared nor wished to offend. It also offered a commission worth several hundred ducats, which after a period of enforced idleness he could ill afford to refuse.[38]

What Aldus may not have understood at once is the nature of the author and the full significance of his work. We can be certain that he soon knew who the author was, for a large part of the text described buildings, inscriptions, triumphs and sacrifices in a detail which demanded illustration, and the programme of illustration which resulted was so closely integrated with the text and with the design of individual pages that it could hardly have been carried out unless the author, the illustrator, and the printer had sat together in consultation.[39] Aldus must also have been one of the first to realise a fact which other readers soon discovered – that the initial letters of each succeeding chapter concealed the author's name in the acrostic "Poliam Frater Franciscus Columna Peramavit". Some copies actually carried the same name – Francesco Colonna – in a short introductory poem,[40] and since Francesco seems to have borrowed money from his Provincial to help with the financing of the project, it is probable that Aldus also had business dealings with him.[41]

At first sight, Fra Francesco must have seemed respectable enough. He was a Dominican, attached to the famous Venetian house of San Giovanni e Paolo, and he was esteemed by Benedetti, who commissioned him to say masses for his soul.[42] He may have been a "sfratato" – a member of an unreformed Order living half in, half out of his community – but even in the time of Giordano Bruno, such people could often find a comfortable niche in Venetian society. Aldus' associates Fra Urbano and Fra Giocondo fell into the same general category, and were accepted everywhere.[43] It could have taken the printer some time to discover that Fra Francesco was a more than usually vicious character, who had twice been called before the highest authorities of his Order and once expelled from Venice on so many charges that the senior members of his community had also been held under threat.

Though he was by this time in his late sixties – he was born in 1433 – Colonna's cup of iniquity was still far from full. In 1516 he was at the centre of a scandal which split San Giovanni e Paolo from top to bottom, involving both the Venetian Council of Ten and the General of the Dominican Order. Fra Francesco accused several of his superiors of sodomy, then retracted and was himself accused and convicted of seducing a young girl.⁴⁴ Banished yet again from Venice, he still managed to return – apparently something of a legend by this time, for when he finally died in 1527, full of years and sin, his misdeeds were enshrined in a novel by Matteo Bandello.⁴⁵

One can only wonder what carnal realities lay behind the symbolic fountains and sublimated obelisks of his romance. Polia, as we have seen, introduces herself as Lucrezia Lelli, and makes her vow of chastity during an attack of plague. The Lelli were indeed a powerful family who held large estates between Padua and Treviso: one of their members, Teodoro, was Bishop of Treviso during an outbreak of plague in 1464.⁴⁶ Whether or not some real love-intrigue lay behind the story, Fra Francesco's character would have excited far more suspicion in his ecclesiastical contemporaries than it does in us. He was not the best of associates for Aldus, who in 1498 had special reasons to be discreet.

The position must have grown steadily more embarrassing as the programme of illustration developed. Because of the absolute necessity of co-operation, we can be certain that the work was done in Venice and at least fairly certain that Aldus, who had the right contacts, chose the craftsman who designed the woodcuts. It is indeed an indication of our extreme ignorance of Aldus' business activities that the master's name has never been discovered. Personally, I am convinced by those who have advanced the claims of Benedetto Bordone, partly because the circumstantial evidence in his favour is strong – we know that he had a workshop in the San Zulian area of Venice, and his application for copyright on his "Triumphs of Caesar" suggests an interest in classical material – partly because several illuminated copies of Aldine editions that I have seen appear to bear traces of his work.⁴⁷

Perhaps because the material was congenial, the illustrator, whoever he was, produced a masterpiece which towers above any contemporary and carries the interdependence of word and picture into a new dimension. Arches, temples, vases, sculptures, inscriptions, chariots were traced out as the writer had described them, not only with expertise but with a kind of zest which gave the completed whole both its brilliance and its danger. For the reader might not

Sacrifice to Priapus from *Hypnerotomachia Polifili* (see note 48).

have been offended by the mere description of a sacrifice to "the lord of the garden, with all his right and proper attributes" even if he had understood what that phrase meant. But when the text was faced by a superbly balanced woodcut of Priapus enshrined, with his thrusting phallus, his ring of exultant worshippers, and his sacrificial calf spilling its blood before the altar, the real meaning of the stilted language needed no explanation.[48] This was a sensuous wallowing in the revived glories of the pagan past, stripped by the force of its illustration of any real pretence to moral symbolism. The illustrations in Rubeo's edition of the *Metamorphoses*, to which the Patriarch of Venice had objected only two years earlier, are by comparison indifferent in execution and innocuous in content, even when they deal with scenes such as the love of Ares and Aphrodite, which had attracted censorious attention since Plato's time.[49]

We can now appreciate the artistry without fear of the paganism, and there were a number of contemporaries – mostly rather disreputable painters, like Giorgione, his pupil Tiziano Vercellio, and a mysterious German visitor named Albrecht Dürer – who were prepared to accept both elements together.[50] But the bulk of steady and orthodox opinion, which Aldus needed to conciliate, will have found the work an obscene, heathen carnival.

The particular circumstances in which *Polifilo* actually appeared gravely aggravated the moral difficulties already inherent in the text. Throughout the spring of 1499 there were rumours of war, confirmed in July as a mighty Turkish armada put to sea and sailed west. It was met off the Peloponnesus by the most formidable fleet Venice had ever assembled, but the running fight which followed during August failed to prevent the Turks breaking into the Gulf of Lepanto and seizing the Venetian fortress. The feeling of disillusion was profound, and public opinion snarled for scapegoats. The fleet-commander Antonio Grimani narrowly escaped execution. Other prosecutions followed during the winter months, and, when the war went no better next year and the vital town of Modon was lost, Venice was gripped by one of those spasms of collective self-reproach which blamed defeat on the just anger of the Almighty.[51] An unsigned letter to the doge denounced public venality and private immorality, calling for repentance before the tide of Turkish success could be checked. It was read aloud in the council-chambers, and published by the vigilant Patriarch Donà.[52] Venice was embarking on a moral, as well as a military crusade: and, by a stroke of disastrous timing which can rarely have been equalled in the annals of publishing, *Polifilo* appeared in December 1499, just as the agitation was getting under way.

Aldus was plainly uneasy about *Polifilo* well before copies were actually on the bookstalls. He printed his own name only in small type, at the bottom of a page of corrections, and a number of surviving copies have the less discreet sections inked out in a style so uniform as to suggest that it was done before the books left the workshop.[53] But since he rarely signed commissioned work at all, it is hard to resist a suspicion that Aldus was also fascinated by the technical virtuosity which he and his collaborators had achieved. We do not know whether there were any direct repercussions. Possibly this was one of the occasions on which high connections could help. Very probably the obscurity and expense of the book, which cost a ducat, scared off the usual buyers of Italian romances, kept the sales at the low level later deplored by Crasso, and so averted the scandal which gathered round a popular edition like Rubeo's *Metamorphoses*.[54] But considering his own circumstances and the atmosphere in Venice, it is hard to believe that Aldus did not feel some need to vindicate his reputation and his abandoned vocation.

The Letters of St Catherine of Siena, which were being prepared for the press at the same time as *Polifilo* and finally appeared about ten months later with the first experimental letters in italic type, appear to have been used by Aldus partly as an atonement and form the last act in this curious publishing drama. The edition was a joint venture. On 17 April 1499 Aldus acted on behalf of Margherita Uglheimer, widow of Jenson's partner and executor, in organising the loan of four manuscripts and a printed text from an unknown monastery. Presumably this last survivor of the great syndicate shared financial risks with the organisation which was now claiming something of the role which her husband and his associates had once occupied.[55] The edition also followed a well established trend: texts of the later medieval devotional writers were enjoying a considerable vogue and two partial editions of St Catherine's works had already appeared during the 1490s. But the editorial work of Fra Bartolomeo da Alzano greatly expanded this material, and Aldus showed himself willing to take some pains to secure the manuscripts he needed, promising sixty ducats to the monastery if they should be damaged.[56]

He also launched the edition with an almost ostentatious degree of publicity. First, an application for copyright stressed the sanctity of the writings and the care that had gone into collecting them.[57] Next, a careful dedication was directed to Cardinal Francesco Piccolomini, an elderly and fairly respectable Sienese cleric who would live to enjoy a few days as Pope after the death of Alexander VI. Aldus took care to play upon the hideous vices of the time, and the need for holy writings to act as preachers in converting Christendom to better ways, especially at a time when the threat from the Turks was above men's very heads. He was making the best of a good chance to display his orthodoxy and moral soundness.[58]

But, if circumstances had dealt harshly with *Polifilo,* in the wider world of business and politics they were turning increasingly in favour of its publisher. Aldus may have been the most enterprising printer in Venice during the later 1490s: but he did not yet enjoy the domination of the Venetian industry and of classical publication which was to be his soon after the end of the century. A glance at Table I (page 112) reveals that his most productive year during this period was 1497, when at least a dozen editions appeared.

This is an impressive total, but it was equalled by Locatellus and an analysis of Panzer's certainly over-conservative *Annales Typographici* shows that Aldus was only one of five or six publishers in Venice who were capable at this time of turning out ten or more editions in a single year.[59] Even in his chosen field of Greek literature and philosophy he had serious rivals. Six of the eleven editions attributed to the Florentine press of Lorenzo de' Alopa are undated, so it is impossible to say precisely how its activity was concentrated. But between 1494 and the end of 1496 Lorenzo was operating with a larger number and better quality of Greek type-founts than Aldus, and with the priceless advantage of direct access to Florentine scholars and libraries. His publications, which included Greek and Latin material, in several cases anticipated Aldus'.[60]

In Venice itself a renegade associate named Gabriel of Brassichella made a direct attempt to undermine Aldus. Zacharias Callierges was cooperative and tactful, avoiding any infringement of the Aldine patents, sharing editors, possibly even concerting plans to some degree. But there was more than an implied threat in the Cretans' comparison of their type-face to Aldus', and in the fact that they could produce four superb folio editions in sixteen months.[61] When Aldus complained about the disasters of the age, he can hardly have known that, in weeding out these various rivals, war and economic catastrophe were being no bad friends to him.[62]

THE CHANCES OF BUSINESS

Lorenzo de' Alopa's organisation seems to have died of slow starvation rather than sudden misfortune, though its affairs have not been fully investigated. Its last publications were two volumes of the Platonic commentaries of Marsiglio Ficino, which appeared at the very end of 1496: by this time, Ficino was sick and disillusioned; Lascaris had been tempted away by the conquering French, and his satellites had dispersed. The driving force had simply vanished.[63]

In contrast to this, the story of Gabriel of Brasichella has an intriguing flavour of drama and espionage. In 1497 he is honourably mentioned by Aldus as a collaborator: on 7 March of the following year he obtained a ten-year copyright on his own projected editions of Pollux, Philostratus, the Letters of Brutus and Phalaris, and the Fables of Aesop; but on 20 May he felt it wise to seek confirmation of his privilege, hinting darkly that his plans were suspected "by those who are too devoted to their own advantage". The new concession was granted, and the Letters of Brutus and Phalaris appeared in June, printed in a type which bore a dangerous resemblance to the Aldine cursive – itself protected by the privilege of 1496.[64] Gabriel disappeared from sight immediately and irrevocably. In September, Alberto Pio was inquiring about Aldus' "lawsuit with the men of Carpi", and we can reasonably infer what this means from the fact that Gabriel's collaborators, Benedetto de Manzi and Giovanni Bissolo, both of Carpi, had been obliged to leave Venice for Milan by the following spring. There must have been a head-on collision between two irreconcilable copyrights, with the victory going to the party with the greater influence: and that issue at least can never have been in doubt.[65] Bissolo and de Manzi did not forgive Aldus, and devoted the next few years to a vain quest for revenge: in 1499 they formed a company with Demetrius Chalcondylas to print the *Suda*, only to have their enterprise snuffed out by the Franco-Venetian invasion of Milan; and in 1506 de Manzi made a brief appearance in Carpi, where he printed two editions with a blatant imitation of the Aldine Italic fount.[66] On this occasion, Aldus does not appear to have taken any serious action. The facts suggest that, of the three men involved, Gabriel of Brasichella may have been a sinister industrial spy of the kind we met in the first chapter: Bissolo and de Manzi were probably no more than victims of a system which was still too vague to realise the implications of the numerous copyrights it was granting.

The press of Zacharias Callierges appears to have been engulfed, along with an unknown number of others, in the widespread commercial crisis which convulsed Venice at the very end of the fifteenth century. In early 1499 the business-community was shaken to its foundations by a series of bankruptcies: from 1500 the number of presses and publications declined steeply. We cannot link cause and effect precisely, but we can be sure that war lay at the origins of the disaster. The campaign against the French invaders in 1495 had stretched Venetian finances severely, and left the Republic with several outstanding military commitments on the mainland. As the government called upon richer citizens for one forced loan after another to maintain its new conquests in Southern Italy or to support Pisa against its Florentine overlords, the flow of money which had been a feature of the earlier 1490s vanished underground. By the summer of 1496 government stocks had declined to sixty-two per cent of their par value. As the threat of another French invasion receded, some business confidence returned, but the rumour of Turkish naval preparations during the winter of 1498–9 was enough to provoke a panic-stricken withdrawal of funds which the banks were unable to meet. At the end of January 1499 the bank of Andrea Garzoni crashed with liabilities of 96,000 ducats. In May, Tomaso Lippomano followed with losses of 140,000 ducats. Within three and a half months, commented one diarist bitterly, the business community of Venice had lost half of its credit-facilities at the mere rumour of war, while all ten of the Florentine merchant-banks had stood firm through five years of war, revolution, and foreign occupation. No worse disgrace could have come from the loss of one of the republic's principal dominions.[67]

In the annals of Venetian economic history, the disasters of that spring have been somewhat overshadowed by the nearly contemporary Portuguese voyages which ultimately re-routed the currents of world-trade. But the impact may at the time have been far worse. There was simply not a ducat to be found, wrote one banker, and the effect of this situation on the publishing-houses, which needed long credit because their funds "could not be quickly collected", is easily imagined.[68] We happen to know that one of the most important and intransigent creditors of the Lippomano bank was Nicholas Vlastos, a Cretan noble who had placed funds at the disposal of Zacharias Callierges, so we can feel fairly certain that this press disappeared in 1499 because investment was no longer available.[69]

But it is natural to see the cash-famine behind a change in the whole pattern of Venetian publishing. The decline in the number of presses operating was considerable: the thirty-six names represented in 1499 dwindled to twenty-seven in the following year, and to seventeen by 1504. The total figure had not climbed back to twenty by the end of the decade. Even more striking is the loss of production. During the last decade of the fifteenth century the total number of editions printed in Venice during any one year was generally between 120 and 150. In 1501 it had slumped back to seventy-one, and by 1504 it was as low as fifty-seven. Though these figures are certainly not exact, it is clear that the Venetian printing industry was sinking into a severe recession, and since it now becomes rare to find any printer producing more than six editions per year, it seems likely that credit-difficulties were creating a sense of caution.[70]

But few economic crises blow nobody any good. In this case the strangest beneficiary was probably the disgraced captain-general Antonio Grimani, who was awaiting trial for his life while his company, which controlled the only available supplies of spice, made 40,000 ducats out of a shortage created partly by the naval incapacities of its own manager.[71] Similarly, Aldus' fortunes appear to have advanced in step with the general recession in printing. In a preface of 1502 he wholly abandoned his usual lugubrious tone and expressed delight at the expansion of the taste for good literature, and at the way in which his labours were being rewarded.[72] Such figures as we have appear to justify his confidence. He printed eleven or twelve editions in 1501: seventeen in 1502, the highest total he ever achieved; eleven again in 1503. Overall, his output over the three years more than doubles that of printers such as de Gregoriis and Tacuinus who had been close competitors only a few years earlier.[73] Luck was probably the main ingredient of success. As was mentioned in the previous chapter, Aldus had exceptionally strong financial backing, and his company's moneys were channelled through the bank of Mafio Agostini, one of the two which survived the catastrophe of 1499. By 1500, the chances of war and politics had pruned away his rivals. It cannot be shown in detail that the labour-force of Callierges and Gabriel of Brassichella passed into Aldus' workshop, but it is certainly true that Greek scholars now devoted their editorial skills exclusively to the only man who was printing Greek texts, and it is likely that compositors will have done the same thing.[74]

Just as Aldus' company was entering the period of its greatest activity, the development of the large variety of types mentioned in the previous chapter was nearing completion. There is a distinct possibility that this was more than mere coincidence: as less money was drawn off towards capital investment in punch-cutting and the striking of matrices, more should have been freed for the day-to-day expenses of publication like paper, copy, and editorial help. Unfortunately, the fragmentary records do not allow us to examine such details. But the deployment of its full range of typographical equipment is enough in itself to give us a number of clues about the commercial strategy which the company was following. In 1502, men still spoke of "writing" a printed page as if it were a letter to a friend. As this now oddly intimate language implies, the type-face provided a much closer link between the printer and his public than it does today: particular styles of type were reserved for particular groups of readers, and we can consequently infer a good deal from a printer's use of types about the section of the market he was trying to reach.[75] In Aldus' case it is vital to make this attempt, since his types had an original and individual quality about them which excited the keenest admiration and rivalry in his own time and has provoked a good deal of disagreement between different scholars of different ages.

To Erasmus, and apparently to most literary men of the sixteenth century, the Aldine italic letters were "those small types, the most beautiful in the world". Stanley Morison saw the Roman fount used for Bembo's *De Aetna* as the opening of "a new epoch in typography", and the Aldine Roman style as dominating "the finest typography of two continents" to this very day.[76] But modern bibliographers have been no less outspoken in their hostility. In his discussion of Greek types, Robert Proctor treated Aldus as a man of horribly bad taste, whose types were "devoid of beauty of form other than that conferred on them by good cutting", and whose success "secured the disappearance of older and purer models". Curt Buhler went still further, and wrote off Aldus' entire typographical programme as a disaster:

His presswork was indifferent, and his types were poor. It has been said – I believe with all possible justification – that his Greek types set back the study of that tongue by three hundred years.... The italic type has by this time found its natural and proper habitat among the footnotes of learned periodicals.[77]

This clash of views is the more serious, because it has been only partly acknowledged and because much depends on the decision. It is not only Aldus' reputation as a printer that is at issue, but his entire relationship to the intellectual and cultural life of his times.

If they are judged purely by the modern standards of visual clarity and harmony of form, Aldus' Greek founts will and must be found wanting. Obsessed by the same dream as Gutenberg and many early printers, he strove to reproduce the most fashionable manuscript-styles and so make good a repeated claim that his letters were "as good, if not better, than any written with a pen". Unhappily, the fashionable Greek script of the fifteenth century was a fussy, flamboyant cursive, full of ligatures and ornamental flourishes, and the effect of copying it can be seen all too clearly in the alphabet which Aldus appended to his first edition of Constantine Lascaris' Grammar. There are seven variant forms of the letter "nu", five of "alpha", "phi" and "omega", four of "beta" and "tau": in all, the twenty-four letters of the alphabet appear in seventy-five forms, while contractions, abbreviations, accents and breathings carry the total number of sorts well into the hundreds. This first, experimental fount was either extended into or wholly recast as an even more elaborate version which is now known as the "Aristotle fount" from its use for that celebrated edition and for the contemporary texts of Musaeus, Theocritus, Theodorus Gaza, and the *Galaeomyomachia*.

Size and complexity were both somewhat reduced for a third type which appears in certain sections of the *Thesaurus* in 1496 and was Aldus' main work-horse for some time thereafter: it was used either on its own or in conjunction with the Aristotle fount, and also had the ambiguous distinction of being copied by Gabriel of Brassichella and his associates. Another and still smaller type was introduced for Dioscurides and Nicander in 1499: this experiment in miniaturism later proved useful for the printing of large prose-texts in double columns, is generally considered more legible than its predecessors, and earned even Proctor's grudging approval. Finally, in August of 1502, Aldus' last distinct fount was brought out for the first edition of Sophocles: this was still further simplified. If we take an overall view of these seven years of development, and treat the "Lascaris fount" and the "Aristotle fount" as products of the same set of matrices and therefore technically a single strike, it seems clear that the general tendency was away from the excessively complex forms of the earlier period towards a greater simplicity and economy. But it remains true that, unless he is a skilled palaeographer or well acquainted with the text he has to hand, the modern reader who attempts to study an Aldine Greek text will soon experience a prickling in the eyes and a woolly sensation behind them.[78]

τούτω. ἢ μᾶλλον θέσει, πανταχῶς· ὅταν, ἤτοι
εἰς σύμφωνον λήγῃ· καὶ τὴν ἑξῆς ἔχῃ ἀπὸ συμ-
φώνου ἀρχομένην· οἷον ἔρνος· ἢ μετὰ τὸ φύσει
βραχὺ φωνῆεν, ἑτέρα ἡ συλλαβὴ ἀπὸ δύο
συμφώνων, ἢ διπλοῦ ἀρχομένη ἐπιφέρηται·
οἷον, ἄγρος· ὄξος. ἢ εἰς δύο σύμφωνα· ἢ εἰς
ἓν διπλοῦν λήγῃ· ἅλς. ὄψ.

Περὶ βραχείας συλλαβῆς.

Βραχεῖα δὲ, ἡ ἔχουσα ἤτοι φύσει βραχὺ φωνῆεν·
οἷον λόγος. νέος· ἢ δίχρονον ἀντελλόμενον
μόνον. φιλία. γυνή.

Περὶ κοινῆς συλλαβῆς.

Κοινὴ δὲ, ἡ δυναμένη μακρά τε λαμβάνεσθαι
καὶ βραχεῖα. γίνεται δὲ τὸ τοιοῦτον ὅταν, ἤτοι
εἰς φωνῆεν μακρόν, ἢ δίφθογγον λήγουσα, εἰς
μέρος λόγου καταπαύσῃ· εἶτα τὴν ἑξῆς ἔχῃ
ἀπὸ φωνήεντος ἀρχομένην· ἐπὶ μὲν γὰρ ἐν —

Aldus' Greek script, from Biblioteca
Ambrosiana, Milan, Ms Graecus, P. 35

Aldus' "Aristotle Fount"

Approximately seven months before Aldus embarked on his own Greek programme, the Florentine press of Lascaris and Alopa published an edition of the Planudean Anthology in a superb uncial maiuscule, which has been universally admired by modern critics for its clarity and boldness, but which its originators felt bound to abandon within eighteen months. Aldus has consequently been condemned not only for his perversity in selecting the inferior cursive pattern, but for his assumed success in driving a far better rival out of the market and determining the style of Greek typography until the uncial could be revived. The view that he provided the manuscript model for his own Greek types – a view with which I am inclined to agree, in so far as I believe a definite decision to be possible – serves only to add point to the accusations by making Aldus personally and totally responsible for everything that is assumed to have gone wrong with the printing of Greek over the last four and a half centuries.[79]

But in the first place, it is surely unfair to hold Aldus so completely responsible for adopting the cursive style. He was working for and with the tight circle of professional Greek copyists and Italian philologists in Venice, Padua and Ferrara, borrowing manuscripts, commissioning copies, and seeking all kinds of grammatical and technical advice. His Greek teacher Adramyttenus, and his main scribal assistants Apostolis, Gregoropoulos and Musurus all used a cursive hand, and it is hardly surprising that they passed the taste for it on to their Italian pupils and patrons. The library of Giorgio Valla, which played an unspecifiable but definite part in Aldus' editorial plans and was later purchased by his patron Alberto Pio, was composed largely of manuscripts written in a similar style. Men like these provided the market Aldus had to satisfy. In commissioning Francesco Griffo to cut four different and increasingly modest versions of the cursive onto punches, he cannot be blamed any more than can a chameleon for turning green against a background of thick jungle foliage.[80]

Second, it is not nearly as obvious as it seemed to Robert Proctor that Lascaris' uncial must always have been more legible than its cursive rival, or that the Florentine company was "forced" by Aldus to sacrifice clarity to fashion. During the late 1530s and early 1540s the French ambassador in Venice, Guillaume Pellicier, bought and dispatched home roughly 200 Greek texts to fill the royal library. Among them was a fine copy of Lascaris' Greek Anthology, heavily glossed by Gianfrancesco Torresani. But when Pellicier's acquisitions were inventoried, the book was separated from the main groups of manu scripts and printed texts, being listed instead among a special composite category of "books which cannot easily be read because of their age".[81] Apparently, the uncial was as difficult for a reader trained in the fifteenth-century cursive as that script is for his modern counterpart. Aldus' aims and achievement must be judged not by some cosmic and all embracing standard of what was best for typography, but by what was required at the time. Clarity, like so much else, exists in the eye of the beholder. In studying the tastes of the fairly restricted market of academics and wealthy patrons which he hoped to reach, Aldus was trying to fit his style of printing to his readers. He succeeded. Lascaris and Alopa tried, as they realised, to swim against the current. They failed.

There is an element of mystery about Aldus' six Roman type-founts, which for some reason has escaped notice. He never sought to protect them from competition – since the basic design was not original, this might have been difficult – and he did little or nothing to advertise them in correspondence. With the important exceptions of Poliziano and St Catherine of Siena, the works printed in Roman type tended to be "occasional" pieces, sponsored by wealthy clients or academic friends, or introductory and ancilliary material within editions of more central importance. There is, in fact, little to suggest that Aldus took this style of printing very seriously. A rather crude, bunched version, which Griffo may simply have cast from existing matrices without cutting the punches, was used for the Latin sections of Lascaris' Grammar, and then immediately discarded. Two clearer, but equally short-lived variants were brought in for the Latin passages of Theodorus Gaza's Grammar and the introductions to Aristotle and Theocritus.

But by this time, Aldus and Griffo had already developed what posterity has come to regard as their masterpiece. In February 1496 Bembo's little essay *De Aetna* saw the light of day, and the type used to print it has become so famous that it is still identified by the name of that otherwise insignificant piece. The relative weight of earlier Roman lower cases was reduced to give the page a light and harmonious appearance, which was further enhanced by the introduction, in 1499, of a delicately proportioned fount of capitals, based on inscriptional models and reduced in scale to fit neatly with the small letters. A slightly reduced version of the lower case was cast for Leoniceno's *De Morbo Gallico* in 1497: otherwise, the basic design was neither altered nor expanded. Yet it was this style, unobtrusively launched in a sixty-page compliment to a personal friend, which caught the attention of the French type-founders Garamond and Simon de Colines around 1530, spread from their workshops across Europe, and holds its place in Western typography until the present day. What has proved Aldus' most permanent contribution to type-design appears to have had the least importance in his own eyes.[82]

But the paradox may be deceptive. If we turn for a moment to the wider cultural and artistic history of the times, then return to the types themselves, we shall find Aldus at the centre of one of the most profound and enduring movements of the Renaissance – the reform of writing. The general outlines of this quest are clear enough: the disputed details lie beyond the range of this study. As Petrarch and his followers pressed their search for the lost Latin classics about a century before Aldus' birth, they came across a number of manuscripts written in the clear, minuscule script of the ninth century and, since they knew no earlier forms, jumped to the conclusion that they had re-discovered the truly classical or "Roman" style. Naturally, they adopted the carolingian model in their own copies. Developed by the early fifteenth-century humanists of the Florentine circle, a clear, rounded hand had by 1430 become a hall-mark of the committed classical antiquarian, pitting what he imagined to be a genuinely Latin script against the angular and ornamental letters of the later Middle Ages which he connected, again quite erroneously, with the "Gothic" destroyers of his beloved Rome.[83] From Poggio and Niccoli the fashion passed in the time of Eugenius IV to the scribes of the papal chancellery, and from them to Sweynheim and Pannartz in Rome, and to Windelin of Speyer and Jenson in Venice. In the hands of the first printers of Italy, a lower case modelled on the neo-carolingian script of the humanist pioneers became the accepted medium for Latin literary texts.

But over the same period a parallel, equally committed, and intellectually better grounded movement was affecting the design of capital letters. The antiquarian craze revealed manuscripts: but it also revealed monuments, and many of these were "antique" in the truest sense. While Poggio and Niccoli were were copying the carolingian script, artists such as Donatello and Ghiberti were decorating their works with inscriptions based on the square-cut capitals of early imperial Rome. So the real and the imagined were linked in a single quest for the truly "Roman" style of writing. By the third quarter of the century, Felice Feliciano and Leon Baptista Alberti were trying to reduce the formation of Latin capitals to an intellectual system, based on the mathematical laws of proportion: and around 1470 their ideas were taken up by a young Franciscan named Luca Pacioli, who was indeed to become the greatest mathematician of his time. There were minor disagreements between these experts about the precise rules governing the height of vertical strokes relative to their width, and about the exact design of complicated "round" letters such as G, Q, and R. But all saw the correct formation of letters as an important part of the cosmic mystery of proportion, the key to understanding each and every science, known to antiquity but lost during the barbarous centuries that came between that happy age and their own. The artists Andrea Mantegna, to whom Feliciano dedicated his own collection of Roman inscriptions in 1463, and Piero della Francesca, to whom Pacioli is said to have owed many of his ideas, gave this conviction visual expression in their use of perspective and their portrayal of the correct proportion between the different parts of the human body.[84] Pacioli himself proclaimed it boldly in words when he added two appendices, one on the measures to be observed in architecture, another on the formation of letters, to his mathematical treatise *On the Divine Proportion*. When he came to Venice in 1508 to lecture publicly on the fifth book of Euclid's *Elements*, he promised excellence in any of the arts and sciences to those who would "hasten to this ever-flowing fountain, the knowledge of proportion". And among those who crowded into the church of San Bartolomeo to hear him we find the names of Aldus and a number of his associates, including Egnazio, Daniel Renier, Fra Giocondo, Ambrogio Leone, and Vicenzo Querini.[85] Sure enough, when we turn back to the capitals of *Polifilo*, we find that their relative height and weight are governed by the 1:10 proportion recommended by Feliciano and only marginally reduced to 1:9 by Pacioli.[86] They were designed, in fact, with a precise awareness of the most sophisticated antiquarian research of the time. Used in conjunction with the "De Aetna" lower case, the "Polifilo" capitals proclaimed Aldus' association with an all-embracing movement to revive the culture of antiquity as loudly, and to his audience as clearly, as any of his rousing humanistic prefaces.

In April 1501 Aldus brought out an octavo-sized edition of Virgil, printed in a style at which he had hinted in the Letters of St Catherine, and which has come to be associated with his name more than any other – the italic. To defend his exclusive right to use it, he sought the

 ROMANORVM

 IVDAEORVM

Tiberius retulit ad Senatū vt inter cætera sacra reciperentur. Verū cū ex consulto patr̄ʒ Christianos eliminari vrbe placuissē. Tiberius p edictū accusatoribus cominatus est morte. Scribit Tertullianus in Apologetico.
Multi Senatoʒ & Equitum Ro. interfecti.
Tiberius in Campania moritur.

Olympias ccIIII.

ROMANORVM · IIII · C · CALLIGVLA ANN · III · MENS · X ·

I.   C. Cæsar cognomento Calligula Agrippam vinculis   XXIIII ·
     liberatum Regem Iudææ facit.   Iud. roʒ
     C. Semetipsum in Deos Transfert.   Agrippa
     Flaccus Liuius Præfectus Aegypti multis Iudæos   Ann · VII
     calamitatibus premit consentienete Alexandrino
     populo. & crebris aduersus eos clamoribus personante. Synagogas quoq̄ eoʒ imaginibus, statuis.
     aris, & victimis polluit. Refert Phylo in eo libro.
     qui Flaccus inscribitur: hæc omīa se præsente gesta:
     ob quæ & legationē ad Caium ipse susceperit.
II. Passienus filius ob fraude hæreditatis suæ necatur.   I
III. Caius Memmi Reguli uxorē duxit, impellens eum   II
     vt vxoris suæ patrē esse se scriberet.
     Pontius Pilatus in multas incidens calamitates propria
     se manu interfecit. Scribunt Romanoʒ historici.
     Caius Petronio Præfecto Syriæ præcepit, vt Hierosolymis statua sua sub nōīe Iouis Maximi poneret.
     Toto orbe Romano sicut Phylo scribit & Iosephus
     in Synagogis Iudæoʒ statuæ & imagines, & aræ
     C. Cæsaris consecratæ.

The italic script of Bartolomeo di San Vito (see page 141)

_VNII IVVENALIS AQVINA
TIS SATYRA PRIMA.

     EMPER EGO AVDITOR
     tantúm? nunquám ne reponam
S   V exatus toties rauca theseide
     Codri?
     Impune ergo mihi recitauerit ille
     togatus?
Hic elegos? impune diem consumpserit ingens
Telephus? aut summi plena iam margine libri
Scriptus, et in tergo nec dum finitus, Orestes?
Nota magis nulli domus est sua, quam mihi lucus
Martis, et æoliis uicinum rupibus antrum
Vulcani. Quid agant uenti, quas torqueat umbras
Aeacus, unde alius furtiuæ deuehat aurum
Pelliculæ, quantas iaculetur Monychus ornos,
Frontonis platani, conuulsáq; marmora clamant
Semper, et assiduo ruptæ lectore columnæ.
Expectes eadem a summo, minimóq; poeta.
Et nos ergo manum ferulæ subduximus, et nos
Consilium dedimus Syllæ, priuatus ut altum
Dormiret. stulta est clementia, cum tot ubique
Vatibus occurras, periturae parare chartæ.
Cur tamen hoc libeat potius decurrere campo,

  Aldus' italic (Venice 1501) cut by Francesco Griffo of Bologna

first known set of privileges on an entire type, rather than a series of titles, probably accelerating his final breach with Francesco Griffo in the process:[87] and the speed with which Griffo and other less reputable competitors broke the monopoly reveals the jealous ambition which Aldus' success excited. Besides Griffo, at least two other contemporaries, Filippo Giunti and Ludovico degli Arrighi, were hailed as inventors of the style or as the first to have used it, and controversy over this famous type, the reason for its being adopted, and the model on which it was based, has continued from that day to this.[88]

But this exclusive concentration on the italic is in fact rather misleading, for both in aesthetic and commercial terms, the "Latin cursive" was a continuation of Aldus' established system of Roman types, not a departure from it. The italic style of writing has a pedigree entirely similar to that of the more formal Roman. The first to have used it regularly was Niccolo Niccoli, who gave his letters a slope and dynamism when he wished to write in a faster, more relaxed fashion than usual. The mid-century archaeologists, Ciriaco d'Ancona and Feliciano, further elaborated the form: by the 1470s and 1480s the cursive script, used in conjunction with the square-cut inscriptional capital, had become the accepted style for the copying of "sillogi" or those personal collections of ancient inscriptions which were by now necessary equipment for anyone who wished to claim an intimate knowledge of the Roman world.[89] The fashion for this kind of research was particularly strong in the Veneto area, and a number of Aldus' associates, including Fra Giocondo of Verona, were affected by it. Over the same period, a taste for the cursive form was also spreading among the professional scribes of the city chancelleries, who seem to have enjoyed the opportunities it offered for a free and flourishing self-expression. The script itself soon became known as the "cancelleresca", and in 1492 the Venetian senate appointed an official instructor for its prospective secretaries in Antonio de' Tagliente, who favoured an exuberant form of italic.[90]

The cursive style had therefore been devised and developed by the same dedicated antiquarians who had popularised the more formal "Roman" style, and was simply the latest form of humanistic writing. In adapting it to print, Aldus and Griffo were riding the tide of contemporary taste and intensifying their appeal to the same group of committed humanist readers. This makes it difficult to see how either of them could have substantiated a claim to be the real "inventor" of the type, and almost as difficult to single out any one scribe whose handwriting might have provided the model for the punches. Tagliente is an obvious candidate, but he has no known connections with Aldus and seems to have affected a more ornate style than that of the earliest italic types. There is more to be said for a recently identified Paduan scribe named Bartolomeo di San Vito who not only wrote a hand very similar in form to the Aldine but can be proved to have dealt frequently with a number of the printer's closest associates, including Fra Giocondo, much of whose "silloge" he copied, the type-founder Julio Campagnolo, and the Bembo family, for whom he copied at least four manuscripts.[91] Whatever the ultimate truth of the matter, this close assimilation to manuscript forms should warn us against treating the Aldine italic as an isolated phenomenon, and should certainly keep us from falling into the erroneous but still popular belief that Aldus hoped to cram more material onto each page by using sloping letters, and so to cut the cost of his editions. If this had been the case, he would hardly have gone to the trouble and expense of having 150 different sorts cut and cast:[92] and far from cramming his margins, he earned some criticism from contemporaries for wasting paper to leave them wide.[93] There is no reason for refusing to take Aldus' boast that both his Greek and Latin cursives were as beautiful as anything written with a pen, at its simple face-value as a statement of his aims. In both languages, he was trying to give his printed texts the respectability of the most fashionable manuscript books. He was trying to shake printing out of the stylistic lethargy into which it had fallen since Jenson's death.

We must now turn from form to matter, and enquire how Aldus' programme of publication was affected by the timely misfortunes of his competitors, and his own deployment of the most characteristically "humanist" range of types yet assembled by any printer. It is usual to say that after 1500 Aldus ventured beyond the devoted but slightly doctrinaire Hellenism of his earlier period and explored the whole ocean of humanist interest in the revived classical languages and the emerging Italian vernacular, expressing in his publications Pico's vision of the divine spark of Reason in Man as the instrument of universal enlightenment.[94] An inspiring picture, certainly, and it derives some plausibility from the facts and figures. The overall quantity of Greek material has, indeed, declined sharply: 4,212 leaves were printed up to 1500, only 2,235 between 1500 and 1503, and it is worth noticing that the proportion of Latin to Greek – 3,839 leaves as compared to 2,235 – almost exactly reverses that of the earlier period. But the range of Aldus' activity during the first years of the new century is astonishing. He was now printing in four languages. His experiments with Hebrew type stopped short with his own *Introductio perbrevis* and a few trial folios for his still-born polyglot Bible. But his Greek texts included five exceptionally important first editions of the fifth-century classical writers Thucydides, Herodotus, Xenophon, Sophocles and Euripides, most of whom had received only the most cursory editorial attention up to that time.[95] We must also reckon with the influx of Latin classics – Virgil, Horace, Martial, Cicero, Lucan, Statius, Ovid and Catullus – who take the places of the rather dingy academic trivia which played so large a part in the earlier Latin programme. Most important of all is the introduction, with the italic script, of the octavo book-form, and its subsequent use for publications in Greek, Latin and Italian. A small volume, mass-produced in editions of up to three thousand copies,[96] reasonably priced and easily carried, it seems a social extension of the humanists' conviction that literature could enlighten wherever it went, and the shameless haste with which the model was copied is the clearest proof of its success.

The octavo has in fact become so closely identified with Aldus' whole achievement that a few preliminary words of caution are needed. First, Aldus did not invent the portable book: he merely adapted it. Second, though he did print four important Greek first editions in octavo, his policy was clearly to use the form for safe and popular titles rather than to treat it as a vehicle for the spread of new material. Third, no contemporary ever said that Aldine octavos were cheap. They must have been relatively less expensive than their larger counterparts, but it is not clear that they were uniformly cheaper than other editions of the same titles, and they were quickly undercut by pirated imitations. The notion that Aldus introduced both the octavo and the italic as a means of price-cutting is a modern inference only, and if the printer knew that he was widely heralded as the originator of some kind of "paper-back revolution", he would probably writhe in his unknown grave.[97]

The smaller sized book already had a long history in manuscript and printed form when Aldus produced his famous text of Virgil in April 1501. In the 1470s Jenson had printed some minute Office books. Early in 1497 Lazzaro di Soardis had applied to the Senate for copyright on his projected editions of the works of Jacopo de'

Voragine, St Augustine, various sermons, and a Meditation on the Passion "in forma piccola et ottavo foglio". Only a year later Antonio di Zanoti included octavos in a petition which sought to protect a complete range of different sized Office-books.[98] But these cases have one feature in common which separates them from Aldus' experiment: all the editions are of a religious or devotional character. Prayer was almost the only occasion which required the individual to carry a book about his person. The scholar was expected to deploy a large folio on his study lectern and it is in this attitude that he appears, usually in the guise of Augustine or Jerome, in some of the most celebrated illustrations of the time. Aldus' originality lay in applying what had been a rather specialised book-form to a new and wider field. The Latin titles which he published in octavo were all eminently safe, some being well-established favourites: the British Museum Catalogue lists eighteen pre-Aldine editions of Horace, eleven of them Venetian; twenty of Valerius Maximus; twelve of the complete poems of Ovid, and eleven of Catullus and the elegists. But virtually all of these are folios, and the vast majority are lumbered with the commentaries of Calderini, Calfurnio or some other contemporary humanist. By pruning away one element – the commentaries – and combining two others – the smaller format and the most acceptable titles – Aldus was freeing literature from the study and the lecture-room.

But was he also putting literature into the hands of men who would not previously have been able to afford such a luxury? Most modern critics would say "Yes": the italic script allowed smaller books, smaller books cost less, and lower prices meant a larger market. Unfortunately, this chain of reasoning rests on no contemporary evidence. When Aldus appealed to the senate for copyright, or wrote a short verse-tribute to Francesco Griffo's brilliant design, or addressed letters of dedication, he did not say that his octavo texts were cheap: he said that they were beautiful, and convenient.[99]

As we have seen, he was copying a fashionable script. It would probably have been both cheaper and less troublesome to work with a reduced Roman type rather than commission a complete new fount,[100] and we cannot take it as certain that the economic, rather than the aesthetic motive was uppermost in his mind unless we can produce evidence that Aldine octavos were actually cheaper than their competitors.

In fact, there is specific evidence to the contrary. In 1484, Francesco da Madiis disposed of a complete Ovid – presumably one of the

Table II. Aldine Publications, 1501–1503

Year	Greek	Latin	Italian
1501		Poetae Christiani, I 4º	
	Philostratus, Vita Apollonii, 73f fol.		
		Virgilii Opera, 228f 8º	
		Horatii Opera, 143f 8º	
			Petrarch, Cose volgari, 180f 8º
		Juvenalis et Persii Satirae, 78f 8º	
		Martialis, 192f 8º	
		Valla, De exp. et fug. rebus, 300f fol. + 336f fol.	
		Aldi Rudimenta Grammatices, 88f 4º	
		Donati Oratio, 4f 8º	
		Io. Francisci Pici De Imaginatione, 39f 4º	
1502	Pollucis Vocabularium, 104f fol.		
		Cicero, Epistulae Familiares, 267f 8º	
		Lucani Pharsalia, 140f 8º	
	Thucydides, 124f fol.		
			Dante, 244f 8º
	Sophocles, 196f 8º		
		Statius, 256f 8º	
	Herodotus, 140f fol.		
			Interiani, Vita de Zichi, 8f 8º

Table II (cont.)

Year	Greek	Latin	Italian
1502 (cont.)		Valerius Maximus, 216f 8º	
		Egnatii Oratio, 8f 8º	
		Ovidii Metamorphoseos, 267f 8º	
		Ovidii Heroides, 202f 8º	
		Ovidii Fasti, 203f 8º	
	Stephani De Urbibus, 80f fol.		
		Catullus, Tibullus, Propertius, 150f 8º	
1503		Poetae Christiani, II* Admonitum, 1f fol.	
		Catalogus, 2f fol.	
	Luciani Opera, 286f fol.		
	Ammonii Commentaria, 146f fol.		
		Bessarion, In Calumniatorem Platonis, 112f fol.	
	Ulpiani Commentarioli, 172f fol.		
	Xenophon, 156f fol. } Plethon		
	Florilegium Epigrammatum, 290f 8º		
	Euripides Tragoediae, 268f 8º		
	190f 8º		
		Originis Homeliae, 182f fol.	

* The parallel text of *Poetae Christiani* is not included in the totals.

large folios mentioned above – for 4 lire 10 soldi. This was exactly the price quoted for Aldus' three octavo volumes in the catalogue of 1513. The same man could have equalled Aldus' price for a Sallust, a Virgil or a Lucretius. As early as 1480 the Paduan bookseller Antonio Moreto was offering the works of Ovid at 4 lire, and the letters of Cicero at 2 lire 10 soldi as against 3 lire 10 soldi for the full set of Aldine octavos.[101]

The evidence is by no means one sided. Moreto's price for a Virgil was 4 lire, more than double Aldus' 1 lire 10 soldi; and there was a fair degree of flexibility in all prices, which could bend this way or that according to the relationship between buyer and seller, or the state of the market.[102] But the uniform cheapness of the octavo, on which all modern critics insist, does not appear to have been noticed by contemporaries. Either Aldus' plan failed, or he introduced the italic with some aim other than that of cramming more letters onto a page, printing a smaller book, and selling it to more people at a lower price.

What sort of market was he trying to reach? We do not have sufficient evidence about purchases to give any sound statistical base, but there are other possible guidelines: correspondence, the ownership of the few copies in each edition which were printed on vellum at special request, above all the men to whom some of the books were dedicated. It is these names which reveal the change in Aldus' circle of contacts, and hint at the tastes he was now trying to satisfy. The academic friends of the earlier period are still much in evidence. But Marin Sanudo, the diarist and statesman, who received no less than five dedications during 1501 and 1502, now bulks larger than anyone, and he is joined by an increasing number of similar men. There are influential Venetian patricians like Antonio Morosini: powerful councillors from the Northern European kingdoms, such as Sigismund Thurz or John Lubranski; scholar-diplomats like Janus Lascaris, now in the service of the French crown.[103] A few of the surviving vellum copies suggest that those who took the trouble to order them did not differ greatly in background or occupation. In London and Manchester there are traces of a superb set of the Latin poets, all illuminated in a style that resembles that of Benedetto Bordone, and all carrying the blazon of the Pisani family.[104] A Petrarch now in London, illuminated in the same style, carries the mill-wheel of the da Molin, one of the most powerful families in Venice during the early decades of the sixteenth century.[105] The library of the French administrator Jean Grolier, famous in its own time and today for the beautiful design of its bindings, was particularly rich in Aldine octavos.[106]

The clue lies in the similar cultural and occupational backgrounds of all these men. All had been thoroughly exposed to Italian influences, generally at Padua: and all were busy men of affairs. They were the kind of men who would criss-cross Europe on the errands of princes and republics throughout the sixteenth century, waiting days for a fair wind or a clear road, pacing ante-rooms for hours in the hope of an audience which was never granted.[107] These were the secular intellectuals of Renaissance Europe: the men who packed the expanding universities to win employment in the services of their governments, making what has been called an "educational revolution" in every country in Europe where their rise to prominence has been described.[108] It was for these men, rather than for any imagined or idealised "popular reader", that Aldus was working. He was not prescient: we have no reason to believe that he foresaw, or did anything to create, the "educational revolution". But he rode upon its tide, and he was clearly aware of the discomforts and difficulties that faced his contemporaries. He sent Ovid to Sanudo in the hope that he would find time to read it in intervals between his more serious work, and in his dedication to the Hungarian councillor Thurz declared that he would soon be turning out whole "portable libraries" in Latin and Greek.[109] But Thurz needed no conversion. He had already written to Aldus expressing his delight in the neat editions of Horace and Virgil, and the ease with which he could now snatch a few minutes relaxation during a busy day at court. Lascaris was hardly less enthusiastic.[110] If Aldus' octavos were not all that has been claimed, if they were an instrument designed to expand the pleasure of the relatively few and wealthy rather than the understanding of the masses, it remains true that they were a vital development in the emancipation of learning.

It is perfectly fair to insist on the idealist bias behind this stage of Aldus' career, so long as we remember that idealism constantly interacted with shrewd commercial calculation and a degree of divine disorder. This delicate balance of tensions achieves its fullest expression in the conception of the literary octavo: it shows in the careful weighting of safe Latin against speculative Greek titles; it even shows in the selection and dedication of the three Italian works. In printing the Trecento Florentine classics, Dante and Petrarch, Aldus may very well have been declaring his faith in the future of Italian as a literary language, and in Tuscan as the purest form of Italian. But he was also cultivating the tastes of certain courtly and academic circles whose rather ponderous efforts to handle the Petrarchan style survive in a number of manuscripts, and one of whose members, Carlo Bembo, supplied both the manuscripts and the costs of the editions.[111] To realise their appeal, one has only to glance at the letters in which that compulsive patroness, Isabella d'Este, added a vellum copy of Petrarch to her shopping-list.[112] Even the short description of South Russia by the Genoese traveller Interiano – a mere windfall which the recommendation of Daniele Clari brought to Aldus – was turned to good use. Dedicated to the fashionable Neapolitan writer Sannazaro, it became a request for corrected copies of that author's own works.[113]

But meanwhile, this rush to publish with Aldus was becoming a force in itself: a positive force, perhaps, since it brought new material forward, but often an embarrassment to both commercial and academic planning, and a severe strain on the printer's nerve. We do not know the exact story behind the edition of Philostratus' *Life of Apollonius of Tyana*: Aldus finished printing the text in March 1501 but did not publish it until May 1504, and sent it out with an introduction which attacked the work point by point and declared it the worst thing he had ever read.[114] For his text of Valerius Maximus and for Bessarion's defence of Plato Aldus received new material when his press-run was already almost complete, and had to print additional leaves.[115] The large-scale edition of the Christian Latin Poets seems to have been turned into a publisher's nightmare by this kind of enthusiasm. The first volume and the first half of the second were in print by January 1501, but the dedication of the second to Daniele Clari carries the date June 1502. Undated works in Greek and Latin, with the quires differently marked, are added at the end of both volumes.[116] The third volume was delayed until June 1504. The most probable explanation is that Aldus had originally planned a fairly modest edition of the shorter works of Sedulius, Juvencus, Arator and Prudentius which would have been contained in a single volume and now stand in the earliest dated sections. Then word got round, scholarly enthusiasm took over, and new material started to flow in: first, a more complete manuscript of Prudentius from England, which upset the balance of the volume; then the Greek works of John of Damascus, Cosmas and Epiphanius which were in due course translated, edited, and compounded with the first volume. This of course meant rounding off the second volume, so Pierocandido Decembrio was deputed to edit and translate the *Homerocentra* and the two volumes were apparently published together some eighteen months late. Meanwhile, manuscripts of Gregory Nazanzenus had begun to appear and to be set in order for another volume: one arrived so late that Aldus simply added two and a half pages of corrections to the Greek text, besought his readers to set the Latin translation right for themselves, and tried to persuade himself with an Homeric tag that things were bound to get easier soon.[117] Nonnus' paraphrase of St John's Gospel, which was to have been published as a fourth volume and was in proof when the third was completed, seems never to have appeared officially.[118]

It was appropriate that the second volume of this confused series was the first to carry Aldus' famous cipher of the dolphin and anchor, the symbol of the ancient proverb "Hasten slowly" which Aldus had declared his motto as early as 1499 and seems to have expounded regularly to his friends.[119] In 1502 it was, in fact, a very neat appraisal of his position. He had achieved much. But his continued success would depend on preserving the balance of two forces which might not always be reconcilable: the enthusiasm of the academic friends who deluged him with manuscripts and requests for new editions, and the business-sense of his partners who wanted to sell more books.

The decline of Aldus' enterprise from the zenith which it had reached in 1502–3 is as obvious to us as it was obvious to contemporaries. Only two dozen editions were brought out between 1504 and the autumn of 1512 – less than had appeared during the previous two years alone. There were more than four years of total inactivity, between December 1505 and December 1507, April 1509 and October 1512. But the process is gradual, wholly different from the sudden collapse of Callierges' organisation in 1500, and interrupted by exceptionally important bursts of editorial work: it is not surprising that critics have hesitated to speak of the company as being in decline, and have preferred to hint at commercial difficulties resulting from the perilous situation of Venice itself during these years.[120]

The programme of Greek publications was maintained: the commentaries of Johannes Grammaticus continued the series of Aristotelian works which had started in 1495, and they were closely flanked by the Latin translations of Theodorus Gaza. Gregory Nazanzenus rounded off the Christian poets. The two volumes of Homer, though

Table III

Year	Greek	Latin	Italian
1504	Iohannes Grammaticus in Aristotelis Analytica, 148f fol.		
		Theodorus Gaza, 274f. fol.	
		Carteromachi Oratio, 15f 8º	
	Gregorii Nazanzeni Carmina...4º		
		Cimbriaci Encomiastica, 24f 8º	
	Homeri Opera I, 277f 8º		
	II, 306f 8º		
	Demosthenis Orationes I, 160f fol.		
	II, 144f fol.		
1505			Bembo, Asolani, 96f 4º
		Augurelli Carmina, 128f 8º	
	Horae Virginis, 160f 32º		
		Pontani Urania, 241f 8º	
		Adriani Venatio, 8f 8º	
	Aesopi Fabellae... 150f fol.		
		Virgilii Opera, 304f 8º	
	(Quinti Calabri Paralipomena Homeri, 172f 8º)		
1507		Hecuba et Iphigenia interprete Erasmo, 80f 8º	

Table III (cont.)

Year	Greek	Latin	Italian
1508		Aldi Grammatica, 192f 4°	
		Erasmi Adagia, 249f fol.	
		Plinii Epistolae, 263f 8°	
	Rhetores Graeci I, 367f fol.		
	II, 209f fol.		
1509	Plutarchi Opuscula, 525f fol.		
		Horatii Opera, 155f 8°	
		Sallustii Opera, 104f 8°	

not a first edition, were rendered almost as important by their octavo form, and had been planned for nearly three years.[121] So, apparently, had the text of Demosthenes' *Orations*: this was a small press-run which encountered many difficulties, but Aldus considered the books finer than any he had so far produced.[122] Together with the Greek Orators who followed in 1508–9, these volumes form a pair of extremely important first editions which assured the survival of Greek rhetoric as certainly as the earlier editions of Herodotus, Thucydides, Xenophon, Sophocles, and Euripides had assured that of history and drama. The *Moralia* of Plutarch, which finally appeared in 1509, were another educational favourite, and had been planned for at least ten years.[123] Whatever his problems, it is clear that Aldus' faith in the educational value of Hellenism was still very much alive and capable of translating itself into action.

The Latin editions are more scanty, and contain a good deal of contemporary trivia. But the text of Pliny's letters gains importance from being based on a very early manuscript, and Erasmus' *Adagia* was one of the most successful books of the age.[124]

Allowing for all this, there are still three factors to be explained satisfactorily. The first is the precipitous decline in the actual volume of material printed. The second is the long stoppage between 1506 and 1507, which cannot be blamed on a war that only began in 1509. The third is feeling among contemporary intellectuals that Aldus was letting them down. "He has done nothing notable since he married", lamented John Cuno at the end of 1505..., "I cannot imagine what is the cause of such a change in Aldus, unless it is Aristophanes' old problem of poverty."[125]

One of the works that Aldus did produce during this period was Bembo's *Asolani*. To us it is a work of great interest: a fascinating glimpse of high society, an important literary experiment, a popularisation of Ficino's theories of love, and an edition which commands attention because of the personalities concerned, and because of its connection with political developments in Rome and Ferrara. But to Cuno, the work was "a few odds and ends in the vernacular, about Love". The unthinkable had happened. Aldus was printing trash.[126]

It is fairly clear that the academic friends for whom Aldus had worked so assiduously before 1500 were principally interested in the Greek editions for which he was now their only source, and that they were prepared to put considerable pressure on him to get what they wanted. As early as 1501 Lascaris sniffed at Aldus' "migration from Greece to Italy", and accused him of vulgar profiteering. Angelo Gabriel demanded the publication of Demosthenes with "almost daily reproaches". Writing from Rome in April 1505 Scipio Fortiguerra was anxious about rumours that Aldus had given up printing Greek texts entirely.[127] As we have seen, he had not done so and never did. But Greek editions were expensive to produce and difficult to sell, especially compared to the neat octavos of the everpopular Latin authors. In the catalogue of 1513, only the largest Latin texts printed before the turn of the century are still represented: the Greek editions right back to Lascaris' Grammar are still available, and offered at cut prices.[128]

We cannot be too surprised at the increasing number of signs that Aldus' partners were beginning to intervene more directly in the running of the company, to warn him against speculative Greek editions, and to press for safer titles like the works of Virgil, which had been cleared between 1501 and 1505. The first hint of trouble came as early as 1503, when a series of translations from the sermons of Origen was published "at Andrea Torresani's expense, by the zeal and learning of Aldus Manutius". The formula, normally restricted to limited partnerships, is unique among Aldine publications and seems to suggest that additional funds had been needed to cover the cost of the edition.[129] It was Torresani who informed Fortiguerra in 1505 that Greek was being abandoned: and at the end of the year John Cuno reported that the bookseller was threatening to accept no more Greek texts for sale unless costs could be met more satisfactorily.[130]

Tensions such as these could now be embraced by some jargon-phrase like "board-room battle", and it would be a mistake to inflate them into a full-scale crisis. We have only the humanists' account, and humanists did not love Torresani. The problems were almost certainly real, since the industry as a whole was in a profound recession and some of Aldus' most successful publications were being ruthlessly undercut by cheap counterfeits. It was a time to keep a close watch on cash-flow. Aldus must also have been in a state of distressing personal uncertainty. For some years he had been negotiating for a place at the imperial court, and in 1505 his hopes seemed on the verge of fruition as his friends redoubled their efforts and Maximilian kept nodding affably.[131] Large undertakings may have seemed to have little point. Whether Aldus, rather than his intellectual friends, had any serious clash with Torresani in the meantime seems extremely doubtful. It is unlikely in view of Andrea's overwhelming influence in the company, and still more unlikely in view of the fact that Aldus married his partner's daughter Maria in January 1505. Dynastic unions of this kind were a frequent expression of solidarity in the press-world: the syndicate of Jenson and John of Cologne had been rivetted together by several of them, and Aldus' marriage may seem even more than usually calculated when we discover that, outdoing cliché or proverb, he was actually older than Maria's father. But the difference in age does not appear to have prevented the union from being both happy and fruitful.[132]

As the winter of 1505 advanced, the hopes of imperial patronage diminished, and Aldus closed ranks with his partner and father-in-law. At some moment which cannot be precisely pinpointed but probably followed soon after his wedding, Aldus abandoned the house in Sant' Agostino and moved in with his wife's family who lived near San Paternian. On 27 March 1506 he drew up a will which named Torresani as principal executor and main beneficiary:[133] next day the two partners signed a legal act which declared all their property and assets unified, allotting four fifths of the total to Andrea and one fifth to Aldus.[134] Shortly afterwards Aldus left Venice on an extensive search for manuscripts throughout Lombardy, encountering the unlooked-for adventure described in the previous chapter but considerably extending his range of influential contacts. Naturally, all press-work was at an end. But the terms of the will and the aim of the journey make it certain that operations were to continue,[135] the linking of hands with Torresani makes it seem unlikely that disagreement was more than superficial, and the 2,000 or so ducats dispersed in the will hardly suggest that economic difficulties had yet reached crisis point. The stoppage in 1506 was almost certainly a case of planned retrenchment. Exhausted by swimming with the dolphin for ten years, Aldus was clinging to the anchor for a breathing-space.

One of the factors which made this intermission necessary was almost certainly the threat of unfair or illegal competition, though the blurred and fragmentary quality of the evidence obscures the exact connections. We have already seen the press-pirate, who cut away the time and expense of editorship by securing advance copies from other workshops, haunting the imagination of the numerous publishers who applied to the Venetian senate for protection. Aldus exerted his great influence to the maximum to defend his position. At the very outset of his career he broke new ground by requesting privileges for his Greek cursive types, rather than his titles: he did the same for his italic types in March 1502, and confirmed both privileges with a comprehensive senatorial decree and a ducal letter, which were issued in the autumn of the same year.[136] Besides these wider defences, he held the standard Venetian copyrights on several individual titles including St Catherine of Siena, The Christian Poets, and Bembo's *Asolani*. As though to give the final touch to his portfolio, Aldus had the protection of his types confirmed and extended by papal bull.[137] Considering the reputation which these privileges have won for the Venetian government as an enlightened body, and the political leverage which Aldus could command, he would seem to have been one of the best protected publishers of his time.[138]

In fact, his experience casts grave doubts on the efficacy of the entire system. The case of Gabriel of Brasichella, when conflicting privileges were issued in favour of Aldus' types and Gabriel's titles, hints clearly at the dangers which might lie in lack of technical knowledge, shortage of legal precedent, and in the sheer number of the copyrights requested. What was a "counterfeit copy"? Did it have to resemble an original – whose priority would of course have to be proved – in every detail, or could it be made respectable by a change in size, in type, or by the discreet introduction of new material? How "similar" did similar type-faces have to be? The situation must have been complicated as much by these technical uncertainties as by the lingering convictions of the manuscript-age, that copying another man's work was more of a favour than an injury.[139]

Beyond the problems of definition lay the problems of enforcement. The printed book proved difficult enough to control after the mid-sixteenth century, when a full apparatus of inquisition existed: in 1500, no single body in Venice had a clear competence in press-cases. Many petitions refer to the Avogadori, or public prosecutors: some allude to the Signori di Notte, who dealt with public order and sexual crimes; the protection of Aldus' italic type was passed to the Council of Ten, a formidable body which was supposed to handle state security. Unfortunately, the few surviving records reveal next to nothing, but the confusion and very partial effectiveness of the copy-rights both make one suspect that there never was much to reveal.[140] The appearance of Aldus' Latin and Italian octavos from the spring of 1501 brought a surge of imitations which came from several different quarters and was far more difficult to counter than the clumsy espionage of an associate who was still in easy reach. The petition for comprehensive protection of both his Greek and Latin types was brought about by the copying of his editions in Lyons and Brescia, and is clear proof that the previous year's copyright had been ineffective. These early imitations – of Virgil, Horace, Juvenal, Martial, Lucan and the Roman elegists – were forgeries of the most bare-faced variety. The complete Aldine texts, dedications and all, were reproduced in a coarse imitation of the italic type, on a poor grade of paper, and with the numerous errors which came naturally from hurried work. The format was octavo. Only a date and the printer's name were missing, and this anonymity seems completely to have foiled Aldus' two efforts to choke off the supply at source by copyright or ducal letter.[141]

In 1503 he changed tack and published an "Admonition against the Lyons typographers", which was in reality an attempt to cut his rivals out of the market by warning customers of the existence of these forged versions, and pointing to means of distinguishing them from the genuine articles. He noted the flaws in the presswork: he criticised the quality of the paper; he listed the errors which had been introduced. Duly admonished, the Lyons typographers remodelled their types, emended their texts, and issued new editions.[142] Working on the widest possible definition of the term "counterfeit", Renouard listed sixty-four pirated editions of Aldine texts published in Lyons between 1501 and 1527, mostly by Barthélemy Troth and an Italian immigrant named Balthazar de Gabiano. The total may be subjective, but there is no denying the gravity of the threat, or the failure of Aldus' privileges to check it.[143]

There was another possible target within much easier reach, but at the same time more furtive and difficult to approach: it is in fact quite possible that one of Aldus' motives for suspending production in 1506 was to prepare his line of attack, since this new threat had been developing during the three previous years and the case seems to have been decided shortly before the resumption of business in late 1507. The rival was none less than Filippo Giunti, member of a Florentine press-dynasty which was certainly as powerful as the Aldine company and probably more successful commercially. Filippo was based in Florence, and produced mainly literary texts: his brother Lucantonio operated in Venice, largely as a bookseller and underwriter, but from 1499 as an independent printer of popular and liturgical works. Their joint assets had doubled in value since 1491, and by 1505 were probably worth between twelve and fifteen thousand ducats.[144]

Though entirely retrospective, the evidence about their – or rather Filippo's – dispute with Aldus does make up a consistent picture. In July 1514 the brothers tried to play on the Florentine sympathies of Pope Leo X and challenge the comprehensive privilege which he had just issued in favour of Aldus' Greek and italic types by claiming that they had been the first to use cursive Latin types. The Pope seems to have tried to satisfy all parties by agreeing to everything in general terms. The ambassador Vettori, clearly puzzled by the technicalities, pressed for samples of their work and advised them to print in a marginally different style, but the subject drops out of diplomatic correspondence in a manner which suggests that the Giunti did not get all they had asked.[145] Venetian records show that they had revealed much less than the whole truth. On 10 October 1516 Filippo Giunti's son Bernardo appealed to the Council of Ten for the removal of a sentence of banishment passed at some unstated time against his father by the Signori di Notte: the charge had been infringement of the Aldine copyrights, which had lapsed with the holder's death.[146] Since there are several references in the correspondence of late summer and early autumn 1507 to Aldus' involvement in a law-suit, it seems likely that the case was heard at this time, and a careful look at Filippo's

E il tempo diffar tutto, & cosi presto;
   Et morte in sua ragion cotanto auara;
M orti saranno inseme & quella, & questo :
   Et quei, che fama meritaron chiara,
      Che il tempo spense; e i bei visi leggiadri
      Ch'impallidir fe il tempo & morte amara;
   L'obliuion, gli aspetti oscuri & adri
   Piu che mai bei tornando lasceranno

Italic of Soncino (Fano 1503), also cut by Griffo

De finibus prediorum sine septis.   Cap. XVIII.

PRAETEREA sine septis fines prædy, sationis, notis ar/
borum tutiores fiunt, ne familiæ rixentur cum uicinis, ac limites
ex litibus iudicem quærant. Serunt alij circum pinos, ut habet
uxor in Sabinis. Alij cupressos, ut ego habeo in Vesuuio. Aly ul/
mos, ut multi habēt in Crustuminio, quod ibi pullulat maxime.
Et ubi est campus nulla potior arbor seritur, qd maximæ fructuo/
sa, quod & sustineat sepem, ac colit aliquot corbulas uuarum, et
frondem iucundissimam ministrat ouibus, ac bubus, ac uirgas p/
bet sepibus, & foco, ac furno. Scrofa. Igitur primum hæc, quæ
dixi, quatuor uidēda agricolæ, de fundi forma, terræ natura, de
modo agri, de finibus tuendis.

Italic of Filippo Giunti (Florence 1515)

publications over the previous years quickly reveals the cause.[147] In August 1503, Filippo Giunti brought out an octavo edition of Catullus, Tibullus and Propertius whose texts, he announced, had "recently been much emended by the most learned Aldus Manutius, and were now revised by Benedictus of Florence". It was in fact an exact re-issue of the Aldine text of 1502, copying both the italic script and the page-composition, but varying the first appearance of the book with a new dedication and a short extract from Crinitus' Lives of the poets. Two months later came a Horace: again, the Aldine format was followed exactly; and again, the addition of a little extra material, and a change in the order of the *Satires* and the *Epistles*, gave the beginning and end a slightly different look. A Petrarch, a Virgil, and Bembo's *Asolani* followed in 1504 and 1505.[148] This was plagiarism of a new and subtle kind, wholly different from the crude forgery of the Lyonnais, and one cannot help feeling a pang of regret that the records of such an important press-trial have not survived. Giunti did not stop printing in italic, but he does seem to have been careful to avoid Aldus' titles in the future.

Success in this case, which was presumably decided some time in the late autumn of 1507, must have given Aldus real encouragement as he prepared to resume operations. Planning appears to have been in hand for some time: Cuno reported before the end of December 1506, that preliminary work on the texts of Plato and Plutarch was being discussed,[149] and when Erasmus made his famous approach to Aldus on 28 October of the following year, he never doubted that the company was in business though it had not produced an edition for nearly two years. This letter is interesting chiefly for the light it sheds on Aldus' reputation, on the very informal business-methods of the age, and on the general relationship between author and publisher. Erasmus had virtually to "sell" his translations of Euripides' *Hecuba* and *Iphigeneia in Aulis*, stressing the high opinion of mutual friends, the ease with which Josse Bade had sold out his edition of the same works, and offering, if not to bear the total cost of printing, at least to accept the responsibility for up to 200 copies. Aldus was given free rein to make such alterations as he felt necessary.[150] But this was precisely the sort of cheap, low-risk work which the printer needed to keep his partners content and to balance the editions of Plutarch and the Greek Orators on which he was concentrating. The text may not have been ready in the ten days forecast by Erasmus, but, after receiving the manuscript some time in November, Aldus certainly completed the eighty printed sheets before the end of the year.[151]

The revived company rapidly gathered momentum. Erasmus arrived in person, and began work on the new edition of his *Adagia*. The scholarly French ambassador Janus Lascaris was kept so thoroughly in the dark by his government that he had ample leisure for literary diversions. A new source of interest and patronage was emerging in Venice's dashing general, Bartolomeo d'Alviano, whose brilliant victory over the imperialists in early March 1508, brought a spring of false confidence and security. A number of Aldus' younger friends gathered at his estate in Pordenone, and in April 1509 the printer dedicated to Bartolomeo the edition of Sallust which he had just completed with the help of a manuscript provided by Lascaris.[152] Then on 9 May d'Alviano's troops were shattered by the French armies on the Adda: city after city declared for the invaders, and in a matter of weeks the mainland state which Venice had built up over the previous century crumbled to pieces before the powers which had confirmed their league at Cambrai during the previous winter. France, Spain, the Empire and the Papacy were all in arms against Venice.

There is obviously no difficulty in guessing why a printing company suspended business on this occasion: it is more a question of finding what the partners hoped to salvage from the wreckage and how they planned to do so. Aldus must have left Venice almost immediately after the disaster, for when Alberto Pio wrote to him on 1 June he was already safely in Ferrara with his family. Alberto advised his old tutor to draw up a legal act, discreetly backdated, declaring that Andrea Torresani's estates near Asola had been transferred to Aldus as part of Maria's dowry.[153] On 1 September Aldus appointed Andrea his official agent in Venice for certain outstanding contracts: and on the 28th, he had the deed which had unified their property dissolved.[154]

This pattern makes it fairly clear that the partners were girding themselves to run with the hare and hunt with the hounds. Andrea would stay in Venice, keep business alive, and no doubt "own" the property if Venice regained her dominance: Aldus would wave his proof of ownership if the League prevailed, and use his considerable influence at the French, imperial and Ferrarese courts to ensure it. The weight of that influence may in fact have made it prudent, rather than merely convenient, for Aldus to leave Venice. His pupil and patron Alberto Pio had been an advisor to the French Crown on the formation of the League of Cambrai: his negotiations with the imperial court had been well known and widely publicised and their main object had been Matthew Lang, Cardinal of Gurk and Maximilian's principal representative in the councils of the League.¹⁵⁵ Aldus was even able to arrange for a personal letter to pass between Maximilian and the Marquis of Mantua, affirming his possession of the threatened estates and calling him the "dear and faithful friend" of the King of the Romans.¹⁵⁶ Though they availed him little, these contacts could have been at the very least compromising in Venice. Printers and intellectuals often had outside links which put them in a good position to supply information.¹⁵⁷

From June 1509 until June 1512 Aldus was once again a wandering scholar, and the most we can say about these years is that they were a time of black disappointment and some personal risk to him. His aims appear to have been three: first, to shrug off or at least delegate his remaining business responsibilities; second, to provide what security he could for a now fast expanding family; third, to found the mysterious academy of which he had been dreaming for at least a decade. The first of these aims seems to be reflected by his appointment of agents in Venice and Milan, and by his renunciation, in April 1510, of certain sums due to him from the Barbarigo estate.¹⁵⁸ The second, and the third, both appear in a new will drawn up on 24 August 1511 in Ferrara. Aldus now had to provide for four children: a five-year-old son, Marco, two girls, Alda and Letitia, and the unborn but imminent Antonius. The will is therefore a family document, which makes no mention of the printing company except indirectly, through the unflagging respect and devotion expressed towards Andrea Torresani: and the 1,700 ducats distributed in dowries alone do not suggest that Aldus' situation had been much affected by the difficulties of the previous five years. His main wish was to settle down and educate his own sons in the academy which he longed to found.¹⁵⁹

In pursuit of this ever fleeting ideal, which we shall try to outline in the next chapter, Aldus wandered around the cities of northern and central Italy during these years like an unquiet ghost. He appears in Milan, Mantua, Bologna, Siena and Ravenna, talking to friends and attempting to lobby influential men.¹⁶⁰ During the latter part of 1511 hopes seem to have risen somewhat as the Pope, who had invited the French into Italy to destroy Venetian power for him, set about forming an almost equally powerful league including Spain,

Venice and England in order to drive the French out again. There was some chance of a return to relatively stable conditions if the plan succeeded. But on 11 April 1512 the French won the bloodily contested battle of Ravenna at such a price that both sides were effectively crushed, no new balance emerged, and northern Italy became a yawning power-vacuum in which war would rage for years to come. By June, Aldus was back in Venice with his family. His estates had been lost. His academy was still in the realm of dreams. Only his presses and his reputation remained.[161]

Yet barely six months later Aldus dedicated his first edition of the odes of Pindar to Andrea Navagero, one of the friends who had persuaded him to return unwillingly to printing, with a letter that expressed surprising confidence and buoyancy. He spoke again of printing in all three of the ancient languages. He called Venice, in spite of all its agonies, "another Athens".[162] It was a theme which became frequent in prefaces, and as early as April 1513 Aldus was showing real astonishment at a growth of the arts of peace in time of war.[163] This gambit was not new, even to him: but when we consider what Aldus had suffered and Venice was suffering, it is impossible not to feel some surprise at the rapid revival of a company whose business manager had intended it to close.

For the Venetians, these were years of almost unbroken disaster. In early 1513 the Republic changed alliances yet again, only to see its French allies shattered in their turn at the battle of Novara in June: in September the flare of burning villages could be seen from Venice itself, as Spanish and imperial troops systematically raped the countryside up to the very edge of the Lagoons. Not until the Franco-Venetian victory at Marignano in August 1515 did even relative stability return, and that was a day Aldus did not live to see.[164] The press, meanwhile, was still deep in its long recession: the twenty or so firms operating were producing only about fifty editions per year.[165] Worse, Aldus' long monopoly of Greek texts was being challenged at several points. After a brief foray into Venetian printing late in 1509, Callierges received an invitation to Rome.[166] In Florence, Bernardo Giunti began a series of Greek editions in 1514.[167] And under the influence of Aldus' old associates, Demetrius Ducas and Gerolamo Aleander, Greek typography was beginning to make headway in both Spain and France, launching a native tradition which must eventually make dependence on Italy unnecessary.[168]

Part of the answer to this paradox of disaster and seeming vitality

Table IV. Publications 1512–February 1515

Year	Greek	Latin	Italian
1512	Lascaris, Grammar, 274f 4°		
	Chrysoloras, Grammar, 148f 8°	Cicero, Ep. Fam, 267f 8°	
1513		Caesar, Commentarii, 296f 8°	
	Rhetores Graeci: I, 99f fol. II, 82f fol. III, 134f fol.		
		Cicero, Ep. ad Atticum, 331f 8°	
	Platonis Opera I, 251f fol. II, 220f fol. Alexandri Aphrodisiei Comm., 141f fol.		
		Perotti Cornucopia 359f fol. Pontani Urania 255f 8° Catalogus tertius 5f fol.	
	Pindari Carmina 187f 8°		
		Strozzorum Poemata I, 100f 8° II, 152f 8°	
1514		Ad Herennium, 245f 4° Catonis De Re Rustica 308f 4°	
	Hesychii Dictionarium 198f fol. Athenaei Dipnosophistae 142f fol.		
		Quintilian – 230f 4°	

THE CHANCES OF BUSINESS   163

Table IV (cont.)

Year	Greek	Latin	Italian
1514 (cont.)			Petrarch, Cose vulgari, 183f 8º
			Sannazaro Arcadia 89f 8º
		Virgilii Opera, 220f 8º	
		Valerius Maximus, 216f 8º	
		Aldi Grammatica, 214f 4º	
	Suda, 391f fol.		
1515		Lucretius, 125f 8º*	

---

* I consider, with Christie, "Chronology of the Early Aldines", p. 220, that this edition belongs to January 1515 and not 1516 according to Venetian usage, as Renouard assumed, p. 74.

lies in the nature of Aldus' editions during these last years. Though quality and quantity are equally impressive – five important Greek first editions, twenty-two editions in twenty-four months – there is an air of sunset glory reflected from a more prosperous past. The works of Plato had been in preparation for an unknown number of years: Musurus was certainly working on Alexander of Aphrodisia at the very beginning of 1509;[169] much of the text of the Greek Orators was derived from a manuscript lent by Lascaris, who naturally left his post as ambassador in Venice when relations with France broke down about the same time;[170] and we know that Fortiguerra was supervising the correction of a text of Athenaeus in Rome during the spring of 1508.[171] It would hardly have been possible to run off these texts so quickly if a good deal of preliminary editorial work had not already been done. Also, ten editions out of the total of twenty-five listed were reissues of titles previously printed by the company. In the Lucretius, the text was completely revised and the format altered: in the poems of Pontano, new material was added.[172] But the impression of tying up loose ends and cutting time and expense remains the same.

Even allowing for this, Aldus' achievement during these last years still looks formidable. The series of Latin octavos is extended with Cicero's *Letters to Atticus,* Caesar's *Commentaries,* and the Latin agricultural writers: contemporary Latin and vernacular poetry find their place with the Strozzis' poems and Sannazaro's *Arcadia*; and his acquisition of the unique manuscript of Hesychius to serve as an exemplar shows that Aldus was still prepared to use his system of contacts to gain new material.[173] Whatever difficulties were thrown in his way by the chances of business or the doubts of his friends it is fairly clear that Aldus' faith in the civilizing force of literature, especially Greek literature, remained unshaken to the very end.

Another explanation of this continuing activity may lie in Aldus' rhetorical description of Venice during this period as "another Athens". While it is difficult to test this phrase exactly without a far more detailed knowledge of Venetian society than we possess, the observation does seem to fit certain general tendencies. The devastation of the mainland cities naturally brought a flood of refugees to Venice. They brought disease and overcrowding with them: but they also brought their skills and interests. The dramatic rise of the Venetian cloth industry, in which Aldus' friend Angelo Gabriel made his fortune, has been traced to the large-scale immigration of craftsmen during the second decade of the century.[174] Another dimension of this movement was the arrival of an unknown number of academics from the deserted university of Padua and other mainland towns. Marin Becichemo, a somewhat theatrical Latinist who had made a reputation for himself in Brescia, was tempted up from Rome by the offer of an official lectureship. From Padua came Raphael Regius, the theologians Hironimo da Monopoli and Maurice O'Fihely, and most important of all, Aldus' friend and principal editor of Greek texts, Marcus Musurus.[175]

In spite of the war or perhaps partly as an anodyne for it, the companionship and rivalry of these academic gladiators began to promote a vigorous cultural life which seems strangely out of keeping with the desperate political position of Venice during the next few years. Interspersed with Sanudo's descriptions of armies manoeuvring and alliances shifting, we find accounts of public lectures, private performances of Roman comedies, of theses being defended and masques performed. Diplomatic activity brought its own indirect benefits, as foreigners whom more serious errands had brought to Venice paused to sample the city's rich intellectual fare. Alberto Pio arrived as imperial ambassador early in 1512. A young protégé of the Hungarian representative named Janus Vyrthesi took time off to attend Greek lectures given by Musurus, and in due course earned Aldus' dedication of the first edition of Athenaeus.[176] The level of activity was such that, in January 1512, the government felt bound to revive the dormant public lectureships, one of them for Musurus: and as if to justify their wisdom, some twenty Greek codices have recently been traced in the Biblioteca Marciana, with colophons which show that they were copied for or dedicated to known pupils of Musurus between 1509 and 1516.[177]

Obviously, we cannot know what this implies for the sale of printed texts. But if we remember that almost all of Aldus' Greek editions were now being edited by Musurus, we may assume that they now had the nucleus of a stimulating market on their very doorstep: probably enough to absorb a good many copies through direct sales or personal recommendation, without more complex methods of distribution, clearly large enough to make Venice seem "another Athens".

But at the same time a very different tone is apparent in Aldus' prefaces: a tone which has been there before, in the many declarations of firmness in the face of difficulty, but which now begins to take on an edge of exhaustion and disillusion. Aldus' dedication of the *Rhetorica ad Herennium* to Andrea Navagero is perhaps the most vivid description of the early publisher's plight which has come down to us:

Apart from six hundred others, there are two things in particular which continually interrupt my work. First, the frequent letters of learned men which come to me from every part of the world and which would cost me whole days and nights if I were to reply. Then there are the visitors who come, partly to greet me, partly to see what new work is in hand, but mostly because they have nothing better to do. "All right," they say, "Let's drop in on Aldus!" So they come in crowds, and sit around with their mouths open, "Like leaches which will not let go of the skin until they have a bellyfull of blood." I say nothing of those who come to recite a poem to me or a piece of prose, usually rough and unpolished, which they want me to print for them.

I have at last begun to defend myself from these thoroughly tedious visitors and their interruptions. When those who write to me have nothing very important to say, I do not reply at all: or if it is important, I reply in few words. I ask my friends not to be offended by this, or to take it in any way other than that intended: for it is not pride or scorn that makes me act in this way, but the need to spend what time I have in editing good books. As far as those who come to greet me, or come for any other reason, are concerned: well, I have taken care to warn them with a notice against bothering me any more, or continually breaking in upon my work and study. A notice stands like some sort of an edict above the door of my room, and the words are these: "Whoever you are, Aldus asks you again and again: if there is anything you want from him, please state your business quickly and get on your way, unless you are going to take his work on your shoulders, as Hercules did for weary Atlas. There will always be something for you, or for anyone else who comes along, to do."[178]

Many have noticed the single-mindedness of these sentences: few have commented on their puzzling, almost tragic overtones. For it was precisely these factors – the range of his international contacts, and the sensitivity of his feeling for scholarly and literary tastes – which had given Aldus' enterprise the ebullience symbolised in the dolphin, and carried it to the triumphs of the earliest years of the century. Whatever his difficulties, he had clung to his conviction that all literature refined, and Greek literature refined most of all. Even during the anxious months of 1505, he had never restricted himself to "safe" editions: and whatever misgivings his partners may have felt at that time, there is no doubt that Aldus carried them with him and by the end of his life had made Torresani a complete convert to his own views. "Now that Aldus has gone, the load he carried seems to have fallen upon me...I have imitated him insofar as I could, and whatever course he, an expert in all the learned sciences, thought he should follow, I too have followed."[179]

Such was Torresani's declaration of intent in 1516. The Aldine press continued to operate under his management, and many of its most important publications – Pausanias' *Description of Greece* in 1516, the Greek New Testament and the first edition of the plays of Aeschylus in 1518, the complete works of Galen in 1525 – either derived immediately from editorial work begun in Aldus' lifetime, or were plainly associated to his ideas. Though he had been a successful printer in his own right for at least ten years before Aldus even came to Venice, Torresani was now content to operate as "father-in-law of Aldus", and he quickly abandoned the "sign of the Tower" which figures in earlier correspondence, for Aldus' "sign of the Anchor".[180] Like Patroclus in the armour of Achilles, he found his friend's devices far more effective than his own. It is an eloquent tribute to the moral and intellectual power wielded by a man who can never have controlled more than the smallest fragment of the company's capital, and it is both sad and surprising that Aldus felt no greater sense of achievement. In fact, the scholarly contacts which he had constructed were very far from useless. Torresani quickly realised that an academic reputation brought prestige, and that prestige brought profit: he spent a good deal of time and effort trying to attract the men of letters whom Aldus had been showing verbally to the door. He failed to do so. Bembo, Musurus, Lascaris and Fra Giocondo drifted away to Rome: Erasmus refused to come south again; and the rather grudging help given by old allies like Egnazio shows that this shift of attention was not simply a question of Venice's being superseded by other centres of publication.[181] When Aldus died, part of the company died with him, and three generations of successors tried to conjure it back into existence by boldly proclaiming their relationship to the dead hero. Why should such a man have felt the profound sense of disillusion expressed in the passage we have just quoted? The explanation must lie in the fact that printing was only one part of Aldus' ambitions – and probably not the greatest part.

NOTES

1 See especially the tributes celebrating the 500th anniversary of Aldus' birth: Robertson and Dazzi, cited under Ch. III, n. 50, and C. Buhler, "Aldus Manutius – the first Five Hundred Years", *Papers of the Bibliographical Society of America*, XLIV, 1950, pp. 209–10.
2 OAME VIII. Plato appeared in 1513, Galen in 1525: RAIA pp. 62, 239. The plan for a trilingual Bible was mentioned by Justin Decadyos in the Greek Psalter, probably in 1497: RAIA p. 260, and Firmin-Didot, *Alde Manuce*, pp. 60–1, for the text.
3 OAME LXXI E. (Vol. I, p. 106.)
4 For the full contents, which include works of Proclus, Synesius, Psellus, Alcinous, Speusippus and Xenocrates, see RAIA p. 13. For Ficino's letter to Aldus, CAM 2.
5 RAIA p. 20. Three translations of Aratus were printed.
6 OAME Vol. I, p. 34: "...quia epicurae sectae dogmata elegantur et docte mandavit carminibus."
7 E.g. OAME III, VIII: CSV pp. 72, 74.
8 L. Minio-Paluello, "Attività filosofica-editoriale dell'umanesimo", in *Umanesimo europeo et umanesimo veneziano*, ed. V. Branca, Fondazione Cini, 1963, pp. 245–63.
9 See Ch. III, n. 34.
10 OAME VIII. On Linacre and his books see below, Ch. VII, passim.
11 Caballi was responsible for fixing the order of the various Aristotelian works, and Aldus followed his canon (Minio-Paluello, *op. cit.*, p. 253): on his presence at Padua see E. Martellozzo Forin, *Acta graduum academicorum ab anno 1501 ad annum 1525*, Istituto per la storia dell'universita di Padova, 1969, pp. 163–4.

12 OAME XII. On Valeriani's influence see Ch. III, n. 38. His grammar was reprinted twenty-three times during the sixteenth century.
13 OAME XI, RAIA pp. 13–14.
14 OAME V, and E. Garin, *Il pensiero pedagogico dell'umanesimo*, pp. 452, for Guarino's recommendation in his *De ordine docendi et studendi*. Selections from Theocritus and Hesiod had been printed by Accursius in Milan around 1480: see A. S. F. Gow, *Theocritus*, Vol. I, Cambridge, 1952, p. xliv, for description.

OAME XIV, for the dedication of Aristophanes, and BP pp. 226–8 for Musurus' letter, which is not printed by Orlandi.
15 OAME XIX. For the controversy and Leoniceno's part see Ch. II, n. 16, above.
16 *Lettere di Ludovico Ariosto*, per cura di A. Capello, Milan, 1887, pp. 1–2.
17 Text in CSV p. 74. Dioscurides appeared in 1499, Stephanus in 1502. RAIA pp. 21, 38.
18 *Ib.*, pp. 329–31, for the full text of this catalogue.
19 Biblioteca Marciana, Venezia, Mss. italiani Cl. XI, 45 (7439), ff. 4v–5v. Some of the relevant entries can be found in the sections reproduced by Brown in *The Venetian Press*, pp. 431f.

I am in all cases following the monetary equivalents quoted by S. Romanin for this period: see his *Storia documentata di Venezia*, Vol. IV, 1973 ed., p. 357, n. 104.

    1 Ducat = 6.4 lire mocenighe
    1 Lira = 20 soldi
    1 Marcello = 10 soldi.
20 All figures are quoted in the petition for copyright: see FD No. 9, pp. 104–5, 20 September 1492.
21 *Omnia Opera*, Platonides, Bologna, 1502, Epistola No. 4: text also printed in L. Dorez, "Alde Manuce et Ange Politien", pp. 323–6. The letter, which is dated 5 April 1498, contains a number of passages that illustrate the relationship between Aldus and his partners and count heavily against any attempt to claim that Aldine publications were cheap. "...cognosco tantam esse in eius sotiis (e.g. Torresani and Barbarigo) avaritiam ut nihil commodi ab eo sperem...Sed scito me ab eo (sc. Aldo) nihil deinceps empturum esse, ut credo, propter caritatem (ut ad eum scripsi) rei parvae quam ipse et sotii magnam faciunt, multum papyri in chartis fere vacuis scriptura consumentis." For Alvise Capello's purchase see Brown, *loc. cit.*
22 RAIA p. 14. Two other short works, *De conversione propositionum* and *Quaestio Averrois...*, were published around the same time as Maioli's and are often bound in with them. For full bibliographical details see J. Dukas, *Notes bio-bibliographiques sur un Recueil d'Opuscles très Rares Imprimés par Alde l'Ancien en 1497*, Paris, 1876. For Aldus' comments see OAME X.
23 *De Tiro* can be attributed to Aldus on typographical grounds only: RAIA p. 259. The subject was an academic dispute about the preparation of a compound called "Theriaca". *De Morbo Gallico* concerned the recent outbreak of syphilis: for the social implications of this see B. S. Pullan, *Rich and Poor in Renaissance Venice*, Oxford, 1971, p. 223.

24 OAME I A. See below, Ch. VI, nn. 29f.
25 FD No. 50, p. 123, 26 June 1496. Dedications were addressed to the doge and to eight different senators. The British Library has a copy on vellum with the arms of the Trevisan family (C 8 h 14).
   On Valla's acquaintance with Benedetti see Valla, Nos. 19, 37, and on his circle Ch. V, nn. 50-2.
26 There are frequent references to this type of publication in Sanudo's *Diarii*: e.g. Vol. IV, col. 20 (Papal Bull for crusade, 1501); col. 50 (funeral oration for Cardinal Zen); col. 266 (order of the Corpus Christi procession). For the background of Reuchlin's mission see P. Amelung, "Bemerkungen zu zwei Italienischen Inkunabeln (Hain 4942 und Hain 13883)" in *Contribuiti alla storia del libro italiano – Miscellanea in onore di Lamberto Donati*, Florence, 1969, pp. 1–9. Copies of the speech are known only in Munich, Stuttgart and Zürich. I know of only two copies of Amaseo's poem, in London and Paris: see Table I.
27 Priced at 9 lire 4 soldi in 1513: P. Leicht, "I prezzi delle edizioni aldine al principio dell'500", *Il libro e la stampa*, Anno VI, fasc. iii, 1912, p. 83. On the use of Hebrew type see citations under n. 71 of the previous chapter.
28 L. Dorez, "La mort de Pic de Mirandole et l'édition Aldine des Oeuvres d'Ange Politien, 1494–98", GSLI XXXII, 1898, pp. 360–4: this ingenious but slightly melodramatic attempt to show that Aldus used the names of Sarti and Ricci for cover, while in fact relying on Pico's secretary for his material, has now been superseded by J. Hill Cotton's sober demonstration that Sarti was associated with the printing of Poliziano's works well before his death: "Alessandro Sarti e il Poliziano", LBF LXIV, 1962, pp. 225–46. CAM 3 shows that Sarti and Ricci had been collaborating for some time by the end of 1497, and that Aldus had only just been drawn in through the agency of Gianfrancesco Pico. For Sarti's literary tactics see also Dorez, "Alde Manuce et Ange Politien...", cit. under Ch. II, n. 20. It should perhaps be added that he took pains to make himself useful by acting as a sort of messenger-boy, as well as a forger: see CAM 20.
29 No attempt will be made to cite bibliography beyond the immediate range of this study. For coverage up to 1950 see L. Donati, "Bibliografia aldina", LBF LII, No. 2, 1950, pp. 189–204 (items 247–352). The question of authorship is exhaustively discussed by M. T. Casella and G. Pozzi, *Francesco Colonna, biografia e opere*, 2 vols., Padua, 1959: their conclusions were, however, questioned by Donati, "Il mito di Francesco Colonna", LBF LXIV, 1962, pp. 247–70. For an invaluable discussion of Aldus' part in the project see C. Dionisotti, *Gli umanisti e il volgare*, Ch. 1: and for an equally valuable discussion of the general problems G. D. Painter, "The *Hypnerotomachia Polifili* of 1499: an introduction to the Dream, the Dreamer, the Artist, and the Printer" – separate intr. to Eugrammia Press edition, London, 1963.
30 A.S.V., Senato, Deliberazioni Terra, Rg. XIII, c. 44r. The continuation of public business suggests that this was a fairly limited outbreak.
31 R. Fulin, "Una lettera di Alessandro VI", AV I, 1871, p. 157. On Locatellus ("presbyter Bergomensis") see Burger, pp. 480–2.

32 See Ch. I, no. 93, above. Sandeis' views are noted in Biblioteca Feliniana Capitolare, Lucca, No. 567. The entire volume is heavily annotated.
33 G. Biadego, "Intorno al Sogno di Polifilo", *ARIV.*, LX, pt. ii, 1900–1, pp. 699–714. M. Billanovich, "Francesco Colonna, il *Polifilo,* e la famiglia Lelli", IMU XIX, 1976, pp. 419–28.
34 On the composition see D. Gnoli, "Il Sogno di Polifilo", LBF I, 1900, pp. 189–212.
35 Dionisotti, *Gli umanisti...*, pp. 1–14. For Aldus' refusals see above, n. 22, and below, Ch. VII, n. 42.
36 OAME VI (*Thesaurus Cornucopiae*). See Dionisotti, *loc. cit.*
37 L. Dorez, "Des Origines et de la Diffusion du Songe de Polifile", *Révue des Bibliothèques*, VI, 1896, pp. 239–83.
38 Billanovich, "Francesco Colonna...", p. 420. Appealing in 1509 for a renewal of his ten-year privilege, Crasso claimed to have spent several hundred ducats on the project. FD No. 173, p. 171.
39 Pozzi, *op. cit.*, Vol. II, pp. 152–3. Also *Francesco Colonna e Aldo Manuzio*, Berne, 1962, pp. 15–17.
40 The acrostic had been noted by 1512, and was noted in a copy later examined by Apostolo Zeno but since lost: Casella, *op. cit.*, Vol. I, pp. 63–4. On the introductory poem, *ib.*, p. 95, and P. Hofer, "Variant copies of the 1499 Poliphilus", *Bulletin of the New York Public Library*, XXXVI, 1932, pp. 475–86.
...Mirando poi Francisco alta Columna
Per cui phama imortal de voi rissona.
41 Casella, *op. cit.*, Vol. I, pp. 44–5, and Doc. 50, p. 124.
42 Billanovich, "Francesco Colonna...", p. 420.
43 On the general problem of the "sfratati" see Casella, *op. cit.*, Vol. I, p. 52, n. 1: A. Stella, *Chiesa e stato nelle relazioni dei nunzi pontifici a Venezia*, Città del Vaticano, 1964, p. 127.
44 Colonna was called before the General of the Order in 1477 and before his Provincial in 1483, though in neither case is the charge specified. Casella, *op. cit.*, Vol. I, pp. 22, 33, and Docs. 17, p. 113, and 25, p. 116. For the incident in 1516 see pp. 68f, and Doc. 81, p. 136.
45 *Ib.*, pp. 50f.
46 Billanovich, "Francesco Colonna...", pp. 421f.
47 I am purposely avoiding involvement in this celebrated controversy, and those interested are referred to Donati's bibliography, cited under n. 29, above. Bordon was suggested by Biadego, *op. cit.* under n. 33, above, pp. 711–12, and is accepted by Pozzi, *op. cit.*, Vol. II, pp. 150–8. Though professionally a miniaturist, he showed great interest in the press: cf. FD No. 26, p. 113 (application for copyright on translations from Lucian, published by Simon Bevilaqua, 1494), No. 141, p. 154 (Triumphs of Caesar – no copies survive), No. 168, p. 168 (World-map – no copies survive), No. 251, p. 206 (Isolario – two known editions by Zoppino, 1528 and 1534). Unfortunately, none of his surviving work seems to shed any direct light on *Polifilo*. Bordon was evidently a most versatile character and is currently attracting

a good deal of expert interest: cf. M. Levi d'Ancona, "Benedetto Padovano e Benedetto Bordone: prime tentative per un corpus di Benedetto Padovano", *Commentari*, XVIII, 1967, pp. 21–43; M. Billanovich, "Benedetto Bordon e Giulio Cesare Scaligero", IMU XI, 1968, pp. 187–256; G. Mariani Canova, "Profilo di Benedetto Bordon miniatore padovano", AIRV CXXVII, 1968–9, pp. 99–121, and *La miniatura veneta del rinascimento*, Venice/Milan, 1969, pp. 122–30. (P. 123 for references to a "bottega".) Copies I have seen which might bear traces of Bordon's influence are British Library C4 D5 (Petrarch, *Cose volgari*, 1501): C4 D11 (*Martialis Epigrammata*, 1501): C4 D10 (Statius, 1502): John Rylands Library, Manchester, 3666 (*Ovidii Opera*, 3 vols., 1502). While it could not be claimed that an identification of Bordon as Aldus' miniaturist would resolve the problem of *Polifilo*, it might create a connection which would strengthen Bordon's claim to be the artist. It should also be said that illuminated Aldines, most of which belong to the period after 1500, have not received the attention they deserve from specialists.

48 Ff. M 5v–M6r (= pp. 188–9 in the edition of Pozzi and L. Ciapponi, Vol. I, Padua, 1964). See also Painter, *op. cit.*, p. 10, for comment on the morality of these and other illustrations.

49 *Ovidii Metamorphoseos vulgare*, Rubeo and Giunti, 1497: F. xxviiir. Painter, *op. cit.*, p. 14, considers that these woodcuts might have been designed by the artist of the *Polifilo* at an earlier stage of his life and with worse assistance. Cf. also ff. ii r, vi r, xxxi r, xxxiv v. For Plato's objections see *Republic* 390 c 6–7.

See Ch. I, n. 93, for the storm roused by this edition.

50 Casella, *op. cit.*, Vol. I, p. 97, with citations.

51 For the details of this "missed victory" and of the entire campaign see F. C. Lane, "Naval Actions and Fleet Organisation, 1499–1502", in *Renaissance Venice*, ed. J. R. Hale, London, 1973, pp. 146–73. See also F. Gilbert's essay "Venice in the Crisis of the League of Cambrai", on pp. 274–92 of the same volume.

52 Sanudo III, cols. 623–5, 631–2, August 1500.

53 Painter, *op. cit.*, p. 10.

54 See nn. 38, 50, above. Crasso's claim that he had been unable to distribute copies could suggest that Aldus kept the supply limited. He made no attempt to publicise *Polifilo* in correspondence.

55 Facsimilies of this, the only surviving business document in Aldus' own hand, can be found in CAM and Castellani, *Early Venetian Printing Illustrated*, p. 32. On Jenson's links with Uglheimer see above, Ch. I, nn. 50f: and on the experiment with italic R. Ridolfi, "Del carattere italico aldino nel secolo XV", LBF LV, no. ii, 1953, pp. 118–22.

56 M. Laurent, "Alde Manuce l'Ancien, éditeur de S. Catherine de Siene", *Tradito*, V, 1947, pp. 357–63. Dionisotti, *op. cit.*, p. 4, on the fashion for medieval religious writers.

57 FD No. 101, p. 141.

58 Painter, *op. cit.*, p. 10.

59 Vol. III, pp. 279f. De Gregoriis, Tacuinus, de Tortis, and Torresani all achieved comparable totals.

60 BMC VI, pp. 665–9. The Greek Anthology, four plays of Euripides, and the satires of Lucian all anticipated Aldine editions of 1503. On the Alopa types see Proctor, *Printing of Greek*, pp. 78–80.

61 Geanakoplos, *Greek Scholars*, pp. 207f. Callierges did not copy the Aldine system of kerning accents. On this and the speed of production see Proctor, *op. cit.*, pp. 117–18.

62 OAME XLVI.

63 CAM 2. On Lascaris see above, Ch. III, n. 8.

64 For Aldus' tribute to Gabriel see OAME VIII: for the two copyrights, FD Nos. 76, 80, pp. 131, 133. The text anticipated a number of the Aldine *Epistolographi Graeci*, and is reckoned among the Greek first editions. RAIA pp. 18–19, and on the infringement of the copyright Proctor, *The Printing of Greek*, pp. 110–12.

65 CAM 7. On the move of Bissolo and de Manzi to Milan see Motta, "Demetrio Chalcondila editore", cit. under Ch. III, n. 43.

66 D. Fava, "L'introduzione del corsivo…", cit. under Ch. II, n. 42. The two Scottist commentaries were in folio, far from Aldus' field of interest, and are now so rare as to suggest that this was never a serious threat.

67 Sanudo, II, *passim*. Gerolamo Priuli, *Diarii*, ed. A. Segre, R.I.S., Tom. XXIV, pt. iii, Città di Castello, 1912, pp. 111–25. Malipiero, *Annali…*, in ASI 7, ii, 1844, p. 715. For comment on the system and the crisis see Lane, *Venice, a Maritime Republic*, pp. 323f.

68 Priuli, *op. cit.*, p. 141. "…non coreva uno ducato." Compare FD No. 58, p. 126, for the printers' difficulties with cash-flow.

69 Sanudo, IV, col. 822, 16 March 1503.

70 Information based on Panzer, Vols. III and VIII.

71 Priuli, *op. cit.*, p. 263, entry of February 1499–1500.

72 OAME XXXII.

73 Figures from RAIA pp. 24–45, omitting editions considered doubtful by the author.

74 Geanakoplos, *Greek Scholars*, p. 128.

75 Zuane Bembo's introduction to Sabellici, *Annotationes veteres et recentes ex Plinio, Livio et pluribus authoribus*, Pencius de Leuco, 1502. On fitting type to reader see Carter, *Typography*, pp. 45f.

76 Allen, I, p. 439. For Morison's opinions see "Towards an Ideal Type", *The Fleuron*, 2, 1924, pp. 57–75: "The Type of the *Hypnerotomachia Poliofili*", in *Gutenberg Festschrift*, Mainz, 1925, pp. 254–8; *The Typographic Book*, London, 1963, pp. 32–3.

77 Proctor, *Printing of Greek*, p. 93: Buhler, "Aldus Manutius…", cit. under n. 1, above, pp. 207–8.

78 This section is based on Proctor, *op. cit.*, pp. 50–1, 93–106, and on Mardersteig, "Aldo Manuzio…", pp. 123–42. Proctor does not cover the years after 1500.

79 Proctor, *op. cit.*, pp. 78–82. For the possibility that Aldus designed his own Greek scripts see the article of Quaranta cited under n. 74 of Ch. III. For illustrations of the uncial and cursive forms see Plates in L. Reynolds and N. Wilson, *Scribes and Scholars*, Oxford, 1968.

80 Geanakoplos, *Greek Scholars*, pp. 120f, 171f: D. Fava, *La Biblioteca Estese nel suo sviluppo storico*, Modena, 1925, pp. 150f; and Ch. V of this study.

81 On Pellicier's mission see A. Franklin, *Précis de l'histoire de la Bibliothèque du Roi, aujourd'hui Bibliothèque Nationale*, Paris, 1875, p. 66. On his acquisitions see Bib. Nat., Ms. Graecus 3064, ff. 33f, reference to the printed Anthology being on f. 56r. It is described exactly as a volume of "epigrams printed in large characters and with scholia": there is no other edition that this could indicate, and the mention of scholia identifies the copy almost certainly as Imprimés Réserves Yb 484.

82 On the development of Aldus' Roman types see Mardersteig, "Aldo Manuzio...", pp. 127–37: for more detailed comment, the works of Morison, cit. under n. 76, above; on the wider context, P. Beaujon, "The Garamond Types – sixteenth and seventeenth-century sources considered", *The Fleuron*, 5, 1926, pp. 131–79.

83 I am avoiding involvement in details of manuscript-dating: see Morison, "Early Humanistic Script and the First Roman Type", *The Library*, Fourth Series, XXIV, 1944, pp. 1–29, and *Politics and Script*, Oxford, 1972, pp. 264f. The chronology is disputed by D. Thomas, "What is the origin of the 'scrittura humanistica'?" LBF LIII, 1951, pp. 1–10. Still more detailed coverage can be found in B. Ullmann, *The Origin and Development of Humanistic Script*, Rome, 1960.

On the rejection of medieval forms see E. Cassamassima, "Litterae Gothicae: note per la storia della riforma grafica umanistica", LBF LXII, 1960, pp. 109–43.

84 Mardersteig, "Leon Battista Alberti e la rinascita del carattere lapidario Romano nel Quattrocento", IMU II, 1959, pp. 285–307. M. Meiss, *Andrea Mantegna as Illuminator – an Episode in Renaissance Art, Humanism and Diplomacy*, Columbia, 1957, pp. 68–78: "Towards a more Comprehensive Renaissance Palaeography", *The Art Bulletin*, XLII, 1960, pp. 97–112.

85 *Divina Proportione, opera a tuti gli ingegni perspicaci e curiosi necessaria, ove ciascuno studioso di philosophia, prospectiva, pictura, sculptura, architectura, musica, e altre mathematice*, Paganinis, Venice, 1508: *Praefatio in V Librum Euclidis*, Paganinis 1509, ff. 30v–31v. (List of names.)

86 Meiss, *Andrea Mantegna*, p. 69.

87 CSV pp. 75–7: and see above, Ch. III, n. 71.

88 On the quarrel with the Giunti see below, nn. 145f: on Arrighi, A. F. Johnson and S. Morison, "The Chancery Types of Italy and France", *The Fleuron*, 3, 1924, p. 29; and for general discussion of the problems L. Balsamo and A. Tinto, *Origini del corsivo nella tipografia italiana dell'500*, Milan, 1967.

89 J. Wardrop, *The Script of Humanism*, Oxford, 1963, pp. 13–18. R. Weiss, *The Renaissance Discovery of Classical Antiquity*, Oxford, 1969, pp. 145f.

90 Wardrop, *op. cit.*, pp. 19f: V. Lazzarini, "Un maestro di scrittura nella cancellaria veneziana", in *Scritti di palaeografia e diplomatica*, Venice, 1969, pp. 64–70.

91 Wardrop, *op. cit.*, pp. 24–35, and Plates 38–9. Wardrop played a large part in identifying San Vito. On his social contacts see S. de Kunert, "Un padovano ignoto e un suo memoriale de' primi anni del Cinquecento (1505–11) con cenni su due codici miniati", *Bolletino del Museo Civico di Padova*, Anno X, 1907, no. i, pp. 1–16.

92 Balsamo, *op. cit.,* p. 36.
93 Urceus, quoted by Dorez in the article cited under n. 21, above: see esp. pp. 323–4.
94 Dionisotti, "Aldo Manuzio umanista", pp. 238f.
95 On the timing of Aldus' experiment with Hebrew type see Ch. III, n. 71. Of the Greek texts, only Euripides had received real attention, four plays being published by Lascaris and Alopa in 1496. Three editions of Lorenzo Valla's Latin version of Herodotus had been published.
96 Dedicatory letter of Gerolamo Avanzio to Marin Sanudo in Catulli, Tibulli et Propertii Poemata, 1502, f Fii v. "Aldus Manutius...ex codice catulliano per me miro studio et incredibili labore emendato tria exemplorum milia politis typis impressurus, me iterum ad hanc operam socio usus est." Quoting only from Aldus' own dedication, Renouard (p. 39) considered that 1,000 copies of each of the three authors were to be printed. But Avanzio's Latin does not appear to me capable of bearing that interpretation. The figure of 3,000 would rank Aldus' editions among the largest of the period: R. Hirsch, *Printing,* pp. 65–7, quotes no case of a larger press-run before the 4,000 copies of Luther's *Address to the Christian Nobility* in 1520.
97 This conviction seems to have originated in the experience of modern printers who observe that the sloping italic occupies less space than the upright Roman. It is now universally accepted by commentators on Aldus' work: cf Firmin-Didot, *Alde Manuce,* pp. 161–2; Hirsch, *op. cit.,* pp. 69–70; Morison, passim in the works cited under nn. 76, 83, above.
98 Officium Beatae Mariae Virginis, John Rylands University Library of Manchester, No. 18497. For the petitions, FD Nos. 61, 74, pp. 127, 130.
99 CSV pp. 72, 76–7. See also Ch. III, n. 68 above.
100 Balsamo, *op. cit.,* pp. 27, 36.
101 Compare P. Leicht, "I prezzi delle edizioni aldine", pp. 77–84, with the passages of da Madiis' accounts quoted in Brown, *Venetian Press,* pp. 431–52, and FD, supplementary piece No. 1, pp. 396–401. K. Wagner's recent article "Aldo Manuzio e i prezzi dei suoi libri", LBF LXXVII, 1975, pp. 77–82 shows that Aldine texts kept their value into the 1520s and 1530s.
102 RAIA pp. 329–31, shows that a "lowest price" was set in the first catalogue. See also Ch. III, n. 59.
103 OAME XXXVI, XXXV, XLII, XXXVIII, XXXVII, etc.
104 John Rylands Library, 3666 1D (Ovid, 3 vols): British Library, C. 4, g. 10 (Juvenal and Persius).
105 British Library, C. 4, g. 5. On the Molin family see Ch. III, n. 85. Alvise da Molin was one of the most powerful men in Venice at the time.
106 These libraries will be examined in greater detail below: see Ch. VII, nn. 91–5 (Grolier), 122–30 (Thurz, Lubranski).
107 On the problems and hardships of travel see Braudel, *Le Méditerranée,* Vol. I, pp. 326 f.
108 J. H. Hexter, "The Education of the Aristocracy during the Renaissance", *Journal of Modern History,* XXII, 1950, pp. 1f: L. Stone, "The Educational Revolution in

England", *Past and Present* 28, 1964, pp. 41–80; R. Kagan, "Universities in Castile, 1500–1700", *ib.*, 49, 1970, pp. 44–71.

109 OAME XXXV.

110 CAM 23.

111 Dionisotti, *Gli umanisti e il volgare*..., pp. 1–14, connects Aldus' "conversion" to Tuscan with his friendship with Pietro Bembo: but FD No. 114, p. 146, shows that it was Pietro's brother Carlo who supplied the manuscripts and petitioned for copyright for the texts of both Dante and Petrarch. These editions cannot therefore be taken simply as a declaration of principle by Aldus. For contemporary experiments with Petrarchan forms and full references to manuscripts see F. Lepori's entry on Paolo da Canal in DBI XVII.

112 Documents in Baschet, pp. 9–11. For comment see A. Luzio and R. Renier, "La cultura e le relazioni letterarie di Isabella d'Este-Gonzaga", GSLI XXXIII, 1899, pp. 1–62, XXXVII, 1901, pp. 201–45: V. Cian, *Un decennio della vita di Pietro Bembo*, Turin, 1885, pp. 90f.

113 Dionisotti, *op. cit.*, p. 13. OAME XLI.

114 OAME XXVI. For comment see Christie, "Chronology...", p. 213.

115 Valerius Maximus was published in October 1502 but apparently re-issued with a new quire incorporating additional material after 28 December: RAIA, pp. 36–7, OAME XLII A, B. CAM 27 for Spiesshammer's letter. On Bessarion's treatise see the appendix to my article "Two Great Venetian Libraries in the Age of Aldus Manutius", BJRL 57, No. i, 1974, pp. 164–6.

116 Vol. I, ff. yyxr – "FINIS. Venetiis apud Aldum mense Ianuario MDI." a i v. Icannis Damasceni in Theogoniam, etc.

Vol. II, f. hh vi r – same formula. F. Ai r – Epstola Severi Sulpitii, etc. The letter to Clari printed in OAME XXIII.

117 This reconstruction is suggested by Christie, *op. cit.*, pp. 208–13, on the basis of RAIA, pp. 24–6. I do not feel entirely happy about the details, since Aldus says in his first and undated letter to Clari in Vol. I (OAME XXII A) that he already has the manuscript of Prudentius and has used it: work on Nonnus was also said in 1504 to have been in hand "iam trennium" (see next note). It is therefore not clear that Aldus originally envisaged a simple, one-volume Latin edition.

Vol. III, ff. oo iv v–v r, contains Aldus' account of the special difficulties of this text.

118 RAIA p. 261. A text of Nonnus was announced at the end of the third volume, but since the few surviving copies lack the promised Latin translation and any preliminary matter, Renouard and Christie, *loc. cit.*, agree that the printed pages were simply circulated privately to friends.

119 L. Dorez, "La marque typographique d'Alde Manuce", *Révue des Bibliothèques*, VI, 1896, pp. 143–60: L. Donati, "Le marche tipografiche di Aldo Manuzio il vecchio", GJB 1974, pp. 129–32. For Aldus' exposition of the proverb see M. M. Philips, *The Adages of Erasmus*, pp. 171f.

120 RAIA p. 51. Firmin-Didot, *Alde Manuce*, p. 283.

121 The project was known to Lascaris in December 1501: CAM 24. On the first edition see Ch. III, n. 41.
122 OAME LVI.
123 Plutarch was mentioned in the unfinished petition presented to the senate in 1498: CSV p. 76.
124 RAIA p. 54. On Pliny see below, Ch. VI, n. 108–9.
125 *Pirckheimers Briefwechsel*, Vol. I, No. 86, pp. 280–2.
126 *Ib.*, for Cuno's verdict. On the influence of the *Asolani*, see E. Panofsky, "The Neoplatonic movement in Florence and Northern Italy", in his *Studies in Iconology*, New York, 1967, pp. 129–69. Identically set copies of the work exist with and without the dedication to Lucretia Borgia: for a detailed account of the bibliography see C. H. Clough, "Pietro Bembo's *Asolani* of 1505", *Modern Language Notes*, 84, 1969, pp. 16–45.
127 CAM 24 (Lascaris), 35 (Fortiguerra) OAME LVI (Gabriel).
128 Leicht, *op. cit.* under n. 101, above. The author points out (p. 79) that copies of Dioscurides and Xenophon, which had been priced at 6 lire 4 soldi in earlier catalogues, were offered at 4 lire in 1513.
129 RAIA p. 44. This interpretation is conjectural, but the formula is usual for publishers such as Lucantonio Giunti who sponsored single editions.
130 *Loc. cit.* under n. 125, above. "Libros enim Gracos a se impressos deinceps socer eius Andreas de Asula, bibliopola, non accepturus erat uti solebat, et ob id necessaria pro impressione retribuere."
131 Since this scheme refers to the academic rather than the publishing side of Aldus' ambitions, it will be dealt with in detail in the next chapter. In the letter cited immediately above Cuno reported to Pirckheimer that Aldus was actually making his preparations for the journey to Germany.
132 Torresani was born on 4 March 1451 which certainly makes him younger than Aldus whether the latter was born in 1447 or 1450. Bernoni, p. 5. Firmin-Didot, *Alde-Manuce*, p. 143, dated the marriage on unknown grounds to 1499, but a letter to Aldus from Alberto Pio, dated 11 March 1505, mentions that it had taken place "during this Carnival". CAM 8.
133 The will is addressed at San Paternian. CSV pp. 92–5.
134 No copy of this document survives, but the date and the general import can be reconstructed from the act which annulled it and from Aldus' second will. Cf. Pastorello, "Testimonianze e documenti...", pp. 174–5, and 195, Doc. III.
135 In his appeal from prison to the Marquis of Mantua, Aldus played on the fact that he had been seeking manuscripts of the most famous Mantuan – Virgil. Baschet, No. XIV.
136 CSV pp. 72–81. On the novelty of the attempt to protect types rather than titles cf. H. de la Fontaine Verwey, "Les débuts de la protection des charactères typographiques du XVIe siècle", GJB, 1965, pp. 24–34.
137 Bulls of Alexander VI, Julius II, and Leo X were printed in the 1513 edition of Perotti's *Cornucopia*: RAIA pp. 63.

138 This interpretation of the press-privileges was strongly stated by Fulin, who assembled the fullest collection: FD pp. 86f (introduction). It was naturally followed by Castellani, Brown and others.

139 For Gabriel, cf. nn. 64–6 above. The problem of definition is stressed by by P. Camerini, "In difesa di Lucantonio Giunta dall'accusa di contrafattore delle edizioni di Aldo Romano", *Atti e memorie della reale accademia di scienze, lettere ed arti in Padova*, Anno CCCXCIII, 1933–4, pp. 165–94. It should also be remembered that the dating of editions was by no means universal at this time. On the difficulties of mental readjustment to the press cf. M. McLuhan, *The Gutenberg Galaxy: the Making of Typographic Man*, London/Toronto, 1962, pp. 86–8.

140 FD Nos. 22, 25, 61, etc. (Avogadori del commun): 95, 96, 97 etc. (Signori di Notte); 111 (Aldus' protection entrusted to the Heads of the Council of Ten). Many others simply refer to the "Signoria". The records of the Avogadori and the Signori di Notte are fragmentary for this period, but those of the Council of Ten are complete.

141 On the suspect editions see RAIA pp. 305–16.

142 A. F. Johnson, "Books Printed at Lyons in the Sixteenth Century", *The Library*, Fourth Series, III, 1922, p. 150.

143 Camerini, *op. cit.* under n. 139, above, pp. 188–94, gives a detailed criticism of Renouard's check-list. Without wishing to enter this essentially bibliographical dispute, I suspect that the author may have swung to the opposite extreme in his efforts to defend the Giunti.

144 See Ch. I, n. 47.

145 The documents are assembled by D. Marzi, "Una questione libraria fra i Giunti ed Aldo Manuzio il Vecchio", printed for Nozze Marpurgo-Franchetti, 1895 and reproduced in *Giornale della libreria*, IX, 1896. In the last letter Vettori was still asking for clarification.

146 A.S.V., Consiglio di Dieci, Misti, Rg. 40, c 122 r–v, 10 October 1516.

147 CAM 65, 23 September 1507: "...litigandi molestiam iniquissimi hominis iniuria ...," 54, 1 November 1507: "extricateve da vostre lite...." It is just possible that 62, 25 June 1507, also refers to the case: Livio Podocataro, a cleric who seems to have had something of a taste for collecting documents, reported from Padua on his efforts to get the "writings of our messer Bernardino" from the Pisani bank. In the petition cited in the previous note, Bernardo Giunti offered to make certain payments to the Pisani.

148 A. M. Bandini, *Iuntarum Typographiae Annales*, Pars II, Lucca, 1791, pp. 5–19.

149 *Pirckheimers Briefwechsel*, No. 139, p. 457, 26 December.

150 Allen, I, Nos. 207, 209.

151 RAIA p. 51. Erasmus' letters were written in October and November.

152 OAME LXVIII. On Alviano's victory and the later disaster at Agnadello see P. Pieri, *Il rinascimento e la crisi militare italiana*, Turin, 1970, pp. 448–76: on the composition of the Pordenone circle, E. Cicogna, *Delle iscrizioni veneziane*, Vol. VI, Venice, 1853, pp. 225f.

153 *Lettere di Paolo Manuzio*, No. XIII, pp. 345–6.
154 Pastorello, "Testimonianze e documenti...", Docs. II, III, pp. 194–6.
155 Francesco Guicciardini, *Storia d'Italia*, Florence, 1963, Bk. VIII, passim.
156 Baschet, Doc. XVIII. Previous representations had been made through the imperial ambassador.
157 There is no evidence in the secret registers of the Council of Ten that Aldus was under any suspicion: but one contemporary printer, Bonino de Boninis, was a well known agent. Cf. G. della Santa, "Il tipografo dalmata Bonino de Boninis, 'confidente' della Republica di Venezia, decano della cattedrale di Treviso", NAV XXX, 1915, pp. 174–206. Aldus' friend Giorgio Valla was also arrested in 1496 under suspicion of passing secrets to Milan. Cf. "Nuovi appunti sul processo di Giorgio Valla et di Placidio Amerino in Venezia nel 1496", same author and journal, X, 1895, pp. 13–23.
158 Pastorello, "Testimonianze e documenti...", Docs. IV and V, pp. 199–201.
159 L. N. Cittadella, *Documenti ed illustrazioni riguardanti la storia artistica ferrarese*, Ferrara, 1868, pp. 307–11. An earlier will was made on 25 June 1510, but the text has not survived. Both daughters, and the unborn child if it was a girl, were allotted dowries of 500 ducats. This was a generous figure, since Maria Torresani had brought Aldus only 430. Smaller dowries of 25 ducats were provided for eight deserving girls. On the academy cf. p. 311: "Prego però Dio, chel me dia gratia che possa io fare tale officio (that of educating his sons) et mandare al executione la Academia, che desidero de fare."
160 The will was drawn up "before riding towards Milan". For the most convenient compilation of references cf. Pastorello, "Testimonianze e documenti...", pp. 179–80.
161 Guicciardini, *Storia d'Italia*, Bk. X, Ch. xiii. On Aldus' return to Venice CAM 77. (Paolo Bombasio to Scipio Fortiguerra.)
162 OAME LXXII.
163 *Ib.*, LXXV, LXXVI.
164 Pieri, *op. cit.*, pp. 500–25. For the moral effects on Venice see Gilbert's essay cited under n. 51, above.
165 Panzer, VIII, pp. 410–24.
166 Legrand, *Bibliographie Hellénique*, Vol. I, pp. 94–7, 134f. Geanakoplos, *Greek Scholars*, p. 213, on the invitation.
167 Bandini, *op. cit.*, pp. 54f. Legrand, pp. 124f.
168 Firmin-Didot, *Alde Manuce*, pp. 588–605, gives an appendix of Greek editions printed in centres outside Venice, and most come at the end of the first decade of the sixteenth century. See below, Ch. VII, nn. 104–10 (France) and 117–21 (Spain).
169 CAM 75. The letter implies that Plato was about to go to press.
170 OAME LXXV (Vol. I, p. 115).
171 CAM 38.
172 RAIA pp. 63, 74. Navagero's text of Lucretius was superior to Avanzio's version and the format was now octavo.

173 On this edition see below, Ch. VI, nn. 111f.
174 On the general problems of the time see Pullan, *Rich and Poor...*, cit. under n. 23, above, pp. 216f. On the cloth industry D. Stella, "The Rise and Fall of the Venetian Woollen Industry", in *Crisis and Change in the Venetian Economy in the Sixteenth and Seventeenth Centuries*, ed. Pullan, London, 1968, pp. 106–26.
175 On Becichemo, see Clough's article in DBI VII: Sanudo XIV, col. 19 (Regius), 635 (Hironimo), 60 (Maurice), XV, col. 517 (rivalry of Regius and Becichemo). On Musurus, F. Foffano, "Marco Musuro, professore di Greco a Padova ed a Venezia", NAV III, 1892, pp. 453–73.
176 Sanudo, XIV, cols. 83, 87 (Alberto Pio), 641, XV, 511 etc. OAME LXXXV.
177 Foffano, *op. cit.*, Doc. V. E. Mioni, "La Biblioteca greca di Marco Musuro", AV Ser. V, XCIII, 1971, pp. 5–28.
178 OAME LXXXII A.
179 RAIA p. 78 (preface to Ptolemy).
180 BP pp. 311, 332, RAIA pp. 82–4. Galen was promised as early as 1497 (OAME VIII). Torresani was operating "in signo ancorae" by 1516: see Allen II, p. 315, and compare n. 78 of previous chapter.
181 See particularly Torresani's letter to Erasmus in 1517, where efforts are made both to secure corrections to the texts of Plautus and Terence, and to tempt the Dutchman to Venice on the chance of securing Musurus' vacant Chair of Greek. Allen II, pp. 589f: *ib.*, p. 588, for hostile references to Torresani by Egnazio. The attraction of Rome under Leo X will be discussed in the next chapter.

V
ACADEMIC DREAMS

Aldus' fame as a printer leads easily to the error of regarding him only as a printer. In fact, he spent more than half of his working life as a professional scholar and teacher, continuing as such for some time after his arrival in Venice. One of the debts which he renounced in 1510 was the sum of twenty-five ducats for the oustanding school-fees of his partner's natural son Santo Barbarigo, who "came to my school for an entire year, ate his dinner at my house, and in the evening went to supper at the house of his said father".[1] We have shown in earlier chapters that Aldus had stood on the edges of the most sophisticated intellectual groups of the later Quattrocento, that he apparently saw printing as a development, rather than a change of his teaching vocation, and that he strove to the very end to gear his editions to the needs of an educational ideal. It will be the business of this chapter to show that he lived and worked in Venice amongst professional teachers, and to describe the effects which their society may have had on Aldus' ultimate ambitions.

What, first of all, did it mean to be a teacher in Venice around 1490? According to the exactly contemporary account of Marin Sanudo, there were three possibilities: you were a salaried lecturer employed by the Republic itself; you were a free-lance schoolmaster; or you were a private tutor in a noble household.[2] The first category was an élite group of three or four men, so prestigious and exclusive as to be largely separable from the others. The second and third lacked any stable composition, and intermingled largely with one another. But the overall numbers were considerable. When the religious authorities called for a profession of Faith in 1587, 258 teachers took the oath.[3] Even when we have reduced this figure to allow for the lower population and less developed education of the previous century, we must clearly reckon with an occupational group of around 100 professional teachers, constantly in flux but kept vaguely aware of an identity by mutual interests and rivalries.[4]

The history of the Venetian public lectureships begins during the first decade of the fifteenth century, when a school of logic and natural philosophy was established near the Rialto as a result of bequests by Tomaso Talenti, one of Petrarch's opponents in the celebrated humanistic dialogue *De sua ipsius et multorum ignorantia*. Somewhat surprisingly, in view of his contribution to Aristotelianism, Aldus appears to have had few connections with this foundation. Perhaps its sternly traditional approach was hostile to his humanist convictions. But it will be sufficient to say that the school was almost immediately successful, and gained such prestige that from 1455 it was constantly in the charge of a Venetian patrician.[5]

Education in the humanities had a later and more difficult start. During the 1440s a broad movement developed to improve the standard of secretarial work in the ducal Chancellery by training young men specially, and in 1446 the Senate decided to hire a school-master, provide lodgings for him near San Marco, and give him the task of instructing sixteen non-noble youths of good character in grammar and rhetoric. But there were the usual delays, disputes and unlucky deaths. It was not until 1466 that the School of San Marco began to realise its potential under the firm guidance of Benedetto Brugnolo, a Veronese pupil of Ognibene da Lonigo who had already served as assistant master and was to hold the headship with the greatest credit until he died in 1502, universally lamented and aged over ninety. In 1460 the Senate determined to complement the work of the School by founding a lectureship in poetry and rhetoric, and produced very similar results. Gianmario Filelfo and George of Trebizond came and left, grumbling, within five years. But the erudite and irascible Giorgio Merula, whose ambiguous relationship with the early presses has already been mentioned, stayed from 1465 until 1482, achieving results which persuaded the Senate to make two appointments rather than one when he left for Milan. The work of Giorgio Valla and Marcantonio Sabellico continued until the end of the century, in Sabellico's case beyond it. With two public lecturers backed by a highly competent and respected grammar-school master, the last fifteen years of the Quattrocento were something of a golden age for Venetian public education.[6]

But as with many Venetian institutions it is far easier to follow the ripples of activity on the surface than the stronger currents below. How, precisely, were the lectureships linked to the school and how were both linked to the Chancellery? What was the range of the curriculum? How widely were the effects felt in Venetian society? Gianmaria Filelfo's appointment in 1460 left the scope of the lectureship virtually unrestricted, obliging him only to deliver "two appropriate lectures daily, one in poetry, the other in rhetoric or history" for the benefit of "our nobles, their sons, and the sons of our citizens".[7] Early documents on the Chancellery school concentrate entirely on the sixteen trainee secretaries. But it is completely clear that the school took in a far greater number and variety of pupils, and also that the apparently unlimited lecture audiences soon acquired a rather clublike quality. Men who never entered the Venetian government service appear to have been Brugnolo's pupils. They included patrician intellectuals like Zuane Querini, Daniel Renier, or Zuane Bembo, and scholars from the mainland cities such as Raphael Regius and Domizio Calderini of Verona, who later lectured to Aldus in Rome. We have no figures: but one of the orators at Brugnolo's funeral revealed that his revered headmaster had first gained experience as one of two "hypodidascali", or assistant masters, working under Giampietro of Lucca during the early and relatively difficult days after the school's foundation. More than half a century later John Colet was to think the high master, his assistant, and a chaplain perfectly sufficient to deal with the 153 boys of his foundation at St Paul's.[8] At the other end of the scale, the daily lectures by the Campanile might seem on the face of it a slightly comic free-for-all, a kind of academic sideshow competing for attention with the hucksters and strolling-players who thronged the Piazza San Marco. But the audiences had a definite identity and esprit de corps. Men spoke of themselves as pupils of Valla or Sabellico. Andrea Mocenigo, a precocious exponent of old-school loyalties, addressed a valedictory poem to Sabellico and received the thanks of both his schoolfellows and his teacher, who gave them all the significant title of "the Academy".[9]

The success of the grammar-school and the lectureships depended on the quality and initiative of the individuals. But it is perfectly clear that from the mid-1480s Venice possessed three individuals who could command the attention of a considerable number and variety of men, while radiating a definite cultural influence in society. Brugnolo as grammar-school teacher was thoroughly qualified to prepare the ground for the lecturers. Devoted to the business of teaching rather than to philological research or controversy, he contented himself with editing or correcting other mens' work. But his scholarship gained the respect of Poliziano, and his pupils record that he taught poetry, rhetoric and moral philosophy in both the ancient languages, with a liberal approach which pointed out but did not remove passages whose pagan background made them suspect. More important still, his personality carried a formidable impact, sufficient to affect the conduct of his pupils.[10]

Sabellico, the second of the two lecturers to be appointed and the speaker during the less important afternoon period, was also the less important contributor to that more rarefied philological scholarship with which this study is principally concerned. Roman-born and educated, he belonged to the purely Latin school of Pomponio Leto, and his tendency to publish racey dialogues or popular accounts of local scenery and antiquities brought him, even before his arrival in Venice, a reputation for sensationalism which he never lived down thereafter. Bilingual scholars such as Ermolao Barbaro and Giambattista Egnazio plainly thought him superficial, and Egnazio said so. Sabellico's correspondence does not suggest that his lectures extended beyond the normal range of Latin prose and poetry, and his publications in this field – some notes on Pliny the Elder, emendations to the text of Valerius Maximus, and a paraphrase of Suetonius' *Lives of the Caesars* – also show a keen eye for the topical and saleable. The term "journalist" would be an anachronism: but it roughly conveys the reputation he enjoyed in his own time.[11]

Giorgio Valla was a man of wholly different stamp: more self-effacing than Sabellico, less forceful than Brugnolo, he left few traces of an activity which affected Venetian cultural life profoundly and perhaps contributed more than any other factor to the intellectual side of Aldus' achievement. Having studied Greek under Constantine Lascaris in Milan and been brought to Venice through the influence of Ermolao Barbaro, Valla was the perfect mouthpiece for that expertise in both Greek and Latin which Barbaro personified and Aldus strove to emulate. The range of his teaching and editorship was vast. He left commentaries on Juvenal, various works of Cicero, Pliny and Ptolemy: Latin translations of Aristotle's *Magna Moralia* and *Poetics,* and of a large variety of later Greek scientific and medical writers; and a massive compilation of views on scientific and mathematical subjects entitled *De expetendis et fugiendis rebus,* which was eagerly awaited at the time and eventually published by Aldus in 1501.[12] His correspondence shows that he lectured on Vitruvius, Archimedes, and the history of Greek poetry:[13] and his manuscripts of Dioscurides, Theocritus and Sophocles are annotated in a manner which leaves little doubt that they were used for teaching purposes.[14] Valla's collection of Greek texts, which survives almost intact in the library of Modena, must have been as important and significant as his teaching, for the manuscripts show that he gathered a loose circle of Greek scribes who enabled him both to expand his own collection and become, in his turn, a focus for the further diffusion of literary material and Greek works in particular. Some of his associates can be identified: Michael Suliardes of Argos copied and signed two commentaries on Ptolemy in 1490 and the poems of Theognis in 1492.[15] A more surprising name is that of Nicholas Vlastos, the highly placed Cretan whom we have already met as financial supporter of the Callierges press in 1499 but who was active twelve years earlier, when he helped Valla and at least two other scribes to copy a manuscript of medical writings.[16] Most of the men are simply script-forms in the surviving manuscripts, and presumably hands to satisfy the numerous requests which were addressed to the compliant Valla. It is well known that Janus Lascaris inspected his library carefully during his long quest for rare Greek texts in 1491, and that Poliziano was fascinated by his manuscripts of Heron and Archimedes.[17] But many other scholars sought his help. Pico and Alberto Pio both sent requests for specific copies. Antiquario, the Milanese secretary, was in constant touch. Constantine Lascaris asked for transcripts of several Greek mathematical writers. Soon after his arrival in Venice Aldus was asked by his friend Niccolo Leoniceno of Ferrara to arrange for some of Valla's books to be copied, and it is clear that Valla's circle provided Aldus both with his entrée to Venetian intellectual society and with the nucleus of what would, in its time, become a following of his own.[18]

But before tracing this process in detail we must say something of the less exalted and lesser known echelons of Venetian education. As has been said, the publicly employed teachers were privileged men with assured positions and a guaranteed salary of 150 ducats per year. But they did not teach a different type of pupil, or indeed live a life which was fundamentally different from that of their less fortunate colleagues. The whole of Venetian education at this period shows a fluidity which is surprising in an hierarchical society and almost incomprehensible to a later age which regards educational advantage as one of the first prizes which money and social position will seek. Two of the best known and apparently most successful free-lance teachers were Fra Urbano Valeriani and Giambattista Egnazio, both of them pupils of Brugnolo. The ease with which they were able to set up their own schools provides some sign of the demand for instruction: Egnazio was barely into his twenties when he began to attract his own group of students, but he attracted so many that Sabellico himself felt threatened and there was a growling exchange of scholarly insults which the audience seems rather to have enjoyed. It was Egnazio's schoolfellow Zuane Bembo who arranged for the publication of both versions in a single volume. This particular incident ended in a touching death-bed reconciliation, and, since Egnazio was no ordinary man, we cannot draw any conclusions from it about the status of the great majority of teachers.[19] But the story does serve to show that the public lecturers enjoyed no special immunities, and formed only the pinnacle of a wider intellectual world in which they might have to compete for attention with the rest.

Sanudo wrote of "teachers in the parishes and in the palaces of the nobles", but it is fairly clear that the distinction was logical rather than real. A number of possible combinations are revealed in the sixteenth-century profession of Faith: some class-conscious individuals allotted part of the day to noble pupils, the remainder to their inferiors; others were allowed to take a dozen or so extra children into the palace class-room as companions for their young charges; many simply opened their own doors to such nobles as cared to come along with the others. A century earlier the situation was probably even less clearly defined. This is certainly suggested by the list of creditors drawn up in 1442 for Vittore Bonapace, whose pupils included the sons of a boatman and a bricklayer as well as two young members of Venice's older noble families.[20] Here again, the degree of social fluidity is startling. Conditions were obviously less secure than those of the public lecturers, but since the normal fees during the fifteenth century ranged from two to four ducats per child for a year's schooling, the master who could gather twenty to thirty pupils could hope to make a reasonable living.[21]

How many patrician families employed a tutor exclusively for their own children is not clear, but it does appear that this was becoming a symbol of prestige, cultivated mainly by those of financial and political influence. Among the most powerful families in Venice at this period were the Corner, whose members included the titular Queen of Cyprus and her brother Zorzi, one of the most widely employed and respected statesmen in the Republic. Zorzi had a history of connections with scholars of an earlier generation such as George of Trebizond and Merula, so when it became known in 1484 that he was seeking a tutor for his sons, the post was eagerly sought. Ermolao Barbaro and Gerolamo Donato were asked to intercede. Bartolomeo Merula, the successful candidate, gained a certain status in Venetian intellectual society, editing a number of Latin texts for the press of Tacuinus during the 1490s and 1500s. When his main charge, Marco Corner, was given a cardinalcy in 1500, Bartolomeo simply became his secretary instead of his tutor and was in due course rewarded for his services by the appointment of apostolic protonotary. Of all his contemporaries in Venice, he is perhaps the man who bears the closest resemblance to the court-humanists of the mainland.[22]

But his case seems to have been exceptional. As a rule, appointments were very short-lived, and carried no guarantee of future favours. Leonardo Loredan, member of a family hardly less illustrious than the Corner and a future doge, brought the Trevisan poet-laureate Francesco di Rolandello to Venice as his sons' tutor in 1478, but retained his services for only about a year.[23] Cardinal Domenico Grimani, son of the doge who would succeed Loredan, employed a whole series of private teachers for his nephew Marin, including Gerolamo Aleander and Aldus' friend Scipio Fortiguerra. He also tried to tempt Erasmus.[24] Short-term, almost informal engagements of this type appear to have been the rule, and they also appear to have been relatively easy to come by: within a single year Aleander's diary records his holding a Latin class for a group of young patricians and receiving offers from two older men.[25]

But the hand-to-mouth existence was not an enviable one. "Poverty forced me to become a slave to noblemen", wrote Fra Urbano's nephew Giampietro Valeriani, who ran through his money in a few months, took to teaching as a last resort, and wrote with the bitterness of a Roman satirist of coughing his way up the backstairs of rich mens' houses. The loss of independence was oppressive, and there was no security to compensate.[26] Those who found their pupils with a genuine literary interest were probably the lucky few. "The boy is a little savage:...he is coming to you to have it knocked out of him", Barbaro warned a prospective tutor of one of his Vendramin cousins.[27] Grinding Latin grammar into a young oaf whose social position could only encourage indiscipline must indeed have been a dreadful way of earning a living.

Possibly the most striking point about this whole picture is the perpetual ebb and flow of personalities, the absence of fixed points, and the readiness of intellectual activity to gather round any focus that emerged. The School of San Marco was of course the most important nucleus, but even it, as we have seen and shall see again, had varied fortunes. Change and instability began at the highest level of society: patrician intellectuals who could have, and did become centres of scholarly activity were kept so busy on foreign embassies that their work was frequently interrupted, and in 1490 Gerolamo Donato drew a significant comparison between his own distractions and the concentrated research which his friend Poliziano could pursue: "Public and private business so tie me down that I do not study so much as steal a few moments. I congratulate you on the time you can devote to the finest arts and letters."[28]

We know too little at present about the cultural attitudes of the leading noble families to be able to tell whether this situation was deliberately planned in some way, or whether it developed naturally out of the social structure of the Republic. But it is only fair to say that the fluidity and instability had a credit, as well as a debit-side. The involvement of patricians on every level of intellectual life as pupils or employers, students or sponsors, no doubt dispersed effort which might have been concentrated, and perhaps stifled discussion which might have become challenging.[29] It also provided an enormous range of opportunities for intellectuals to seek various kinds of employment, for interested groups to cluster round a sympathetic gentleman, and for ideas to pass easily up and down the different ranks of society represented or sideways between many different groups. Fra Urbano's wanderings through the Near East seem to have been made possible by his position as private secretary to the future doge Andrea Gritti, who was then a corn-merchant in Constantinople.[30] Lorenzo Loredan, the pupil of Rolandello and son of the doge Leonardo, became an habitual member of Giorgio Valla's audiences. He clearly used the lecturer as a means of exerting leverage on his fellow-nobles during a career which earned him an ugly reputation as a manipulator: this, in itself, is an interesting comment on the indirect influence which a man like Valla might wield.[31] But meantime Loredan absorbed enough interest to commission a superb manuscript of Pindar's *Odes* from John Rhosos in 1487.[32]

Venetian patronage had many sides: it could also take many directions. Valla and Sabellico seem always to have sent five or six copies of a new work to different interested parties, and the letter of thanks which Valla received from Pietro Barozzi for his translation of Euclid might serve as a model of that discreet and informed persuasion which writers on patronage have often idealised but rarely pinpointed. The Bishop of Padua thanked Valla politely, and hoped that he would soon have time to read Euclid more carefully: he then enquired whether the translator had thought of turning his attention to Archimedes' works on geometry and on bodies floating in water "which would be extremely useful to men in their everyday life if they were available in Latin".[33] Even the diplomatic missions of which Donato complained had their uses: Bernardo Bembo's travels gave him opportunities to assemble one of the century's most important collections of bibliographically useful, rather than ostentatious, manuscripts, which in due course became available for study by scholars such as Poliziano and Aldus.[34] Whatever its faults, Venetian "free enterprise" did provide some kind of framework up which a vigorous intellectual and cultural life could grow on its own.

Of the nature of that life we are very imperfectly informed, and it is only possible to reconstruct it by a kind of romantic involvement in the enthusiasms of the time. As a starting-point we should remind ourselves of the strongly personal nature of all medieval teaching and the importance of the spoken word. Latin and Greek were still living languages, and much attention was paid to their correct pronunciation. Everything centred around a dialogue: the master read aloud from a text, the students recited what they had learned back to him, and a number of Valla's manuscripts still bear traces of this intoning of principal parts and explanation of difficult words. Then, from 1470, the flow of printed texts began, and from 1480 the flow became a torrent. By 1493 Raphael Regius, one of the most esteemed classical scholars at the university of Padua, could declare that any student who had passed beyond the earliest stages might now buy his own copy and jot down his own notes. Ultimately, this invasion by the mass-produced book would demolish the entire structure of group-learning by undermining the dependence of scholars upon each other and beckoning them away, as individuals, to a well equipped study.[35] But for a while the printed text was a fascinating new toy. It encouraged its owners to enquire, compare and discuss, whirling the enthusiasm of the groups into a fierce spiral of intellectual energy which the teachers did not need to command and seem to have been unable to control. Sabellico's emendations to Pliny were being broadcast and discussed by his students long before he published them.[36] And when

Valla was asked by Antiquario when his edition of Vitruvius was appearing, he had to reply that he had no idea: he had plans to publish when his lectures were finished, but some of his students had been taking such careful notes that, for all he knew, the text might appear complete with commentary at almost any moment.[37] Obviously, evidence like this is subjective, piecemeal, and difficult to assess precisely: but when we combine it with the anxieties of men like Filippo di Strata, and the constant complaints about the rush to print, we seem to be in the presence of an almost uncontrollable burst of enthusiasm for the world of classical antiquity.

Such excitement could not be kept within the formal bounds of school and lecture-room: of its own accord, it frothed over into the wider social world beyond, and an interest in the ancient world soon became a mark of fashion as well as a badge of intellect. High Renaissance Venice was rich in clubs and associations, from the glamorous patrician clubs, with their jewelled costumes of parti-coloured velvet and their water-born banquets on the Grand Canal, down through sober gatherings of lawyers to open-ended groups of friends like the fifty-nine "good and learned men" whom Zuane Bembo listed at the end of his collection of ancient inscriptions.[38] As we have seen, such informal groups could easily focus on a popular teacher or an influential patrician. So a lecture might continue as a heated argument under the portico of the Ducal Palace, like that described by Sabellico in *De Latinae Linguae Reparatione*: as a languid afternoon reading Quintus Curtius in the Corners' formal garden;[39] or as a visit to the bewitching poetess Cassandra Fedele, whose recitations formed the centre-piece of doge Barbarigo's public banquets, and whose very appearance reduced Poliziano to stammering helplessness.[40]

Many of the topics of conversation, which are fairly well known to us from correspondence or dialogues, now seem restricted and arid: the precise words in which the elder Pliny described King Mithridates' antidote against all known poisons no longer poses a question of pressing medical importance. But we cannot afford to forget that a knowledge of classical literature underlay every area of academic specialisation, that the boundaries of ancient literature had expanded prodigiously over the previous century, and that the Greek and Roman authors could command the hearts, as well as the heads, of their disciples. An interest in the ancient botanical writers could easily become an experimental interest in botany, as happened in the cases of Ermolao Barbaro and Andrea Navagero.[41] Mathematics might mean a study of Euclid and Archimedes, or gazing at the stars through a clear summer sky in the hills above Verona, with copies of Aratus and Virgil to hand.[42] Literary experiments of various kinds were extremely popular, and here judgement becomes most hazardous because the range of choice was so wide. One young poet named Lydus Cattus dramatised a lovers' quarrel as a legal hearing, which he then set out in an agonising pastiche of Latin and Italian, hexameters, elegiacs and terza rima. He dedicated it to Vicenzo Querini, whose interests also turned towards poetry and the directions it should take. But Querini and his friends Paolo da Canal, Nicolo Tiepolo, and Andrea Navagero experimented with Petrarchan forms, collaborated in the preliminary stages of Bembo's *Prose della volgar lingua*, and so played a direct part in settling the subsequent development of the Italian language.[43]

Beyond Venice itself lay the academic empyrean of Padua. The story of the university's steady progress during the fifteenth century is still known only in general outline, and we shall in any case be concerned less with formal academic affairs than with the social life which developed round their edges.[44] From the moment in 1407 when the Venetian government obliged its subjects to pursue their studies at Padua unless they intended to go to one of the Northern universities, interest appears to have built up gradually. Many noblemen took degrees: many more went simply to savour the atmosphere. By the end of the century Sanudo's diary describes numerous invasions of friends and relatives from Venice to celebrate the award of a doctorate with days of feasting, and a local proverb foretold that the ferry which plied daily up and down the Brenta would sink if it did not carry a monk, a whore, and a student: so close had connections between the university and the metropolis become.[45] Each autumn the Northern visitors poured down from the other direction: numerous Germans, whom the Republic favoured as its best customers and who still lacked really prestigious universities of their own; but also Poles, Hungarians, Englishmen and others.[46] The aim of the wealthy student was to

"Keep house and ply his book, welcome his friends,
Visit his countrymen, and banquet them".[47]

Poorer scholars had to rely on patronage. But since the Northerners sometimes rented entire palaces to house personal followings of twenty or thirty, and the Venetian nobles regularly brought their own tutor/servants, there was a variety of opportunities. Aleander and Giampietro

Valeriani both went to Padua as personal attendants to young noblemen whom they had already taught and served in Venice.[48] No doubt the poor student's life had its grim side, but on the whole contemporary descriptions of Renaissance Padua reflect the kind of yearning nostalgia for a world of sophisticated calm which one associates with the romantic novels of a later age. Ermolao Barbaro gave an hour-by-hour account of his routine during an interval of academic repose in summer, 1484. The morning was spent in intensive study of Aristotle and the Greek orators or poets: then came a light lunch of broth, eggs and fruit; afterwards, more relaxed reading or dictation, followed by conversation with any friends who cared to call for a literary or philosophical discussion; finally, a supper of roast game, a stroll in his botanical garden to ponder the herbal lore of Dioscurides, and so to bed.[49] Against such a background texts, coins, and inscriptions could be examined, poems or speeches recited and criticised as easily as in the Venetian circles, and by many of the same men: indeed it is often difficult to say which society was an extension of which, for the foreign visitors joined in wherever they could, eager to make their mark on these cultured Italians by offering something of their own experience. Constantly in search of some new focus, the circles whirled and regrouped like the spindles of conversation at a Tolstoyan soirée.

This, then, was the world to which Aldus came in 1490 and he fitted into it with the effortless grace of one who knows something of his worth, is equipped with impeccable introductions, and has a rare facility for avoiding enmity. Whether or not he knew Giorgio Valla already, it is in Valla's circle that he first appears. During the summer of 1491 Leoniceno mentioned Aldus to Valla twice as a man to whom manuscripts might be passed for copying, and though in this case he seems to have been acting on behalf of Leoniceno and Poliziano, it is hard to believe that he did not turn the resources of Valla's library and the skills of his Greek scribes to some future use.[50] Poliziano definitely appreciated his help. The name "Alto Manuccio" is scrawled in the margin of his notebook alongside those of the procurators Alvise Barbaro and Leonardo Loredan: of Antonio Pizzamano, the friend of Domenico Grimani who would later organise the purchase of Pico's library; and of the two young nobles Pietro Bembo and Angelo Gabriel, pupils of Valla who would shortly depart to study Greek with Constantine Lascaris in Messina, and bring back with them the manuscript-copy for Aldus' first publication.[51] Slightly more than a year later Aldus was asked by the Hellenist Codrus Urceus to pass on his greetings to Sabellico, Raphael Regius, and the patrician Daniel Renier. Codrus mentioned discussion of certain joint plans which linked him to both Aldus and Leoniceno: he explained that his Greek scribe was otherwise engaged, and that there would be some delay before the Greek manuscripts required could be sent to Aldus; and he gave some useful advice on a difficult line of Theocritus. Aldus was now completely accepted in Venetian academic society, and stood very close to the centre of its network.[52]

It is unfortunate that we do not know the exact connection between the "entire year" of teaching that Santo Barbarigo received from Aldus, and the printing-contract which father and tutor signed in 1495: but the general sequence of events is clear enough. With the aid of his contacts and the discreet self-advertisement of the *Epistola ad Catherinam Piam,* Aldus was able to establish himself very quickly in the large group of free-lance teachers who kept their own premises and took in an assortment of pupils. His work left time for scholarly pursuits: and, whether the teaching or the printing contract with Barbarigo came first, he was evidently able to take advantage of that opportunist Venetian patronage which, as one of its critics acidly remarked, made learning into a business commodity not basically different from a sack of pepper.[53]

When Aldus' workshop went into production, it seems to have inherited its tone more from the humanist background of its manager than from predecessors or contemporaries in the world of printing. Producing a clear judgement on such an emotive and intangible issue is naturally difficult: and Aldus may have distorted our vision in the carefully devised introductions which he added to almost all of his editions, and in which stress was always laid on the care and collaboration that had gone into the text. Previously, the introduction had been a matter for the academic editor: the printer was lucky to receive more than a few words of praise for the singular qualities which separated him from his shoddy and avaricious colleagues. As a result, we know virtually nothing about the personal relationships between Jenson and Torresani on the one hand, Merula, Sabellico, Squarciafico and many more on the other.[54] But the mere fact that Aldus made the change suggests a new approach. The discussion of the correct order of Aristotle's works, or the collation of manuscripts in Padua and Ferrara, are plainly activities which derived immediately from the philological work of Valla's scribal circle. The close coincidence of the earlier Aldine editions with contemporary academic tastes is hardly surprising, and it is also noticeable that many of the printer's first editors and contributors – Bembo and Gabriel, Leoniceno and Alessandro Benedetti – were associates or pupils of Giorgio Valla.[55] But the situation was changing, and there is perhaps some sign of what was happening in William Latimer's desperate appeal for the return of his borrowed bed:[56] Aldus' house in Sant'Agostino was becoming a place where scholars came not only to leave corrected proofs, but to eat, sleep and talk. In other words, it was becoming an intellectual centre in its own right.

The stages by which this process was accomplished are so subtle and delicate that they cannot be completely unravelled now. The decisive year was almost certainly 1502, but the four or five which preceded were hardly less important, and from 1495 on the fortunes of Aldus and his associates become so thoroughly entangled with the greater events of the period that they can only be explained against a European background. The underlying fact is that, even as Aldus was organising his company and publishing his earliest editions, the foundations of the intellectual world that had produced him were crumbling. One of his idols, Ermolao Barbaro, died in exile during the summer of 1493. Pico della Mirandola, the "phoenix among men" and Aldus' first patron, passed away as the French armies tramped into Florence on 17 November 1494. Poliziano had gone the same way barely two months before. Ficino, as we have seen, survived long enough to cast an eye over the Aldine text of some of his translations, but his single letter to the printer is haunted by references to ill-health, famine, and books scattered abroad in a city to which he dared not return for fear of plague and violence.[57] The exile of the Medici and the dispersal of their court-circle were now accomplished facts, and Ficino's letter sounds the death-knell over an epoch of Florentine culture. Other centres had been as severely stricken. In 1495 the French had swept away the Aragonese kingdom of Naples: the royal library was carried off as plunder, only to be plundered again on the battlefield of Fornovo, then yet again by various individuals when it reached France.[58] In 1498 Rome lost Pomponio Leto, for whose make-believe imitations of Cincinnatus Aldus had little sympathy, but who had dominated Roman intellectual life for a generation.[59] The library of the dukes of Milan was carried off to Blois by the French conquerors in 1499: and in 1502 the famous collection of the Montefeltro dukes of Urbino was looted by the troops of Cesare Borgia.[60] It is not surprising that Aldus' prefaces are full of flames, war, the loss of friends and the destruction of books: not only scholars, but entire cultural centres were being swept away.[61]

It is true that Venice escaped foreign occupation and political upheaval, becoming something of a haven for scholarly and even princely exiles. But she did not escape as completely from the general misfortunes as her historians have often assumed. We have already seen how the expenses of war sparked the commerical crisis of 1499, and how that crisis affected the printing industry:[62] at the same time the triumvirate of public teachers which had enriched Venetian intellectual life at so many points during the previous fifteen years, began to break down. During the spring of 1496 the Council of Ten became alarmed about a leakage of information to Milan, and instructed one of its secret agents to enquire among the schools for a certain "Placidio", and approach him with a pretended offer of employment as a nobleman's tutor. The trail led to Placidio Amerino, a pupil and close friend of Giorgio Valla. Both were immediately arrested. No case was brought against Valla since the evidence against him was not thought conclusive, and he was held in custody for only a few months: but his editorial work and teaching were badly interrupted, and it seems probable that his health and prestige also suffered. His correspondence dwindles, and he died in early 1500.[63]

Though the loss of Valla was in itself a severe blow to Greek studies in Venice, the chaos which followed it may well have done more damage and certainly had a greater effect on the fears and ambitions of Aldus' friends. Sabellico was naturally elevated to the senior public lectureship. There remained the question of the vacant post, and as Giambattista Scita, Raphael Regius, Demetrius Chalcondylas and Constantine Lascaris were named as possible candidates, the atmosphere became sticky with an intrigue which illustrates more clearly than any rhetoric the influence which these public lectureships exercised in Venetian society. Aldus' old friend Scita was appointed in March, but apparently failed to keep his audiences content and was sacked after barely a month.[64] Next came Gregorio Amaseo, who managed to survive for three years: but he had the disadvantage of being another Latinist, and the slightly shabby quality of his appointment brought rivals such as Regius into his lectures to shout down every point he made.[65] Finally, his election was declared out of order because there had been no proper advertisement of the post or competition for it, and yet another candidate was produced in Gerolamo Calbero of Forli, whose recent services on an embassy in Hungary gave him some political leverage. A competition was staged: no contestant appeared; and Calbero was declared elected. But he, too, seems to have been a bird of passage.[66] Some kind of stability returned in 1504 when Gerolamo Donato hectored the Senate into appointing Leonicus Tomaeus, the Paduan Hellenist, after a contest with Musurus,[67] but in the meantime Benedetto Brugnolo had died and Sabellico was sinking into a last illness which prevented him from lecturing.[68] No successors were appointed. Public instruction in the humanities had suffered a series of bad blows.

Throughout Italy, scholars reacted to the changing times in the only possible ways: by regrouping wherever they could, and often by endeavouring to close their ranks with the help of some half-formal organisation. In Naples, the statesman Giangioviano Pontano gathered the relics of Panormita's old circle around him, read his poems to them, and apparently composed a statute as well as a formal ceremony of admission to his "Academia Pontoniana".[69] In Rome interest began to centre on a wealthy young dilettante named Angelo Colocci who seems already to have had some acquaintance with the Neapolitan circle, bought his way into papal service in 1497, and in due course also bought Leto's villa on the Quirinal. He cut a wide swathe across Italian cultural life during the next three decades, and we shall meet him again.[70] In Venice, Aldus became the natural rallying-point. Probably in its early stages the process was wholly spontaneous: interested noblemen such as Marin Sanudo called in at the print-shop in Sant'Agostino to find how plans were proceeding; foreign visitors like Linacre made their ways home and spoke to their friends, who in their turn wrote respectfully, as did William Grocyn and Conrad Celtis, or came to present their greetings personally, as Reuchlin did in the summer of 1498.[71] Greek expatriates unhesitatingly used Aldus' workshop as a mail-box.[72] And the collapse of the Callierges/Vlastos organisation, following immediately on the death of Valla, left Aldus as the main hope of a Venetian Hellenism which seemed threatened on every side.

But the dreams which would lead to a regrouping were already in the air. Some of Aldus' earliest collaborators – Fortiguerra, Arsenios Apostolios and Marcus Musurus – had worked in Florence under Chalcondylas or Poliziano and known something of Ficino's circle.[73] Alberto Pio's ambitions knew no bounds. Shortly before his house in Carpi was sacked by a howling mob of his cousin's partisans, he was promising to establish Aldus in his principality as chief of "an Academy where barbarism would be left behind, and sound literature and sciences studied".[74] We have positive proof that these dreams had taken some more solid form in Venice by the late summer of 1502: in August, the first edition of Sophocles was published with the colophon "Venetiis in Aldi Romani Academia", and in November the ducal letter of Leonardo Loredan mentioned among Aldus' other services to literature the fact that "he now even has a New Academy". These references are in their turn explained by a single surviving sheet, now in the binding of a volume in the Vatican library and bearing at the head of its Greek text the imposing title ΝΕΑΚΑΔΗΜΙΑΣ ΝΟΜΟΣ – the Statute of the New Academy.[75]

This document has been published on a number of occasions, translated, and discussed with every degree of exaggeration and understatement: but we are still very far from understanding it, for the words plainly say much less than they mean. Read at its face-value, and aligned with what we know of similar and contemporary associations, the forty-nine line statute appears almost entirely devoid of significance, or indeed of anything except enthusiasm. Seven names are mentioned: those of Aldus himself, who is called the "leader"; of Fortiguerra, who appears to have drafted the document; of a certain "John the Cretan", who may be either Rhosos or Gregoropoulos; then those of Baptista Egnazio, Paolo da Canal, Hironimo Menochio, and Francesco Rosetto. The signatories bind themselves to speak only in Greek when in one another's company, to pay a small fine if they lapse, and to collect the fines until they are sufficient to finance an "Academicians' banquet". There are some generally worded clauses on admitting other "philhellenes", or visitors who may wish to learn the language, and the statute closes with an oblique reference to "many others who are longing to learn and eager for a New Academy". But there is no hint of how members might qualify, or of what form the instruction would take.[76] In early 1498 the lawyers of Udine submitted to the Venetian Senate a statute which covers six full folios in the register, giving details of qualification, election, subscriptions, the conduct expected of members, and the procedure for a wide range of social activities. The academies of Leto and Pontano apparently possessed statutes, which have not survived. But contemporaries write of the ceremonial acceptance of a new member after he has proved his worth by a formal recitation: he is crowned with laurel; he is given a new, Latinised name, which is then inscribed in the register of the academy; then the company adjourns to a banquet, during which odes are sung in honour of the new academician.[77] Aldus' association, with its fussy preoccupation with Greek accents and its parties financed from a sort of swear-box, sounds a rather shabby and makeshift affair in comparison.

To put the statute in its true perspective we must first remember the crucial importance of the spoken word in contemporary language teaching: what seems frivolous and pedantic now was vital to the plans of a company which, as we have seen, consisted largely of professional teachers and their more interested students. Next, though the plans as they are recorded are those of teachers and involve only the teaching of Greek, it is fairly clear that the activities of the group came to include a good deal more than the conversation of which the statute speaks. We catch occasional glimpses of meetings, with the academicians sitting in tense conversation round the fire: there is a lecture on a Greek grammarian, an examination of some Latin text, or a simple discussion of the intellectual life of the times.[78] Very probably the recitation of speeches and poems of which we hear in the academies of Pontano and Colocci, also played some part in the Aldine circle.[79] Its bias may have been more philological, and it must certainly have been a useful forum for the preparation of work for the press: but there is no reason in the statute or elsewhere for believing that the activities of the academy were restricted by those of the print-shop.

Such descriptions as we have of the Aldine circle suggest that it hardly differed from the loosely organised groups of friends which we have already seen clustering round an influential figure in Venice or Padua. Indeed we know from a poem of Giampietro Valeriani that at least five of Aldus' closest associates belonged to some kind of poetic sodality in Padua during the early years of the sixteenth century,[80] and the printer himself was plainly accepted in the university's highest society. In 1502 Aldus dedicated his edition of Valerius Maximus to John Lubranski, whose virtues he had first realised at Padua

...when I was sitting in a group in your lodgings...along with our friend Raphael Regius, a man full of learning and integrity, and a few others: you promised, whatever the cost, to send and search for books in the land of the Dacians, where men say there is a tower full of ancient books.[81]

Lubranski was Bishop of Poznań, councillor to the King of Poland. The discussions of the Aldine Academy were probably as many-sided as those of the mercurial groups from which it had sprung. But the existence of a statute, and the very sound of the word "Academy", with its magical echoes of Platonic Athens, do seem to have generated a new sense of excitement and purpose. A Venetian noble, Bernardo Zorzi, wrote anxiously to Fortiguerra of the Academy's health: an imperial bishop's secretary swore an oath "by our New Academy"; a Cistercian, Henry Urbanus, wrote from Erfurt imploring Aldus to accept him among "the swarm of your friends".[82] Whatever its puzzling qualities, we must face the fact that this statute was meant seriously and taken seriously. We must also recall that, unlike any of its predecessors or contemporaries, it was circulated in print.

There is a strong possibility that the statute was designed to advertise as well as organise, and that this may explain both its vague format and its publication. As we have seen, Aldus' editorial activity reached its zenith between 1502 and 1504: but the loss of Valla and Brugnolo meant that there was no longer a Hellenist among the public lecturers to provide discreet publicity for new works.[83] Remembering the strongly didactic bias of the statute, and the turbulent state of the School of San Marco during these years, it is hard to resist the view that Aldus and his associates were trying to keep the claims of Greek scholarship in the public eye, and the idea gains strength when we find that Fortiguerra, who drafted the statute, was also one of those who hoped to secure the disputed lectureship.[84] If publicity was one of the aims, then the evidence suggests that this aim was achieved. We know that the edition of Demosthenes which appeared in November 1504 had been preceded by a series of lectures delivered by Fortiguerra.[85] During January the same scholar had pronounced a rousing *Oratio de laudibus literarum Graecarum*, in which he laid due stress on Aldus' services to humanity in providing more sound texts than had been available at any time since the fall of the Roman Empire.[86] At the same time foreigners were being taught Greek, as the statute had promised. The German Dominican and friend of Reuchlin, John Cuno, lived and studied with Aldus at Sant' Agostino, and the notes which he took from John Gregoropoulos' lectures on Aristophanes survive as proof of his activity.[87] It is very tempting to regard Leonico Tomeo's appointment to the vacant lectureship in December 1504 as the culmination of a campaign mounted by Aldus and his circle. Though there is not the slightest positive evidence for this, the colophon "In Aldi Academia" does vanish at the end of that year. The almost contemporaneous arrival of Lascaris as French ambassador to Venice must have given Greek studies a powerful stimulus from without.[88]

Unfortunately, Aldus' career during the next twelve months presents so complex a pattern that it is foolish to pretend we can understand his motives precisely. The disappearance of the colophon could be due to negative rather than positive factors: the commerical problems noticed in the previous chapter, for instance, or intellectual disagreement between Aldus' associates over the true aims of their Academy. Committed classicists such as Fortiguerra or Cuno seem to have regarded Greek as all-important. But Bembo, his literary companions from Padua, and Aldus himself all had interests both in contemporary Latin literature and in the directions which the still unformed Italian vernacular might take.[89] Perhaps the most important factor was a shift of emphasis: for just as mention of an Academy in Venice was dying away during 1505, more ambitious plans were beginning to take shape elsewhere. The world of the statute was simply swallowed up in a golden vision.

About seven months after his visit to Aldus during the late summer of 1498, John Reuchlin composed a rapid note to his Italian colleague. Since he was referring to a private conversation, Reuchlin had no need to be explicit, but his account of efforts to interest the King of the Romans and others in "your cause" and his conclusion: "Accept the truth in a few words, my Aldus: we are not worthy of you",[90] leave the main issue in little doubt. Even before he and his associates declared their aims in Venice, Aldus had plans to move to the Empire. During the following years these plans were steadily elaborated. In June 1503 Aldus referred in a letter to Conrad Celtis to a scheme which would make Germany "another Athens for the men of our time", and which he had recently set out in detail for a mutual friend, Johan Spiesshammer of Vienna. Infuriatingly, the letter to Spiesshammer has disappeared and though it is obvious that lobbying was being intensified, the plans themselves remain vague. The dedication of Theodorus Gaza's translations from Aristotle to Matthew Lang, a powerful imperial councillor, looks like a calculated gesture by Aldus: and barely two months later, in May 1504, he received a short note from another contact in the imperial chancellory, the secretary John Collauer, who promised to do everything in his power to encourage the interest of both Lang and Maximilian himself.[91] By the end of July Aldus was confident enough to claim imperial citizenship when he approached the ambassador on behalf of his imprisoned servant Federigo da Ceresara.[92] But not until the following August did the direction of all this manoeuvring come into the open. In a short dedication of Pontano's *Urania,* Aldus thanked Collauer "for the support you have given to my plan for founding an Academy, at the court of Maximilian Caesar", and even mentioned personal letters on the subject from Lang and Maximilian. But he had also to admit that nothing definite had been arranged as yet:[93] and there is some suspicion that the dedication itself was an attempt to force the issue, for the negotiations of the next few months have a slightly desperate quality which one connects naturally with the gradual retrenchment of the company. During the autumn John Cuno was dispatched to Germany with letters to Maximilian, Lang, and Collauer, but by early December Aldus was still waiting for a reply, and wrote directly to Collauer in a state of considerable alarm.[94] A fortnight later Cuno reported to Willibald Pirckheimer that Aldus was actually preparing for the move to Germany:[95] but at the end of the following February Jacob Spiegel, secretary to the Bishop of Trieste, was promising Aldus to use his imminent mission to the imperial court as a means of settling a situation that was still unresolved.[96] A month later the printer closed his workshop at Sant'Agostino, made a will, merged his assets with those of his partner Torresani, and set off on a journey for his own purposes. The implication must be that he had now abandoned hope of imperial patronage: and by the end of the year, even the optimistic Cuno was disillusioned.[97]

The crucial letter to Spiesshammer is lost, the dedication to Collauer is expressed in the most general terms, and our only account of Aldus' plans is contained in the letter which Cuno wrote to Pirckheimer on 21 December 1505:

Aldus is preparing to move to Germany, to found a New Academy under the protection of the King of the Romans, in some place determined by him. With him will be various other men, some highly learned in Greek and some in Hebrew, who, while Aldus prints all the best books, will instruct the youth of Germany not only in sound scholarship, but, as Aldus claims, in military skill and exercises, so that those who are well versed in literature may not be proved unwarlike.

This is plainly the language of a scholarly dream-world, and it is not surprising that the mention of Hebrew and military exercises in the same sentence has led some critics to relegate both Cuno's summary and the scheme it describes to a world of humanist fantasy.⁹⁸ But we cannot escape from the problem so easily. Cuno had lived with Aldus for several years, he was acting as his official messenger, and his Latin states explicitly that the plans stemmed from Aldus. The phrase "military exercise" need not be pressed: it probably meant no more than the fencing, dancing and javelin-throwing which had played a part in the educational system of Vittorino da Feltre and derived ultimately from the "music and gymnastics" of Plato's *Republic*.⁹⁹ Hebrew was a new, but growing force in contemporary education. Pico's interest had lent the subject prestige, and probably suggested to Aldus a field of publication which he never exploited successfully but never entirely abandoned.¹⁰⁰ The language had its place in the curricula of the "trilingual colleges" founded by Cardinal Ximenes at Alcala in 1502, at Oxford by Bishop Fox in 1516, and at Louvain by Erasmus' friend Jerome Busleyden in 1517.¹⁰¹

It is not the ideas which Cuno records that are surprising: it is their connection to Aldus. For the association of such advanced educational ideas with the printer suggests that his ambitions ranged far beyond the world of the press and the rather makeshift statute which he and his friends had drafted around 1502. Even allowing for the extravagance of Cuno's language, it is plain that he was not describing an open-ended group of philological enthusiasts, like Aldus' circle in Venice, or a literary society, like Pontano's Academy or the "Sodalitas Danubiana" of Celtis and Spiesshammer, which Aldus will certainly have known by reputation.¹⁰² This was to be an educational institution, with a salaried staff and its own press, relying on royal patronage, not the chances of the market. A number of contemporaries dreamed similar dreams: Ximenes actually realised them at Alcala, where the trilingual college printed the first Bible in Latin, Greek and Hebrew. Celtis came fairly close in 1501, when he persuaded Maximilian to establish a "Poets' College" to provide instruction in literature and mathematics within the Arts Faculty of the University of Vienna. We have no means of knowing if Aldus' plans were connected in any way to those of Celtis: but we do know that Maximilian, on whom the success of both schemes ultimately depended, lacked funds for every project he undertook.¹⁰³

Coming immediately after a year of growing commerical uncertainty, the breakdown of negotiations with the imperial court must have been a severe blow to Aldus and it is not surprising that he suspended business during 1506. By the time of Erasmus' visit in 1508 the very word "academy" had become a household joke: Aldus would utter it in a squeaky, broken voice, hinting that he would be senile if he ever lived to see such an institution.[104] But in fact he never abandoned hope, and the difficulties of his later years seem, if anything, to have given the fleeting ideal an even stronger hold over his mind. Barely a year after the collapse of the German project there are signs that other possibilities were being explored. The evidence is so scarce that it is hard to evaluate precisely, and there is the further problem of guessing how far the various contacts or intermediaries were interested in Aldus' plans, and how far they were pressing their own designs. But Aldus seems to have been ready to explore almost any possibility.

Some of the schemes were obviously unrealistic, and recognised as such at the time. The younger Aldus – not always a very reliable witness – mentioned that his grandfather had once received an advantageous offer from the Prince of Salerno, and a letter of July 1507 from another Neapolitan nobleman, the Duke of Atri, gave the printer a clear invitation. The scholarly traditions of the Neapolitan court were extremely strong. But the kingdom was a battleground, and liable to remain so as long as the Franco-Aragonese dispute over the crown remained an open issue: the Duke of Atri himself had just returned from a long period of captivity in Spanish hands.[105]

Milan suffered from many of the same drawbacks, though Aldus received from this quarter some far more specific proposals, which he seems to have considered seriously. He visited the city during his travels in 1506, received an enthusiastic welcome, and made a great number of friends including the influential secretary Jacopo Antiquario, a correspondent of both Poliziano and Giorgio Valla, the novelist Matteo Bandello, and various members of the French administration such as Jean Grolier and Jeffroy Charles. Some important plans were apparently laid, and one of the participants remembered them with eager concern in June 1511. About the same time Aldus received a letter from Bandello which, though different in detail and much less precise in form, bears some resemblance to Cuno's report of Aldus' plans in 1505. The contacts, Bandello claimed, were now complete: "...we may see in our time an Academy which will be the main means of keeping good Greek and Latin literature alive in Italy...What shall I say of the vernacular tongue?"[106] In a courtly rather than scholarly circle, Hebrew would have to be sacrificed. But when Aldus drew up a new will on 24 August 1511,[107] he was "about to ride to Milan", and it is natural to connect this journey with Bandello's new initiative.

Events soon swept away whatever plans were developed: the following April brought the Pyrrhic victory of Ravenna, and the position of the French conquerors in Italy collapsed so rapidly that by the end of June Milan was even less secure a centre than Naples had been. The other main prospect, Ferrara, was in hardly better case. It will be remembered that Aldus' connections there reached back for more than thirty years, and that when disaster struck Venice in May 1509 he immediately sought refuge in Ferrara. The humanist tradition of the Este court was strong: literary patronage was given a further stimulus by the vivacious and pleasure-loving duchess Lucretia Borgia, who at some time between 1509 and 1512 made Aldus a spontaneous offer to "establish at your own expense and from your own resources the Academy which I have striven to found for so many years – if only the times will allow it".[108] In 1513 the printer thanked his patroness warmly, and sang the praises of that notorious lady's bounty and holiness as loudly as any court humanist. But he knew how many uncertainties were covered by that phrase "if only the times will allow it". Ferrara had joined the League of Cambrai, and inflicted a humiliating reverse on the Venetians during the winter of 1509: but when the Pope shifted alliances during the following year, Ferrara clung to the French cause and was left trapped between the vengeance of a resurgent Venice and the ambition of a Pope who regarded the duchy as a rebellious subject state, and placed it under an interdict.[109]

The times allowed little room for the arts of peace. When Aldus drew up his new will in 1511 he made arrangements for his son to be educated by Giambattista Egnazio, but added "I pray God to grant me the favour of taking this task upon myself, and of bringing into being the Academy which I long to create".[110] The prayer, and the circumstances in which it was made, show both the strength of Aldus' ambitions and the pathetic position in which he found himself.

But one possible centre, the papal court, offered a better chance. The negotiations here cannot be treated as a unity, for they extend over six or seven years, cover two pontificates, and appear frigid and feverish by turns. As early as April 1507 the indefatigable Scipio Fortiguerra was beginning to lobby some of the influential cardinals whose patronage he had enjoyed since leaving Venice in the autumn of 1504, and Aldus may have been assessing the usefulness of these preliminary contacts when he made a hurried journey to meet Erasmus in Siena as the Dutchman travelled north in the late summer of 1509.[111] But attention soon began to focus on Angelo Colocci, by now Procurator of the Sacred Penitentiary and a growing force in Roman cultural life. Though the extent of his own learning remains uncertain, he advanced his reputation as a patron by protecting men of letters who were in difficulty or by sponsoring editions of their works, and by the summer of 1510 Fortiguerra reported to Aldus that he had the "greatest confidence" in Colocci's support.[112] But the web of connections was exceedingly fragile. The letter just mentioned, and another written by Colocci himself in May of the following year, show that this promising patron was no more than another intermediary through whom pressure was being applied to the papal secretary Sigismondo Conti. Also, though Colocci wrote of doing everything he could for Aldus, and of bringing the New Academy to Rome as soon as the court reassembled, he spoke in the same letter of a scheme to establish a Greek press in Rome and mentioned the name of Zacharias Callierges.[113] One wonders how large a part Aldus really had in plans which were soon swept aside by the political events of the winter and the following spring.

The revival of the printing company during the second half of 1512 must certainly be linked to the disappointment of these various hopes and the turbulence of the Italian mainland after the Battle of Ravenna. It will be remembered that, commercially, the company staged a remarkable recovery: Aldus' academic dreams recovered as quickly, and for many of the same reasons. Musurus' presence at the School of San Marco brought back the Greek scholarship, the editorial activity, and the copying of manuscripts which had passed from the institution with the death of Giorgio Valla. But Musurus was only the main feature of an intellectual scene that was beginning to show much of the richness and variety of an earlier age. The architect and antiquarian Fra Giocondo of Verona, who had returned from France in 1504 to become military engineer to the Republic of Venice, brought with him extensive notes on the ancient grammarians, the Roman agricultural writers, and the text of Caesar, all of which became available for discussion and publication.[114] Andrea Navagero, one of the young poets from the Paduan circle, was now temporarily set on the career of a professional scholar: working in the closest collusion with Aldus on the texts of Cicero, Quintilian, Lucretius, Virgil and Ovid, he emerged as one of the ablest Latin editors of his time and, as librarian of the Marciana, played a great part in the re-organisation of the long-neglected manuscripts.[115] Egnazio, meanwhile, had been made a public notary:[116] Fra Urbano was still active. That feeling of co-operation between intellectuals and the press which had produced the ebullience of 1502 was making itself felt once again. The circumstances had of course changed greatly, and Aldus did not bring back the old colophon "ex Academia": but a certain buoyancy appears when, in January 1513, he dedicates a volume to Navagero, and wishes Pindar "to come from our Academy under your name".[117]

Some two months later the bellicose Pope Julius II, whose political ambitions had done much to ruin Aldus' hopes and plunge Europe into war, died and was replaced by the younger and more pacific Leo X. For Aldus, as for many other men of letters, it was a moment full of golden visions. Not only was the new pontiff Giovanni dei Medici, son of Lorenzo the Magnificent, pupil of Poliziano, Ficino, and Fra Urbano: during his exile after the fall of his brother Piero in 1494 he had made a number of friends in Venice, was known to have a particularly high opinion of the patrician ascetic and one-time poet Vicenzo Querini, and almost immediately appointed Pietro Bembo his apostolic secretary.[118] In early August, Bembo was instructed to contact Musurus about the possibility of establishing a Greek College in Rome, and Aldus seems to have felt that his moment had come at last.[119] A month later the first edition of Plato's complete works appeared, and was dedicated to the Pope with one of the most elaborate addresses ever to come from the Aldine press. Musurus' Greek elegiac poem has been considered one of the finest written since the decline of classical civilization: and Aldus' Latin letter is one of the most comprehensive statements of the humanist position to be found outside Erasmus. He reminded the Pope of his past, and the favours his father had shown to Ficino. He pointed to the opportunities which the future might hold for a Christendom at peace with itself, to the part which learning might play in promoting that peace and in extending Christian knowledge among converted infidels and newly discovered peoples: and finally, he asked the Pope for funds to establish the Academy which would create and propagate the necessary learning.[120]

The Pope's reply – or failure to reply – to this eloquent request is a matter of considerable mystery. For the Greek College was founded. Its premises were established in Angelo Colocci's house on the

Quirinal, its organiser was Janus Lascaris, and its first professor Musurus. The institution itself had an educational aim with which Aldus would certainly have sympathised: ten or more young Greek expatriates were to be instructed in both their own language and Latin as a nucleus of teachers from whom the proper pronunciation and use of Greek could be learned.[121] If it were not for the fact that he never received any further communication on the subject, we might fairly consider this College the realisation of all Aldus' dreams, especially when we find that it had its own press. But the press was run by Aldus' old colleague and competitor, Zacharias Callierges. It must be admitted that we know relatively little about the preparatory stages of the Greek College, that Callierges' first Roman edition, the Pindar of August 1515, appeared more than six months after Aldus' death, and that Aldus' apparent failure to sway the Pope may simply have been an accident of time.[122] But even before Bembo wrote to Musurus, Paolo Bombasio had suspected that Aldus and all non-Greeks would be excluded from the new College, and if there had been the slightest gesture in the printer's direction during the year and a half of life that remained to him after September 1513, some hint of it would surely have survived.[123] Perhaps if Aldus had lived to see the flourishing Greek College dissolved by a Pope who lacked his predecessor's humanist interests, he would have realised that patronage offered no surer support than commercial sense: and if he had known that, within a year or so, Callierges and Lascaris would be dumping their Greek texts in hundreds on an apathetic market, he would have agreed that his own diversified programme of publications had its advantages. But the black despair which shows in the *Ad Herennium* of March 1514 may well derive in part from a final disappointment of his academic dreams.[124]

On the face of it, these dreams would appear to have brought Aldus repeated disappointments, and very few tangible results. A loosely organised system of scholarly exchange and co-operation with the press had existed long before 1500, and it is hard to see how the statute of 1502 could have altered it significantly. In any case, that document seems to have been little more than an improvisation: whatever it brought into being soon passed into oblivion, and greater plans had been afoot even before the statute was drafted. But those plans in their turn all came to nothing. Aldus' appeals to Leo X and Lucretia Borgia, his own will, and even some of the tributes paid to his memory, all speak of the Academy as a vision constantly fading.¹²⁵

However, judging a dream such as this by severely practical standards is misleading. At its face value, the statute of 1502 may seem affected, trivial, even a shade ridiculous. But as a comment on the enthusiasm of the men who drafted it, the statute carries a significance far beyond its mere words. The word "Academy" became a rallying-point for men of many different nations, an illusion perhaps, but still a kind of fiery pillar which gave both purpose and direction to scholarly endeavour. In the dream of an Academy we have the symbolic union of what had been divided worlds – the world of business and the world of letters – in the pursuit of an ideal – the spread of literacy and learning.

NOTES

1 Pastorello, "Testimonianze e documenti...", Doc. v, p. 201.
2 *Cronachetta*, written 1493, published for Nozze Papadopoli-Hellenbach, Venice, 1880, pp. 50–52.
3 Archivio della curia patriarcale di Venezia, single filza entitled simply "Professioni di fede richieste agli insegnanti, 1587". I am most grateful to Professor Paul Grendler for bringing this document to my attention, as it contains the only complete figure available.
4 On the growth of Venetian population during the sixteenth century see K. J. Beloch, "La popolazione di Venezia nei secoli XVI e XVII", NAV, Nuova serie, III, 1902, pp. 5–49. Though badly stricken by the plague of 1576, the population in 1587 was still at least 50% higher than in 1500. A bold attempt was made to calculate the average number of teachers operating before 1500 by E. Bertanza and G. Della Santa in their documentary study *Maestri, scuole e scolari in Venezia fino al 1500*, Monumenti storici publicati dalla R. Deputazione veneta di storia patria, Serie I, Vol. 12, Venice, 1907. Working from the mention of some 850 different names in notarial records over the period 1287–1497, they suggested that fifty to sixty teachers were probably active in any one decade.
5 B. Nardi, "Letteratura e cultura veneziana del Quattrocento", in *Civiltà veneziana del Quattrocento*, Fondazione Cini, 1956, pp. 99–145. In 1502 Egnazio thanked Francesco Bragadin, lecturer at the Rialto school, for his patronage in the preface to his *Racemationes*: but this is the only link I have discovered between the Aldine circle and the philosophy school.
6 On the Chancellery school see in general Nardi, *op. cit.*, and A. Pertusi, "Gli inizi della storiografia umanistica nel Quattrocento", in *La storiografia veneziana al secolo XVI, aspetti e problemi*, ed. Pertusi, Florence, 1970, pp. 269–332. O. M. T. Logan, *Culture and Society in Venice, 1470–1790*, London, 1972, has useful references. On the leading individuals see Gabotto/Confaloniere, *Giorgio Merula*,

and J. Monfasani, *George of Trebizond, a Biography and a Study of his Rhetoric and Logic*, Leiden, 1976.

7 Relevant documents printed in Segarizzi, *op. cit.*, under Ch. II n. 36, pp. 641–3.

8 Alexandri Falconis Veneti sacerdotis in obitu clarissimi rhetoris Benedicti Brugnoli omnibus eiusdem academiae discipulis epicedium, 4 fols. 4to, undated, Bernardino de Vitalibus, Venice (contains information on pupils): Ioannis Querini Nicolai ad Hieronymum Raymundum consolatoria oratio pro obitu eximii ac integerrimi viri Benedicti Brugnoli utriusque praeceptoris, 8 fols. 4to, no date or printer (note on "hypomagistri"). The foundation statute of St Paul's School is printed in full in J. H. Lupton, *A Life of John Colet, D.D.*, new edition, New York, 1974, pp. 271f. It is an indication of Brugnolo's influence and popularity that at least two other funeral tributes were paid to his memory, one by Sabellico (Sanudo, IV, col. 282, 7 July 1502), another by Egnazio (said to have been published by Aldus, 1502: see previous chapter, Table II. I have not seen a copy of this edition.)

9 Sabellici, *Opera Omnia*, Vol. IV, pp. 389–90.

10 Falconis, *op. cit.* (good opinion of Poliziano): Querini, *op. cit.* (variety of Brugnolo's teaching, and his moral impact).

On Brugnolo's editorial work see A. Zeno, *Dissertazioni vossiane*, Vol. II, Venice, 1753, pp. 70f: Io. M. Mazzuchelli, *Gli scrittori d'Italia*, Vol. II, pt. iv, Brescia, 1763, pp. 2134–6. He was responsible for editing Ambrogio Traversari's translation of Diogenes Laertius, various works of Cicero, Priscian, George of Trebizond's *Libri rhetoricorum*, Giustiniani's *History of Venice*, and Perotti's *Cornucopia*.

11 A. Zeno, introduction to *Istorici delle cose veneziane*, Vol. I, Venice, 1717, pp. xxixf, xxxvii, xl. (Attacks on his *De vetustate Aquileiae*, 1482, and Barbaro's suspicion of his Venetian History.) M. A. Sabellici *Annotationes veteres et recentes ex Plinio, Livio, et Pluribus Authoribus*, J. Pentius de Leuco, Venice, 1502: this is a composite volume of academic abuse edited by Zuane Bembo; Egnazio's attack on the "vulgarity" of Sabellico's work can be found in the introduction to his *Racemationes*, f. 77v. It is only fair to record that Sabellico's historical work gave the impetus to a complete Venetian "school". Cf. F. Gilbert, "Biondo, Sabellico, and the beginnings of Venetian Official Historiography", in *Florilegium Historicale – Essays Presented to Wallace Ferguson*, Toronto, 1971, pp. 276–93, and Pertusi, *op. cit.* under n. 6, above, esp. pp. 319–32.

12 On Barbaro's involvement in Valla's appointment see *Epistolae*, lxi (Vol. I, pp. 77–9). On Valla's editorial activity, Heiberg in ZFB XVI, 1896 ("Valla"): and on his place in the scientific thought of the time, P. Rose, "Bartolomeo Zamberti's Funeral Oration for the Humanist Encyclopedist Giorgio Valla", in *Cultural Aspects of the Italian Renaissance*, pp. 299–310.

13 Valla, pp. 70, 93.

14 Biblioteca Estense, Modena, Ms. Graeci α P 5, 17 (= 115), α U 9, 19 (= 99). The notes give explanations of difficult words, paradigms of irregular verbs, etc.

15 Ib., Ms Graeci α W 9, 6 (= 131) f. 42r (Theognis). α T 9, 6 (= 40) f. 189 (Commentaries on Ptolemy).

16 P 5, 17, f. 185v, was signed and dated 1487 by Vlastos. See previous Ch. n. 69, for his association with Callierges.
17 See Muller, "Janos Lascaris", *op. cit.* under Ch. III, n. 8, at pp. 382–4. For Poliziano's comments, *Prose vulgari*, ed. del Lungo, pp. 79–80.
18 Valla, pp. 61 (Pico), 62, 88 (Lascaris), 63 (Alberto Pio).
19 On Fra Urbano see Ch. III, n. 38, above. On Egnazio's quarrel with Sabellico, n. 11 of this chapter, and on his career in general J. B. Ross, "Venetian Schools and Teachers, Fourteenth to Early Sixteenth Century: a Survey and a Study of Giovanni Battista Egnazio", *Renaissance Quarterly*, XXXIX, no. 4, 1976, pp. 521–60.
20 See n. 3, above. On Bonapace, B. Cecchetti, "Libri, scuole e maestri, sussidii allo studio in Venezia nei secoli XIV e XV", AV XXXII, 1886, p. 357.
21 V. Rossi, "Maestri e scuole a Venezia verso la fine del medioevo", *Rendiconti del Reale istituto Lombardo di scienze e lettere*, Ser. ii, XL, 1907, pp. 765–81, 843–55. This is a review article of the work of Bertanza and Della Santa cited under n. 4, and uses the data revealed by those scholars.
22 On the role of Barbaro and Donato see Barbaro, *Epistolae* xli, Vol. I, pp. 56–7. The remainder of the information is derived from Merula's various dedications to Marco Corner: e.g. Q. Curtius, *De Rebus Gestis Alexandri*, Tacuinus, 1496; Ovidii, *Tristia*, 1507. By this time he was protonotary and "a secretis".
23 A. Serena, *La cultura umanistica a Treviso nel secolo decimoquinto*, Miscellanea di storia veneta, Ser. III, Vol. iii, Venice, 1912, pp. 82–91.
24 CAM 33 (Fortiguerra to Aldus, 2 December 1504): Allen, IX, pp. 204f.
25 *Journal Autobiographique*, ed. H. Omont, Paris, 1896, pp. 37–9. Under 1499–1500 Aleander mentions offers from Sebastiano di Priuli, archbishop of Nicosia, Nicolo Michiel, a leading statesman, and his small Latin class. His assignment with the Grimani, which is mentioned by Fortiguerra in the letter cited above, came in 1502. J. Paquier, *Jerome Aléandre de sa Naissance à la fin de son Sejour à Brindes* (1480–1529), Paris, 1900, pp. 15–20.
26 *Praeludia*, Tacuinus, Venice, 1509, ff. 59r–61v. "Calamitatem suae vitae deplorat." This volume of poems shows that Valeriani taught members of the Gritti, Donato and Contarini families.
27 *Epistolae*, lxxv, Vol. I, p. 95, 12 February 1486. My translation is free, but coveys spirit of the original: "Puer natura ferociusculus...edomandus tibi creditur."
28 Politiani, *Opera Omnia*, Aldus, 1498, Epistolarum Lib. II, No. 12. On Barbaro's classes on Aristotle see Ch. III, n. 37, above, and on his constant employment as a Venetian ambassador n. 6 of Branca's study in *Renaissance Venice*, ed. Hale, pp. 238–9.
29 On Venetian readiness to clamp down on any institutions that threatened to get out of hand see Nardi, *op. cit.* under n. 5, above, at p. 116 (Rialto school prevented from gaining university status). On patrician attitudes, M. L. King, "The Patriciate and the Intellectuals: power and ideas in Quattrocento Venice", *Societas*, V, no. 4, 1975, pp. 295–312.

30 Ch. III, n. 38. On Gritti's activities see J. C. Davis, "Shipping and Spying in the Early Career of a Venetian Doge, 1496–1502", *Studi veneziani*, XVI, 1974, pp. 97–108.
31 Valla, p. 91. Lorenzo Loredan was later singled out for particular criticism by the diarist Priuli: RIS Tom. XXIV, pt. iii, Bologna, 1938, p. 40.
32 Biblioteca Estense, Modena, Ms. Graecus N. 7, 17.
33 Sabellici *Opera*, Vol. IV, col. 355, shows that copies of *De Venetae Urbis Situ* were sent to Sebastiano Badoer, Leonardo Loredan, Tomaso Trevisan, Marcantonio Morosini and Gerolamo Donato. For Valla's exchange with Barozzi, Valla, pp. 83–4.
34 On the sections of this library now in the Vatican see Nolhac, *Bibliothèque de Fulvio Orsini*, passim, but pp. 237–9 for Poliziano's observations: on the sections now in the British Museum, C. Clough, "Pietro Bembo's Library Represented in the British Museum", *British Museum Quarterly*, XXX, No. 1, 1965, pp. 3–17.
35 Regius' comments can be found in his introduction to Ovid's *Metamorphoses*, Locatellus, Venice, 1493. On the effect of the printed book on one of the most important props of oral communication, see Frances Yates, *The Art of Memory*, London, 1969 ed., pp. 130f. Regius delivered one of the most severe blows to the prestige of Memory by attacking the attribution of the *Rhetorica ad Herennium* to Cicero.
36 Introduction to *Adnotationes Plinianae*, Pencius de Leuco, Venice, 1502.
37 Valla, p. 70.
38 On the patrician clubs see L. Venturi, "Le compagnie della Calza, secoli XV–XVI", NAV, Nuova serie, XVI, 1908, pp. 161–221: F. Mutinelli, *Annali urbani di Venezia*, Venice, 1841, pp. 283–6 (statute of the "Sempiterni"). An interesting charter submitted by an association of lawyers in Udine is contained in A.S.V., Senato, Deliberazioni Terra, Rg. XIII, ff. 30–36v, 23 January 1497–8 (M.V.). It is part social, part charitable, providing for legal aid to the poor, various joint activities, and a roll of membership. Zuane Bembo's silloge is now Ms Latinus 10801 in the Stätsbibliothek, Munich: ff. 149–150r contain a list of "viri docti et probi", ff. 185v–186v a shorter list of "compatres".
39 Bartolomeo Merula's introduction to Q. Curtii *De Rebus Gestis Alexandri*, Tacuinus, 1496.
40 C. Cavazzana, "Cassandra Fedele, erudita veneziana del rinascimento", *Ateneo veneto*, Anno XXIX, ii, fasc. i, July–August 1906, pp. 73–91, 361–72. Cassandra's *Epistolae et Orationes*, Padua, 1636, show that she was in touch with several crowned heads and most of the leading intellectuals of the age.
41 On Barbaro see below, n. 49. On Navagero, M. Cermenati, "Un diplomato naturalista del Rinascimento, Andrea Navagero", NAV, Nuova serie XXIV, 1912, pp. 164–205.
42 Navagerius sive De Poetica, Dialogus Hieronymi Fracastorii, in Navagerii *Opera Omnia*, Padua, 1718, pp. 229f. The dialogue records the reactions of Navagero the poet and Bardellone the mathematician (see below, Ch. VI, n. 112) to the summer sky.

43 Lydii Catti Ravennatis *Opuscula*, Tacuinus, Venice, 1502. Querini's sonnets are preserved in Biblioteca Marciana, Venezia, Ms. italiani cl. IX, 203 (6757), ff. 93r–94v.
44 Records of degrees awarded during the first half-century are available: C. Zonta and I. Brotto, *Acta Graduum Academicorum Gymnasii Patavini ab anno 1406 ad annum 1450*, Padua, 1922. A thorough account of the Venetian government's policy and its increasing involvement in university affairs has been compiled by G. de Sandre in "Dottori, università, Commune a Padova nel Quattrocento", *Quaderni per la storia dell'università di Padova*, Vol. I, 1968, pp. 15–47.
45 H. Brown, *Studies in Venetian History*, Vol. II, London, 1907, p. 116.
46 On Venice's favourable treatment of Germans, see de Sandre, *op. cit.*, pp. 18–19. A. Veress, *Matricula et acta Hungarorum in Universitate Patavina Studentium, 1264–1864*, Budapest, 1915, p. v, shows that the number of Hungarians attending Padua more than doubled during the second half of the fifteenth century. On the Poles see the various articles collected in *Relazioni tra Padova e la Polonia*, Padua, 1964: and on the English, G. Parks, *The English Traveller to Italy*, Rome, 1954, pp. 631–4.
47 Shakespeare, *The Taming of the Shrew*, Act I, scene i, ln. 191–2. The atmosphere of contemporary Padua, and the subtle relationship between master (Lucentio) and tutor/servant (Tranio) is perfectly conveyed in this play. See Brown's article "Shakespeare and Venice", in the volume cited above, pp. 159–80, and B. Brunelli, "Shakespeare e lo studio di Padova", AV, Nuova Serie I, 1922, pp. 270–83.
48 Sanudo, XXXII, col. 132, report of 13 November 1520. For some of the establishments kept, see the information supplied in E. Martellozzo Forin, "Note d'archivio sul soggiorno padovano di studenti ungharesi, 1493–1563", in *Venezia e Ungheria nel Rinascimento*, ed. V. Branca, Florence, 1973, pp. 245–60. On Valeriani and Aleander cf. nn. 25, 26, above: immediate reference is to f. 24r of *Praeludia*.
49 *Epistolae*, xlix, Vol. I, pp. 60–3.
50 Valla, pp. pp. 71–2. A prior acquaintance between Aldus and Valla is suggested by Bertoni, *La biblioteca Estense*, p. 118.
51 Stätsbibliothek, Munich, Ms. Latinus 807, f. 42v. Parts of this vital manuscript, which contains Poliziano's personal notes on his journey during 1491, were published by G. Pesenti, "Diario odeporico-bibliografico del Poliziano", *Memorie del Reale istuto lombardo di scienze e lettere*, Classe di Lettere, scienze morali e storiche, XXIII–IV, Ser. III, fasci. vii, Milan, 1916, pp. 229–39. Unfortunately the script of the original is virtually unmanageable, being written in a kind of shorthand and in no clear order. On Pizzamano and his role in the purchase of Pico's library see Lowry, "Two Great Venetian Libraries...", pp. 128f, and on the presence of Bembo and Gabriel in Messina, Valla, p. 62.
52 Schück, Doc. v, pp. 117–20.
53 The view of the Venetian attitude to learning is that of Giovanni da Ravenna, and is quoted by De Sandre, *op. cit.*, p. 19. See Ch. II, nn. 28f. for the interpretation of the *Epistola*, and n. 1 of this Chapter for references to Aldus' school.
54 Merula was quite prepared to be caustic about printers even in a dedication to one of Jenson's editions: see the preface to *Scriptores Rei Rusticae* in BP, pp. 145–8. The

relationship of earlier humanists with printers was raised by F. Gabotto, *Vita di Giorgio Merula*, p. 62: the author argued that, because the scholars concerned worked for several printers, they could not be compared to Aldus' committed assistants. In fact, Musurus worked for Callierges as well as Aldus, so we are driven back to purely personal considerations.

55 OAME VIII. Valla, passim.
56 CAM 87.
57 *Ib.*, 2. OAME VII, VIII, show Aldus' admiration for Pico, Barbaro, and Poliziano, and his reaction to their deaths.
58 D. M. Robathan, "Libraries of the Italian Renaissance", in *The Medieval Library*, ed. J.W . Thompson, Chicago, 1939, pp. 569f.
59 See Ch. II, n. 9, above.
60 Robathan, *op. cit.*, pp. 536f (Urbino), 552f (Milan).
61 OAME XIX, XLVI, etc.
62 Ch. IV, nn. 67f, on the commercial crisis. On the lure of Venice after the collapse of the mainland centres see Geanakoplos, *Greek Scholars*, pp. 115f, and for Aldus' dedication to the exiled Guidobaldo da Montefeltro, OAME LI.
63 G. Della Santo, "...processo di Giorgio Valla", cit. under Ch. IV, n. 157. Valla died on 24 January 1499/1500: Sanudo, III, cols. 90–1.
64 Sanudo, III, cols. 90–1 (the contenders), 178 (Scita's appointment).
65 *Ib.*, cols. 249, 429 (Amaseo replaces Scita), 1146 (confrontation between Regius Amaseo).
66 *Ib.*, V, cols. 333, 433.
67 *Ib.*, VI, col. 117.
68 *Ib.*, IV, col. 282 (death of Brugnolo), VI, col. 198 (Sabellico excused further lecturing). For comment see Gilbert, *op. cit.*, under n. 11, above.
69 E. Percopo, "La vita di Giovanni Pontano", *Archivio storico per le provincie napoletane*, Nuova series, Anno XXII, 1936, pp. 231–4.
70 The literature on Colocci is substantial, and growing. Of the older studies the most useful is still G. Lancellotti, *Poesie italiane e latine di Monsignor Angelo Colocci, con più notizie intorno alla persona di lui e sua famiglia*, Iesi, 1772. This has been brought up to date by several recent studies of V. Fainelli, e.g. "Il ginnasio greco di Leone X a Roma", *Studi Romani*, Anno IX, 1961, pp. 379–93: "Aspetti della Roma cinquecentesca – le case e le raccolte archeologiche del Colocci", *ib.*, X, 1962, pp. 391–402; and his edition of F. Ubaldini's *Vita di Mons. Angelo Colocci*, Studi e Testi No. 256, Città del Vaticano, 1969. This work contains exhaustive bibliographical coverage. Material on Colocci's archaeological collections can be found in Weiss, *Renaissance Discovery of Classical Antiquity*, and on his library in Nolhac, *Bibliothèque de Fulvio Orsini*.
71 OAME XV (Sanudo): BP p. 240 (Grocyn): RAIA p. 17 (Reuchlin's visit), 515 (Aldus' reply to letter from Celtis).
72 Firmin-Didot, *Alde Manuce*, pp. 499f.
73 Geanakoplos, *Greek Scholars*, pp. 111f, 170–1.

74 OAME VIII. On the situation in Carpi see Ch. II, n. 38, above.
75 RAIA p. 34 (Sophocles): CSV p. 78 (ducal letter). The only copy of the statute is in the binding of Barbarini Stampati IV, 13, a copy of *Etymologicum Magnum*.
76 The statute was first published by J. Morelli, *Aldi Manuti scripta tria longe rarissima...*, Bassani, 1806, pp. 47f. Cf. also RAIA pp. 499–503 (Latin and French translations), Firmin-Didot, *Alde Manuce*, pp. 435f, CSV pp. 100–2 (Italian translation). The most extravagant discussion is that of Firmin-Didot: the most cautious that of M. Ferrigni, *Aldo Manuzio*, Milan, 1925, pp. 140f; the most balanced that of M. Brunetti, "L'Accademia Aldina", *Rivista di Venezia*, VIII, 1929, pp. 417–31. My own article "The 'New Academy' of Aldus Manutius – a Renaissance Dream", BJRL 58, No. 2, 1976, pp. 378–420, contains a number of errors and in general suffers from the faults of having been written in an over-polemical frame of mind. But it can be consulted for some destructive criticism of existing views.
77 Ubaldini, *Angelo Colocci, ed. cit.*, pp. 14–16, with Fainelli's notes *ad loc.*
78 OAME XXXVIII (Sophocles, 1502), XLIII (Ovid, 1502), XXIV C. (Lascaris, *Grammar*, undated).
79 See the letter of Sadoleto quoted by Ubaldini, *Angelo Colocci, ed. cit.*, p. 68.
80 *Praeludia, ed. cit.*, f. 14v.

> ...Canalis, citharae decus supremum,
> Cultus Naviger, elegans, canorus,
> Emunctus Trypho, perpolitus, acer,
> Motensis vehemens et eruditus,
> Expromptus Maro, floridus, decorus,
> Borges grandiloquus venustulusque,...

Navagero and Paolo da Canal are immediately recognisable. Trypho is probably Tryphon Dalmata, who was employed by Alberto Pio (CAM 8). Andrea Maro was famed for his extemporary verse and contributed some lines to the opening of *Hypnerotomachia Polifili*. Motensis refers to Motta, the birthplace of Aleander. Gerolamo Borgia was a Neapolitan humanist who played some part in the preparation of Aldus' edition of Sannazaro's *Arcadia*. The manuscript cited under n. 43, above, may contain some of the relics left by this and similar circles.

81 OAME XLII.
82 CAM 42 (Zorzi, 26 April 1505): *ib.*, 58 (Jacob Spiegel, secretary to Bishop of Trieste, 27 February 1506); Schuck, No. XIII, pp. 131–3 (Urbanus, 29 November 1505).
83 Valla, p. 93, shows Valla passing on information about the Aldine text of Aristotle and other recent editions. Sabellico sometimes recommended future editions in his lectures: *Opera Omnia*, Vol. IV, p. 359.
84 CAM Nos. 32, 33, 11 October, 2 December 1504. My interpretation of these letters is not foolproof, as Fortiguerra used the term "Academy" ambiguously, and it is not always clear whether he is reproaching Aldus or the Venetian government for their neglect. But the use in the second letter of the official language "è presa la parte" would appear to refer to official government business, probably discussion of the contest between Leonico and Musurus. Cf. n. 67, above.

85 Mention in Aldus' introduction to Apollonius of Tyana, in OAME XXVI (Vol. I, p. 48).
86 *Ib.*, and RAIA p. 46.
87 H. D. Saffrey, "Un humaniste Dominicain, Jean Cuno de Nuremburg, precurseur d'Erasme à Bâle", *Bibliothèque d'Humanisme et de Renaissance*, XXXIII, 1971, pp. 19–62.
88 Sanudo, VI, col. 101, 22 November 1504.
89 Throughout this section cf. Dionisotti, *Gli umanisti e il volgare*, pp. 1–14.
90 Nolhac, CAM 14. For details of the negotiations that followed see M. von Kleehoven, "Aldus Manutius und der Plan einer Deutschen Ritterakademie", LBF LII, 1950, pp. 169–77: for the retort of L. Donati, "La seconda Accademia Aldina ed una lettera ad Aldo Manuzio trascurata da bibliografi", *ib.*, LIII, 1951, pp. 54–9; for an English summary, Lowry, "The 'New Academy...'", pp. 404–8.
91 *Der Briefwechsel des Konrad Celtis*, ed. H. Rupprich, Munich, 1934, p. 517. RAIA p. 45 and OAME XLVIII, for the dedication to Lang. CAM 30 for Collauer's letter.
92 A. S. Mantova, Carteggio Estero (Carteggio ad inviati), Busta 1440 bb.13, letter of the imperial ambassador to Federigo Gonzaga, 25 July 1504. "Illustrissime Princeps et Domine Observantissime, post commendationem – Quando apud hoc Illustrissimum Dominium Venetorum a Caesarea Maestate orator missus sum, venit ad me D. Aldus Romanus, vir vite non mediocri doctrina et bonarum artium professione perinsignis atque praeclarus, *qui se etiam a Caesarea Maestate pro Achademia bonarum scientiarum constituenda nuper conductum esse ait* [my italics]. Eum igitur tamquam Caesareum servitorem et scientiarum peritia celebrem omni favore dignum dicens, tam ipsum quam Fredericum quendum de Ceresara consanguineum suum, Illustrissimo Domino vostro non commendare non potui. Dixit enim ipse Aldus hunc Fredericum superioribus annis proprium fratrem ei vim inferentem in sui ipsuis defensionem veluti coactum occidisse, eumque postea, causa cognita, ab Illustrissimo Domino vostro remissionis gratiam impetrasse: nunc vero aliquorum persecutione qui ipsius Frederici bona sitiunt, ex eodem crimine rursus captum et incarceratum fuisse. Cum igitur existimat meas veluti Caesaris oratoris preces apud Ill.mum D. vostrum ipsi Frederico profuturas, ut paucis ad eum scriberem vehementer institit. [The request for clemency is now repeated, along with the usual formalities.]" For the background of the incident and the dispatch of the Papal nuncio see above, Ch. III, n. 91.
93 OAME LVII.
94 "Lettere inedite dei Manuzii, raccolte dal dottore Antonio Ceruti", AV XI, 1881, p. 269. Cuno's mission is mentioned in the letter.
95 *Pirckheimers Briefwechsel*, Vol. I, pp. 280–2. See below, n. 98.
96 CAM 58: and cf. OAME Vol. II, pp. 354–5, for a useful note.
97 *Pirckheimers Briefwechsel, ed. cit.*, Vol. I, p. 457. On the interpretation of Aldus' actions in early 1506 see previous chapter, nn. 127f.
98 Text from *loc. cit.* under n. 95. Cf. Donati, *op. cit.* under n. 90, for a sceptical approach.

99 See Platina's Life of Vittorino in E. Garin, *Il pensiero pedagogico dell'umanesimo*, Florence, 1958, p. 678.
100 For Aldus' unbroken interest in Hebrew publication see his introduction to Pindar in OAME LXXII: the "Introductio perbrevis ad Hebraicam linguam" was reissued in 1514. RAIA p. 69. On the general field of Hebrew typography see the work of J. Bloch cited under Ch. III, n. 52.
101 P. S. Allen, "The Trilingual Colleges of the Early Sixteenth Century", in *Erasmus – Lectures and Wayfaring Sketches*, Oxford, 1934, pp. 138–63, is still the fullest general treatment of the subject, and, since Allen was a fellow of Bishop Fox's foundation, that aspect is well covered. There is much information on Alcala in the earlier pages of M. Bataillon's *Érasme et l'Espagne*, Paris, 1937, and some of this finds its way into Geanakoplos, *Greek Scholars*, pp. 229f. On Louvain a special study is available: H. de Vocht, *History of the Foundation and Rise of the Collegium Trilingue Lovaniense, 1517–1550*, 4 vols., Louvain, 1951–5. For similar though somewhat later experiments in France see A. Lefranc, *Histoire du Collège de France depuis ses origines jusqu'à la fin du Premier Empire*, Paris, 1893.
102 L. Spitz, *Conrad Celtis, the German Arch-Humanist*, Harvard, 1957, pp. 45–62.
103 *Ib.*, pp. 68f. On Maximilian's constant financial difficulties and his dependence on the banking-houses of Augsburg see R. Ehrenberg, *Capital and Finance in the Age of the Renaissance*, translated from the German by H. Lucas, London, 1928.
104 Erasmus told the story a number of years later: Allen III, p. 404, No. 868, and Lowry, "The 'New Academy'...", p. 415 for comment.
105 *Lettere volgari di Aldo Manucci*, Rome, 1592, Ep. I, p. 1. CAM 64. Neither letter contains any mention of an academy.
106 For the full text of the letter and discussion of the circumstances, cf. Donati, *op. cit.* under n. 90. On Aldus' visit to Milan and his acquaintances there see the introductions to Plutarch's *Moralia* and Horace, both of 1509, in OAME LXVI, LXVII. CAM 84 may contain an oblique reference. The writer may have been Ventura Benassai.
107 Text in L. N. Cittadella, *Documenti ed illustrazioni riguardanti la storia artistica ferrarese*, Ferrara, 1868, pp. 309–11.
108 On Aldus' movements after the Battle of Agnadello see previous chapter, nn. 158f. The tribute to Lucretia Borgia was made in the dedication of the poems of Tito and Ercole Strozzi: OAME LXXIII. On the position of Lucretia and her reputation at this time see M. E. Mallett, *The Borgias*, 1971 ed., pp. 232f.
109 *Ib.*, p. 238. The Estensi were in the strict sense papal vicars, who had been able to establish a large measure of independence during the later Middle Ages: but that independence was threatened by the territorial ambitions of the Renaissance Papacy, and eventually eclipsed in 1597.
110 Cittadella, *op. cit.*, p. 311.
111 Fortiguerra had entered Cardinal Grimani's household by December 1504 (CAM 33) and later passed into the service of Cardinal Farnese, Franciotti della Rovere, and Francesco Alidosi: A. Chiti, *Scipione Fortiguerra, il Carteromacho* – studio biografico con una raccolta di epigrammi, sonetti e lettere di lui e a lui

dirette, Florence, 1902, pp. 22f. For mention of Aldus' trip to Siena, Allen, I, p. 462.

112 CAM 41. On Colocci, see refs. under n. 70, above.

113 CAM 43. This project for the establishment of a Greek press is linked to Evangelista de Tosinis by J. Ruysschaert in an ingenious article: "Trois recherches sur le XVIe siècle Romain", *Archivio della società romana di storia patria,* Ser. III, xxv, fasc. 1, 1971, pp. 11–29.

114 On Aldus' re-entry into business see previous chapter, nn. 162f. Fra Giocondo is known to have assisted with Caesar, the new edition of *Cornucopia,* and the *Scriptores Rei Rusticae* (OAME LXXIV, LXXX C, LXXXIII – CAM 86). His research in France also aided the edition of Pliny's *Letters* (OAME LXIV, and Ch. VI, n. 108), and he seems to have played some part in persuading Aldus to resume printing (OAME LXXII). In spite of his public and private importance, he remains a very mysterious figure: R. Brenzoni, *La lettera autografa di fra Giocondo ad Aldo Manuzio,* Verona, 1962, and *Fra Giovanni Giocondo veronese,* Florence, 1960.

115 For Navagero's earlier poetic activity see above, n. 43. OAME, Vol. II, p. 363, has a good note on his editorial activity. On his work as librarian of the Marciana, which did not begin until after Aldus' death, see my article "Two Great Venetian Libraries", pp. 136–7.

116 Cicogna, *Delle iscrizioni veneziane,* Vol. I, Venice, 1824, pp. 341–2.

117 OAME LXXII.

118 There is much useful information on the intellectual influence at work in the court of Leo X during these years in F. Gilbert's article "Cristianesimo, umanesimo, e la bolla 'Apostolici Regiminis' del 1512", RSI Anno LXXIX, fasc. i, 1967, pp. 976–90.

119 Text in Legrand, *Bibliographie Hellènique,* Vol. II, p. 321: cf. also I, p. cxvi.

120 For this dedication see either OAME LXXVIII, BP pp. 286–96, or Legrand, *Bibliographie Hellènique,* Vol. I, pp. 101–12. Orlandi does not print Musurus' poem.

121 Fainelli, "Il ginnasio greco..." cit. under n. 70, above.

122 Geanakoplos, *Greek Scholars,* pp. 214f.

123 CAM 78, 2 July 1513.

124 Fainelli, *op. cit.,* pp. 391–2. Ruysschaert, "Trois recherches...", cit. under n. 113, above, pp. 21–2, quotes notarial acts showing Callierges' efforts to dispose of 778 copies of Pindar and 981 of Theocritus as early as 1516. Lascaris appears to have been making similar efforts in an undated draft: Vaticanus Latinus, Ms. 1413, f. 63r-v.

125 Epigram of Pirckheimer, quoted in Firmin-Didot, *Alde Manuce,* p. 415, n. 2:

> Posset ubi tandem concepta Academia condi
> Nullus in hoc Aldo cum locus orbe foret,
> "Seclum"ait "insipiens, tellusque indigna, valete"
> Atque opus in Campos transtulit Elysios.

VI
AUTHORSHIP AND EDITORSHIP

Aldus' description of the gawping idiots who crowded into his workshop to read their execrable compositions would hardly suggest that he had a very high opinion of the literary men of his own time.[1] In their different way, his plain texts of the ancient authors carry the same implication: the learned modern commentaries which had delighted the editors of the 1480s and 1490s were of no ultimate importance; the unadorned words of the classical master, restored as nearly as possible to their original purity, were what really concerned him, and he sought to establish his reputation on his informed and accurate editing of Greek and Roman authors.

At the outset of his printing career he dreamed of texts which would be more accurate than the exemplars on which they were based: in terms reminiscent of Poliziano or Merula, he spoke of comparing numerous exemplars, adding nothing and removing nothing, but printing the text in its purest possible form. He wanted his books to be both beautiful and correct, and towards the end of his life admitted that he had never produced an edition which fully satisfied him.[2] Like many of his contemporaries, Aldus longed to raise his own age to the cultural level of the ancient world by restoring the traditions of that world.[3] And in spite of occasional private reservations, his contemporaries publicly acclaimed his efforts. "He sets nothing in his bronze letters unless it is correct", enthused Gerolamo Bologni: Aldus was "the most glorious of all makers of books, in any age", the "rescuer of Greek and Latin literature". The ducal privilege issued in 1502 by Leonardo Loredan paid tribute to Aldus' "extreme diligence and care in correcting books in Latin and Greek".[4] Though there have been occasional whispers of doubt, his reputation as the first responsible scholar-editor of classical texts has stood the test of time on the strength both of these tributes and of certain preconceptions about the situation of the publishing world in

Venice. The main business of this chapter will be to submit Aldus' fame as a scholar to some more searching scrutiny.[5]

But before proceeding to such a detailed examination, we must raise a question which is bound to affect our judgement in some degree, and which has a great interest of its own for an age which values originality far above authority. This is the matter of Aldus' relations with the writers of his own day. Considering his expressed and implied views of them, it is something of a surprise to find that, of the 124 editions printed in his lifetime, more than a third were the works of authors who had lived during the previous century and a half.[6] Of the forty-two which make up that proportion, twenty-five were the works of living men. These totals are of course distorted by the three editions of Aldus' own Grammar, his catalogues, and the warning to the plagiarists of Lyons, the last two being no more than printed circulars. The remainder include works of such diverse character and value that we should certainly avoid the error of classifying them together as "contemporary literature". But this is not the point. What matters is that Aldus had numerous opportunities of working directly with authors, that he took some of these chances and passed others by, and that for a substantial number of his editions, perhaps including his famous texts of Petrarch's *Cose volgari,* he had access to autograph copies.[7] This extensive co-operation with the literary world, and the survival of a number of personal letters which illustrate it, give us a unique opportunity of watching the relationship between author and publisher at a crucially important period in the history of communications, and of watching the effect of printing on the part played by both.

It has been pointed out by a number of experts that writers of the manuscript-age possessed a concept of originality which, by the finnicky and rather self-obsessed standards of our own age, seems astonishingly vague and easy-going. Books were so comparatively few, memories so prodigiously long that turns of phrase or entire passages could pass from hand to hand like a common currency, and the borrower might be doing a favour by spreading another man's ideas.[8] The mechanics of communication tended to blur the outlines of individuality. Savonarola's sermons and Giorgio Valla's lectures were taken down by members of their audiences and circulated in versions which cannot have been more than generally accurate paraphrases. If, as often happened, an author passed copies of his work round among his friends, then revised it and repeated the process, there might be several different copies in circulation with equal claims to authenticity. Quite separate drafts of Bessarion's *In Calumniatorem Platonis* existed during the cardinal's own lifetime.

With its capacity first to stabilise a text by standardising the version, then to circulate copies on a massive scale, the press brought a violent change to this relaxed atmosphere, provoking two apparently opposite but associated reactions. Passing a work to the press meant losing effective control of it, and the "once for all" quality of the decision scared a number of literary men into the delays, the perpetual revisions, and the evasiveness which have been among the less endearing features of their profession from that day to this. Aldus himself was a case in point.

But the diffusion of 500 copies or more carried a promise of immediate literary fame that many found hard to resist, and that soon brought out the pathetic hacks who tried Aldus' patience so hard. Many of the authors who dealt with him did, indeed, show an inordinate eagerness to get their names into print, and to get their work printed by the man who seemed likely to secure the widest diffusion and the greatest prestige.

We have already had occasion to notice some of the symptoms of this rush to publish, and a realization of the change brought about by the new medium seems to have grown up rapidly among those who worked for the Venetian presses. As early as 1481 Squarciafico imagined the spirits of dead authors in the Elysian Fields lamenting that "their works would perish if they were not printed, since this art compels all writers to give way to it". Only five years later Sabellico took out the first known author's copyright:[9] and by the 1490s the more plentiful correspondence reveals a fairly definite movement, in which writers are not only jostling the publishers but are being jostled from behind by their own friends and admirers. Pietro Bembo, the student-aristocrat who returned from Messina in 1494 with a manuscript of Lascaris' Greek Grammar corrected by the author and an account of his own expedition up Mount Etna, bears a strong resemblance to the "sleek young man with a ready tongue and a good store of learning" whose quest for literary fame Urceus had attacked. Aldus published the two pieces within the next twelve months, and so played a direct part in launching one of the most brilliant careers of the time.[10] Alessandro Benedetti was such a determined writer that he sent a preliminary copy of his *Diaria de bello Carolino* to Giorgio Valla for criticism barely a month after the Battle of Fornovo, and long before the French invaders had actually left Italy. One wonders how much time he had to spare for the wounded.[11] Valla's own great work, *De expetendis et fugiendis rebus,* was held up by his disgrace, and eventually seen through the Aldine press by his adopted son Gianpietro, after Valla's own death: but he had been under pressure to publish it for nearly ten years.[12] The same sort of pressure appears in Lorenzo Maioli's insistence that Aldus should satisfy the demand for his *Epiphyllides in dialecticis* in spite of the imperfections which the work contained, and in sinister anticipation of the adage "Publish and be damned".[13]

If this sort of excitement occasionally overboiled and created intolerable tensions, we should perhaps not be too surprised. The hunger for publicity could reach the point where a minor editor named Alessandro Sarti simply inserted a complimentary reference to himself into the letters of Poliziano. The immortal longings of people like the Vicentine schoolmaster who sent Aldus his translations from Gregory Nazanzenus six months after that author's works had been printed, must have a constant strain.[14] No doubt far more of these requests were made than the few we can trace now. But those which have survived share one intriguing quality – their very deferential tone. Erasmus was not the international figure he would soon become, when he asked Aldus to print his translations from Euripides: but he was no stranger to the publishing world, and it is surprising to watch his cautious approach, through personal compliments and references to mutual friends, to the matter in hand. His remark "I should think my studies had received the gift of immortality, if they saw the light of day printed in your types"[15] is a powerful comment on the importance which the printer was fast acquiring in the literary world. Rhetorical words, certainly: but I doubt if writers of Sabellico's generation would have seen the need for rhetoric.

How did Aldus treat his responsibilities? It is hard to detect a clear pattern, partly because his interests were so comprehensive. He showed very early in his career that he was prepared effectively to "commission" a new work from a new author if he saw the need for it. Fra Urbano Valeriani's Greek Grammar, the first to be written with a Latin text to support it, was produced at Aldus' "request, or rather insistence", printed in January 1497 and presumably in preparation for some time before that.[16] At the same time he was courting the personal assistance of established authors, in the hope of issuing their work in more correct editions. The approach to Marsiglio Ficino seems to have had only a moderate success: the old philosopher made a couple of corrections to his translations from Iamblichus and approved a suggestion of Aldus', besides promising a complete index of emedations when the basic presswork was finished. But his complaints about the difficulty of finding books, his readiness to leave everything to "your good faith and judgement", and the generally lugubrious tone of the letter all show that his heart was not in the matter.[17] Aldus apparently had no better luck with the Neapolitan writer Jacopo Sannazaro: his request for corrected copies was tactfully embedded in the dedication of a short work entitled *Vita e sito de' Zichi*, an account of life in the steppes of South Russia which had recently been brought to Aldus by its Genoese author Giorgio Interiano, and was published in October 1502.[18] Interiano was himself a friend of Sannazaro, and the whole manoeuvre was plainly a reaction to the commercial success of an extremely incorrect edition of the *Arcadia* which had been printed in Venice by Bernardino da Vercelli in June of the same year. But Sannazaro was in France at the time, and from indirect evidence he seems to have been rather hostile to the idea of publishing his work in its present form. The matter was soon taken out of his, and Aldus' hands. When he returned from the French court in 1504 his *Arcadia* had already been published from the revised, autograph manuscripts which Sannazaro had left behind in Naples, and which were put to use by his determined colleague and well-wisher, Pietro Summonte. Aldus remained on good terms with Sannazaro, and dedicated to him the edition which he finally produced in September 1514: but he had little to do except re-issue and simplify Summonte's text. It was to be expected that the neat Aldine octavo would become the more successful text, and, sure enough, it was more widely copied than the Neapolitan version during the sixteenth century. But it must also be admitted that the attempt to monopolise and capitalise upon the prestige of the author's name had failed, and the whole episode casts a strange light on the ethics which governed publication during this hectic period of the transition into print. Not once had Sannazaro been directly involved, and Aldus appears to have been the only editor to approach him formally.[19]

The works of Sannazaro's contemporary and close friend, Giangioviano Pontano, had an even more complicated history. In this case there was no question of any arbitrary action, since the author was only too anxious to publish and sent copies of his three main poetic works, *Urania, Meteora* and *Horti Hesperidum* to Aldus some time during the late summer of 1502. The printer was enthusiastic. He dedicated his edition of Statius to Pontano in August, offering to publish anything else which the talented author chose to send him.[20] But the sheer eagerness of both parties seems to have worked against them. Aldus was plainly hoping for more before proceeding to edit what he had, and Pontano may have encouraged these hopes by speaking in a letter to his agent in Venice, Suardino Suardo, of a "well corrected" copy of the *Horti Hesperidum,* and by sending a number of shorter poems which apparently went astray in transit. Another manuscript was prepared by Pontano himself, but this, too, disappeared for a full year when the messenger who had been bringing it to Venice fell ill and died in Padua some time during the summer of 1503.[21] The matter languished, to be revived some two years later and almost simultaneously by Aldus and the conscientious Summonte. On 2 August 1505, the Neapolitan wrote what must be termed a masterpiece of tactful reproach. He reminded Aldus of Pontano's commission: he sent two new pastoral poems for inclusion; he broke the news that he had embarked on the publication of Pontano's lyric cycles on his own initiative; and finally, he hinted that his distinguished colleague might return the exemplars sent him by the author, if they were going to be of no further use. When he was greeted by the news that *Urania, Meteora* and *Horti Hesperidum* had already been printed and that Aldus was hoping to add some of the lyrics as a continuation, Summonte expressed his delight, waived his monopoly of sales in the Kingdom of Naples, and only asked for publication of the Venetian edition to be suspended for a few weeks until his own had been cleared. This request must have arrived too late for Aldus to be able to comply. But there was in any case only a partial overlap between the two versions. Summonte did not print the longer works, and the Aldine text, based on the author's final draft, remains fundamental. Aldus used earlier exemplars of the shorter, *Neniae, Tumuli* and *Epigrammata,* where Summonte had access to the latest revisions. The affair had been conducted with a sense of propriety and consideration which is rare in the annals of early publishing. But, as the reader can easily tell, it is still a story of confusions, crossed purposes, and neglected undertakings: one which shows how little an author's wishes might matter, how precariously his works were poised above an abyss of extinction, and how completely their preservation now depended on the press.[22]

The soliciting of authors which appears in these cases does not seem to have been Aldus' usual method. As a rule it was not necessary, since the men concerned beat their own path to his door and the publisher could make his choices according to his own very personal criteria. So far as they can be reconstructed, these were roughly as follows. First, did the author have any claims on him? Second, did he have connections which Aldus did not wish, or could not afford, to neglect? Third, had he anything interesting to offer? The rush of minor works by the Aristotelian editors Leoniceno and Maioli during the later 1490s looks very much like a return of favours: much the same might be said of Bembo's *De Aetna* and *Asolani,* for he had provided invaluable help with the manuscripts of Lascaris' Grammar, of Petrarch's *Cose volgari,* and of Dante's *Commedia.* Giorgio Valla, whose *De expetendis et fugiendis rebus* Aldus published posthumously in 1501, had done much to introduce the printer to Venetian high society: and Reuchlin, as we have seen, was trying to perform a similar service by promoting the idea of an imperial academy.[23] Alessandro Benedetti was a close associate of Valla: and Aurelio Augurello, whose poems were printed immediately after the *Asolani* in 1505, was an old family client of the Bembo.[24] In his first approach to Aldus, Erasmus laid careful stress on his friendship with Grocyn, Linacre, Latimer and Tunstall, and whatever the Dutchman's personal qualifications, Aldus took due note.

Some writers carried overpowering recommendations in their own pedigree: this was clearly the case with Gianfrancesco Pico della Mirandola, nephew of the famous Giovanni Pico and a relative of Alberto Pio. It also applied to Adriano Castellesi, whose dramatic poem *Venatio* Aldus published in September 1505, and who badgered him with various corrections for some months afterwards.[25] Apart from being a patron of Filippo Beroaldo and Fortiguerra, Castellesi was a cardinal. In other cases the influence of rank could be exerted less directly. Aldus definitely had a personal regard for Ercole Strozzi, who had once been a pupil of his: but when he edited Strozzi's poems in 1513, the printer had known for three years that Lucretia Borgia, who received the dedication, had been keenly interested in the project and wanted him to undertake it.[26]

Considerations of this kind did not invariably decide the issue: we have seen Aldus objecting to the crude composition of Maioli's work, and he returned a resolute "No" to Conrad Celtis' request for a version of his pupils' poems on the "Triumphs of Maximilian", in spite of the German's editorial help and his influence at the imperial court.[27] But broadly speaking, the system preached by Aldus was "Hand washes hand, and finger finger": or, as our cruder age would say, "You scratch my back, and I'll scratch yours".[28]

If this treatment of authors seems arbitrary, quirkish, and based on personal rather than literary merits, much the same must be admitted about Aldus' treatment of their works. As we have seen, he made something of a fetish of the precision and accuracy of his texts, and the accidents of fate have decreed that we should be allowed, in two cases at least, to check his claim to have followed a manuscript written or corrected by the author and to see at close range what that claim implies. In his introduction to Lascaris' grammatical writings, Aldus was mildly disparaging about the printed versions already in circulation: the manuscript brought from Messina by Bembo and Gabriel was corrected by the hand of "Constantine himself in around one hundred and fifty places"; with its aid he had been able to "remove some sections, correct many, and add a great deal".[29] The Latin translation had been added "on his own initiative", to help those whose study of Greek was only just beginning. Now the manuscript which Aldus used can be identified almost beyond doubt as No. 1401 in the Greek holdings of the Vatican Library. It is glossed unevenly, but in places quite heavily, in a hand which is definitely that of Constantine Lascaris: at the base of its end-page it carries the significant date "1494, 25 Novembris", almost exactly the time when Bembo and Gabriel must have returned from Messina; it came to the Vatican from the collection of Fulvio Orsini, the Roman scholar who bought substantial parts of Pietro Bembo's library from his illegitimate son Torquato Bembo; and, sure enough, a number of the glosses added in the writing of Lascaris can be shown to have found their way into the Aldine version.[30] But a more careful scrutiny of the manuscript quickly reveals that Aldus said less, and implied more, than he might have done. This was no specially prepared copy, to enable a favoured printer to supersede earlier and unsatisfactory editions: the description "well used text-book" would be more appropriate, and a letter which Lascaris wrote to Giorgio Valla during the relevant period shows no sign whatever that he knew of the project.[31] The manuscript has been used by a number of different pupils, who have left doodles, snatches of poetry, even some of a sermon translated into Greek and Italian, on the opening leaves. Lascaris seems to have worked through the text less to correct the Greek than to make it more comprehensible to his beginners, for the majority of the "one hundred and fifty places" which Aldus mentioned were not, in fact, altered, but simply clarified by the insertion of a few Latin words. Most of the explanations appear to have been derived from the translation of Giovanni Craston, which had been printed alongside the Greek text by Bonus Accursius in the Milanese edition of 1480.

What, then, of Aldus' version? In the first place, he did not reproduce this new manuscript though, as he seems to have realised, it extended the range of examples offered by existing printed editions.[32] Apart from his inclusion of a few glosses or expansions such as that noted above, Aldus followed Accursius' text, and since the manuscript was not used as copy and does not appear to have been taken into the print-shop, we must assume that it served only as a quarry from which occasional alterations could be carried into the Milanese edition which must have served as exemplar. Since the manuscript represented a slightly different draft of the work concerned, this was a very arbitrary procedure. But Aldus' Latin translation was prepared in an even stranger way. His words implied, without stating it exactly, that this version was his own. In fact it was a re-touching of Craston's text, once again from the Milanese edition of 1480, and could hardly be called so much as a paraphrase: the verbal changes – "at" for "sed", "tenue" for "lene", "ad minimum" for "saltem" – are not only superficial in themselves, but frequently go against the explanations of Lascaris, on which Aldus had based the claims of his own edition. Scissors and paste had far more to do with the publication of this text than science and scholarship. When the hybridisation, the thinly disguised plagiarism, and Aldus' free adaptations stand revealed, the whole provides an astonishing illustration of the liberties which an editor could safely and respectably take.

Many of the same points could be made, perhaps even more emphatically, about Aldus' text of Petrarch's *Cose volgari*, though it must be said at once that this argument involves a number of fundamental uncertainties about the inter-relation of manuscripts into which this study could not hope to venture without intolerable digression. What is quite certain is that, from the earliest stage, all those involved with this edition claimed that it was derived from an autograph copy, and that these claims were almost immediately called into question. When Isabella d'Este's agent Lorenzo da Pavia called at the printshop towards the end of July 1501, shortly before the edition was published, he was able to see and handle the highly prized authority. The petition for copyright, lodged in this case by Pietro's brother Carlo Bembo, made the boast official: Aldus' colophon made it public; and when the claim was challenged, the printer composed a spirited defence which was attached as an introduction to all copies sold thereafter.[33]

We have already examined this piece as a statement of Aldus' liberal views on the fluidity of language: but its immediate purpose was to insist that the text was based on an autograph manuscript, that Bembo had other specimens of Petrarch's handwriting which proved that fact, and that the authenticity of such a source could not be doubted. Unfortunately, the editors had a crucial gap in their defences which has been open to sceptics from that day to this: Bembo did not at this stage own the manuscript. Lorenzo da Pavia explained that it was the property of a Paduan, and Aldus was careful to say only that he had "obtained it from" or "seen it with" the Venetian nobleman. We know that in 1544 Bembo succeeded in buying, again in Padua, a copy of Petrarch's *Sonnets* and *Canzoni* partly written, partly dictated by the author, and from Fulvio Orsini's description this can now be identified with Vaticanus Latinus No. 3195: but have we any guarantee that this was the same manuscript, and that it was accessible to Bembo and Aldus in 1501?[34] It is true that a number of the important variants on which Aldus made a stand in his introduction – "Bavarico" for "barbarico", for instance – do derive from the autograph. But experts have noticed that Aldus' text is in detail very much more similar to that of Vaticanus Latinus No. 3197, a contemporary manuscript copied and annotated by Bembo himself at roughly the time when the Aldine edition was in preparation. Bembo consciously introduced deviations from the original readings in around 160 passages, intervening fussily in details of spelling by insistence on initial aspirates and on the Latinised form "et", occasionally altering the entire meaning of a passage, as in verse 24 of the Canzone "A qualunque animal..." where he read "destin" for Petrarch's "desir".[35] Aldus faithfully, and perhaps not surprisingly, followed his own editor. Did they really have direct access to the autograph?

Faced with the curious paradox of the evidence and judging it by the high editorial standards of their own time, modern critics of Petrarch's works have resolved the problem in one of two ways: some have suggested that Bembo and Aldus did, indeed, consult the original, but far less closely than they claimed, that the foundation of the Aldine text was Bembo's own copy (i.e. Ms. 3197), and that the notes which cover the pages of that manuscript are the results of Bembo's recension of the autograph for the edition of 1501;[36] others have cut the knot and assumed that Bembo misled Aldus, or that both were lying.[37]

The first of these possibilities is very doubtful, since it is more likely that Bembo corrected his own manuscript after he got possession of the original in 1544: the second seems to me to brush aside both the conviction of Aldus' own defence and the commerical risks which his claims might have involved, if he had known them to be false. In any case, do our explanations need to be so intricate or so desperate? The example of Lascaris' Greek Grammar shows that even a manuscript which had passed through the author's hand qualified for no special treatment, but simply as a source for one or two eye-catching corrections such as those defended by Aldus in his introduction to Petrarch. The manuscript of Lascaris was Bembo's property: the Petrarch, as we know from Lorenzo da Pavia, belonged to a Paduan gentleman who "esteemed it highly", and it is quite possible that the Aldine editors only had time for the most cursory recension. They clearly did not "copy its form, letter by letter", as Aldus claimed. But we have seen repeatedly in this study that printers' claims, whether to have used a particularly authoritative manuscript or to have worked "most accurately", must be treated with great caution and according to the very elastic editorial standards of the day.[38]

Nor is it fair to lay all the blame on the printers and editors, for many references make it clear that the easy attitudes of the manuscript-age died a hard death, and that authors not only condoned, but expected, a large amount of intervention from their publishers. We have seen Ficino virtually shrugging off his responsibilities and leaving everything to Aldus. Erasmus was quite content to admit alterations to his translations from Euripides, and later in life caused a good deal of embarrassment to his assistants in Basel by leaving them to take editorial decisions which they felt most reluctant to accept.[39] In the field of vernacular literature, where there were still no clear rules of grammar and orthography, the printer might find an even heavier load placed on his shoulders, not only by some uncertain author, but by his own compositors who must have been mortally confused by the constant minor variations of spelling. In his dedication of Interiano's *Vita de' Zichi* Aldus admitted to correcting the orthography at the writer's own request.[40] He seems to have done much the same to Sannazaro's *Arcadia*, for critics have noticed that his widespread assimilation of dialect forms to Tuscan usage merely continued a process which had been begun by Summonte and by the author himself.[41] Against its background, the treatment of Petrarch is not too surprising.

What has been said above may well seem a sophistic attempt to divert the reader's attention from the damning evidence of the texts themselves, when they are confronted with the claims that were made about them. But it is a simple matter of fact that Aldus' treatment of writers and their works, which seems unsympathetic, arbitrary and authoritarian to us, seemed the height of courtesy and consideration to his contemporaries. Erasmus' famous tribute in the *Adagia* has been mentioned many times already in this study, and one could argue fruitlessly and endlessly over his debt to Aldus, and Aldus' to him. There is no doubt that constant repetitions of that passage have done much to fix the printer's reputation in the minds of posterity: but it is equally true that the 1508 edition of the *Adagia* was nearly four times the size of its predecessor, and that the publication of this work saw the definite transformation of Erasmus from a promising minor author to an international literary figure. This was not, of course, the sole responsibility of Aldus: it derived indirectly from the cultural ambience he had created, from the visits of interested friends such as Janus Lascaris, Musurus, Egnazio and Fra Urbano, from the manuscripts they provided, and from the advice they had to offer.[42] But the credit for creating the friendly and co-operative atmosphere was clearly given to Aldus. Here, perhaps, the impact of his mysterious Academy was felt most fully. It had never been planned as a literary forum, and at the time of Erasmus' visit its fortunes were at a low ebb. But by grafting the fashionable discussion-groups of Venice or Padua onto the world of printing, it became a natural focus for the exchange of ideas and information, and placed Aldus where Erasmus described him, at the centre of an extremely widespread and influential network.

We have less florid, but possibly more significant evidence of its range and force in a letter written at roughly the same period by Matteo Bandello. Referring to the plans for an Academy and probably to Aldus' visit to Milan in 1506, he continued:

I know that it will please you to hear how my short stories are coming along, since you have read one or two, praised them, and urged me to collect as many as I could: well, I can tell you that I have now written many, and I am now sending you one....Let me also assure you that when I have brought them to a conclusion, I shall send them to you and to no one else....[43]

As it turned out, Aldus never did publish Bandello's *Novelle*. But it is interesting to find him acting as mentor to an author who went on to become one of the most lively and successful Italian writers of the century, and one cannot help wondering how far his underground influence really extended. What part, for example, did he play in the discussions on the future of Italian as a literary language which were led by Pietro Bembo and his circle? We have no means of knowing. But we can be quite sure that Aldus was a much more active and positive force in the literary world of his time than he would ever have admitted.

In spite of the unexacting standards of contemporary opinion, we must agree that Aldus' handling of the works of Constantine Lascaris, Petrarch and Sannazaro does not inspire much initial confidence in his qualities as a Greek and Latin textual critic. Here, however, his reputation rests on different and rather more solid foundations: not simply on his own assertions or the tributes of his admirers, but on certain basic facts about the material which was, or should have been, available to him in Venice. In 1468 the Papal legate Cardinal Bessarion, a Greek intellectual who had accepted the re-unification of the Eastern and Western Churches negotiated in 1439, bequeathed his library to the Venetian Republic. The size of the collection was impressive enough. The total of 752 manuscripts bore comparison with many of the princely libraries of the period, and the 482 Greek items formed an exceptionally large proportion.[44] But it was the quality of the material and the terms of the bequest which gave the acquisition its special importance for Venetian cultural life. Unlike many of his contemporaries, Bessarion did not equate the value of a manuscript with its appearance and the amount of costly decoration it contained. He claimed in his will to have made a planned effort to save as much of the Greek heritage as he could after the fall of Constantinople, and to have collected "not numerous books, so much as the best books, and individual copies of particular works: and so I brought together almost all the works of the wise men of Greece, especially those which were rare or difficult to find".[45]

His collection did, indeed, cover almost the entire range of classical Greek philosophy, rhetoric, drama, and history. He also gained possession of a number of items which remain almost as precious to the classical heritage today as they were in Bessarion's own time: the famous "Venetus A", a tenth-century manuscript of Homer which is still the main source for the text of the *Iliad* and the early commentaries on it; the slightly later, but hardly less important "Venetus V" of Aristophanes; Planudes' autograph copy of the Anthology which was named after him; the earliest known copy of Athenaeus' *Deipnosophistae*.[46]

Cardinal Bessarion's attitude to this treasure was extremely generous. He seems to have been much influenced by that belief in the civilising force of literature which was common among the intellectual liberals of his time, and took particular care in his deed of gift to ensure that the government turned his books into a truly public library. There must be "free access to all who wish to read and study", so that "the minds of many may be enlightened, and the books of use to all, and to posterity".[47] The implications of this for the editorial effort which Aldus set in motion some twenty years later need no further comment. The Biblioteca Marciana offered the best, and most comprehensive range of Greek codices available anywhere in Western Europe at the time. The ideals and intentions of its founder were almost exactly those of Aldus himself. It is not surprising that generations of scholars have written of the Aldine Greek editions as the extension of Bessarion's manuscripts into society at large, and assumed that they were excellent because of the undoubted excellence of the exemplars on which they were based.[48]

Though the Venetian government accepted the Cardinal's gift in language as gracious as his own, its subsequent treatment of his bequest soon became a minor scandal to which a committed group of senators returned sporadically and ineffectively over the next half-century. The books were stored temporarily in the ducal palace itself, where their presence caused such inconvenience that in 1485 they were stacked behind a wooden partition, still in the boxes in which they had been brought from Rome. Efforts in the early 1490s to get the manuscripts properly housed proved a failure: the bulk of opinion seems to have been reflected by Domenico Malipiero, who brushed the whole issue aside with the entry in his diary, "They [the books] were not worth much, since you could buy printed copies."

Pilferage quickly took over from the very limited circulation, and the librarian Sabellico seems to have been unable or unwilling to prevent it.[49] By the time he died in 1506 losses had become so severe that the senate attempted to ban loans entirely, but the decline in the activity of the public lecturers during these years meant that no one was in overall charge, so the situation merely grew worse. When the nobleman Andrea Navagero became librarian in 1515, manuscripts from Bessarion's collection were being found for sale on the bookstalls of the Merceria. But by remorseless pressure on individuals and patient lobbying of public bodies, Navagero and his successor Pietro Bembo gradually reduced the chaos to some kind of order, and when Sansovino secured the contract to design the present library building in 1537, the long ordeal of the manuscripts was nearing its end. But they did not finally come to rest until nearly a century after the original bequest, and they had come very close to destruction in the meantime.[50]

This of course does not mean that Aldus could not have used the Greek texts. It is quite clear that books were accessible to those with the contacts and the influence to get them, and the leverage which Aldus was able to exert through his partners and friends among the governing class has been one of the constant themes of this study. The appointment of Navagero as librarian is significant enough: during the previous three years he had worked extensively with Aldus on the Latin poets, and attained an importance in that field which was hardly less than Musurus' in Greek. Poliziano was refused entry to the library in 1491, but there may have been political reasons for that, since Venetian and Florentine relations were very strained at the time.[51] We have exactly contemporary evidence that the Paduan lecturer, Leonico Tomeo, was able to borrow a manuscript and retain it in his possession for nearly forty years.[52] If Aldus never mentions the Marciana, that need not surprise us too much: any material that he did use will almost certainly have been obtained through private contacts, and in contravention of the increasingly restrictive measures which hedged the library round. Such tactics could not be declared publicly.

But incredible though it may seem, all the signs suggest that Aldus never gained access to the Marciana, or at least never learned enough about its contents to use them as a regular and reliable source. Sometimes his own words provide a clue. When editing parts of Theophrastus in 1497, and Quintus of Smyrna in 1505, he lamented his difficulties with the "torn and defective" manuscripts which were the only exemplars he could find in the whole of Italy. Clearly, he cannot have been referring to the complete, unstained and carefully written codices of the works concerned which survive to this day in the Marciana, and the texts which he printed prove that he did not know of them.[53] The steadily expanding evidence of textual criticism reinforces the argument time and again. Renouard noticed that Aldus omitted twenty-three letters of Crates, which he could have found in the Marciana, from his collection of Greek letters:[54] detailed research on the texts of Aristophanes, Plutarch, and Athenaeus has proved that he was unable to refer to the vital manuscripts of those authors which Bessarion had collected;[55] and his edition of Bessarion's own *In Calumniatorem Platonis* is perhaps the strangest case of all. This was one of the instances where Aldus claimed to have had an autograph manuscript brought to him, and the Marciana contains three manuscripts of the relevant work, at least one of which was definitely in the collection at this time and has been corrected by the author. Not only did Aldus fail to use this source: he printed a draft of the work which differed entirely from that presented by the Venetian codices.[56] It has yet to be proved that any of the editions produced during Aldus' lifetime was derived from the manuscripts of Bessarion's collection, and even if it could be so proved the counter-examples would still forbid us to make any general conclusions about the excellence of his editions on the basis of the Marciana and its unquestionable virtues. Even for his Greek editions, Aldus had no special privileges. He had to rely, like his contemporaries, on the open market.

A word of caution here – like most open markets in Venice, the manuscript-market was exceptionally rich, and Aldus' high social connections enabled him to exploit it at every level. Bernardo Bembo, the excellence of whose library has become a recurrent theme in this study, showed much of Bessarion's discernment in his quest for early manuscripts of individual authors. He owned a fourth-century Terence, to which Poliziano paid reverent tributes in 1491, a ninth-century Lombardic codex of Virgilian extracts, and autographs of a number of the works of the fifteenth-century Florentine writers: his equally careful and much less preoccupied son Pietro added some valuable Greek items, including a twelfth-century manuscript of Pindar's *Odes*.[57]

These books were among the lucky few which have survived: we know of others, equally important, which have not, and of private libraries which may in their time have equalled or surpassed Bembo's. Giorgio Valla's much admired manuscript of the Greek mathematical writer Heron has perished.[58] So has the "venerable" Homer once owned by Urbano Valeriani, who must have assembled part of his Greek library actually in Greece.[59] When Musurus prepared the Aldine text of Aristophanes in 1498, he certainly had access to a manuscript of the comedies which had once been owned by the celebrated early humanist Francesco Barbaro, and passed down to his descendants Ermolao and Alvise. This library, and that of Alessandro Benedetti, were both visited by Poliziano and Lascaris during 1490 and 1491. Both are now dispersed.[60] Of the collection assembled by the Gabriel family, which Poliziano also inspected, or by Daniel Renier, who definitely possessed Greek texts and made them available to Aldus, we now know nothing whatever.[61]

But the lesson is clear enough: the neglect of the Marciana does not by itself mean that material of the same, or comparable quality was not available elsewhere. By a curious paradox, these "private" libraries appear to have been far more accessible to the public than the Marciana, whatever the terms of Bessarion's will and the Senate's undertakings to him. During the 1450s a nobleman named Gerolamo da Molin was operating something very like a lending library, with a brisk circulation of literary, religious and philosophical texts among his fellow-patricians and other interested parties such as students and clerics.[62] Judging from his correspondence with Leoniceno, Valla seems to have been running his library in much the same way in the 1490s: Aldus, as we have seen, played some part in the process and by his involvement in it placed himself strategically at the junction of many other channels of communication.[63] So his ability to find a variety of good material need not be seriously questioned, in spite of his own complaints of insuperable difficulties: the real problem is to find what use he made of his opportunities.

Sometimes, the opportunities themselves were poor and Aldus frankly admitted it. If his texts of Theophrastus and Quintus of Smyrna were each based on a single damaged exemplar, we should not be surprised to find that the texts are of rather inferior quality:[64] but we should notice that Aldus did not differ from his contemporaries in his willingness to base an edition on such narrow authority. His method of work, too, excites occasional suspicion: he is too rushed to eat or wipe his nose; Erasmus is too busy to scratch his ears, and hands the drafted pages of the *Adagia* straight to the compositors; Navagero revises the notoriously difficult text of Quintilian "hurriedly, with little rest", to satisfy the demands of the press-operators.[65] Can there have been time for a proper collation of manuscripts, and had there been much progress since de Bussi revised the text of Silius Italicus in a fortnight?[66] Some of the texts hardly suggest it. The Theocritus of 1495 exists in two separate versions, both based on Accursius' Milanese edition, into which some variants were introduced from an undistinguished manuscript now in the Vatican library. In his first version, Aldus was able to print only thirteen lines of the Idyll "Megara", so he filled out the gap by inserting a section of the earlier "Lament for Bion": but some time before the press-run was completed another manuscript was produced, two quires reprinted, and the necessary additions and corrections made.[67] This is still the scissors and paste world of Lascaris' Greek Grammar.

Was the process always as haphazard as this, and what different stages did it involve? Occasionally, we are able to follow the editors step by step in the pages of a surviving press-copy – a manuscript which by the page-markings and corrections in its margins, the smudges and finger-marks on its surface, reveals that it was used actually by the compositors to set up the text. Naturally, there are not many of these specimens: the eleven traced so far account for less than a tenth of Aldus' output, and several of them are no more than bundles of fragments which have been "passed to the printers to be ripped apart, and to die like vipers in the act of birth" – the fate which Aldus considered normal for an exemplar.[68] But these eleven span the twenty years of his publishing-career from the first volume of Aristotle down to the Hesychius of 1514, and they can supply us with three vital clues to the editorial techniques which were being applied: in the manuscripts themselves we can judge the quality of the material that Aldus and his associates had at their disposal; from the notes and corrections they added we can form an opinion of their philological skills; and from the correspondence between the corrected manuscripts and the printed versions we can see how far they succeeded in transmitting their knowledge through the compositors onto the paper, and so eventually to the public.

Appropriately, the great edition of Aristotle on which Aldus based his bid for fame now offers the best opportunities of reconstructing his method, and since these have recently been exploited to the full by Professor Martin Sicherl, I can confine myself to summarising his arguments, adding a few observations of my own, and referring the specialist to his exhaustive researches.[69] The largest range of material refers to the two volumes of the scientific works of Aristotle and Theophrastus which appeared in 1497. For the *De Historia Animalium* Aldus' main source was a manuscript now classified as Suppl. Graec. No. 212 in the Bibliothèque Nationale of Paris. It was copied by an unidentified scribe at a time which can be dated roughly to 1450-69 from the water-marks in the paper, and carries quire-markings for the section of the third volume that extends from f. b 3 up to d 20. The text is now fragmentary, and the pages disordered. The codex itself is a composite jumble of extracts which no doubt was part of the debris in the workshop and probably came to Paris, along with several others owned by the Torresani, as a result of purchases made by the French ambassadors during the 1530s.[70] But as a witness to Aristotle's text it is by no means without value. Though a recent copy in Aldus' time, it was derived from the oldest known manuscript of the *De Historia Animalium*, the thirteenth-century Marcianus Graecus 208 which must still have been in Cardinal Bessarion's possession when the copy was taken. Corrections were introduced to the printed edition from two other sources, the fourteenth-century Vaticanus Graecus 262 and Ambrosianus I 56 supra, which was copied for the wealthy Florentine dilettante Palla Strozzi and presents a different version of the manuscript-tradition. Altogether, the assessment of the Paris manuscript and the text based on it is very evenly balanced. Aldus had some good material to hand, and he tried, as he claimed, to establish the correct tradition by comparing different witnesses. But when we descend to details, his methods and those of his collaborators still seem very arbitrary. In a four-page section of the printed text Sicherl reckons that the Aldine editors corrected their press-copy at proof stage on twenty-five occasions and introduced eleven new errors on their own account.[71] Finally, one cannot help wondering why they failed to use the archetype, Marcianus Graecus 208, which must have been in Venice at the time.

In this case, Aldus worked from manuscripts which were already in existence: in others, he had to multiply the risk of error by having copies specially made for the press. This happened with the botanical works of Theophrastus, whose "single, mutilated exemplar" we have already seen causing their publisher a good deal of anxiety. By a strange irony, both the original and the copy which Aldus had made have survived to provide an illustration of the dangers of working rapidly from inferior material. The original is identified by Sicherl as Graecus 2069 in the Bibliothèque Nationale: it was once the property of Aldus' friend, Niccolo Leoniceno, for whom it appears to have been copied during the 1460s or 1470s; and sure enough, it lacks the end of *De Causius Plantarum*. The press-copy, now MS. 17 in the Greek collection of the Harvard library, is another composite codex containing various fragments rescued by John Cuno during his stay in Venice: his notes and directions indicate that the contents were already fragmentary and in disorder by 1509. Both from the water-marks and on wider historical grounds, we can probably date this particular section to the early 1490s and to the intense period of preparatory work which is reflected in Leoniceno's letters to Valla.[72] The use of a very ordinary paper, the amount of abbreviation, and the lack of any ornament, all suggest that the unknown scribe worked at speed: so does the fact that he omitted three passages in *De Causis Plantarum*, and had to enter them in the margin later. More serious still, the Harvard manuscript makes it quite clear that there were as yet no accepted symbols or procedures for correcting copy before printing. At times, the editor tried to help the compositors and succeeded only in confusing them. On f. 132v, the manuscript, with a rather indistinct abbreviation, read ἆρος καὶ θέρους ("in spring and summer"). Correctly but perhaps unnecessarily, the editor expanded this to ἔαρος καὶ θέρους: the puzzled compositors printed ἀέρος καὶ θέρους ("of the *wind* and summer"), compounding the error and wholly distorting the sense of the Greek. Then at other times, the printers were given no guidance at all: Sicherl lists ten passages, in both the *Historia Plantarum* and the *De Causis Plantarum*, where the printed text differs from the Harvard manuscript and from other possible sources on no visible grounds whatsoever.[73] One can only assume that the editors had indulged in a carefree bout of conjecture when the text was already in proof. If *De Historia Animalium* is an uncertain witness to Aldus' methods, the works of Theophrastus provide unambiguous evidence of poor material, subjective or arbitrary editorship, and lack of coordination between editors and compositors.

The further we search, the more marked these tendencies become. For the *Metaphysics* of Aristotle, which they printed along with Theophrastus' botanical works, the Aldine editors used what is now Graecus 1848 in the Bibliothèque Nationale. This was evidently a manuscript to which they attached some importance: apart from the quire-markings for the fourth volume, it shows few signs of damage; it was written by Michael Apostolis, one of the best known scribes of the mid-fifteenth century, and since it carries the signature of Gianfrancesco Torresani, Andrea's son and successor, there is every likelihood that it once formed part of a family- or company-collection before passing into the French Royal Library. But the manuscript was still used in a very free and easy fashion by the editors: Sicherl notes seventeen doubtful passages in the first three chapters of the work where the Aldine agrees with its exemplar, and eleven where it differs, six of these being simple omissions.[74] Once again, we have the obvious hints of haphazard conjecture and careless presswork. By the time we reach the *Nichomachean Ethics,* which formed part of the final volume and were printed in 1498, the evidence becomes absolutely damning. We have in this case only a short section of the exemplar for comparison: seven folios of the Harvard manuscript, which seem to have been copied in the later 1480s by the Cretan scribe Thomas Bitzimanos and cover the early chapters of the first book up to 1,102 a 14. But even within this narrow compass Sicherl has detected 112 places where the Aldine deviates from the manuscript: twenty of these appear to be simple printing errors; the remains are random corrections introduced from other authorities or editors' emendations jotted down at proof-stage. It is clear that this text, and those of several minor works such as the pseudo-Aristotelian *De Physionomia* and Porphyrius' *Eisagoge,* of which the Harvard manuscript also preserves a few fragments, are hopelessly and incurably contaminated.[75] Our conclusion must be that, at this stage of its development, Aldine editorship was more like an academic wheel of fortune than a controlled system of scholarly criticism: when the editors had good material, they generally had it by accident; they had little or no idea of how to use it; and they still had a lot to learn about communicating with their press-operators. The availability of Greek scribes in Venice, long considered as one of Aldus' main advantages, seems to have served mainly to flood the market with inferior copies.

Similar conclusions are suggested by fragments of a manuscript which was used as copy for the *Epistolarum Graecarum Collectio* of 1499 and is now Suppl. Graecum 924 in the Bibliothèque Nationale. This is another composite codex, whose history appears to be rather different from that of its counterparts in Paris: the opening folio bears the inscription "Beati Rhenani sum", and since Beatus Rhenanus studied under Cuno in Basel, it is likely that we have here another of the irrepressible Dominican's gleanings from his years in Venice and Padua.[76] The second component of the manuscript, covering only folios 33r to 39v, is the most important for the present enquiry. It carries an incomplete text of thirty-two amorous letters of Philostratus, copied rather hurriedly on a paper which can be dated from its five-petaled watermark to 1499 and which must therefore suggest that this apograph was taken specifically for the Aldine edition.[77] The pages are marked for quire u of the edition, and there is a note at the beginning directing the compositors to set the heading in capital letters. Beyond this, the editorial instructions are very scanty.

Only six passages have been glossed, one with no more than a Latin note to identify the festival of the goddess Flora. There is the same failure to distinguish between emendations and observtions which we have already seen in Theophrastus, the same inconsistency in transferring them into print, and the same tendency to compound errors as a result. On line 11 of f. 34r, for example, the editor corrected the meaningless ἀπέβλαβεν to ἀπέλαβεν: in the printed text, the word had changed to ἀπέβαλεν.[78]

But there is a new and still more revealing feature in the arrangement of the material itself. At the end of f. 39v the text simply gives out with the prophetic words "Now what am I going to do?": at 40r it is taken up, but on a different and much smaller paper and in another handwriting; the fragmentary letter is finished, and some more added; then at the bottom of 41v the compositors are directed to "look for the rest in the large quire". There are no page-markings in this new section, but eight passages have been modified, some with an almost unbelievable lack of taste and understanding. On line 9 of f. 41v the text read ἐμοὶ δὲ μόνοις πρόπινε τοῖς ὄμμασιν ("Drink to me only with thine eyes"). The editor wanted to change ὄμμασιν (eyes) to χείλεσιν (lips), but fortunately the compositors knew better, so the lack of communication in this case worked out to everyone's advantage.[79] The light shed on the method of collecting copies is the striking feature here. We can actually watch the editors run out of material, hastily fill out the gap, and shuffle the new piece in somehow with what they already had. When we combine this with what we already know of their hurried, uneven emendation and their failure to give clear instructions to the printers, the overall prospect becomes alarming.

Only a few of these fears can be dispelled by turning to the next two Aldine editions whose genesis we can study in any detail – the Sophocles of August 1502 and the Euripides which appeared in February of the following year. In both cases, we have direct evidence that the editors worked from at least two manuscripts: but it is equally clear that they worked in a very unsystematic style. For the text of Sophocles, they had both a fourteenth-century codex which is now No. 48 in the Greek holdings of the National Library of Vienna, and the somewhat later Graecus No. 731 of the Leningrad Public Library, which, though containing only the *Ajax, Electra,* and *Oedipus Tyrannus,* carries the crucial page-markings that prove it to have been the Aldine press-copy.[80] The Soviet philologist Fonkich has collated the printed text of the *Ajax* with both manuscripts, and drawn up a table of readings which shows that the editors were usually responsible enough to follow their earlier and better authority. But it also shows that the Leningrad manuscript itself contains much that is unmetrical or ungrammatical, and that it has been systematically corrected from its counterpart only from line 357. Stranger still, there are suggestions that an even better exemplar lay somewhere in the background: at line 1,000 the editors discarded the δειλαῖος of both their manuscripts for the reading δυστηνός preserved in the earlier tradition, and we are left wondering what further material they had to hand, but above all why they used it so unmethodically.[81]

For Euripides, the evidence is less complete but entirely similar in type. Two manuscripts were used in the workshop, and a few of their scattered leaves now survive in Supplementum Graecum Nos. 212 and 393 of the Bibliothèque Nationale. Only a few hundred disconnected lines from three plays – *Hecuba, Orestes* and *Phoenissae* – can be found in these codices, but it is clear enough that they were recent copies from the hand of one of the Gregoropoulos family, derived from different exemplars and unconnected to the capital tradition of Bessarion's twelfth-century Marcianus 471. Once again, the vigilant Cuno's magpie-like quest for bits and pieces has saved these fragments from destruction. As with Sophocles, the Aldine editors definitely checked their authorities against each other, following 393 rather than 212 in twenty-one passages contained in both authorities. But there is the same absence of care and method. Corrections were clearly introduced from other sources, and yet there are still seven passages in 212 where basic errors, including the spurious feminine form εὐτεκνοτάτην at Hecuba line 581, have passed unchallenged into the printed edition.[82] We can at least point to these two editions as clear proof that Aldus and his team were collating manuscripts as they claimed to be doing: but we have still no sign of their using any worthwhile authorities, and as we watch them veer giddily from one source to another, or produce a correction to both exemplars from no known source whatever, their method of procedure becomes more and more puzzling.

The first edition of Plutarch's *Moralia,* which appeared after a long period of gestation in 1509, suggests a few answers to these open questions, and they are not reassuring. The surviving press-copy in this case was a far more solid authority than anything we have examined so far: a fine, thirteenth-century manuscript now in the Biblioteca

Ambrosiana of Milan, its parchment folios present the strongest contrast to the tattered fragments rescued by Cuno from the workshop floor.[83] But there is no doubt that it went into the print-room: from from f. 29v to 34r, then again from 84v, it carries the page-markings of the Aldine text, most of the material falling in volume II of the edition. Though not numerous, the corrections are sufficient to show that at least one other manuscript has been used and that the editor, whom we know was Demetrius Ducas, worked competently enough within the limits imposed on him. In altering the meaningless ἄμως πλάσαι on f. 85v of the manuscript to ἀπέσπασται, or the weak ἡ τῶν ὅρων ἀκαιρία on f. 120v to λόγων, he may possibly have been working by conjecture. But the passages added to the text on ff. 29v, 33v, 84v and elsewhere, can only have come from another manuscript. It is in fact less the critical treatment of the exemplar that excites interest here than the general use made of it in finalising the printed version. Above the sections between ff. 34v and 84v which lack page-markings and emendations, is scrawled the word "stampato" – "already printed".

Our inference must be that the process of criticism and emendation did not precede that of printing but advanced jerkily alongside it, step by alternating step: and that this particular manuscript, the earliest we have so far found in Aldus' hands, was used not as part of a coherent recension but simply as a source of some new grist which could be ground straight into the mill. There is further evidence for this in the fact that one of the assistant editors, Gerolamo Aleander, was collecting material on his own account before the Aldine text appeared, and published his own improved version of some of the essays four years later in Paris.[84] It is hard to avoid the conclusion that Aldus' editorial method often seems puzzling precisely because there was no method in it: printing classical texts was first and last an exercise in improvisation.

The evidence of these Greek editions brings us once again to the problem of reconciling Aldus' reputation and his claims with the actual quality of the texts he produced. We have already seen how little the boasts of copying Petrarch's forms "letter by letter" from an autograph were worth. Are the claims to have checked and corrected exemplars of the classical authors, and to be ready to redeem every single error with a gold piece, based on as narrow a foundation? Aldus was by no means above criticism in his own time. As early as 1498 Codrus Urceus mistrusted a number of the readings adopted in Aristotle's scientific works:[85] in 1513 Michael Hummelberg hinted that a number of the Greek passages in Erasmus' *Adagia* were suspect;[86] and in 1528 another editor of Petrarch, Alessandro Vellutello, openly accused both Pietro Bembo and the now deceased Aldus of lying about their authority for the Sonnets, Canzoni and Trionfi.[87] It is also worth recalling that in 1503 the rival printer Soncino suggested that Aldus had claimed far more than his due measure of credit for the types designed by Francesco Griffo.[88] Have we now reached a position where the evidence of his own editions can be used to set Aldus in the dock as a prince among literary charlatans, a man who turned the resources of his business partnership to buying prestige, and hid his deficiencies behind a barrage of social and intellectual contacts? Is the whole mystique of Aldine editorship a vast confidence trick?

The first and perhaps the surest defence against such charges must lie in the conventional nature of the original claims. As we have seen repeatedly in this study, the boasts of having access to special material, of working with exceptional care or of facing insuperable difficulties, were all parts of the publisher's stock in trade, and Aldus cannot be blamed for dressing his own windows in what was plainly the accepted style. When he appealed to the Senate for copyright in 1492, Paganino de' Paganinis spoke of the four doctors of theology whom he had hired to perfect his edition of Nicholas of Lyra's Commentary on the Bible: but in 1485 he had bought a copy of the work concerned from a public bookstall.[89] In 1506 Johan Amerbach wrote of his search for the works of Augustine throughout the libraries of Italy, France and Germany: but a year earlier he had instructed his sons, then students in Paris, to look out for certain texts in the university bookshops.[90] Without suggesting that the editions concerned were prepared entirely on this basis, we may surmise from these cases that between the boundaries of strict truth and actual falsehood there was a broad area of what we might term "permissible hyperbole". Aldus, like his contemporaries, made use of that area. If he also used the language of more developed textual criticism, and led some of his modern readers to expect the scientific scholarship of Lachmann, Bentley or Housman, then that is the fault of the readers and the changing times – not of Aldus.

Yet even without this retreat into questions of terminology, it could still be shown from Aldus' personal correspondence that his editorial method followed many of the paths of which he spoke and produced many of the effects of which he dreamed. He was capable of working with the utmost patience and caution. He did everything in his power to encourage academic co-operation and the exchange of information, both securing and retaining the services of the leading classical philologists of the time, Musurus and Navagero. These efforts in their turn brought a good deal of new material to the surface, fulfilling the hopes expressed by Aldus himself in 1496 and by his predecessor de Bussi a quarter of a century earlier.

So much of this chapter has traced the preparation of editions at breakneck speed and with an apparent minimum of care that it is only just to point out that the picture has a different side. Texts of Plato, Pausanias and the Suda were being mentioned more than a dozen years before they were eventually published, and Erasmus worked in 1508 on an edition of Terence which was finally printed by Andrea Torresani in 1517.[91] In these cases, we have no means of knowing how far the work had gone: but sometimes we can follow its progress in fair detail. From his appeals for release to the Marquis of Mantua, we know that Aldus' journeys in Lombardy during 1506 had been part of a search for manuscripts of Virgil's *Catalepton,* and he appears to have been bringing a good deal of material back to Venice with him.[92] From this, a master-copy was compiled and entrusted to Fortiguerra, who a year later was taking advantage of his contacts at the Papal court to see what manuscripts could be found in Romagna and the March.[93] Aldus was still working on the project only a few months before his death, and in the autumn of 1514 received a detailed letter from the Neapolitan scholar Parrhasius who suggested emendations to more than fifty passages. The printed edition appeared in 1517.[94]

Athenaeus' *Deipnosophistae* was even longer in preparation. The final version appeared in August 1514, edited carefully but on the strength of rather indifferent manuscript-authority by Marcus Musurus.[95] We know that Aldus had been negotiating to buy an exemplar through Fortiguerra as early as 1505, and that a copy was being made for him in Rome during the spring of 1508: but the Pierpoint Morgan Library possesses a single printed sheet, carrying the Epitome of Book 1 and set up in a type which Aldus did not use after 1499.[96] Even though the plan clearly did not develop steadily, and was probably in abeyance for quite long periods, fifteen years were needed to bring it from the experimental stage to eventual fruition. No doubt the editorial efforts involved would seem hopelessly ill-coordinated by modern standards. Fortiguerra passed his copy of the *Catalepton* to a friendly bishop named Fabrizio Varano who had a few emendations of his own to offer and in due course passed the exemplar on to an associate in Urbino for further suggestions. There is no evidence that any of these men had worked on the same manuscript as Aldus, and little to show how their separate investigations were linked to the common goal. On what basis, for example, did Aldus adopt almost exactly half of the emendations proposed by Parrhasius and reject the rest, but often with a measure of compromise which suggests that he did not want to offend a valuable associate too much?[97] Here as in his treatment of authors, there is a strong suggestion that personal factors were very relevant: that Aldus preferred to assemble opinions rather than variant readings, and that he had a better understanding of men than of manuscripts. But even allowing for this lack of understanding and organisation, the sheer intensity of the research was enough to promote knowledge of the material that was available and so, indirectly, to begin refining the techniques of using it.

In their more flamboyant moments Aldus and his colleagues probably exaggerated the extent of the help they received from "Poles and Hungarians" who sent valuable manuscripts from long-lost "castles in the land of the Dacians".[98] In or outside Italy, intellectual co-operation was a constant gamble, subject to both the misfortunes and the misunderstandings that we have already met. The trick was to spread the stakes widely enough to be sure of drawing some winners. Sometimes the editors failed to recognise their own luck. Early in 1500, more than a year before this first octavo was published, Aldus submitted some printed sheets of Virgil to the judgement of his Florentine friends. Pietro Ricci was enthusiastic: he wrote back to approve the whole scheme, and to offer corrections of his own to six passages in the *Aeneid*. All his suggestions were sound, and there is the strongest possibility that they were based on the fifth-century Codex Mediceus, to which he might well have had access: but his strongest argument for the readings he proposed was that they had been approved by Poliziano or Ermolao Barbaro. He did nothing to show the identity or the importance of his manuscript authority, and it is not entirely surprising that neither in 1501 nor in 1514, when he had the shrewder judgement of Navagero to guide him, did Aldus show any eagerness to incorporate these daring conjectures, as they must have seemed, in his own text.[99]

In direct and bitter contrast, Aldus often overvalued a relatively modest prize. He was delighted with his exemplar of Prudentius, which had been summoned "all the way from Britain, after lying there neglected for eleven-hundred years and more".[100] It is a rather sad comment on the naïve enthusiasms to which even the most serious scholars were still subject. What Aldus received from England was probably an apograph taken from an eleventh-century codex, and there is every indication that he could have done better had he directed his research towards Milan or Rome.[101] At times, this painstaking quest for what should have been immediately available reaches almost comical proportions. In 1508 and again in 1513, Aldus paid eloquent tributes to Janus Lascaris and his late patron, Lorenzo de' Medici, for their efforts in bringing manuscripts of the Attic orators back from Greece, since the printer realised that in securing access to this material he had made a very lucky coup.[102] By rights, the manuscripts should have been in the private library of the Medici, but the death of Lorenzo, the comparative indifference of Piero, and the collapse of the régime in 1494 had made it possible for Lascaris to retain them indefinitely.[103] So Aldus had every reason to feel pleased – with Lascaris for preserving the manuscripts, with himself for having sought Lascaris' friendship at an early stage, and with Louis XII for sending the Greek to Venice as his ambassador. But would Aldus have felt so lucky if he had known that copies as good, if not better than these, should have been easily available to him in Bessarion's library, within a few minutes walk of his own front door?[104]

We can make two points in the attempt to cheer this landscape of false trails, abandoned bridgeheads, and vast, unnecessary detours. First, it could be argued that the journey in itself was as important as the destination or the direction, since it gradually increased the stock of information about what was available and where: so, by painful and uneconomical stages, the confusions into which Aldus and his contemporaries so obviously fell were bound to become easier to avoid. Second, the sheer extent of the explorations was almost certain, on the simple law of averages, to reveal one or two important discoveries. We can follow these processes in two of Aldus' later editions, the Pliny of 1508 and the Hesychius of 1514.

Based on an imperfect Italian manuscript-tradition, the early editions of the letters of Pliny the Younger contained only the first seven books and book nine. But by about 1500 rumours of an important new source in France were beginning to circulate. Aldus to have got wind of them quickly, no doubt through the good offices of Fra Giocondo: the letter which Lascaris wrote to the printer from Blois on Christmas Eve, 1501, contains clear reference to a manuscript of Pliny which

Aldus had asked his correspondent to investigate, and by 1502 another of his associates, Gerolamo Avanzio, had secured copies of part of book ten and included them in a new edition.[105] But Aldus was prepared to wait. With Fra Giocondo well established as architectural advisor to the French Crown and another dedicated classicist, Guillaume Budé, starting his career in the royal chancellery, Aldus was able to rely on that delicate personal touch which had been useful to him on so many occasions.[106] When Fra Giocondo returned from France in 1504 to become military engineer to the Venetian Republic, he brought his own apograph of the French manuscript with him. But by now, an even greater prize was within reach. Aldus had quickly established a close relationship with Lascaris when the Greek arrived in Venice, and in 1505 a friendly nobleman named Alvise Mocenigo was dispatched to represent the Republic at the French court.[107] Now armed with a double leverage, Aldus got the original codex into his hands and printed the complete text. The manuscript, he reported, was on vellum and written in a style so antique that he could only believe that the copy had been made in Pliny's own time.[108] This patently exaggerated description of what must have been a fifth- or sixth-century uncial codex, combined with the confession that he found the script very difficult to read, gives us a sharp reminder of the limited palaeographical skills which Aldus could apply to his task. But here, unfortunately, the trail becomes blurred. A fragment now in the Pierpoint Morgan library has been thought to come from the famous Paris manuscript, but is too short to yield enough information for a definite conclusion:[109] and in any case Aldus' text contains some errors so obvious and bizarre as to leave lingering suspicions that, whether he followed the Morgan manuscript in its complete state or some other now vanished authority, he followed it in the same erratic and eclectic style as he followed Ricci's emendations to the *Aeneid*.[110] But perhaps these detailed and unanswerable technicalities are less important than the simple fact that Aldus had taken part in a significant antiquarian discovery, and had broadcast its results on his presses. This was what he had longed to achieve, and the feeling of exhilaration in his preface is unmistakable.

The story of the text of Hesychius' *Lexicon* is much simpler and illustrates not only the workings of Aldus' information service, but a feature of his editorship which should have been suspected but has never been investigated – its development over the course of his lifetime. There is, and apparently was in Aldus' time, only one complete copy of the work concerned.[111] It became the property of the Biblioteca Marciana during the eighteenth century, but in 1514 belonged to a Mantuan gentleman named Giangiacomo Bardellone, a scholar and mathematician who was well-known in the intellectual circles of the Gonzaga court, and also acquainted with a number of prominent Venetians including Andrea Navagero and Gasparo Contarini.[112] In his dedication Aldus spoke only of Bardellone's generosity: but it was probably through his network of contacts that he heard of the manuscript and got it into his hands. He and his editor Musurus have been much criticised for their treatment of a unique book, which belonged to an influential friend.[113] They did not trouble to take an apograph but used the original, like the Ambrosian Plutarch, as a print-room copy, so that Musurus' corrections and the inevitable daubs of ink still stain its pages. Without denying that their conduct implies lack of respect for a valuable authority, I think it is only fair to point out that this attitude was general, and ought not to shock us. Aldus and Musurus treated Bardellone's Hesychius more kindly than Erasmus and Froben treated the Dominicans' New Testament in Basel a few months later,[114] and there is no sign that Bardellone, who received the dedication, was in any way put out. He may even have been pleased to have the corrections of a scholar as prestigious as Musurus on his own copy.

In fact, the modern scholar has every reason to be grateful for these corrections. They were transferred into print only about five months before Aldus' death and a comparison of this last surviving press copy with earlier versions such as the Harvard Aristotle gives us a chance of seeing whether the technique of the editors and the skill of the compositors had developed during the interval. A glance puts an end to any thought of treating "Aldine editorship" as a unified and coherent method, for we might be in different worlds. The editors of Theophrastus, admittedly working on an apograph of their own, corrected only nine passages in over forty folios and glossed about the same number. Musurus regularly corrected or glossed twenty or thirty passages on a single side of folio. His emendations were often extremely shrewd, and the most recent editor pays a grateful tribute to him.[115]

But there is more than the quality of the scholarship to be considered. We have seen how the vagueness of the corrections and the lack of instruction from the editors often confused the compositors of the earlier Aldine texts and led to compound errors. By 1514, this problem has been brought under control. I cannot claim to have collated the manuscript completely with the printed text, but two dozen emendations, selected at random from different sections of the *Lexicon*, proved in every case to have been followed exactly by the printers.

There is no reason to be surprised by the development. Most of Aldus' editions were probably the work of a team rather than a single scholar, the sum-total of many mens' opinions rather than one man's observations. But Musurus worked almost continually with Aldus from 1497 at the latest until the printer's death, and spent much of the rest of his time expounding the Greek authors in Venice or Padua. Navagero appeared on the scene rather later. But between the battle of Agnadello and his abrupt return to public life in 1523, he became an almost compulsive editor of the Latin classics, working on the texts of Virgil, Cicero, Quintilian, Lucretius, Ovid, Terence, and others.[116] Men like these can hardly have worked for fifteen or twenty years under the conditions described by Erasmus without learning a few more philological tricks to guide themselves, and a few new methods of communication to guide the members of what had to be a closely interlocking team. Aldus' editorial method, such as it was, did not spring fully armed from his own head: it had to be developed over the course of many years.

The reader who has persevered thus far with this most intricate section of an already intricate study will, I hope, have realised by now that in this field of editorship I have found it almost impossible to be both accurate and fair. It is not just that the material is scarce: the rules have changed. By our standards, there cannot be the slightest doubt that Aldus overstated his claims. He savaged the texts of contemporary authors when he was claiming to follow them letter by letter. He failed completely to recognise the real status and importance of the ancient authorities he professed to revere. Worse still, he expressed his claims in the most persuasive language. So the modern textual critic has two options. He accepts Aldus' claims in general terms, but does not turn to him as a serious authority: or he approaches a text that Aldus once edited, armed with wholly new technological aids and marching ahead of a coherent system of manuscript-catalogues, palaeographical handbooks and accumulated philological expertise. He knows Aldus' reputation. He turns to his text, hoping for dazzling feats of scholarship; failing to find them, he treats these primitive efforts with a gigantic condescension, forgetting to ask how far the formidable armoury which he can deploy was prepared by the exchange of information that Aldus and his friends encouraged. Accustomed to think of Aldine editorship as a coherent system, he then finds it easy to condemn that system on the strength of one or two examples.

But if Aldus treated the works of Petrarch, Sannazaro and Pontano with a high hand, he did so because he was expected, indeed obliged to do so. Another contemporary editor, Pietro Summonte, agonised over the various forms of Neapolitan place-names which he found in Pontano's autographs and ended by assimilating them to the only standards he could find – those of Latin usage.[117] There were no rules of vernacular orthography, and the responsibility of imposing them fell largely on the editor. And if Aldus seems naïve in his treatment of Greek and Latin manuscripts, we must remember, first, that information about manuscripts was a good deal harder to come by in 1500 than it is today, and second, that a powerful current of opinion thought that reference to manuscripts implied a lack of confidence in one's own judgement. Aldus clearly never discovered what was in the Marciana. When Parrhasius sent his long list of emendations to the *Catalepton*, he felt it necessary to begin with a defence of having spent so much time comparing exemplars: some, he knew, preferred to show off their own knowledge of Latin by telling the world what Virgil should have said.[118] In 1493 Matteo Bossi had sent Poliziano an ancient Ausonius, with a hint of apology in his letter: "But I have noticed on a number of occasions that age in books is something that you admire as others do in wine."[119] An interest in early manuscripts and palaeography was not yet seen as an essential part of critical scholarship: it was a donnish eccentricity, like a taste for vintage port. If we set him against this background, we can feel some surprise at Aldus' achieving as much as he did.

What must definitely be abandoned is any notion of Aldine editorship as a single grand system, an "arcanum imperii" which set classical scholarship on a new course. An Aldine text is as good as its exemplar, its editor, and the use he made for it, and every case has to be treated independently. Aldus' services to scholarship lay less in improving the quality of texts, though he certainly achieved that in certain cases, than in vastly extending the quantity of material available for general study. And it is only fair to say, in conclusion, that he did not deny his deficiencies. Five years after the appearance of his text of Demosthenes, he was still checking its readings against Florentine manuscripts with the help of Decembrio.[120] In his text of Stephanus of Byzantium, he entirely omitted one quire-marking because his manuscript was faulty, and he wished his readers to have the opportunity of filling out the missing section, if they were lucky enough to find it.[121] And he introduced the custom of marking passages which he could not fathom with asterisks.[122] In his more sober moments, Aldus saw himself simply as a transmittor of a great tradition, and his enterprise as a component in a far larger process. He also had one quality lacked by many far greater editors of the classics – that of admitting that he could be wrong.

NOTES

1 Preface to *Rhetorica ad Herennium* (OAME LXXXII). See also the section quoted in Chapter IV, n. 178.
2 Preface to Theocritus and Hesiod, 1496 (OAME V): to the *Grammatici Veteres*, 1496 (*ib.*, IV); and to Plato, 1513 (*ib.*, LXXVIII). For comparison with the principles stated by Merula and Poliziano see Kenney, *The Classical Text*, pp. 7f.
3 OAME XI, A.
4 Museo Correr, Venezia, Fondo Cicogna, Ms. 949, No. 56 (Bologni): CAM, 38, 47; CSV p. 78. But for some sharp criticism of Aldus' texts see Urceus' letter to Battista Palmeri, printed in Dorez, "Alde Manuce et Ange Politien", pp. 323–6.
5 Kenney, *The Classical Text*, p. 17, and references for some critical comment. But cf. R. Bolgar, *The Classical Heritage and its Beneficiaries*, New York/London, 1964 ed., p. 375, for a generally favourable verdict on Aldus' work.
6 There is bound to be an arbitrary element in the total: I have counted the volumes of Aristotle, but not the two-volume texts of writers like Euripides and Homer, as separate editions.
7 OAME XXX. See also I A (Lascaris' Greek Grammar), L B (Bessarion's *In Calumniatorem Platonis*.) Cases such as Erasmus' *Adagia* or Reuchlin's *Oratio* are made obvious by the circumstances: both men were in Venice at the time.
8 H. J. Chaytor, *From Script to Print – an Introduction to Medieval Literature*, Cambridge, 1945: E. P. Goldschmidt, *Medieval Texts and their First Appearance in Print*, London, 1943: M. McLuhan, *The Gutenberg Galaxy – the Making of Typographic Man*, Toronto/London, 1962, esp. pp. 81–140.
9 On this "semi-oral" transmission see Ch. I, above, nn. 86–8. Shepherd, "Francesco Filelfo...", p. 25 (Squarciafico) and FD p. 102, No. 3 (Sabellico).
10 RAIA pp. 1–4, 7, and Ch. I, *loc. cit.*
11 Valla, p. 75 (acknowledgement dated 9 August 1495: the battle had been fought on 6 July).
12 *Ib.*, p. 64: Antiquario seems to have known about the work as early as 1491. Privilege on the edition, dated 1501, in FD p. 146, No. 117.
13 OAME X.
14 Dorez, "Alde Manuce et Ange Politien", pp. 311–19. CAM 31.

15 Allen I, p. 439.
16 OAME XII.
17 CAM 2.
18 OAME XLI. See also Dionisotti, *Gli umanisti e il volgare*, pp. 13–14.
19 Though Summonte dedicated his edition to Sannazaro, the terms in which he did so make it clear that he had presented the author with a fait accompli: on this see A. Mauro, "Le prime edizioni dell' *Arcadia* di Sannazaro", *Giornale italiano di filologia*, IV, 1949, p. 350. "E per questo senza altra sua ordinazione, anzi forse, se io mal non estimo, non senza qualche offesa de l'animo suo...ho pensato essere cosi utile come necessario darle subito in luce, facendole imprimere...." Also the same editor's notes to Sannazaro, *Opere volgari*, Scrittori d'Italia No. 220, Bari, 1961, pp. 427–8. Aldus' dedication, OAME LXXXVIII, makes no mention of autograph copies.
20 OAME XXXIX A.
21 CAM 28, 31 December 1502. These are apparently the dealings mentioned in Aldus' dedication of his own edition to Suardo: OAME LVII C.
22 CAM 47, 48: OAME LVII. For background and comment see G. Oeschger, notes to Ioannis Iovani *Carmina, Ecloghe, Elegie, Liriche*, Scrittori d'Italia, No. 198, Bari, 1948, pp. 485–92.
23 See above, Ch. IV, nn. 22–4, and Ch. V, nn. 50–3.
24 On Benedetti see above, n. 11: on Augurello, the article of R. Weiss in DBI 4.
25 OAME XXVIII (Pici *Liber de Imaginatione*): LIX (*Venatio*). On the latter see also CAM 22, 36.
26 OAME LXXIII: compare CAM 81 (letter of Equicola, 10 March 1510, informing Aldus of the project).
27 Schück, p. 124, Doc. IX.
28 OAME XL, LVII.
29 OAME I.
30 On the identity of the manuscript see Nolhac, *La Bibliothèque de Fulvio Orsini*, pp. 152–3. For an example of a gloss transposed see f. 11v = Ald. a v: Συναίρεσις δέ ἐστι δύο φωνηέντων φυλαττομένων συναλοιφή· οἴη Δημοσθένει, εἰ κρᾶσις δέ ἐστι δύο φωνηέντων ἀλλοιουμένων συναλοιφή, οἴη Δημοσθένεα.
31 Valla, p. 62. Lascaris mentions Bembo and Angelo "Michiel" (sic), but not their taking a copy of his grammar.
32 The examples of conjugation given by the manuscript (ff. 16v–17r) are a good deal more numerous than those offered by Aldus (a viii, f.).
33 Baschet, Doc. V, p. 10 (Letter of Lorenzo da Pavia): FD No. 115, p. 146 (Copyright petition); OAME XXX. It is not known at what stage this defence of the edition was added: see RAIA p. 28.
34 P. de Nolhac, "Le canzoniere autographe de Petrarque", Communication faite à l'Academie des Inscriptions et Belles-Lettres, Paris, 1886: *La Bibliothèque de Fulvio Orsini*, pp. 279f.
35 G. Mestica, "Il Canzoniere del Petrarca nel codice originale a riscontro col Ms. del Bembo e con l'edizione Aldina del 1501", GSLI XXI, 1893, pp. 300–34.

36 *Ib.*
37 G. Salvo Cozzo, *Codice Vaticano 3195 e l'edizione aldina del 1501*, Rome, 1893: "Le rime sparse di Francesco Petrarca nei codici vaticani latini 3195 e 3196", GSLI xxx, 1897, pp. 375–80; *Le rime di Francesco Petrarca,* Florence, 1904, p. vii. Followed by G. Carducci and S. Ferrari, *Le rime di Francesco Petrarca,* Florence, 1899, pp. xviii–xxi. Salvo Cozzo's main argument, that a critic as responsible as Bembo would not have altered an autograph as arbitrarily as the Aldine text suggests, is almost definitely mistaken: his second point, that later drafts of Bembo's *Prose della volgar lingua* show signs of his only recently securing access to the autograph, still does not exclude the possibility of the editor's having been able to extract a few variants from it for the 1501 edition.
38 See above, n. 33, for references to Lorenzo da Pavia's letter. On editorial standards see above, Ch. I, nn. 84–8.
39 See n. 15, above: also A. Horawitz, ed., *Briefwechsel des Beatus Rhenanus,* Leipzig, 1886, Ep. 47, pp. 74–5.
40 OAME XLI.
41 Mauro in Sannazaro, *Opere volgari, ed. cit.* under n. 19, above, p. 28.
42 The 838 adages of the Paris edition became 3,260: M. M. Philips, *The Adages of Erasmus,* p. 75; pp. 185–6 for the tributes to collaborators.
43 *Tutte le opere di Matteo Bandello,* a cura di Francesco Flora, Milan, 1952, Vol. I, pp. 154–5. On the background of the letter and of Aldus' visit see Ch. V, n. 106.
44 All documents relating to the bequest, and a full inventory of the library, are collected by H. Omont, *Inventaire des Manuscrits Grecs et Latins donnés à Saint Marc de Venise par le Cardinal Bessarion en 1468,* Paris, 1894. On the unusually large proportion of Greek material see P. Kibre, "The Intellectual Interests reflected in Libraries of the XIVth and XVth Centuries", *Journal of the History of Ideas,* VII, No. 3, 1946, pp. 260–2; only the Vatican possessed an equal number of Greek texts at this date.
45 Omont, *op. cit.,* p. 10.
46 On the selection and range of Bessarion's library, and his scholarship, see Reynolds and Wilson, *Scribes and Scholars,* pp. 124f. On particular items see R. Sabbadini, *Le scoperte dei codici latini e greci ne' secoli XIV e XV,* Vol. II, Florence, 1967, pp. 67f: *Aristophane,* ed. V. Coulon, Paris, 1958, pp. xiiif; A. S. F. Gow and D. L. Page, *The Greek Anthology,* Cambridge, 1965, Vol. I, p. xxxviii.
47 Omont, *op. cit.,* pp. 18–19.
48 C. Castellani, "Il prestito dei codici manoscritti nella biblioteca di S. Marco a Venezia nei suoi primi tempi e le consequenti perdite dei codici stessi", ARIV Ser. VII, 8, 1896–7, p. 318: "È finalmente cosa notissima che quasi tutte le edizioni greche e latine che gli Aldi fecero...furono condotte sopra testi esistenti nella libreria publica." See also the citations under Ch. III, n. 4. As recently as 1972 an exhibition at the Marciana set the Aldine Greek first editions alongside the manuscripts which were supposed to have served as exemplars.

49 *Annali veneti*, in ASI 7 pt. ii, 1844, p. 655. Only seven loans were recorded between 1474 and 1493: G. Coggiola, "Il prestito di manoscritti della Marciana dal 1474 al 1527", ZFB xxv, 1908, p. 52.
50 L. Labowsky, "Il Cardinale Bessarione e gli inizi della Biblioteca Marciana", in *Venezia e l'Oriente fra tardo medievo e rinascimento*, ed. A. Pertusi, Florence, 1965, pp. 159–82: Lowry, "Two Great Venetian Libraries...", pp. 133–9.
51 *Prose volgari*, p. 79.
52 Labowsky, "Manuscripts from Bessarion's library found in Milan", *Medieval and Renaissance Studies*, v, 1961, pp. 117–26.
53 OAME IX: Marcianus Graecus, No. 260. See Lowry, "Two Great Venetian Libraries...", p. 143, and the independent conclusions of N. G. Wilson, "The Book-trade in Venice, ca. 1400–1515" (in press).
54 RAIA p. 18.
55 Wilson, *op. cit.*
56 Lowry, "Two Great Venetian Libraries...", pp. 164–6. OAME L B.
57 Nolhac, *La Bibliothèque de Fulvio Orsini*, pp. 183–5 (Greek items), 237–9 (Latin), 279f (Florentines): V. Cian, *Un decennio della vita di Pietro Bembo*, pp. 79f: P. Floriani, "La giovinezza umanistica di Pietro Bembo fino al periodo ferrarese", GSLI CXLIII, 1966, pp. 25–71: C. Clough, much invaluable personal advice and conversation, besides his paper "The Library of Bernardo and Pietro Bembo", forthcoming in a volume of studies edited by A. Hobson.
58 Card. G. Mercati, *Codici Latini Pico Grimani Pio e di altra biblioteca ignota del secolo XVI essistenti nell'ottoboniana e codici greci Pio di Modena*, Studi e testi, 75, Citta del Vaticano, 1938, pp. 204–5.
59 Castrifrancanus, *Oratio...*, cit. under Ch. III, n. 38.
60 Now Biblioteca Estense, Modena, Ms. Graecus v. 5, 10 (= Gr. 127). The manuscript carries the signatures of Musurus, Andronico Manolesso, Alvise and Francesco Barbaro. It is uncertain when Francesco acquired it. On the use of this codex see N. G. Wilson, "The Triclinian Edition of Aristophanes", *Classical Quarterly* LVI (N.S. XII), 1962, pp. 34–5. On Poliziano's inspection of the Barbaro library see Pesenti, "Diario odoeporico-bibliografico...", p. 237: on Lascaris' visit and Benedetti's collection, K. Müller, "Janos Laskaris", *op. cit.* under Ch. III, n. 8, at pp. 385–6.
61 Pesenti, *loc. cit.* On Renier's library and Aldus' use of it, see OAME XXXVII (Thucydides).
62 B. Cecchetti, "Una libreria circolante a Venezia nel secolo XV", AV XXXII, 1886, pp. 161–8.
63 See above, Ch. V, nn. 50–1.
64 F. Vian, *Histoire de la Tradition Manuscrite de Quintus de Smyrne*, Paris, 1957, p. 7: Theophrastus, *De Lapidibus*, ed. D. Eichholz, Oxford, 1965, pp. 48–9.
65 Ch. III, n. 83, and Ch. IV, n. 3 for references. OAME LXXXVI, for the introduction to Quintilian.
66 See Kenney, *The Classical Text*, p. 13, for this and other references.

AUTHORSHIP AND EDITORSHIP 253

67 The variants were classified as two versions of the same edition by RAIA pp. 5–7. For the fullest description see BMC v, p. 554: the fact that the British Library has six copies of the first version and three of the second excludes any serious possibility of error in arranging the quires. The most authoritative modern editor, A. S. F. Gow, identifies Aldus' sources with Mss. 1311 and 1379 of the Greek holdings of the Vatican, but did not consider either of them worth including in his own recension. *Theocritus*, Vol. I, p. xlv.

68 OAME VIII (Vol. I, p. 16).

69 *Handschriftliche Vorlagen der Editio princeps des Aristoteles*, Mainz, 1976.

70 See below, Ch. VII, n. 114.

71 *Op. cit.*, pp. 19–28, on *De Historia Animalium*: p. 28 for these figures.

72 *Op. cit.*, pp. 42–50. On the preliminary editorial work that was going ahead at this period see above, Ch. V, n. 18.

73 *Op. cit.*, p. 49.

74 *Op. cit.*, pp. 29–35. Statistics from p. 32. On Apostolis see Geanakoplos, *Greek Scholars*, pp. 73–110.

75 Sicherl, *op. cit.*, pp. 36–41. Statistics from p. 37. On the smaller fragments see pp. 50f. Since the relevant material is very detailed and at times conjectural, I have not included it here.

76 C. Astruc and M.-L. Concasty, *Bibliothèque Nationale, Catalogue des Manuscrits Grecs*, Tom. III, 1960, pp. 23–5. On Cuno's teaching in Basel see below, Ch. VII, nn. 59–61.

77 Astruc and Concasty, *loc. cit.*

78 Page u ii r, ln. 21 in printed edition. See also lines 8 and 10 of the same page, where one editorial conjecture ($\phi\acute{v}\lambda\lambda o\iota\varsigma$ for $\phi\acute{\iota}\lambda o\iota\varsigma$) is adopted while another ($\chi\rho\acute{o}\nu o\varsigma$ for $\theta\epsilon\acute{o}\varsigma$) is rejected.

79 Page T vi r, ln. 8.

90 A. Turyn, *Studies in the Manuscript Tradition of the Tragedies of Sophocles*, Illinois Studies in Language and Literature, XXXVI, Urbana, 1952, p. 175. B. Fonkich, "On the Manuscript Tradition of the Aldine Edition of the Tragedies of Sophocles", *Vizantiskij Vremennik*, XXIV, 1964, pp. 109–21 (original in Russian).

81 *Ib.*, pp. 113–16. A full apparatus criticus for the *Ajax* is provided, with the siglum Lg. indicating the Leningrad manuscript, Y its Viennese counterpart.

82 M. Sicherl, "Die Editio Princeps Aldina des Euripides und ihre Vorlagen", *Rhein Museum*, 118, 1975, pp. 205–25.

83 Ms. C. 195 infra (= 881). For description see A. Martini and D. Bassi, *Catalogus Codicum Graecorum Bibliothecae Ambrosianae*, Tom. II, Milan, 1906, pp. 981–2.

84 On Ducas' editorship see Geanakoplos, *Greek Scholars*, pp. 223f: on Aleander, B. Hillyard, "Girolamo Aleandro, editor of Plutarch's Moralia", *Bibliothèque d'Humanisme et Renaissance*, XXXVI, 1974, pp. 517–31.

85 For the text of this letter see Dorez, "Alde Manuce et Ange Politien", pp. 323–6. For Aldus' claims see references under n. 2, above.

86 *Die Amerbachkorrespondenz*, ed. A. Hartmann, Basel, 1942, Vol. I, No. 482, p. 455.

87 G. Salvo Cozzo, *Codice Vaticano 3195...*, pp. 8–13. The charge was repeated even more explicitly by Lodovico Dolce in a letter to Varchi in 1553.
88 Cf. Ch. III, n. 69.
89 FD No. 9, p. 104. Biblioteca Marciana, Mss. it. Cl. XI 45 (7439), f. 18v. Entry from the daybook of Francesco da Madiis.
90 *Die Amerbachkorrespondenz*, Vol. cit. p. 276, Ep. 293 (Introduction to edition of Augustine): p. 232, Ep. 246.
91 OAME XI. See also Ch. IV, n. 181.
92 Baschet, p. 30, Doc. XIV. For a full account of this incident see Ch. III.
93 CAM 37. The existence of a master-copy is an inference only, but perhaps a fair one from Fortiguerra's allusion to "quelli opusculi di Virgilio".
94 RAIA p. 190. On Parrhasius' career see C. Jannelli, *De vita et scriptis Auli Jani Parrhasii Consentini, philologi saeculo XVI celeberrimi, commentarius*, Naples, 1844. A fully annotated text of the letter can be found in E. Pastorello, *Inedita Manutiana*, Florence, 1960, pp. 11–21.
95 OAME LXXXV. In his notes the author wrongly states that the Venetus A manuscript was used for this edition. See *Les Deipnosophistes*, I et II, ed. A. Desrousseaux and A. Astruc, Paris, 1956, pp. xliii–xliv.
96 CAM 35, 38. C. F. Buhler, "Aldus Manutius and the printing of Athenaeus", reprinted from GJB 1955 in *Early Books and Manuscripts*, Pierpoint Morgan Library, 1973, pp. 220–2.
97 Cf. notes 92, 93 above. Pastorello's footnotes trace the adoption or rejection of Parrhasius' readings. Verse 38 of the *Copa* is a particularly interesting case: for the weak "Mors autem veniens" of his manuscripts Parrhasius proposed "Mors aurem vellens". Aldus compromised with "Mors autem vellens", losing much of the point of the conjecture.
98 See for example OAME XLII A (dedication of Valerius Maximus to Lubranski, 1502).
99 CAM 4. It is interesting to notice that Aldus immediately adopted the reading "...potest electro" at Aeneid VIII, 402, and that Ricci referred this reading to Poliziano. Aldus adopted "...quin protinus omnia" at *Aeneid* VI, 33, in 1514 but not in 1501. My suggestion that Ricci had seen Mediceus is purely conjectural, since he is never more specific about his source than "In vetustioribus codicibus invenio...". On this continuing failure to recognise and use a vital authority see Kenney, *The Classical Text*, pp. 13, 48–9. Mediceus was used eclectically by de Bussi and by Aldus, who included some of its readings in an appendix of corrigenda.
100 OAME XXII A (Vol. I, p. 34).
101 J. Bergmann, *Corpus Scriptorum Ecclesiasticorum Latinorum*, Vol. 61, Vienna, 1926, p. xlix: H. Thompson, Loeb edition of Prudentius, Vol. I, Harvard, 1949, pp. xiv–v. Bergmann identifies Aldus' exemplar as a codex now in Boulogne, but does not rank it among the earliest or most significant authorities.
102 OAME LXV, LXXV. Müller, "Janos Lascaris".
103 E. Piccolomini, "Delle condizioni e delle vicende della Libreria Medicea privata dal 1494 al 1508", ASI Ser. III, XIX, 1875, pp. 101–29.

104 Omont, *Inventaire*, cit. under n. 44, above, pp. 129–87. See Nos. 274, 304 (Lysias): 300 (Aeschines): 306 (Isocrates). See also Bolgar, *The Classical Heritage*, App. I for a chronological index showing the availability of different authors.

105 CAM 24 (Lascaris' letter). For the earlier editions and Avantius' copy see p. 37 of Lowe and Rand's study, as cited under n. 108, below.

106 L. Delaruelle, *Guillaume Budé – les origines, les debuts, les idées maitrisses*, repr. Geneva, 1970, pp. 81–90 (Material on Fra Giocondo and Budé).

107 Sanudo, VI, col. 182: Mocenigo's election was on 10 June 1505. *Ib.*, col. 442, 8 October 1506: Fra Giocondo reports on fortification of the Ionian islands.

108 OAME LXIV (Vol. I, p. 94). Aldus does not even appear to have been aware of the more general use of papyrus during the lifetime of Pliny. The same section contains reference to Fra Giocondo's apograph.

109 I have with some hesitation relegated a major controversy to a footnote, since the issues appear to me too uncertain to be applied directly to the judgement of Aldus' editorship. E. A. Lowe and E. K. Rand, *A Sixth-Century Fragment of the Letters of Pliny the Younger: a Study of Six Leaves of an Uncal Manuscript Preserved in the Pierpoint Morgan Library*, New York, Washington, 1922, identified the Morgan fragment with the remains of the Paris manuscript and consequently as Aldus' exemplar. But Rand's collation of the fragment with the Aldine (pp. 41–3) shows clearly that Aldus followed conventional humanist spellings rather than those of the fragment, and does not really justify his speaking of a "striking similarity" (p. 43) between the two texts. This weakness was exploited by E. Merrill, "The Morgan Fragment of Pliny's Letters", *Classical Philology*, XVIII, 1923, pp. 97–119: the author revealed 47 differences of reading between the Aldine and the Morgan fragment, also pointing out that the provenance of that manuscript was uncertain. Rand argued that the divergences were not significant: *Harvard Studies in Classical Philology*, XXXIV, 1923, 79–119, XXXV, 1927, 137–169. But the indifferent quality of the presswork was further illustrated by G. Winship, "The Aldine Pliny of 1508", *The Library*, Fourth Series, VI, 1925, pp. 358–69, and A. Case, "More about the Aldine Pliny of 1508", *ib.*, XVI, 1935, pp. 173–87. Current editorial opinion seems to accept the identity of Aldus' exemplar with the Morgan fragment in its complete form, but very cautiously: see R. Mynors' Oxford Classical Text, 1963, and A. N. Sherwin-White, *The Letters of Pliny*, Oxford, 1966, p. 84. Whatever the truth of the matter, there is no doubt that Aldus adopted some very odd readings. See next note.

110 Cf. Mynors' text, p. 67, ln. 13: MS. "parva si non cotidie fiant". Aldus reads "sint" for "si non". P. 68, ln. 3: Aldus reads "mirabilis" for the "mira" of the entire tradition. P. 68, ln. 8: Aldus reads "illic accubat" for the "lotus accubat" of the fragment.

111 OAME LXXXIV (Vol. I, p. 143), "Nemo enim est, quod sciam, qui extare alium audiverit". Biblioteca Marciana, MS. Graecus 622 (851).

112 Fracastoro's dialogue, *Navagerius sive De Poetica*, is built around an expedition into the hills above Verona made by Bardellone, Navagero, and the della Torre brothers. *Andreae Navagerii patricii Veneti, oratoris et poetae clarissimi Opera Omnia*, Padua, 1718,

pp. 229f. For contacts with Contarini H. Jedin, "Contarini und Camaldoli", *Archivio italiano per la storia della pietà*, II, 1959, Ep. XIII, pp. 42–3. Further bibliography in OAME, n. 1 *ad loc.*

113 Brown, *Venetian Press*, p. 45. Kenney, *The Classical Text*, p. 18. Rather unfairly, Professor Kenney extends the condition of the manuscript to the quality of the scholarship.

114 Universitätsbibliothek, Basel, MS. Graecus AN IV, i ex B VI 25.

115 *Hesychii Alexandrini Lexicon,* recensuit et emendavit Kurt Latte, Hauniae, 1953, pp. xxv, xxxiii etc.

116 Aldus' introduction to *Rhetorica ad Herennium* (OAME Vol. I, p. 130) gives a half-serious picture of Navagero's badgering him for more work on the Latin poets. For Navagero's career and works see Cicogna, *Delle iscrizioni veneziane*, Vol. VI, 1853, 173f. Though he is frequently mentioned by more modern critics, I know of no other comprehensive study.

117 C. Pascal, "Una lettera pontoniana del Summonte ed un autografo inedito del Pontano", *Atti del Reale Accademia Pontoniana*, LVI, 1926, pp. 178–86.

118 Pastorello, *Inedita Manutiana*, p. 11. "Non me fugit, hoc observandi genus ex collatione exemplarium a quibusdam irrisum: quasi iudicio potius oporteat niti."

119 *Familiares et Secundae Epistolae,* Vicentius Bertochus, Mantua, 1498, Ep. LX (unpaginated).

119 Pastorello, *op. cit.*, pp. 5–6, No. 203.

120 Colophon on f. L viii r. "Nota, lector, deesse in libro quarternionem ZF, quia non extat reliquum cappae litterae: relictus est igitur locus, ut si forte quispiam quod deest, aliquando invenerit, illud commode huic libro queat adiungere."

122 OAME XXXIII.

VII

THE GREAT DIFFUSION

It is not possible, I think, to make an exact calculation of the number of copies that Aldus distributed through Europe with the help of his academic friends and the less welcome services of entrepreneurs like Jordan von Dinslaken. Most authorities accept 1,000 copies as the normal size of an Aldine press-run, and allowing for the fact that certain editions, such as that of Demosthenes' *Orations*, may have been smaller, this figure would still give us a basis for reckoning Aldus' total output between 100,000 and 120,000 copies. But I suspect that the actual number may be considerably higher. Avanzio's introduction to the octavo edition of Catullus can only mean that 3,000 copies were being produced, and what was done with one popular Latin text may well have been repeated with others.[1] One-thousand copy editions were being turned out in the 1460s: but no printer is known to have produced more than 3,000 copies of a single edition until the feverish controversies of the early reformation expanded demand still further.[2] There can be no doubt that Aldus was the most active member of the most active printing industry in Europe, at least between 1499 and 1504, then again after 1512: if he was producing editions of up to 3,000 copies, then he must be regarded, on purely numerical grounds, as the most important focus for the distribution of literature to contemporary Europe.

But the variety and timing of Aldus' editions were even more important than their mere numbers. The octavo-sized Latin text may not, in fact, have been borne of an attempt to cut prices and reach a wider public, and the works published in this way were available in a large variety of other editions. But the convenience of handling such books may have been a powerful enough factor in extending a knowledge of the authors concerned. And whatever the quality of the texts as texts, Aldus' dominance of early publication in Greek was, and is, complete. He produced first editions of ninety-four classical and post-classical Greek writers. If some of the works published were spurious, and some of the authors of little value, their numbers still include Plato and Aristotle, the historians Herodotus, Thucydides and Xenophon, Desmothenes and all the minor Attic orators, besides all the Greek dramatists except Aeschylus, whose works were to appear only after Aldus' death.[3] It amounts to an almost complete cross-section of the Greek literary heritage as reconstituted by the fifteenth-century humanists and transmitted to the modern world.

It is this process of transmission, combined with the sheer bulk of his work, which raises the most important questions about Aldus' whole position in the cultural history of Western Europe. Historical turning-points are out of fashion these days: so are heroic individuals. But Aldus' career straddles a period of turbulent cultural and political change in a most suggestive way. He was organising his company and preparing his earliest editions as Poliziano and Pico lay dying, and as the French armies marched into Florence behind Charles VIII:[4] he was working on Greek and Latin texts provided by Janus Lascaris until the very moment when the power which that ambassador represented smashed the last independent military and political force in Italy on the battlefield of Agnadello;[5] he died just six months before the Franco-Venetian victory at Marignano brought the first stage of the foreign invasions of Italy to a close.[6] He was therefore making the fruits of a century and a half of intellectual activity available in bulk at precisely the time when the courtiers and dilletanti of the Northern kingdoms arrived in force to sample them. Anyone can argue, without fear of being proved wrong, that if Aldus had not taken it upon himself to put the heritage of Greece into print, someone else would have done so, and that in any case the survival of that heritage was already assured. But the company of Barbarigo, Torresani and Manutius represented a fusion of economic and intellectual power which could not easily have been copied, and the fortunes of the Medici library or the Marciana during this period show how vulnerable the most apparently secure centres could be. In the event, it was Aldus who did the job and Aldus who got the credit for it from his contemporaries. He was producing a library, wrote Erasmus, which was not limited by place or time as the great libraries of the past had been and which knew no boundaries except the boundaries of the world. Thomas More went even further, and sent Raphael Hythlodaye beyond the limits of the known world to introduce the Utopians to Greek from the neat, portable Aldine editions which he carried in his luggage.[7]

The international quality of Aldus' circle of acquaintances has been noticed at many points in this study; it is worth noticing here that most of the men involved either were already, or soon became leading figures in equally influential circles in their own countries – Grocyn, Linacre and Latimer in England; Reuchlin, Celtis and Mutian in the Empire; Lefèvre, Budé, and, by adoption, Aleander in France; Erasmus everywhere. The careers, the correspondence, and sometimes even the libraries of these great men show us a good deal of what they owed to Aldus and what he owed to them: and this evidence enables us at least to set a finger on the pulse of one of the most important cultural arteries that connected Renaissance Italy to Renaissance Europe.[8]

Rather surprisingly, the first group of foreign visitors to establish a definite and sustained intellectual link with Aldus were Englishmen. "Surprisingly", because the predominance acquired in the universities by the followers of the English philosophers Scotus and Ockham during the later fourteenth and fifteenth centuries had earned the bitter enmity of those Italian champions of classical literature, whose interests Aldus so strongly represented. To the humanists, the term "British" stank, not wholly without reason, of obscurantism and entrenched academic privilege.[9] Aldus was well aware of all this, and when he paid his personal tribute to Linacre and Grocyn in 1499 he wrote in tones of barely suppressed astonishment:

Once a barbarous and uncultivated learning came to us from Britain, took over Italy, and still holds our citadels: but now I hope we shall have the Britons to help us in putting barbarity to flight, and that we shall receive from them a truly polished and Latin learning; and so the wound will be cured by the very spear that inflicted it.[10]

Exactly how and when the connection was formed is not clear, though it is certain that Thomas Linacre was the vital figure. He appears to have come to Italy with William Sellyng, ambassador to Rome, in 1487, but to have moved fairly quickly to Florence where he was joined by his compatriot and Oxford-contemporary William Grocyn.[11] The two men basked in the sunset glory of the Laurentian circle for a year or two, either acquiring or greatly increasing their proficiency in Greek under the tutelage of Chalcondylas and Poliziano. Then their ways parted for a while. Grocyn appears to have returned to England in 1491, and though he came later to regard Aldus with the highest respect and to make some editorial contribution to his work, it is most unlikely that the two men ever met.[12]

Linacre moved on from Florence to Padua in quest of the medical degree which he eventually took on 30 August 1496.[13] He must have been working with Aldus by this time, since his name is mentioned in the preface to the third volume of Aristotle which appeared at the very beginning of the following year and must have been in preparation for months, if not years beforehand.[14] A bond of cooperation may well have been suggested by mutual acquaintances in Florence, and it seems to have grown up soon after the Englishman's arrival in Padua. It is a pity that we cannot measure the range of Linacre's work more precisely, for it would be interesting to know if he played any part in the compilation of the Harvard manuscript: unfortunately, he was a member of a rather ill-defined editorial team and his contribution is submerged in the completed whole. But it is clear that Aldus esteemed that contribution highly, and that the relationship between the two men was close. Linacre's name stands in the preface before those of all the other scholars involved: the tribute states specifically that he worked in Venice, so he may well have lodged with Aldus as his friend Erasmus would do a decade later; and when Aldus dedicated his text of the *Astronomici Veteres* to Alberto Pio in 1499, he spoke of his prince's "warm friendship" with Linacre, whom he had introduced as an unknown foreigner only two years earlier. Evidently the cultured barbarian was thought worthy of presentation in the most exalted company.[15]

Before tracing these connections back to England and watching their effects, we should make a point which can be applied with little change to all the foreign visitors who clustered round Aldus' workshop. The central figure – Linacre in this case – was merely the nucleus of a system which extended indefinitely outwards. If William Latimer, soon to be tutor of Reginald Pole at Oxford, knew Aldus well enough to lend him someone else's bed, we can scarcely believe that this was the only commerce between them. In 1507 Erasmus mentioned Cuthbert Tunstall, later bishop of London, among the mutual friends who had praised his translations from Euripides, and Tunstall was certainly in Padua during the first few years of the sixteenth century when he encouraged the studies of another English visitor, Richard Pace.[16] Pace is credited with reciting an oration in praise of Greek literature in Venice during 1504, and there is an overwhelming temptation to link this in some way with the campaign which was launched by some of Aldus' friends during that very year.[17] The evidence is entirely circumstantial. We have only Erasmus' passing mention of a link with Tunstall, and no mention at all of a link with Pace. But the importance of a tightly-knit group of five or six young men with a common cultural background in England and Italy, strong interests in the classical revival, and a range of high social contacts, is obvious enough by itself. Intellectual movements are made by such people.

When Linacre returned some time in 1498 his reputation had grown prodigiously, and he was appointed tutor to Prince Arthur, immediate heir to the throne.[18] But the traveller had brought back more than a prestigious degree and an assortment of happy memories. The library of New College, Oxford, still contains a magnificent set of the Aldine edition of Aristotle, printed on vellum and carrying in each volume the neat inscription "Thomae Linacri". No other complete set now exists on this costly material: but only the first volume is missing from the nearby library of Corpus Christi, where one of the survivors carries the signature "Wm. Grocyni".[19] It is worth remembering that, even on paper, the works of Aristotle were priced at eleven ducats and formed one of the most expensive editions printed during the fifteenth century. On vellum, they must have cost at the very least five times that amount, and whoever footed the bill, these two sets represent a colossal investment in Italianate scholarship and its future in England.[20]

Still more significant, the books were not for show and they were probably not alone. Both sets contain a considerable amount of annotation which shows that they have been used for study or teaching, and the New College copies are flanked by a number of other early Aldines glossed in a very similar hand. A *Thesaurus Cornucopiae* and an Aristophanes could perhaps have come back with Linacre in 1498: copies of the *Epistolographi Graeci* and the Satires of Lucian would have to have followed later, but as we shall see in a moment the channels of communication between England and Venice were considerably widened in the years after Linacre's return.[21] What part, one wonders, did these or similar books play in the public lectures and personal instruction which both Grocyn and Linacre seem to have offered to an enthusiastic group of students in London during the first years of the sixteenth century? Here again, a definite answer is just out of reach. The young Thomas More calls Grocyn "my master in learning", Linacre "the dearest partner of my endeavours" and adds the significant detail that towards the end of 1501 he "shelved his Latin books to take up the study of Greek".[22] It is unfortunate that he never said precisely what form his studies took, and that our very incomplete knowledge of the libraries assembled by his two instructors makes a reconstruction still more difficult.[23] But the Greek texts which More made his hero Raphael give to the Utopians are a very suggestive collection: Plato, Aristotle, Theophrastus, Plutarch and Lucian; Hesychius' Dictionary; the grammars of Gaza and Lascaris; Homer, Aristophanes, Euripides and Sophocles; Herodotus and Thucydides – all are Aldine editions, and there is even an arcane joke about the state of Theophrastus, perhaps in recognition of Linacre's efforts with the only available manuscript. Though its meaning is subtly submerged, this entire passage acknowledges More's debt to Aldus as gratefully as the more florid letter which Grocyn sent in 1499.[24]

Even without exact information from the earliest years of the century, we can be certain that Aldus' influence on English humanism grew steadily over the next two decades. His books arrived no longer as windfalls, but as part of a regular traffic: More was referring in the passage we have just examined to texts published in Venice only a year or so before he wrote *Utopia,* and his young protégé John Clement, one of the first scholars of St Paul's School and a prominent humanist-physician of the next generation, seems to have owned many books "of Aldus' prynt", including the vital editions of Aristotle and Plato.[25] But the most solid and enduring monument to this cultural contact is the library of Corpus Christi College, Oxford. Founded in 1516 by Bishop Richard Fox, Corpus was the first institution in England, and, after Cardinal Ximenes' university of Alcala, only the second in Europe to be dedicated exclusively to the study of theology through the medium of the three ancient languages, Latin, Greek and Hebrew.[26] We have seen how the dream of such a college haunted Aldus' own imagination and it is not surprising that Bishop Fox's enterprise was greeted with cries of enthusiasm by Erasmus. Had Aldus been able to see that his own publications would account for almost all the Greek items in the library of this new foundation – twenty-four volumes out of the thirty-three listed – he might perhaps have found the disappointment of his own hopes easier to bear. As early as 1518 authorities took delivery from London of a consignment of Aldine texts from which few significant literary or philosophical works were excluded.[27]

So far, our evidence has tended to highlight the cultural dominance of the Italian scholar-printer over his English customers and their rather abject dependence on his services and his example. Before passing on, it is as well to remind ourselves that the picture has another side. Linacre was saluted as a valued collaborator from whom Aldus hoped to receive "other most useful works in medicine and philosophy",[28] and though most of the traffic in books between Aldus and his friends probably did travel north, a number of requests for help came with it and a fair amount of material came back to balance the account. Aldus sent unsuccessfully to England for a copy of Bruni's translation of Aristotle's *Ethics*: his exemplar of Prudentius came from England;[29] and the author of the *Adagia*, perhaps Aldus' most successful contemporary publication, came armed with introductions from English friends. Though the Italian scholar was very conscious of his literary superiority and though his English associates made no direct effort to contest it, the link between them was one of partnership, not total dependence.

Turning now towards Aldus' impact on the intellectual life of the German-speaking countries, we must turn also to problems of a quite different order. English students were not exotic rarities in the Italian universities: but they were usually rare enough to know one another, to hunt in a pack while they were abroad and to seek each other's company when they came home. Though the search for Italian influences may not always have a clearly-marked trail to follow, it is at least straightforward. But the number of Germans studying at Padua or Bologna might run into hundreds in any single year. A substantial minority had acquired the taste for Greek either within the universities or in the more fashionable atmosphere of Ficino's circle in Florence.[30] And the busy German colony in Venice was equipped to supply and eager to encourage any demand for luxury goods from the south. Not surprisingly, the channels of interest in Aldus' programme of publications are varied and complex, sometimes combining into a single flood of enthusiasm, sometimes overflowing into wide meanders which in time become independent, but related centres of activity. Sometimes, we appear to be dealing with the simple longing of the esthete to own and enjoy any exciting new book that came on the market. But it is certain that Aldus' professional example affected some of his German colleagues deeply, and some of the humanists, like their English counterparts, plainly treated the printer as an ally in their more ambitious struggles for a reform of education and society. The difference was that for the Germans the test would come sooner.

Aldine texts must have been quite widely available in Germany from an early date, for there was no lack of dealers like Jordan von Dinslaken, the Frankfurt fairs were active, and booksellers like Johan Amerbach of Basel were handling Venetian editions years before Aldus started printing.[31] But our first positive evidence about the reception of the first Greek texts comes only from the final years of the century, and from the immediate environment of Heidelberg. It is from here that any discussion of Aldus' impact on German intellectual life must begin. By the central 1490s, a combination of chance and sympathetic patronage had brought together one of those ill-defined groups of enthusiasts whose efforts to rebuild the world of Pericles or Augustus have formed so large a part of the present study. Activity, as usual, centred on the Chancellery and the university: Johan von Dalberg, Bishop of Worms and sometime Chancellor of the Palatinate, cast a beneficent eye over the proceedings; the professor of Law, Johan Wacker, made his house available for meetings, and the theologian Jodocus Gallus, later an eager partisan of the scheme to bring Aldus to Germany, added the weight of his authority. Less permanent but equally active members included the Hellenist Reuchlin, the mysterious abbot Trithemius of Sponheim, and that hot-headed apostle of German nationalism and purified Latin poetry, Conrad Celtis. As with all such associations, the hopes and dreams of this "Societas litteraria Rhenana" are extraordinarily difficult to understand or define. It may have been the Italian background of Reuchlin and Celtis, particularly Reuchlin's knowledge of both Greek and Hebrew, that led the participants to make a cult of the three ancient languages and of the mystical learning which Reuchlin had imbibed from Pico in Florence. In 1495 Celtis called the group an "Academia Platonica", in obvious imitation of Ficino's circle. But their aims appear to have included the discovery and publication of unknown manuscripts and in this, as in their taste for Greek and Hebrew, the members of the "Societas Rhenana" anticipated the plans of the Aldine Academy by six or seven years and may even have encouraged its formation. The difficulty was that, for all their enthusiasm, none of the German scholars except Reuchlin knew anything beyond the barest rudiments of Greek and Hebrew or possessed the means of learning more.[32] It is not surprising that the rumour of grammars, dictionaries, and even an *Introductio perbrevis ad Hebraicam Linguam,* produced a shiver of excitement in Heidelberg.

Against this background we must read the first letter of Aldus to

Celtis, which carries the date of 13 October 1497 and is a reply to an earlier approach from the poet. Aldus was delighted to hear "that Greek literature is being studied there too, and that my works have found such favour amongst you": he arranged for the texts Celtis had ordered to be supplied through his agent; he enclosed copies of Fra Urbano's new grammar as a gift; and he looked forward to the promised visit of his correspondent. This letter is intriguing, first, because it shows how readily a fire-brand like Celtis would appeal to an Italian tradition which he frequently and eloquently urged his fellow-countrymen to discard, second, because it suggests that instruction in Greek was becoming a regular function of the German group and that a relatively extensive circle of "young men" was benefitting.[33]

We can prove independently that this was the case. The library of the University of Basel contains a somewhat unprepossessing manuscript with the title *Varia de Re Grammatica* and notes that it was written by an unknown Ioannes Drach of Speyer during 1498. The first seven folios carry the section of Constantine Lascaris' Grammar that deals with Greek nouns, the Greek and Latin texts both being those of the Aldine edition: the eighth folio copies the title-page of that edition exactly, and is immediately followed by the parallel texts of Phocylides, the Lord's Prayer, and the Ave. On the twentieth folio we find Herodian's treatise *On Numbers,* drawn this time from the edition of Theodorus Gaza's Grammar. The remainder of the manuscript is taken up with short introductory Greek dialogues by Reuchlin and his dedications of them to Dalberg.[34] As a comment on the value attached to Aldus' editions, whose printed texts were being copied back into manuscript, this unimpressive little book takes on a new importance. The unknown name of Drach hints, like Aldus' letter, at a fair number of pupils. One of them was certainly the ubiquitous Dominican John Cuno, who appears in a letter of Gallus during 1499, hurrying to nearby Speyer with a "virginalis cursus" – apparently the Aldine *Horae Beatissimae Virginis,* which had appeared two years earlier.[35]

It is already evident that Aldus' influence on this first and crucial stage of Greek studies in Germany was immense, and later events would prove that this influence was neither superficial nor temporary. If Cuno's name has floated in and out of this narrative like a lietmotif, that is because he spent most of the remainder of his life studying with Aldus, trying to arrange for the printer's move to Germany, and, when that scheme had failed, spreading his fame and his methods. The scope of Reuchlin's learning made him the most respected scholar of his time in Germany, and a target for the Inquisition in the most bitterly-fought controversy of the years before the Reformation. He included Aldus' letters in the collection which he published as one of his weapons in that pamphlet-war, and bought his friend's texts at a pace which filled more than half his Greek library – twenty-eight volumes out of fifty-five – with Aldines.[36] Even Abbot Trithemius, who warned against the short life of print, and had such books copied back onto vellum for the library of Sponheim, proves on closer investigation to have acquired Aldine editions of Musaeus, Theocritus, the *Grammatici Veteres,* the Greek Orators, parts of Aristotle and Theophrastus, and the Grammars of Lascaris and Theodorus Gaza.[37]

The enthusiasm of the Heidelberg circle soon spilled over and spread outwards, perhaps losing some of its force in the process of diffusion but quickly extending the common cult for Hellenism, improved philology, and scholarly publication over a much wider area. Some of the activity we have already seen and a good deal of it led nowhere. Reuchlin's visit to Venice during the summer of 1498 was made possible by his mission to Rome on behalf of the Elector Palatine, and the first, still-born negotiations to tempt Aldus to the Empire must have derived largely from the excitement of the previous two or three years.[38] But the "Societas Rhenana" was beginning to break up. Conrad Celtis moved away to Vienna during 1497 – indeed the lost approach to Aldus may have been written from Vienna – and soon became involved in plans for Aldus' future which, as we have seen, were rather similar to Reuchlin's and equally unsuccessful. Celtis was at best a headstrong and volatile character, and it is never quite clear what part the Italian printer played in his vast schemes for an interlocking system of "literary sodalities" reaching throughout the Empire. None of his plans achieved much positive success, and it is noticeable that his name drops out of the direct dealings between Aldus and the imperial court a good two years before they collapsed. But in spite of the disappointed hopes of 1506 and the rather shame-faced silence that followed, Celtis did a great deal to encourage contact between Venice and Vienna, and laid foundations on which an interest in Aldus' programme of publication could grow up of its own accord. He founded a "Societas Danubiana" on the pattern of the Heidelberg circle and including, like its predecessor, a number of members of the university. He lectured on Homer, and pressed unsuccessfully for the appointment of a professor of Greek. In 1501 he persuaded Maximilian to establish a special "Poets' College" within the Arts Faculty of the University, and this group, with its professors of Poetry, Rhetoric and Mathematics, its library, its astronomical spheres, and its right to confer the poetic crown of laurel, was soon centred on Celtis' own house.[39] How far these activities depended on Aldus' editorial help is not clear, but he certainly kept in close touch with developments in Vienna. In the autumn of 1499 he received a formal visit from Vincent Lang, who was soon to become Celtis' assistant at the Poets' College and on this occasion was presented with two copies of Musaeus.[40] During 1501 Aldus sent copies of his new octavo-sized texts of Horace and Virgil to Celtis, with a specific request to explore the market, and later in the same year he dispatched Fra Urbano's Greek Grammar and a Dictionary in response to a demand for some introductory material. Celtis also appears to have been one of the few who was shown some experimental pages of the ill-fated trilingual Bible.[41] The positive results of all this intellectual exchange were probably less impressive than they might appear at first sight to have been, for Celtis was more of a "public-relations man" than a scholar and it is doubtful whether he could have turned Aldus' Greek texts to anything like the good effects achieved by Reuchlin in Heidelberg. He seems also to have made wildly extravagant, even impossible promises of editorial help: of lists of Greek manuscripts which never arrived, or of the later books of the *Fasti* which Ovid himself may never have completed. The only offer to take solid form was a collection of short poems by his students in honour of Maximilian, which Aldus turned down point-blank with the rather specious excuse that they might be politically compromising. Perhaps he was really assessing their literary merits.[42]

Overall, the hectic enthusiasm of Celtis was probably less important to Aldus than the more sober academic or commerical co-operation which it threw open to others, and the general admiration of the printer's aims which it encouraged. There are a number of references to the activities of a Viennese bookseller named Leonard Alantsee, who appears to have combined his work as an intermediary between Aldus and Celtis with a fair amount of trading on his own account.[43] Johan Spiesshammer or "Cuspinianus", whose house provided a centre for the "Societas Danubiana", filled out a number of the gaps in the editorial collaboration which Celtis could only promise. He turned to Aldus for help with a Latin version of Dionysius Periegetes, and though the printer was unable to provide a copy of the translation required, he suggested emendations to eleven passages which puzzled his Austrian correspondent and was able to offer a Greek codex to help with the restoration of the Latin. An avid student of the natural sciences, Spiesshammer pressed Aldus for texts of Dioscurides, Hippocrates' *Aphorisms,* and a Latin version of Theophrastus' treatise *On Gems*: and in the same letter he enclosed twenty-four sections of Valerius Maximus' *Dictorum et Factorum Memorabilium Libri* which had been missing from the edition that Aldus published in October 1502. In April 1503 the printer filled out and re-issued his text, adding a letter to salute Spiesshammer as a true "benefactor of the Republic of letters".[44]

Up to a point, Aldus' contacts with Vienna resemble his exactly contemporary association with Linacre's circle in London. There is the same exchange of vital material at the centre, the same aura of good-will radiating outwards: the imperial secretary Collauer and his student-protégé Fruticenus may not have succeeded in bringing Aldus to Vienna, but there is no reason to suppose that they were any less eager to read and own his books than Grocyn, More, or John Clement.[45] The difference is that, whereas the English scholars appear to have accepted Italian intellectual leadership unhesitatingly and flaunted their abject condition as "Britons, cut off from the whole world", Celtis had always given his followers an aggressively nationalistic lead and urged them to throw off their cultural dependence on Italy.[46] The eagerness with which he sought Aldus' help and friendship reveals both the hollowness of the rhetoric and the extent of the printer's influence.

The final breakdown of the negotiations for an "Imperial Academy" in 1505–6, Celtis' gradual collapse before remorseless attacks of syphilis, and the rapid deterioration of Venetian relations with Maximilian during 1508, naturally sent Aldus' dealings with these first German friends into one of the long, meandering detours of which we spoke earlier. But the force of the Heidelberg circle was by no means spent and when, from 1510, its lingering current gathered strength again in Basel, the effects were not dissipated so quickly. From his first studies with Reuchlin, John Cuno moved to Venice in 1504 and for the next eighteen months received instruction in Greek both from Aldus and from other members of his circle. Possibly embarrassed by his failure to secure a position for Aldus, possibly turned loose by the suspension of business in 1506, Cuno transferred his attention to Padua and the lectures of Musurus, which he followed for another two years at least. Throughout the period, he was presumably indulging his curious passion for collecting used press-copies and whatever his reasons were, the assorted manuscripts must have given him another means of communicating an atmosphere which he had imbibed deeply, over a considerable period, and in both its academic and commerical centres.⁴⁷ Cuno knew the Aldine circle as few foreigners can have done. His arrival in Basel towards the end of 1510 brought Beatus Rhenanus hurrying back from Paris to hear him, drew an urgent request from his old teacher Reuchlin to persuade him to stay, and provoked a sigh of relief from Johan Amerbach.⁴⁸

The moment could hardly have been more opportune, for the wars of the League of Cambrai and Aldus' second suspension of business had recently broken a pulse of interest that had been growing steadily stronger for a dozen years or more. How much actual contact there had been between Basel and Venice is not clear: Reuchlin, who knew both Aldus and Amerbach well, could have acted as intermediary. But whatever the background, the interaction of the two presses on one another between 1495 and 1515 provides a striking example of the respect with which Italian literary fashions were treated in the North. Both commercially and academically, the Basel concern had an enormous start. Amerbach had been in business since 1476. He held a Master's degree from Paris, and had learned his trade with Anton Koberger, the first great printing entrepreneur and probably the most successful publisher of the fifteenth century.⁴⁹ At a time when the Venetian printers were facing the snubs and silences of Sabellico, Amerbach was in regular and friendly contact with scholars such as Reuchlin, Jakob Wimpfeling, and Sebastian Brant, and was already receiving the kind of tributes which were soon to be heaped upon Aldus.⁵⁰ Johan Froben, his partner from 1491, was a far more sensitive and capable successor than Torresani would prove to be.⁵¹

But in spite of their priority and their advantages, the Balois appear to have greeted Aldus' Greek texts with the same breathless excitement as their contemporaries in Heidelberg. Amerbach must have been quick to invest in the first Grammars, for in the winter of 1498 he sent a copy specially to his sons at their school in Schlettstadt, and the university library of Basel still possesses three – two of Lascaris' version, one of Valeriani's – which bear his signature.[52] One of these volumes also carries the names of his son Boniface, of Johan Froben, and of Froben's son, and its heavily annotated pages suggest that this was a much-valued and much-used family heirloom.[53] Occasional references in Amerbach's personal correspondence over the next few years hint at the growth of this influence from beyond the Alps. Requests for copies of Poliziano's complete works in 1501 and of Bessarion's *In Calumniatorem Platonis* in 1503 show that, in his capacity as a bookseller, Johan was now dealing regularly in Aldine texts.[54] In 1506 he addressed one of many hectoring letters to his elder sons Bruno and Basilius, who by this time were studying in Paris: amongst many other reproaches, he criticised the barbarous handwriting they had learned and urged them to cultivate a more "Roman" – in other words, a more Italianate and humanist – style.[55] A year later Bruno wrote to his father of the Greek lectures which François Tissard had recently initiated, and of his own eager attendance.[56] And by 1508 it was the turn of the youngest son, Boniface, to be pestered by his father for the return of Aldus' *Latin Grammar* – apparently another prized possession.[57] But the most interesting symptom of this interest in Aldine publications is supplied by a copy of the fourth volume of the *Poetae Christiani Veteres,* which contains Nonnus' paraphrase of St John's Gospel and in this case carries notes to show that it was bought by the Amerbach family from Froben. We know from Aldus' own introduction to the third volume that he never officially published the fourth, since he was unable to complete the Latin translation: the few sets of the printed sheets that got into circulation were apparently passed "under the counter" to privileged, pressing or very well connected individuals. Froben appears to have found the means of becoming such a man.[58]

So Basel was fertile ground for Greek studies long before Cuno arrived, and whatever his personal responsibility, there is no doubt that the intellectual life of the city soon came to look more and more like that of Aldus' Venice. Johan Amerbach, who was almost equally preoccupied with editing Jerome and educating his three sons, tackled both problems at once by inviting Cuno into his household as editorial assistant and family-tutor. In Basel as in Venice, the print-shop quickly became a sort of research-centre. Other interested scholars began to call and learn from the far-travelled Dominican, and the nucleus of the group is hardly distinguishable from the editorial team which Erasmus named in the dedication of Jerome's works that was ultimately directed to Leo X. At the centre stood the three young Amerbachs, Froben himself, and the devoted Beatus Rhenanus, now so stricken with the whole environment of Basel that he had settled down there and erected a funerary monument to Cuno's memory. Nearer the periphery we find Cantiuncula, Professor of Law at the university, and Wilhelm Nesen, later a member of Busleyden's trilingual college at Louvain.[59]

So far as we can reconstruct it, Cuno's teaching appears to have relied on the spirit rather than the letter of Aldus' example. The dispersion of his library unfortunately began immediately after his death in early 1513, so we cannot be sure of the working-tools he had to hand: but the selection preserved by Beatus Rhenanus suggests that printed copies played a surprisingly small part compared to the manuscripts that Cuno had copied for himself in Padua, or the debris he had collected from the second-hand market and the print-shop floor. Perhaps, as Erasmus seems to suggest, Cuno took his vows of poverty rather too seriously and could not afford new books.[60] There is certainly nothing to show that he was being used as the sort of sales-contact that Celtis had been, and neither of the two patristic texts which he edited after his return from Italy has any direct Aldine predecessor.[61] His main functions were probably to encourage the general respect for Italian philological methods and the taste for Aldine publications which had been growing up in Basel for some time, and, judging by the behaviour of his pupils, he achieved a large measure of success. Johan Amerbach had sampled Aldus' introductory Greek texts: his third son Boniface became a collector of Aldine editions. The library of the university of Basel still possesses an almost complete range of the classical and neo-classical works printed by the Venetian company, bearing the inscriptions "Ex libris Amerbacchiorum" or "Bonifacii Amerbacchii liber" in that neat, humanistic hand which old Johan, for all his growling homilies, never managed to cultivate. Even when his father already possessed a particular work, Boniface took care to buy the Aldine version as well:[62] and his personal copy of the Aldine Book of Hours seems to have acquired the almost mystical qualities of a family Bible, in whose pages he recorded the most important events of his own life – the dates of his birth and his doctorate of Law, the deaths of his brother Basilius and of his greatest friend Erasmus. It is a striking proof of the value attached by one of the most distinguished Northern European scholars of the age to the work of his Italian predecessor.[63]

\# hora prima no[c]is mortuus e[st]
Erasmus Roterodamus vir *[illegible]*

Iulius habet dies 31. Lu[na]
Iouis na 30.

```
15  g  1  Calendis    Iulii
 8  A  2  Sexto nonas Iulii
    b  3  Quito no.   Iulii
16  c  4· Quarto no   Iulii
 5  d  5· Tertio no   Iulii·
    e  6· Pridie no   Iulii
13  f  7· Nonis       Iulii·
 2  g  8· Octauo idus Iul·
    A  9  Septimo idus Iul.
10  b 10  Sexto  idus Iul·
    c 11· Quito  idus Iul·
18  d 12· quarto idus Iul·
 7  e 13· Tertio idus Iul·
```
B   iiii
Mors matris chariss[imae]
Anno 1518.

A leaf from Boniface Amerbach's Book of Hours, with a note Erasmus' death.

Froben's attitudes, personal or professional, are much harder to define exactly. He took over the Amerbach press after Johan's death in 1514, and re-issued a number of Aldine editions during the following years: the series in fact starts with Erasmus' *Adagia* in 1513, and continues with an octavo text of Aesop's *Fables,* Theodorus Gaza's Greek Grammar, Erasmus' translations from Euripides, and Fortiguerra's *Oratio de Laudibus Literarum Graecarum.* The prominence of works designed to encourage or assist Greek studies is obvious. But the overall number is relatively small, and Froben did not fall into the mere plagiarism of the Lyons printers or the more subtle imitation of Giunti.[64] Also, his overwhelming commitment to Erasmus and the impossible task of deciding what Erasmus himself owed to the Aldine circle between them remove Froben's own attitude to his Italian colleague too far from any solid point of reference. The vital point is that his entire publishing career represents a gradual drift towards Italian styles of printing: he began work in 1491 with Gothic founts; during the first and second decades of the new century he used Amerbach's bold Roman types, and also possessed a Greek fount which, though less acceptable to contemporary scholars, bore obvious resemblances to the Aldine cursive. Finally, in 1519, he introduced two close copies of the Aldine italic which were the first legitimate ventures into this style by a Northern publisher, and were soon being widely imitated by others. When Erasmus commented in a later edition of the *Adagia* that Froben was carrying on the work of Aldus, he was paying more than a vapid compliment to both parties.[65]

The duration of the contact, the fame and commitment of the scholars involved, and the importance of the centres affected naturally give the Heidelberg circle and its successors a particular claim on our attention. But there were numerous other channels through which Aldus' influence could spread into the Empire, and several other scholars whose letters reflect the same excitement with the new publications. Two groups must be scrutinised in some detail: first, because their very different motives show the variety of tastes that Aldus could satisfy, second because their concern with his work moves the printer into fascinating conjunction with the most important artistic and religious movements of his age.

Willibald Pirckheimer of Nuremberg does not appear to have suffered greatly from Reuchlin's immortal longings, or to have seen much need for the high-pressure salesmanship which Celtis sought to employ on behalf of the liberal arts. A bluff, boisterous, sensuous dilettante, born of a considerable line of Italian travellers and book collectors, his main interests were in literature and the enjoyment of the most sumptuous library his purse could provide. During his own sojourn in Italy he indulged these tastes so thoroughly that even his father expostulated, and after some three years in the giddy intellectual whirl of Padua Willibald was obliged, in 1491, to abandon the lecture halls of Calfurnio and Pomponazzi for the more sober atmosphere of Pavia. But he could still work up little enthusiasm for the law, and the Greek classes of Demetrius Chalcondylas were dangerously accessible. In 1495 Willibald returned home without his doctorate and devoted his life to matrimony, civic responsibilities, and the pursuit of the Hellenic studies with which he was now, he confessed, completely captivated.[66] It is most unlikely that he ever met Aldus: he followed every development of the printer's plans, but always from a certain distance and without the close personal involvement that shows in the correspondence of Reuchlin or Spiesshammer. Willibald had an unquenchable thirst for Greek texts: Aldus offered the best means of gratifying it. This was an uncomplicated economic relationship, and therein lies its main interest.

"I have every Greek book printed in the whole of Italy"[67] boasted Pirckheimer in a letter to Celtis during 1504. The gradual dispersal of his library in the course of the seventeenth century means that we cannot now test this claim absolutely, but we can use it to illustrate the total dominance that Aldus acquired over this field of publication after 1500. Pirckheimer began collecting very early, and owned copies of Accursius' Aesop and the Florentine first edition of Homer, besides Lorenzo di Alopa's texts of The Greek Anthology, Lucian, and Apollonius, and Callierges' *Etymologicum Magnum*. He always kept himself fully informed about production in different centres. But the thirty Aldine volumes which he possessed wholly outweigh the Greek contribution of any other contemporary press, and if we include two editions published after Aldus' death and a sprinkling of Latin texts, the overall figure can be expanded to forty.[68]

The purchase of this range of books, even by a private individual operating indirectly, appears to have posed no problems whatsoever: as Pirckheimer commented almost casually in 1501, there were always one or two of his Imhof relations at the Fondaco dei Tedeschi in Venice who would be glad to act as agents.[69] No doubt many German buyers could have said as much. What occupied Pirckheimer far more was securing the most accurate information about the latest publications, and for this purpose he employed a variety of semi-official agents. At the beginning of the century he relied chiefly on a young relative named Anton Kress, a law student who, like himself, shuttled between Padua and Pavia and could always be sent a shopping-list or a request to scrutinise some rumour in the literary world, such as the imminent appearance of Aldus' trilingual Bible.[70] The contact apparently worked well: in March 1503 Willibald remarked complacently to Conrad Celtis that he had recently acquired a large quantity of Greek books and was busy with the texts of Herodotus and Thucydides, which Aldus had printed during the previous summer.[71] But Kress must have returned to Germany about this time for, from 1505, Pirckheimer was relying on two temporary residents actually in Venice. The first, not surprisingly, was the ever-valuable Cuno, who was much embarrassed by Aldus' reduced programme of Greek editions but kept his client's interest alive with anecdotes about the plans for an imperial academy and later about the projected editions of Plato and Plutarch.[72] The second was no less a person than Albrecht Dürer, who was then examining the style of the Venetian painters, aided by a loan from Pirckheimer. Most unfortunately, Dürer's letters speak only in general terms of investigating the bookshops, giving no specific information about what he was buying, or when.[73] But we have solid evidence of his close involvement with his friend's library in the twenty volumes – eleven of them Aldine – which are listed in the inventory as containing illumination in his hand. Sometimes, as in the volumes of Aristotle, there is simply a coat-of-arms or a few decorative motifs: but on the first page of the Aldine Theocritus there is a complete landscape in miniature, representing the two shepherds whose songs form the bulk of the first idyll and showing at least some acquaintance with the Greek text.[74] It is fatally easy for the mind to run riot at this point: to imagine the great master among the undefined throng of well-wishers at the print-shop, perhaps poring over the woodcuts of the *Hypnerotomachia* and arguing about the potential of the classical style with Benedetto Bordone. But we must be responsible. There is no way of proving that Dürer did more for Pirckheimer than stroll down the Merceria with his eyes open, and flick his brush this way and that across an end-page when he returned home. Nothing is going to turn him into a member of the Aldine academy, or coax cabbalistic mysteries out of his sketch-books. But his illuminations, and the whole of Pirckheimer's library, remain a powerful symbol of the direction that intellectual tastes were taking in the South-German towns, and of the immensely fertile cultural exchange with Italy that was now becoming possible.

The mention of Dürer leads on to what is arguably the most important of all Aldus' links with Germany, though its precise effects are almost impossible to define. Some time in the early months of 1520 the painter wrote in the following terms to Georg Burkhard, secretary to Elector Frederick the Wise of Saxony and Luther's principal ally at court:

> God helping me, if I ever meet Dr Martin Luther, I intend to draw a careful portrait of him from the life and to engrave it on copper, for a lasting remembrance of a Christian man who helped me out of great distress. And I beg Your Worthiness to send me for my money anything new that Dr Martin may write.[75]

As this letter implies, Burkhard or Spalatinus acted as intermediary for many different men on many different matters: one of his functions had been to advise the Elector on the formation of a comprehensive library for his cherished university of Wittenberg, and to make purchases on his behalf. He turned straight to Aldus. So we are brought to the very core of one of the greatest questions of sixteenth-century history: the relationship between humanism and reform, Renaissance and Reformation. What did Aldus contribute to the cultural environment that generated Luther's theses?

The story has a typically protracted and convoluted course, which derives from the varied experiences of Conrad Muth or Mutian – a problematical figure in himself, since he was subjected to widely different cultural influences from the Brethren of Deventer on the one hand and the scholars of Italy on the other, and left few writings to show where his own biases lay. He spent nearly ten years in Italy, from 1494 until 1503, and studied in most of the main centres: but there is no clear proof that he met Aldus face to face.[76] What is certain is that he acquired the fashionable taste for Greek literature and an almost reverential respect for the printer who was now providing the only means of pursuing it. On his return to Germany Mutian became a canon of the town of Gotha, and, thanks in part to the nearby university of Erfurt, soon became the centre of yet another busy cell of ambitious Hellenists. He recommended Aldus' Grammar to them. He stressed the importance of reading the Greek text alongside the Latin – a method of study which Aldus made possible.[77]

And in 1510 the cosmic disasters of European war paled in Mutian's eyes beside the fact that the Alpine passes were closed to traffic and that "liberal studies were lying dead, bereaved of Aldus' help".[78] One of his pupils, the monk Henry Urbanus, was so carried away that he wrote direct to Venice begging for copies of Pollux, Xenophon, Bessarion, and the *Etymologicum Magnum,* besides a place in Aldus' personal circle. One of the others, Spalatinus, contented himself on this occasion with sending his greetings.[79] But he had apparently imbibed all his teacher's respect for the Italian printer, and he did not forget it when, through Mutian's influence, he acquired the post of tutor to the Elector of Saxony's nephew in 1508.[80]

The notion that the University of Wittenberg always had a humanistic bias – that it was established in 1502 by an unusually secular charter and with statutes which gave surprising prominence to literary studies – can perhaps be exaggerated rather too easily. It remains true that the new foundation contained a large proportion of men with an Italian educational background, and that Greek found a regular place on the curriculum at a time when it was still rare in other German and indeed European universities. A succession of Hellenists runs unbroken from Nikolaus Marschalk, a pupil of Mutian himself and also an enterprising printer, to Philip Melanchthon.[81]

But the vital factor was probably Elector Frederick's determination that his university should be a thoroughly up-to-date institution: this demanded a good library, and in 1512 Frederick took Mutian's advice to throw open and expand his personal collection for the benefit of the university at large. Naturally, the Elector turned to his talented tutor/secretary Spalatinus for detailed advice, and naturally, the secretary was instructed to write to the printer whose texts he so strongly recommended from his personal acquaintance with them.[82] Two requests for catalogues were dispatched to Venice during the spring of 1512, but Aldus later claimed to have received neither: very probably he did not, since both were sent within weeks of the Battle of Ravenna.[83] So in December Frederick himself lent weight to his secretary's two notes, paying gracious tributes to Aldus' services to the learned world and leaving us with an interesting vignette of the prince tapping on the craftsman's door less than a generation after the death of men who had hardly been prepared to admit that printed books existed. Even this was not the first time he had written to Aldus, though the previous approach, which apparently was made in 1505, must have been made on his own behalf rather than the university's.[84] The outcome of all these hopeful dealings is still rather less clear than one would like. Spalatinus mentions in his notes for 1515 that Aldus was dead by the time a definite order arrived, and that the books were forwarded by Andrea Torresani. But catalogues were still being sent and enquiries made in Venice by a Franciscan named Burkhard Schenk between 1516 and 1518, so we must assume the purchase of Aldines was not concluded by the first contract:[85] and since the inventories drawn up by Spalatinus in 1536 did not identify individual editions, we cannot make a precise calculation of the number of Aldine texts that eventually found their way into the library.

However, we do have the material for an informed guess. During 1512 and 1513 an unknown agent named Wolf Fries, acting for Spalatinus, bought 153 volumes which included a large proportion of Italian humanistic writings and a specially listed section of twenty "Aldus Druch". Some of the items must have been wrongly described: but we can clearly identify all the volumes of the *Poetae Christiani,* the works of Firmicus, a volume of Aristotle, the Grammars of Lascaris and Aldus himself, Craston's *Lexicon,* Plutarch's *Moralia,* and the contemporary works of Pontano and Poliziano. The spurious volumes can be balanced by the works of Giorgio Valla, Dioscurides, and probably Erasmus' *Adagia,* which somehow slipped from their intended place on the invoice. Between ten and fifteen percent of Fries' purchases were Aldines, and their isolation proves that they were valued above the rest.[86]

Turning now to Spalatinus' tantalisingly incomplete catalogue, we can be at least fairly sure that these basic holdings were expanded by the works of Aristotle and Plato – which are described as "recently printed" – by Pindar and Homer, by Thucydides and possibly by Lucian. Finally, since the Elector's letter expressed an interest in Latin, as well as Greek and Hebrew texts, we can surmise that the baldly mentioned texts of Virgil, Horace, Ovid, Juvenal and others conceal an unknowable number of the famous octavos.[87] Luther himself was no Hellenist, and Aldus cannot have made much direct contribution to his intellectual development: but to Carlstadt and later Melanchthon the printer had much to offer. Mutian put the situation very succinctly when he observed that the Elector of Saxony had bought his Greek library in Venice and opened it in Wittenberg.[88] It is intriguing to find such a firmly laid foundation of Italian learning beneath a movement for reform that based much of its popular appeal on a rejection of all things Italian.

The muster-roll of Aldus' friends in France contains a number of individuals whose characters are now becoming familiar: the dilettante, collecting like a magpie for reasons which justify themselves; the scholar on the make; the committed reformer, dreaming of a new era of enlightenment; even the professional imitator, eager to capitalise on a fashionable style. But the overall pattern of the relationship was somewhat different from those we have examined so far. Though a good many Frenchmen did come to study in Italy, the intellectual and literary traditions of France were far more prestigious and much more deeply entrenched than their equivalents in England or the Empire. This is not to say that those traditions were particularly healthy during the years around 1500 – a number of Frenchmen came to Italy because they felt in need of new sources of inspiration. But while Reuchlin and Cuno beat a path to Aldus' door, our evidence suggests that it was Aldus who took the initiative in seeking scholarly contacts within France, and the spread of his reputation there certainly depended as much on refugees from Italy as on French visitors returning from the peninsula. Though occasional manuscripts might arrive from London or Vienna, the editorial balance of trade with these centres appears to have been heavily in Venice's favour. Between Venice and Paris it was far more evenly poised. International politics also complicated the situation more than was ever the case in dealings with distant England, or with the Empire, whose commercial cities often acted quite independently of their nominal overlord. From 1509 until 1512, Venice and France were deadly enemies. But from 1499 until 1509 the two powers were in alliance, and the French controlled the neighbouring duchy of Milan until 1512. Naturally, there was a large contingent of administrators there, and the frequent shuttling of diplomatic missions to and fro between the two centres allowed for a good deal of informal contact. Aldus did not miss his chances of cultivating this moneyed and influential clientele, and they showed that for all their native traditions and Gallic pride, they were as susceptible to the charms of Italy as their English and German contemporaries.

The illuminated copy of Amaseus' *Vatacinium,* the friendly tone of the dedication of Bessarion's *In Calumniatorem Platonis,* and Aldus' familiarity with the reading-habits of the ambassador, are clear proof that some sort of link had been formed with the jurist Accursius de Mayner, who represented the French crown in Venice from the summer of 1499.[89] Unfortunately, the trail ends immediately. But his visits to Milan in 1506 and again in 1511, the dedications he addressed to the secretary Antiquario and the diplomat Jeffroy Charles, the probability that Milan was considered as a centre for the Academy, are all indications that Aldus was carefully extending his circle of acquaintances among the rulers of Lombardy.[90]

It must have been in 1511 that he met the man who perhaps comes nearer than any other to Michelet's vision of the French visitor to Renaissance Italy – Jean Grolier.[91] Like many contemporary French patrons and collectors, including the Briçonnets from whose number he chose his bride, Grolier's family had risen from relative obscurity through the rapidly expanding financial administration of the Crown. His father Estienne was Élu of Lyons in 1494, and Treasurer of Milan from 1499. Jean, who succeeded his father in 1510, lived and died in royal service. He was besieged in the Castello of Milan in 1512, and captured at Pavia in 1525: he was involved in the foundation of the Collège Royale during the 1530s; and he survived a charge of embezzlement in 1561. During this eventful career he became so sensitive an esthete and so committed a collector that even the fragments of his library form some of the most prized holdings of the Bibliothèque Nationale and the British Museum, besides having given his name to a style of ornamental binding and a bibliographical society. His ancient coins and cameos have long diappeared: so have nearly nine-tenths of his books. But of roughly 350 surviving volumes, almost a half are Aldines, forty-two of them from the lifetime of Aldus the Elder. Grolier's zeal makes even Pirckheimer and Boniface Amerbach look mean. He had four copies of the 1501 edition of Juvenal and Persius, four of *Polifilo,* and no less than six of the first octavo edition of Martial.[92] He bought many copies on vellum, and frequently bore the added expense of illumination: and since the work often bears a strong resemblance to that executed for members of the Venetian nobility, there is a real possibility that special orders were prepared for him in the Aldine workshop itself.[93] His relationship with the press was definitely close, personal, and lasting: in 1515 Musurus dedicated the posthumous edition of Aldus' Greek Grammar – the printer's "last daughter", as he put it – to Grolier, and asked for the Frenchman's help in persuading Torresani to maintain the standards set by his late partner. This, apparently, was given, for in 1521 Grolier received the dedication of Terence which had been promised to him by Aldus, and in the following year he sponsored a new edition of Budé's celebrated treatise *On the Ass,*[94] which he wished to have modelled on the Poliziano of 1499. In the meantime he also kept in touch with past members of the Aldine circle such as Battista Egnazio.[95] It is indeed strange and surprising that Grolier's activity has remained the province of bibliographers, while attracting so little attention from historians, for no career gives a better notion of the lengths to which a French dilettante would go in his quest for the material signs of Italian culture, and no library offers a surer measure of the part played by Aldus in satisfying such demands.

But whatever his merits as a bibliophile, Grolier was no intellectual, even in the eclectic and gentlemanly fashion of Pirckheimer. Though the survivors of his Aldine collection may not be fully representative, there is a suggestive scarcity of Greek editions, and it is in fact extremely difficult to plot the stages by which Aldus began to affect the scholarship, rather than the taste of France. The architect Fra Giovanni Giocondo was caught by the French working on a villa for the Aragonese king of Naples, and accompanied the retreating invaders to Paris as royal adviser on buildings in 1495: but, though he was to exercise an immense influence on Latin texts after 1508, there is nothing to suggest that Aldus knew him at this early date.[96] The Greek philologist and editor Janus Lascaris also joined the French court about a year later. He had probably met Aldus in Venice during the early 1490s, but the letter which he sent the printer from Blois at the end of 1501 contains a strong note of surprise that contact had been made "across such a distance and after such a time". It is most unlikely that there had been any link between the two men, or between the print shop and the French court circle, during the interval. More significant still, Lascaris' reply reveals that Aldus had written to him for advice on his octavo editions and for manuscripts of Pliny and Terence, so we appear to have discovered a decisive shift in the cultural wind from the south that has prevailed thus far in our study.[97]

A good deal has been said in an earlier chapter about Aldus' use of manuscripts from France, but we must stress the crucial importance of Lascaris and Fra Giocondo as intermediaries, besides making the general point that, without this connection, the Aldine editorial programme would have been very different. The much praised and publicised edition of Pliny's *Letters* was based on an early exemplar investigated and transcribed, along with six other volumes, by Fra Giocondo in Paris. The Attic orators and an unknown quantity of other Greek material was made available by Lascaris during his long embassy in Venice, and, though the Greek codices were misplaced waifs from the Medicean collection rather than migrants from France, Lascaris was thanked along with Fra Giocondo for providing two "very ancient" manuscripts of Sallust for the octavo edition of 1509. These definitely came from Paris.[98] Other references prove that Fra Giocondo used his time in Paris to transcribe the third section of Nonius Marcellus' *Compendia,* unpublished before the appearance of Aldus' new *Cornucopia* in 1513, to revise the text of the *Scriptores Rei Rusticae,* and to consult manuscripts of Caesar which he considered better than any known in Italy.[99] Many European countries made some contribution to Aldus' programme, and the printer generally made a special, slightly florid acknowledgement: with France, no such gesture was necessary or possible, because the contribution was too great and too regular.

But during the same years of the first decade, and through the same intermediaries, Aldus' influence was percolating into French intellectual circles. In Paris, as in Heidelberg, the ground had been well prepared, and there was an active circle of men with advanced literary and philological interests. Pico himself had studied in Paris during the latter half of 1485, and the philosopher Lefèvre d'Etaples had returned the courtesy with a visit to Florence and Rome during the early 1490s. Some sort of basic instruction in Greek – its quality, admittedly, is very uncertain – was offered, at a price, by a wandering Spartan named George Hermonymus.[100] Lascaris and Fra Giocondo were lionised. The architect was soon dividing his time between the Pont Notre Dame and a course of informal lectures on Vitruvius, while the Greek was persuaded by an eager young secretary called Guillaume Budé to provide some teaching if he had time and to lend his books if he had not.[101] We cannot, unfortunately, say how many of the early Aldine Greek texts passed into France at this time by means of the contact which the printer had opened with Lascaris: but it is clear that the hopes and interests of the Parisian circle began to polarise on Venice during the first five or six years of the sixteenth century. Lefèvre came to Italy for the Jubilee of 1500, and made a detour to visit Aldus.[102] Budé followed a year later, apparently as a member of a French mission in Venice: he did not specifically claim to have met Aldus, but since he was attached to Accursius Mayner, dined with the family of Ermolao Barbaro, and discussed literary topics with them, it is hard to believe that there was not some contact.[103] But for unmistakable proof of this growing influence we must wait until 1507. In the spring of that year François Tissard of Amboise returned to Paris after a period of study in Italy and provided funds for Gilles de Gourmont to print the first complete Greek texts in France. The material he selected was openly and avowedly derived from Aldine precedents: the gnomic poets and Hesiod's *Works and Days,* which both appeared in 1507, were copied exactly from the Aldine edition of 1495.[104] At almost the same moment Erasmus was hinting to his room-mate in Venice, Gerolamo Aleander, that a shrewd and adventurous man might be able to turn all this enthusiasm to good account, and it is not surprising that the needy Aleander took his advice. He arrived in Paris on 4 June 1508.[105]

We have now reached one of those points where the precise weighting of merit and responsibility becomes exceedingly delicate. Aleander lodged with Aldus occasionally over a number of years, and did some work on the text of Plutarch's *Moralia,* Erasmus' *Adagia,* and probably other publications. But he was in no sense the printer's dependent or creature. Most of his studies were supervised by Musurus, and he was gifted with immense linguistic and educative powers of his own.[106] So Aleander's achievements in Paris over the next five years – the enthusiasm of his students, the courtiers who came to hear him, the lecture-halls packed to the door two hours before he arrived, and immobile with anticipation after he had finished, his election in 1513 as Rector of the University, the first Italian to hold the post since Marsiglius of Padua two centuries earlier – must all be considered his and his alone.[107] They concern us only coincidentally. What cannot be doubted is that those successes were based on the foundation laid by Aldus' Greek editions. Aleander brought three cases of books with him from Italy and in July of 1508 reported anxiously to Aldus that they had been mislaid, and that he could not begin formal teaching without copies of Lascaris' *Erotemata*: could Aldus please dispatch twelve of the vital Grammars immediately, together with six Lexicons and six or more Lucians? At this stage, Aleander was decidedly caustic about the primitive efforts of Tissard, even though he was grateful for the helpful advice given by Budé and Lefèvre.[108] But the uncertainty of communications with Venice and the cost of transport soon showed him that he would have to rely on the local printers, and with the outbreak of war in the spring of 1509 a shift of loyalties became imperative. Before the Battle of Agnadello was fought, Aleander was in harness with Tissard and de Gourmont.[109] But the productions of the new team still followed Aldus' footsteps exactly. A text of Plutarch's *Moralia* appeared on 30 April 1509: in 1512 came Chrysoloras' *Erotemata* and a reprint of Craston's *Lexicon* which, though much expanded by Aleander, was still basically the Aldine edition of 1497; a Theocritus, a Lucian, and Theodorus Gaza's Grammar followed in 1513; and a year later came Fra Urbano's Greek Grammar, a work both commissioned and printed by Aldus.[110] But by this time Aleander had abandoned his position in Paris and entered the service of the Bishop, Etienne Poncher.[111]

Aleander's departure, followed in barely more than a year by Aldus' death, brought this period of intensive contact between the Venetian print shop and the Parisian lecture rooms to an abrupt close, and left a great many unanswered questions behind. Though the interest of the French in Greek scholarship and Italian techniques is obvious enough, it found much of its expression in local copies rather than imported originals, and we cannot be at all sure of the numbers of Aldines that actually reached Paris.[112] Aldus definitely received a great deal of valuable material in return, but the intermediary role played by adventurers like Lascaris, Fra Giocondo, and Aleander, who moved sure-footedly from country to country and from patron to patron, blurs the boundaries between the French and Italian traditions. Like two colours in an aquatint, they simply touched, and merged. To see the full measure of Aldus' impact on French scholarship and book-production as well as French taste, we must wait almost a generation after his death.

The long and successful series of plagiarised octavos produced by the Lyons presses are ample proof of the popularity of the smaller format and the italic type at the lower end of the French market. The lapse of the copyright after Aldus' death legalised the imitation of the type, and the appearance of two treatises on writing styles by the scribes Arrighi and Tagliente during the 1520s naturally encouraged experiment. The French printers were slower than Froben in taking this opportunity: but Simon de Colines produced a text of Catullus in italic in 1529, and he was gradually followed by others, notably Gryphius of Lyons with his "Great Italic" in 1537 and Robert Estienne who interspersed his texts with italic passages until, with the *De Re Rustica* of 1543, he initiated a complete series of classical texts in italic.[113] Over the same period the Aldine Roman types were being studied and imitated by many of the same men. The intermediary in this case appears to have been an antiquarian fanatic named Geofroy Tory, who returned to Paris some time in the early 1520s after a long stay in Italy and much earnest reading of the *Hypnerotomachia Polifili*. His views on the proper formation of antique letters were embodied in a work named *Le Champ Fleury,* which he published in April 1529, and which drew heavily on earlier Italian examination of classical inscriptions. The tradition that he "taught" the typefounder Garamond has never been substantiated: but by the early 1530s Colines and Estienne, both of whom dealt regularly with Garamond, were using Roman founts modelled on the type in which Aldus had printed *De Aetna,* and it was from Garamond's workshop that this style spread rapidly across Europe during the second quarter of the century. When Garamond took to printing on his own account in 1545, his first aim was to "copy the italic script of Aldus Manutius". The ghost of Aldus had now secured a dominant position in French typography as well.[114]

Still more striking is the acceptance of the Aldine printed text by critics of the most exacting scholarly and esthetic tastes. We have seen the beginnings of this process with Jean Grolier: but it can be followed at a higher level, and on a different scholarly plane, in the formation of the French Royal Library. Anxious to establish his place among the most discerning and munificent patrons of the time, Francis I appointed Budé his librarian in 1522, and it was probably through Budé's influence that instructions were sent to Jean du Pins and Guillaume Pellicier, successive French ambassadors in Venice, to buy or secure copies of all the Greek texts they could find for the new library at Fontainbleau. Pellicier's list of purchases still survives. It starts with a catalogue of around 150 manuscripts, then continues with fifty-five printed texts. Of these, thirty-one are Aldines, sixteen of them from the lifetime of the elder Aldus. No more than two editions are recorded from any other printing-house.[115] The volumes were incorporated into the library over a period of twenty years or so, and most of them can be clearly identified by the ornate royal binding and the intertwined initials of Henry II and his mistress Diane de Poitiers.[116] In absolute terms their numbers are not, perhaps, very large. But they illustrate yet again the dominance of the Aldine press over this field of scholarship and they draw an emphatic line through Vespasiano's hope that printed texts would feel ashamed in the company of manuscripts. If the Most Christian King could collect such books and have his personal coat of arms stamped on them, no lesser bibliophile need fear a pang of conscience.

In France, the Empire and England, we can follow the progress of Aldus' influence fairly confidently through the correspondence of his patrons and quantify it up to a point through the growth of their libraries. Lack or loss of these two crucial sources prevents us from following the same path much further. In several other countries we may feel the strong awareness of an Aldine presence: but we cannot always tell how it came to be there, how deep an impact it made, or how long it lasted.

Every one of these difficulties applies to Spain. There are a number of indications that Aldus had some influence there: he was apparently on the most familiar terms with the household of the Spanish ambassador in Venice,[117] and when he stopped business in 1509 one of his Greek editors, Demetrius Ducas, was invited to teach at the new trilingual college which Cardinal Ximenes had founded at Alcala in 1508.[118] There is proof of the task that Ducas was facing in the fact that, when he arrived in 1513, the university possessed only fourteen Greek texts: but there is also proof of Aldus' reputation in the fact that at least seven, and possibly ten of them were his publications.[119] During the five years of his teaching, Ducas was also involved in the publication of the famous "Complutensian Polyglot" Bible, and it is highly significant that the maiuscule Greek and Gothic Latin types which were used to print the New Testament in 1514 were abandoned in all subsequent volumes for a Roman-style of Latin fount and a Greek cursive that followed the pattern set by Aldus in the 1490s.[120] Was the magnetic force of the Venetian publishing house reaching out through its emissary? The eye of faith longs to find a connection: but the sad truth is that we have only loose ends. The ambassador Giambattista Spinelli, at whose table Aldus discussed Petrarch, was a Neapolitan noble, not a Spanish hidalgo, so we cannot assume that his tastes were communicated to his government. Nothing is known of Ducas before he appears as co-editor of the *Rhetores Graeci* in November 1508 and Plutarch's *Moralia* in March of the following year. By May the Aldine circle was no more. It is just possible that Ducas was the principal editor of the Polyglot New Testament, though I am bound to say that the evidence for this seems very slight, and the time it allows for the work very short: it must remain true that we have no reasons for linking any changes made by Ducas in the text or the typography back to Aldus, even if Ducas' responsibility could be established in the first place.[221] The connection between the two men was simply too short-lived. We might also doubt if Cardinal Ximenes, who regarded Greek only as a means to the understanding of the Scriptures, would have been prepared to allow free-rein to the more widely-based scholarship of

Aldus. Even if he did, the inquisitors of the later sixteenth century would not have permitted many traces to survive.

Turning now from the Western to the Eastern extremities of Europe, we find a rather different range of problems, for here there is no questioning the fact of Aldus' influence or its hold over men of the highest social position. He had many Hungarian friends, remarked the printer to Philip Csulai, ambassador in Venice: in fact they dated back to his own schooldays with Battista Guarino in Ferrara.[122] There was every opportunity for this sort of contact, for the period from around 1490 until the disastrous Battle of Mohacz in 1526 saw a peak of Hungarian interest in Italian classicism, and no less than forty future royal secretaries are known to have studied in Bologna, Padua, Pavia and Ferrara.[123] Aldus was known and respected by the most powerful of them. Sigismund Thurz, son of a Hungaro-Polish family which controlled vast mining interests as well as a number of bishoprics, studied from 1489 under Raphael Regius in Padua: around the turn of the centuries he visited Aldus in Venice and became an honoured friend; he was one of the first patrons to receive sample copies of the new octavos, and in 1502 his request for a similar edition of Cicero's *Letters* was answered in a specially drafted dedication. By 1506 he held four bishoprics, the prefecture of Transylvania, and the post of secretary to the King of Poland.[124]

Not very surprisingly, Aldus' reputation in both Poland and Hungary was rising during these years. The new Queen of Hungary, Anne de Foix, passed through Venice on her way to Buda in 1502 and one of her courtiers, who is known only as "Johannes Capellanus", wrote at least twice to Aldus and sent a catalogue of Greek codices in the famous library of Matthias Corvinus.[125] Probably in 1507 another Hungarian student at Padua, Stefan Brodarich, was encouraged by his patron Gyorgy Szatmari to have a selection of the works of John Pannonius published by Aldus: Szatmari was Bishop of Varad, patron of Thurz as well as Brodarich, and Brodarich himself went on to become Chancellor of the Kingdom of Hungary.[126] Philip Csulai himself later became secretary to the king and Bishop of Pecs: and the friendship which grew up between him, his protégé Vyrthesi, and Aldus from around 1512 must be seen merely as the culmination of a long process. With contacts such as these, Aldus' influence must have reached as close to the centre of power as it did in any European country. But what came of it all? Erasmus might speak in general terms of Hungarians bringing their manuscripts, and

Capellanus might send catalogues, but the only positive sign we have of literary co-operation is Brodarich's enquiry about a seven-year-old request for an edition of John Pannonius – which Aldus tactfully ignored. And even as Aldus was extolling their virtues in 1513 and 1514, time was running out for the Magyar lords. In that very year, a savage peasant-revolt split Hungarian society, leaving it open to the deadly onslaught of Suleiman the Magnificent in 1526. Csulai died with his king on the battlefield of Mohacs. Brodarich, who as Chancellor had been responsible for such defence as there was, escaped to reflect grimly on the misfortunes of himself and his countrymen.[127] How many relics of Aldus' once potent influence perished in the Turkish conquest, we cannot know: but most of the editions which survive in Hungarian libraries appear to come from a later period, and we can only assume that contact with Venice was almost completely broken.[128]

Poland presents a rather different picture: apart from the enthusiastic travellers to Italy who are by now a familiar part of the pattern, we have to reckon with a determined cadre of humanist exiles who strove to plant a colony of Hellenists in the university of Cracow. Between them the two groups seem to have achieved a considerable measure of success, and we have both letters and figures to show that Aldus occupied a central position in their plans. During the last two decades of the fifteenth century classical studies had been given considerable encouragement in Poland by a member of Pomponio Leto's circle named Filippo Buonaccorsi Callimacho who sought refuge in Cracow after the disgrace which had overwhelmed him in Rome, and secured employment as tutor to the son of King Casimir. In 1489 Conrad Celtis visited the Polish capital and – inevitably – founded a literary society whose activity continued well into the next century.[129] It is hardly surprising that there were a number of distinguished Polish visitors in Italy around the turn of the century. One of them, Sigismund Thurz, we have already met. Another, John Lubranski, must have been thoroughly imbued with Italian ideas by the time he met Aldus, since he had already studied at Cracow with Callimacho and at Bologna with Beroaldo when he made a second, leisured expedition to Italy as Bishop of Poznań and royal councillor. In October 1502 Aldus dedicated the octavo edition of Valerius Maximus to him with an evocative description of the Bishop's entertaining him in his room in Padua, and expansively promising to mount an expedition in search of manuscripts which were said to be shut away in a tower somewhere in Moldavia.[130] If the expedition ever took place, the tower must have been empty: but in 1507 Lubranski was still showing the keenest interest in Aldus' personal fortunes.

In the meantime events in Cracow itself had taken an independent and more positive turn.[131] A wandering Italian lawyer named Sylvius Amatus drifted north from Vienna some time in 1504, and he was soon followed by a Pistoiese humanist called Constanzo Claretti who had learned some Greek at Bologna under Codrus Urceus. In all but their determination to establish Greek studies in Cracow the two men quarrelled like cats, but during 1505 Claretti managed to interest Erasmius Ciotek, Bishop of Piock, in the scheme, and to persuade a prominent Cracow bookseller named John Haller to act as agent for the import of the necessary books.[132] Towards the end of the year Sylvius wrote to Aldus asking for the immediate dispatch of 100 copies of Lascaris' *Erotemata* and promising a further 100 sales in due course: Haller made independent contact a few months later, in the spring of 1506. Unfortunately, it is not clear how far this particular channel of communication was exploited. Haller made no mention of Greek texts, adding instead an order for 250 Latin books, none of which had been printed by Aldus: and about a year later, in September 1507, Claretti wrote to Venice asking for some cheaper anthologies of the Greek classics, since few of his students could afford complete texts.[133]

But it is still certain that a large number of Aldine texts found their way to Poland, and that Aldus' influence on the intellectual life of the country went far beyond the surface of the page. Of the twenty-nine editions published before 1500, twenty-two are represented to this day in the Jagellionian library of the University of Cracow: where the purchasers can be identified, they are always men of influence in the university or the Church, one of the foremost being a friend and client of Lubranski named Nicolai Czepiel.[134] Shortly before his death in 1520, Lubranski himself established a "New Academy" in Poznań, and though we are not fully informed about its activities, it definitely taught Greek and there is every likelihood that it was modelled on the polished intellectual circles which the Bishop had known in Venice and Padua earlier in the century.[135] Aldus' impact on Polish scholarship was enduring: as late as 1559 Paulus Manutius wrote to thank the Bishop of Cracow, Andrej Zebrzydowski, for the continuing respect shown to his father's memory.[136]

Nowhere complete, the picture is consistent almost everywhere. Though we cannot say precisely how many Aldine texts reached any one country in Europe, the demand for them was so obvious and so universal that Erasmus' tributes to the library that would fill the world now appear as a simple recognition of the facts. At the same time, Aldus was almost as anxious to get manuscripts from his northern friends as they were to get printed books from him: in the event, only France contributed a significant quantity to his programme, but the appearance of Pliny's *Letters* in Paris encouraged dreams that other treasures would emerge from the Scottish or Danubian mists, and Aldus saw himself as leader of a general literary revival, not a campaign for Italian supremacy. He received far less than he had hoped for, and been promised, from abroad. Meanwhile, the fashionable cult for Greek, the prestige of Padua and his own tactful search for the right sort of friends, combined to raise Aldus' personal reputation ever higher. By the time of his death, Europe was filled not only with his books but with eager, committed groups of his admirers, who strove to reproduce in London, Vienna, or Poznań the glittering world of high scholarship and good company which they had once known in Italy.

NOTES

1 The estimate of 1,000 copies is based on the introduction to Euripides (OAME XLVI). But there is a hint in the preface to Demosthenes that fewer copies ("admodum quam pauca") were printed (*ib.,* LVI, Vol. I, p. 88): and it is most unlikely that occasional pieces such as political or funeral orations were printed in large editions. On Avanzia's introduction to Catullus see Ch. IV, n. 96: the relevance of the wording does not appear to have been noticed by Renouard and the passage is not reproduced by Orlandi.

2 Hirsch mentions a 3,000 copy edition of Guarino's Grammar in 1508: *Printing,* p. 65. For the enormous expansion of printed material during the early years of the reformation see A. G. Dickens, *The German Nation and Martin Luther,* London, 1974, pp. 112–115.

3 This is a "catch-all" estimate, including individual authors whose works form part of a collection and others such as Euripides whose works had been partly, but not completely edited before. Numbers of the letters printed in the collection of 1499 would certainly be considered spurious today. The works of Aeschylus were finally published in 1518: RAIA p. 193.

4 Pico died on the very day when the French armies entered Florence, 17 November 1494. P. Villari, *Life and Times of Gerolamo Savonarola,* Florence, 1888, p. 232.

5 Cf. Ch. IV, n. 152, Ch. VI, nn. 102–3. Work on the Greek orators must have continued over the interval between Lascaris' leaving Venice and the appearance of the edition in 1513.
6 The periodisation is that of Pieri, *La crisi militare*, and A. Renaudet, *Préréforme et Humanisme à Paris pendant les Premières guèrres en Italie*, Paris, 1916.
7 M. M. Philips, *The Adages of Erasmus*, pp. 180–1. More, *Utopia*, ed. P. Turner; London, 1965, p. 100.
8 For bibliography on the polemics between Italians and Northern Europeans see G. Manacorda, "Notizie intorno alle fonti di alcuni motivi satirici", *Romanische Forschungen* XXII, 1908, pp. 733–60. On particular countries Dickens, *The German Nation*, pp. 21–48: H. Hornik, "Three interpretations of the French Renaissance", in W. Gundersheimer, ed., *French Humanism, 1470–1600*, London, 1969, pp. 19–47: F. Simone, *The French Renaissance*, trans. G. Hall, London, 1969.
9 E. Garin, "La cultura fiorentina nella seconda metà dell'300 e i 'barbari Britanni'", *Rassegna della letteratura italiana*, Anno 64, No. 2, 1960, pp. 181–95. G. Parks, *The English Traveller to Italy*, pp. 448–54, comments on the large number of manuscripts of English scholastic writers surviving in Padua and on the widespread study of authors such as Michael Scot and John of Holywood.
10 OAME XVII (Dedication of *Astronomici Veteras* to Alberto Pio).
11 Parks, *op. cit.*, pp. 457f. R. Weiss, "Notes on Thomas Linacre", in *Miscellanea Giovanni Mercati*, Vol. IV, Città del Vaticano, 1956, pp. 373–80.
12 Grocyn's letter, which Aldus published with the *Astronomici Veteres*, implies that Linacre had acted as intermediary. Text in BP, pp. 240–1. There is some possibility that Linacre and Grocyn had begun to study Greek at Oxford in the 1480s, as Linacre received two Greek books as part of a bequest in 1489: J. Bennett, "John Morer's Will: Thomas Linacre and Prior Sellyng's Greek Teaching", *Studies in the Renaissance*, XV, 1968, pp. 70–89.
13 On the dating of Linacre's time in Italy see P. Allen, "Linacre and Latimer in Italy" cit. under Ch. III, n. 84, and R. J. Mitchell, "Thomas Linacre in Italy", *English Historical Review* L, 1935, pp. 696–8, on the date of his doctorate.
14 OAME VIII, and on the dating, Christie, "Chronology of the Early Aldines", cit. under Ch. III, n. 2.
15 Allen, *op. cit.*, p. 515.
16 CAM 87. Allen I, p. 438. G. Sturge, *Cuthbert Tunstall – Churchman, Scholar, Statesman, Administrator*, London, 1938, pp. 8–17.
17 This incident is mentioned by Pace's biographer J. Wegg, *Richard Pace, a Tudor Diplomatist*, London, 1932, pp. 5–12. But no copy of the speech is cited, and Pace makes no allusion to Aldus in his later dialogue *De fructu doctrinae*. On the situation in Venice at the time see Ch. V, nn. 83–7.
18 See Linacre's dedication of Proclus *De Sphaera* to Arthur, in BP p. 242.
19 New College Ω 7.1–6: Corpus Christi, Φ B 5: 8. For other isolated copies on vellum see D. Fava, "Libri membranacei stampati in Italia nel Quattrocento", GJB, 1937, pp. 55–84. They are considerably rarer than assumed by Renouard

since the three volumes he mentions in the Riccardiana of Florence are in fact on a high grade of paper. RAIA p. 9.
20 See Ch. IV, n. 19. It is unfortunately not possible to say exactly how much the full set cost on vellum, and Aldus probably allowed for a fair degree of flexibility with extraordinary publications. But the proportional costs of vellum and paper can be roughly compared from Aldus' quotations to Isabella d'Este-Gonzaga: copies of Catullus and Lucan cost 1 lire on paper, 3 ducats on vellum. Some allowance must be made for the fact that Aldus was offering illuminated copies in this case, while the Oxford Aristotles are all plain texts. Baschet, Doc. XII, p. 26.
21 New College, Ω 6.7 (Aristophanes), 6.6 (Cornucopia), 4.4 (Epistolographi), 5.6 (Lucian).
22 E. Rogers, ed. *St. Thomas More: selected Letters*, Yale, 1961, No. 2, p. 6, No. 1, p. 2. For further evidence see P. Hogrefe, *The Life and Times of Sir Thomas Elyot, Englishman*, Iowa, 1967, pp. 52f.
23 Weiss, *op. cit.* under n. 11, above, refers to a number of books once owned by Linacre but admits that his library as a whole cannot be reconstructed. There is a partial inventory of Grocyn's books in the Muniments Room of Merton College, Oxford: see M. Burrows, "A Memoir of William Grocyn", *Oxford Historical Society Collectanea*, Vol. II, 1890, pp. 332f. Editions are unfortunately not identified, and a number of important items, including the Aristotle, are missing. Rather than a complete inventory, the list probably records what Linacre and Lupset found among their friend's effects at the time of his death in 1520.
24 *Utopia*, ed. cit., pp. 100–1. Compare Raphael's anecdote about the monkey tearing up his Theophrastus with Aldus' comments on his exemplar: OAME, Vol. I, p. 16. Grocyn's tribute to Aldus was printed with the *Astronomici Veteres* and can be found in BP pp. 240–1.
25 A. Reed, "John Clement and his Books", *The Library*, Series IV, Vol. VI, 1925–6, pp 329–39.
26 For references to Aldus' plans and the wider European context see Ch. V, especially notes 101–3.
27 On the background to the College's foundation and the formation of its library see J. R. Liddell, "The library of Corpus Christi College, Oxford, in the Sixteenth Century", Oxford B.Litt. thesis, 1938, and in *Transactions of the Oxford Bibliographical Society*, XVIII, 1938, pp. 385–416.
28 OAME, I, p. 28. Specific mention was made of Linacre's translations of Simplicius' commentary on the *Physics* and Alexander of Aphrodisias' on the *Meteora*.
29 *Ib.*, p. 22. Ch. VI, n. 100, above.
30 C. Malagola and E. Friedlander, *Acta Nationis Germanicae Universitatis Bononensis ex Archetypis Tabularii Malvezziani*, Berlin, 1887, pp. xxxvi–xxxvii. G. Knod, *Deutsche Studenten in Bologna, 1289–1562*, Strassbourg, 1899, lists 4,398 different names. Scholars like Agricola, Reuchlin and the Pirckheimers definitely knew Greek, and a letter of 1491 from Marsiglio Ficino to Reuchlin suggests that there was a more or less

standing arrangement enabling young Germans to go to Florence "tamquam ad academiam". See Ch. III, n. 9, above.

31 *Amerbachkorrespondenz*, Vol. I, p. 39, Ep. 29. On Dinslaken and other dealers see Ch. III, nn. 96–9.

32 For recent English accounts of the formation and membership of the "Societas Rhenana" see H. J. Cohn, "The Early Renaissance Court at Heidelberg", *European Studies Review* I, No. 4, 1971, pp. 309f: L. Spitz, *Conrad Celtis, The German Arch-Humanist*, Harvard, 1957, pp. 45f (46 for reference to the "Academia Platonica"). On individual members see L. Spitz, *The Religious Renaissance of the German Humanists*, Harvard, 1963, pp. 60–80.

33 *Der Briefwechsel des Konrad Celtis*, ed. H. Rupprich, Munich, 1934, p. 288, Ep. 24. Also printed in RAIA p. 515.

34 Universitätsbibliothek, Basel, F. VI 54. Description in H. Omont, *Catalogue des Manuscrits Grecs des Bibliothèques de Suisse*, Leipzig, 1886, pp. 29–30, No. 67.

35 Reuchlin, *Briefwechsel*, Ep. LXVII, pp. 59–61. Saffrey, "Un humaniste Dominicain...", pp. 20–2.

36 Aldus' letter is printed in Schuck, pp. 128–30. On Reuchlin's library see K. Preisdanz, "Die Bibliothek Johannes Reuchlin", in *Festgabe Johannes Reuchlin*, ed. M. Krebs, Pforzheim, 1955, pp. 80–2: on the general context J. H. Overfield, "A New Look at the Reuchlin Affair", *Studies in Medieval and Renaissance History*, VIII, 1971, pp. 167–207.

37 *Index Graecorum Voluminum Ioannis Trithemii Abbatis Sponhemensis*, undated item in *Paralipomena Opusculorum Petri Blesensis*, Cologne, 1624, pp. 777–94. (I am grateful to Henry Cohn for this reference.) On Trithemius' attitudes see Buhler, *The Fifteenth-Century Book*, p. 35.

38 On this incident see Ch. IV, n. 26.

39 Spitz, *Conrad Celtis*, pp. 68–70.

40 *Briefwechsel*, ed. cit., No. 256, pp. 435–43.

41 Schück, Doc. VII, p. 123.

42 *Briefwechsel*, ed. cit. p. 568, Ep. 115.

43 *Ib.*, pp. 288, 451.

44 CAM 27: OAME XLII B.

45 CAM 30, 63.

46 *Fünf Bücher Epigramme von Konrad Celtes*, herausgegeben von K. Hartfelder, Berlin, 1881, pp. 19, 20, 23, 26, 28, 84–5. On the nationalistic bias of Celtis' writings see Spitz, *Conrad Celtis*, pp. 21f, 72f, and for more general comment, Dickens, *The German Nation*, pp. 33–5.

47 On Cuno's experience in Venice, see Ch. V, especially Saffrey's article "Un humaniste Dominicain...", cited under n. 87.

48 A. Horawitz, ed., *Briefwechsel des Beatus Rhenanus*, Ep. 21, pp. 38–9. *Amerbachkorrespondenz*, Vol. I, p. 411, Ep. 443. (Dated 1 December 1510: Reuchlin congratulates Amerbach on the arrival of Cuno as an "oneris sublevamen" and promises to persuade him to stay.)

49 For this background see C. Heckethorn, *The Printers of Basel, in the XV and XVI Centuries, their biographies, printed books and devices*, London, 1897, pp. 27–47.
50 *Amerbachkorrespondenz*, Vol. I, Ep. 34, 39 etc. See Ch. I.
51 Heckethorn, *op. cit.*, pp. 87f.
52 *Amerbachkorrespondenz*, Vol. I, Ep. 89, p. 95. Universitätsbibliothek, Basel, DD VII, 10, DD VI, 8a (Lascaris): BC III, 112a (Valeriani).
53 DD VI, 8a. This is a composite volume, in which the Grammar is bound with Dionysius Bertochus edition of Craston's Lexicon (Reggio, 1497). The signatures are inside the front and end-boards.
54 *Amerbachkorrespondenz*, Vol. I, Ep. 143, p. 132: Ep. 199, p. 190.
55 *Ib.*, Ep. 265, p. 251.
56 *Ib.*, Ep. 358, p. 333. It will be shown below that Tissard's teaching and publishing was based entirely on Aldine material.
57 *Ib.*, Ep. 388, p. 354.
58 Universitätsbibliothek, Basel, F.K. IX, 12. On the problems of this entire edition and the extreme rareness of the last volume see Christie, "Chronology of the early Aldines", pp. 210–13.
59 Erasmus' dedication (see Allen, II, Ep. 335, p. 88) names those involved with the edition before his own arrival and compares interestingly with Sturm's life of Beatus Rhenanus, where a wider circle of names is mentioned. See Horowitz, *ed. cit.* under n. 48, above, pp. 3f.
60 *Ib.*, Ep. 41, p. 68, shows that some of Cuno's books passed to Willibald Pirckheimer, though the greater part was apparently incorporated in the library of Beatus Rhenanus, which is now in the public library of Schlettstadt. The Aldine holdings are not substantial, and they cannot be traced directly to Cuno. See A. Horowitz, *Die Bibliothek und Correspondenz des Beatus Rhenanus zu Schlettstadt*, Vienna, 1874. Saffrey "Un humaniste Dominicain...", pp. 35–6, n. 51, mentions a glossary of the works of St Cyril (Schlettstadt MS. 105) and a manuscript of extracts from Aristophanes (Trinity College, Cambridge, MS. R 1, 42), besides Cuno's own lecture-notes on Gregoropoulos' classes on Aristophanes (see also *Scriptorium*, IV, 1950, pp. 104–7, for the note of V. Olerdoff). The parallel texts of Aristophanes and Lucian mentioned by Bruno to Boniface Amerbach (*Amerbachkorrespondenz*, Vol. II, Ep. 571, p. 81), cannot have been Aldines. For the suggestion that Cuno may have been too poor to buy new books see Wilson, "The Book-Trade in Venice".
61 Saffrey, *op. cit.*, pp. 41–2. The works concerned were a translation of Ps. Gregory of Nyssa's *De Natura Hominis* and Gregory Nazanzenus' eleventh discourse. A translation of St Basil's thirty-eighth letter was included. All edited by Matthias Schurer, Strassbourg, 1512.
62 For a general guide to the family library see Universitätsbibliothek, Basel, MS. C. VI, 33 ("Amerbachiana"), insert 25. CB III, 23 (*Rhetorica ad Herennium*, 1514) and BD VII, 61 (Chrysoloras, *Erotemata*, 1512) are interesting cases of Boniface's buying the Aldine version when the family library already possessed two earlier editions.

63 MS. AN VI, 36. (Boniface's notes are sufficiently copious for the book to be classified as a manuscript.)
64 For a useful checklist see Heckethorn, *The Printers of Basel*, pp. 91f, with immediate reference to Nos. 74, 75, 78, 84, 110. Froben was charged with plagiarism by Allen, "Erasmus' Relations with his Printers", *The Library*, XIII, 1916, pp. 318–19, but I think this view relies too much on the mistaken belief that Froben printed the *Adagia* in italics in 1513: in fact, this edition is a large folio in Roman type, and it should be remembered that Aldus had no specific copyright protection on the title.
65 For this account of Froben's career see Heckethorn, *loc. cit.*: A. F. Johnson, *Type-Designs: their History and Development*, London, 1934, p. 130; H. Carter, *Typography*, pp. 118–20, and Plate 79.
  For Erasmus' compliment to Froben see Philips, *The Adages of Erasmus*, pp. 185–6. It was included in editions after 1515.
66 This account of Pirckheimer's background is based on the fundamental article of H. Rupprich, now translated and re-printed as "Willibald Pirckheimer: a Study of his Personality as a Scholar", in G. Strauss, *Pre-Reformation Germany*, London, 1972, pp. 380–435. *Pirckheimers Briefwechsel*, Vol. I, Ep. 40, p. 122, shows Willibald extolling the superiority of Padua over Pavia as a centre of liberal studies: in Ep. 43, p. 137, he confesses his absorption in Greek literature.
67 *Briefwechsel*, Ep. 63, p. 206.
68 E. Offenbacher, "La Bibliothèque de Willibald Pirckheimer", LBF XL, No. 7, 1938, pp. 241–63. An inventory compounded from various library and sale catalogues is printed on pp. 251f. On individual copies and their present location see W. Eckert and C. von Imhoff, *Willibald Pirckheimer, Dürers Freund im Spiegel seines Lebens seiner Werke und seiner Umwelt*, Cologne, 1971, pp. 85f. In January 1503 Pirckheimer asked Kress to see if any further Greek editions were being prepared in Milan: *Briefwechsel*, Ep. 57, p. 190.
69 *Ib.*, Ep. 43, p. 137.
70 *Ib.*, Ep. 40, 43, 44, 57. It is interesting to find that Pirckheimer asked for news of the trilingual Bible at almost exactly the moment when Aldus admitted to Celtis that the project was in preparation: p. 123, and above, n. 41.
71 *Ib.*, Ep. 59, p. 195.
72 *Briefwechsel*, Ep. 86, p. 280, Ep. 139, pp. 436–8.
73 For an account of Dürer's visit to Venice and translations of his letters to Pirckheimer see W. Conway, ed., *The Writings of Albrecht Dürer*, London, 1958, pp. 45–60, especially 47, 54, 58. Dürer in fact never states definitely that he bought anything. The literature is too vast to allow for more than a single citation, but on the general importance of his stay in Venice see T. Pignatti's article "German and Venetian painting..." in Hale, *Renaissance Venice*, pp. 244–73.
74 Numbers based on Offenbacher's inventory; see also his text, pp. 243–5, and Eckert/Imhoff, *loc. cit.* The Theocritus miniature is reproduced on Pl. VIII, facing p. 89.
75 Conway, *op. cit.*, p. 89.

76 On Mutian's background the difficulties of understanding it see Spitz, *The Religious Renaissance...*, pp. 130f.
77 *Der Briefwechsel des Mutianus Rufus*, ed. C. Krause, Kassel, 1885, Ep. 35, pp. 42–3, Ep. 111, p. 136. "Eme tibi Rudimenta Manutii, ut scribere discas."
78 *Ib.*, Ep. 140, p. 193.
79 *Ib.*, Ep. 40–3, pp. 46–8. Also in Schück, Docs. XIII, XIV, pp. 131–4.
80. M. Grossman, *Humanism in Wittenberg, 1485–1517*, Bibliotheca Humanistica et Reformatorica, Vol. XI, Nieuwkoop, 1975, pp. 20–1.
81 Grossman, *op. cit.*, pp. 37–54. I confess to an uneasy feeling that the authoress uses the label "humanistic" in a very elastic sense.
82 *Ib.*, pp. 100–12.
83 *Urkendenbuch der Universität Wittenberg*, ed. W. Friedensburg, Vol. 1, Magdeburg, 1926, p. 68. The letters were written on 25 March and 1 May 1512. Neither was known to Pastorello. On the political situation in Northern Italy at this time see Ch. IV, n. 161. For Aldus' claim to have received none of the letters see Schück, Doc. XVI, pp. 135–6.
84 For the text of this letter (which was also unknown to Pastorello) see G. Buchwald, "Archivalische Mittheilungen über Bucherbezuge der Kurfustlichen Bibliothek und Georg Spalatinus in Wittenberg", *Archiv für Geschichte des Deutschen Buchhandels*, 18, 1896, pp. 10–11. Also printed by Grossman, *op. cit.*, p. 107, n. 28. Aldus mentions a previous letter from the Elector in his reply to Spalatinus, cited in n. 83.
85 Grossman, *op. cit.*, pp. 107–10.
86 Inventory of Fries' purchases printed in Buchwald, *op. cit.*, pp. 7–10, with Aldine entries on p. 9. As Grossman rightly comments, the proportion of Italian humanistic authors is large and includes contemporaries like Ricci, Beroaldo and Mancinelli as well as established figures such as Valla and Platina. A number of translations into Italian are listed. It should be noticed that the list of Aldines includes a Eusebius (which Aldus never published) and a copy of the printer's own Greek Grammar (which did not appear until 1515).
87 Spalatinus' inventories can be found in E. Hildebrandt, "Die kurfurstliche Schloss- und Universitätsbibliothek zu Wittenberg, 1512–1547", *Zeitschrift für Buchkunde*, 2, 1925, pp. 158–64.
88 Quoted by the same author, *op. cit.*, p. 121. "...illustrissimus Fridericus Graecam comparaverit bibliothecam Venetiis et Wittenburgi publicaverit ornatissime."
89 See Ch. IV, n. 26, and OAME L, A.
90 Dedications of Plutarch, 1509 (OAME LXVI) and Horace, 1509 (*Ib.*, LXVII). See also Ch. V, nn. 106, 107, and Donati's article "La seconda Academia Aldina...".
91 A copy of Erasmus' *Adagia* contains a note by Grolier recording a meeting with Aldus: this must have occurred after 1508. See M. Le Roux de Lincy, *Recherches sur Jean Grolier, sur sa Vie, et sa Bibliothèque*, Paris, 1866, p. 212. On the different views of French reactions to Italy see Hornik's article, cited under n. 8, above.
92 Biographical information and figures from Le Roux de Lincy, who gives an inventory of surviving copies, pp. 181–297. See also H. M. Nixon, *Bookbindings from the Library*

of *Jean Grolier: a Loan Exhibition, 23 September–31 October, 1965*, British Museum special catalogue; G. D. Hobson, *Notes on Grolier with a Eulogy of the late Dr. Theodor Gottlieb*, London, 1929. For some ideas on the interest of the French royal administrators in Italian humanism and its French counterparts see E. Rice, "The Patrons of French Humanism, 1490–1520", in *Renaissance Studies in Honor of Hans Baron*, ed. A. Molho and J. Tedeschi, Florence, 1971, pp. 689–702.

93 A full investigation of Grolier's illuminated copies would require an independent study: Bibliothèque Nationale, Paris, Vélins 2070 (Lucretius, 1515) and Vélins 2091 (Martial) bear a considerable resemblance to a Petrarch illuminated for the Mocenigo family (Vélins 2142) and to other items in the British Library and the John Rylands Library. See Ch. IV, n. 47 for references.

94 Dedications printed in Le Roux de Lincy, *op. cit.*, pp. 438–40 (Greek Grammar), 447 (Terence) and 449 (De Asse). See also p. 434 for Grolier's letter to Francesco d'Asola on this last edition.

95 Le Roux de Lincy, *op. cit.*, p. 49.

96 On Fra Giocondo see references under Ch. V, n. 114, above.

97 CAM 24. For bibliography on Lascaris see Ch. III, n. 8, above.

98 On the Pliny and the Attic orators see above, Ch. VI, nn. 102–3, 108–9. On the manuscripts of Sallust see OAME LXVIII.

99 RAIA pp. 60, 63, 66. Since Fra Giocondo's comments are not quoted by Renouard or Orlandi, it is worth reproducing them here: C. Julii Caesaris, *Commentariorum Libri*, 1513, f. C ii v. "...conquisivi multa tota Gallia exemplaria, quod multa eo semper ex Italia translata sunt atque ea minus praedae exposita ac bellis fuerunt, multo incorruptiora volumina cuiusque generis reperiuntur...."

100 There are numerous studies of French intellectual life at this time, but it will be sufficient to cite Renaudet's classic *Préréforme et Humanisme...*, pp. 120–7, 142–57, and the recent work of D. McNeil, *Guillaume Budé and Humanism in the Reign of Francis I*, Travaux d'Humanisme et Renaissance, No. CXLII, 1975, pp. 8–10.

101 L. Delaruelle, *Guillaume Budé – les Origines, les Débuts, les Idées Maîtrisses*, reprinted Geneva, 1970, pp. 73–4.

102 Renaudet, *op. cit.*, pp. 389–90.

103 Budaei *Opera Omnia*, Basel, 1557, repr. Farnborough, 1967, Vol. II, p. 143.

104 The two fundamental articles on this stage of Parisian printing are H. Omont, "Essai sur les Débuts de la Typographie Grecque à Paris, 1507–1515", *Mémoires de la Société de l'Histoire de Paris et de l'Île de France*, XVIII, 1891, pp. 1–14: M. Jovy, "François Tissard et Jerome Aléandre: contribution à l'Histoire des Origines des Études Grecques en France", *Mémoires de la Société des Sciences et des Arts de Vitry-le-François*, XIX, 1899, pp. 318–457 (all introductions reproduced). See esp. p. 340 "Aldus, qualem eum Venetiis novi et suis scriptis percepi..." (intr. to Greek Grammar, 1509).

105 J. Paquier, *Jerome Aléandre de sa Naissance à la fin de son Séjour à Brindes, 1480–1529*, Paris, 1900, pp. 26–8.

106 See Paquier, *loc. cit.,* and CAM 51–6, esp. 55.
107 For a full account, with ample quotations, see Paquier, *op. cit.,* pp. 37–52.
108 CAM 57. The three cases of books are mentioned in Aleander's *Journal Autobiographique,* ed. H. Omont, Paris, 1896, p. 11.
109 The difficulty with expenses was stressed in Aleander's introduction to Plutarch's *Moralia:* see Omont, "...la Typographie Grecque...", p. 55.
110 For full lists see Omont and Jovy, *opera citata.*
111 Paquier, *op. cit.,* p. 56.
112 Aleander definitely mentions a number of Aldines among the 62 items of "Books left at Blois" in November 1514 (*Journal,* p. 12), but these were presumably his own, and his introduction to Plutarch states that the numbers of texts brought from Italy "would hardly suffice for three or four students of Greek".
113 Carter, *Typography,* pp. 117–36. S. Morison, "Towards an Ideal Italic", *The Fleuron,* 5, 1926, pp. 93–129: Morison and Johnson, "The Chancery Types...", *op. cit.* under Ch. IV, n. 88, pp. 41f: E. Armstrong, *Robert Estienne,* pp. 48–9.
114 A. F. Johnson, "Geofroy Tory", *The Fleuron* 6, 1928, pp. 37–66. See also Garamond's preface quoted in "The Chancery Types...", pp. 49–51, and in general Beaujon, "The Garamond Types", cit. under Ch. IV, n. 82.
115 Bibliothèque Nationale MS. Graecus 3064, ff. 59v–61r. On this purchase see also Ch. IV, n. 81, above.
116 The volumes I have been able to identify with reasonable certainty from the inventory are: Aristotle, 5 vols (Rés. 29, Vélins, 469–73), Dioscurides and Nicander (Rés. T 138/27a), Athenaeus (Rés. Z 29), Aristophanes (Rés. Yb 47), Epistolographi (Rés. Z 650), Demosthenes (Rés. X 279), Hesychius (Rés. X 44).

Volumes of Stephanus, Thucydides, Gregory Nazianzenus, Ulpian and the Greek Anthology are mentioned by the inventory but cannot be identified from any distinctive bindings or glosses.

Copies of Herodotus (Rés. J 10), Euripides (Rés. Yb 804), Plato (Rés. R 8), the Suda (Rés. X 53) and Homer (Vélins 2046–7) carry the royal arms and binding but are not mentioned in this particular inventory. Possibly they were acquired by du Pins or the other agent who was active at this time, an Italian named Gerolamo Fondulo. See Franklin, *op. cit.,* pp. 66f.

Copies of Poliziano (Rés. Z 296), Bembo's *Asolani* (Rés. Z 2459), Pontano (Res. 1050–1) and Erasmus' *Adagia* (Res. Z 243) carry the salamander crest of Francis I and prove that the incorporation of Aldines into the royal library began before the systematic collection of Greek texts in the 1530s and 1540s.
117 OAME LXXXVII A (Petrarch, 1514).
118 On Ducas' career in general see Geanakoplos' invaluable chapter in *Greek Scholars,* pp. 223–55.
119 M. Bataillon, *Érasme et l'Espagne,* Paris, 1937, p. 22, n. 2. The five volumes of Aristotle, the Grammar of Fra Urbano, and the volume of the Astronomici Veteres, are definitely Aldine: the Vocabularium, the Cornucopia, and the Psalter are less certain, as is the Grammar of Lascaris.

THE GREAT DIFFUSION

120 K. Woody, "A Note on the Greek Fonts of the Complutensian Polyglot", *Papers of the Bibliographical Society of America*, 65, 1971, pp. 143–9.
121 Geanakoplos, *Greek Scholars*, pp. 239–43. The author's attempt to attribute the introduction of the New Testament to Ducas on stylistic grounds seems to me ingenious rather than convincing, and I find it hard to believe that Ducas had the decisive voice in the preparation of a text which appeared in January 1514 if he had been at Alcala only since the previous year.
122 OAME LXXVII (Cicero, Ad Atticum, 1513).
123 G. Bonis, "Gli scolari ungheresi di Padova alla corte degli Iagelloni", in *Venezia e Ungheria nel Rinascimento*, ed. V. Branca, Florence, 1973, p. 237. On the period in general see I. N. Goleniscev-Kutuzov, *Il Rinascimento italiano e le lettere slave dei secoli XV e XVI*, Moscow, 1963, trans. and reprinted Milan, 1973, pp. 193f.
124 On Thurz's mixed background and career see Bonis, *op. cit.*, pp. 232–3, Kutuzov, *op. cit.*, p. 195. On his relations with Aldus see OAME LXXVII (reference to friendly contact during his time at Padua): CAM 23 (praise of the octavo and request for a Cicero in the same format); OAME XXXV (dedication of Cicero).
125 CAM 88 (undated). Capellanus refers to a previous letter.
126 *Ib.*, 85. The letter refers back from 1512, and mentions Csulai as a contact to whom the completed work may be passed. On Brodarich see Bonis, *op cit.*, p. 236 and Kutuzov, *op. cit.*, pp. 191–2. On the background influence of Szatmari see G. Hraban, "Alde Manuce et ses amis Hongrois", French résumée of article in *Magyar Konyvszemle*, LXIX, 1945, pp. 38–98.
127 Hraban, *op. cit.*, and Kutuzov, *op. cit.*, pp. 191–2.
128 P. Gulyas, "Catalogue déscriptif des Aldines de la Bibliothèque Szechenye du Musée Nationale Hongrois", *Magyar Konyvzemle*, Ser. 2, Vol. 15, 1907, pp. 17–33, 149–65, 241–56, 331–51: Vol. 16, 1908, pp. 51–72, 148–65.
  For another Eastern European catalogue see L. Bica and I. Marza, "Carti aldine in Bibliotheca Batthyaneum din Alba Julia", *Apulum*, XI, 1973, pp. 311–50.
129 C. Morawski, *Histoire de l'université de Cracovie*, transl. P. Rongier, Vol. III, Cracow/Paris, 1905, pp. 122–6: Kutuzov, *op. cit.*, pp. 198–9, 282–3.
130 OAME XLII. On Lubranski's background see S. Lempicki, *Renesans i humanizm w Polsce – Materiały do Studiow*, Cracow, 1952, pp. 50f, and Kutuzov, *op. cit.*, p. 327.
131 CAM 61.
132 Lempicki, *op. cit.*, pp. 51–4: Morawski, *op. cit.*, pp. 125–9.
133 CAM 59 (Sylvius), 60 (Haller), 65 (Claretti). Lempicki's attempt to coax Aldine titles out of Haller's order is brave, but vain, since the Pole asked for Ciceronian texts with commentaries and Aldus invariably printed plain texts.
134 Lempicki, *op. cit.*, pp. 54–5.
135 *Ib.*, p. 50: Kutuzov, *op. cit.*, p. 327.
136 Pastorello, *Epistolario*, No. 929.

CONCLUSION

It is the range and depth of these scholarly contacts which give the true measure of Aldus' achievement. Printers had traded as widely as he did in Jenson's time, and there is no doubt that Aldus' rivals, the Giunti, were commercially far more successful. But from the moment in 1496 or 1497 when Codrus Urceus set him in a special category, Aldus has been seen as a man apart by scholars, by writers, and by bibliophiles. Even when his quarrels with Alberto Pio and Aleander were leading him to drown the memory of his Italian friends, Erasmus could not deny that he had longed to have the *Adagia* published "by a celebrated house".[1] Right through the sixteenth century, collectors like the English mathematician and wizard John Dee carefully identified the volumes in their libraries that came from the Aldine press, isolating them from the thousands of others which bore only a date and the name of a city.[2] During the golden years of French classicism, Jean Racine sketched the characters of his own formidable heroines in the margin of an Aldine text of Sophocles' *Electra*;[3] and it was only natural that the name of Aldus should have been one of the first to attract eighteenth-century antiquarians like Zeno and Manni, or the collectors of the same and a later period such as Cracherode, Lord Spencer, and Augustin Renouard.[4] From them the current of interest in Aldine studies flows in an unbroken series of studies, bibliographical articles, and laboriously collected documents, down to the present day. The most embittered revisionist – and I may at times have cast myself in that role – would find it hard to reduce Aldus' reputation to a skilfully orchestrated programme of self-advertisement. His prestige grew spontaneously, and in his own lifetime: it survived attacks in his own lifetime; it has not only survived, but increased, in the four and a half centuries since his death.

But it has to be admitted that a good deal of recent research makes it hard to find the bed-rock on which that prestige must originally have rested. Even in his simple capacity as a designer of types and a producer of printed books, Aldus' place in the European tradition is far more ambiguous, more narrowly based, and far less closely connected to his own aspirations than his uncritical eulogists have suggested. Amongst illustrated texts *Polifilo* will always count as a masterpiece, and the roman type in which it was printed has been treated by Stanley Morison as a model of visual clarity and a pattern for future typographers. But Aldus did not base his programme on a quest for visual clarity: he never sought copyright on any of his roman types, and he bore no ultimate responsibility for *Polifilo*, which was sponsored and financed by the outsider Leonardo Crasso. Aldus' bid for fame was founded on the Greek and Latin cursives which he publicised widely and protected by no less than six copyrights from the Venetian senate and three successive popes. Admired and imitated in their own time because of their close resemblance to the most fashionable handwritten forms, these types are now either neglected or condemned by scholars and typographers for precisely the same reason: like the script of Apostolis, Musurus, or Tagliente, they are decorative rather than legible. So if Aldus succeeded in setting standards for his own century, then we have to admit that those standards are now discarded: if he supplied a model for the fine roman printing of a later age, then he did so largely by accident. And even in the first years of the sixteenth century, the division of credit between Aldus as designer and Francesco Griffo as caster was a matter for dispute. We cannot hope to settle the question conclusively, but it is significant that Aldus never remodelled his types after Griffo left Venice in 1502.

The reputation for accurate scholarship on which both the printer and many of his assistants staked so much is now severely tarnished, if not wholly defaced. It must be regarded as certain that Aldus never gained direct access to the Greek codices bequeathed to Venice by Cardinal Bessarion. Possibly this was through failure to appreciate their value: more probably it was the result of political confusion and bad luck; whatever the reason, the fact itself removes one of the main supports on which the assumed excellence of Aldine texts has been carried. Detailed examination of individual editions will probably press ahead for some time to come, but it may never be possible to say how far the merits or deficiencies of a particular text should be attributed to Aldus himself, for the system of collective editorship blurred responsibility. What excites suspicion is the functioning of that system. Aldus sought and adopted corrections from Ricci or Erasmus or Parrhasio in the most haphazard fashion, and with only the most cursory interest in the manuscript authorities from which they had worked. Most of his exemplars were recent copies borrowed from the libraries of his friends, and he shifted from one to another as if he was composing a scrap book rather than editing a text. Even in the cases of Petrarch and Pliny, where chance and friendship brought capital manuscripts into his hands, his method of using them appears, on the evidence, to have been arbitrary and subjective. The lucky coincidence of an editor like Musurus with an authority like Bardellone's Hesychius could produce important results. But for most of his career Aldus seems to have followed the modish taste for personal opinion and assumed linguistic expertise rather than the harder and more recently discovered paths of textual and philological analysis. It is doubtful if he, or any of his associates, had progressed as far as their idol Poliziano in understanding the means by which the relationship between different manuscripts can be traced, and the status of the archetype determined. Even the Academy in which Aldus and his friends are supposed to have developed their critical methods, appears, in so far as it ever existed, to have been little more than a short lived social club.

As an advocate of mass enlightenment and social improvement Aldus' position is more secure. If we sneer at his declared ideals, we must devise another explanation for his entering the printing trade, and his apparent lack of financial reward makes this a difficult task. But we must keep both his ideals and their implementation in careful perspective. Though the number and the diffusion of his texts is impressive enough, the notion that he introduced the octavo to bring down book prices and reach a wider public is quite simply mistaken, and there are more subtle reasons for doubting whether he had any clear vision of what mass literacy implied. Like his friend Erasmus, Aldus would have paid lip service to the edifying image of the "virtuous poor", singing the psalms at their work. But he had no more contact than Erasmus with the realities of popular culture, and he would probably have shared much of Erasmus' contempt for those, like the friars, who did. For in his background and his social values, Aldus was a courtier. He spent much of his adult life in the polished atmosphere of Carpi and Ferrara: he longed for imperial Vienna even during his most prosperous years in Venice; he chose his correspondents, as far as he could, from the academically useful or politically powerful. Linacre and Reuchlin, Celtis and Thurz, Grolier and Lubranski, were all men who stood close to thrones.

He would drop any task, Aldus politely told Elector Frederick's secretary Spalatinus, to reply to a learned friend or a great prince.[5] Provincial schoolmasters like Gerolamo Bologni or needy students like Candidus Romanus do not often seem to have been so lucky.[6] For his own workers Aldus had neither time nor sympathy. His interest in Italian vernacular literature, though genuine and far-sighted, was also strictly bounded by works which were acceptable in the best company: there is no suggestion that he had any acquaintance with the culture of the piazza or the wine-shop. Perhaps a clerk or artisan occasionally tried to impress his fellows by investing one-and-a-half lire in an Aldine octavo, though he would have had to dig deep into his wages to do so: but he is far more likely to have bought one of the cheap imitations from Brescia or Lyons, more likely still to have preferred the spicy romances or saints' Lives that Francesco da Madiis offered, and most likely of all to have joined the audience of one of the street-singers whom Filippo di Strata so cordially despised. Whatever he may have been intellectually, as a person and a publisher Aldus was not the stuff of which social crusaders are made.

But these very deficiencies – his élitist attitudes, his frantic experiment, his isolation from the best available sources of material – must raise Aldus to a far greater eminence as an individual than his misguided admirers have ever done by submerging him in a liberal tradition. It has been implied again and again that the Venetian printing industry carried him along on the tide of its own success and that, consequently, Aldus had only to add a finishing touch. But as we saw at the beginning, the industry was going through an embarrassing period when Aldus arrived in Venice. It lacked constructive direction from above: it was being undermined by savage competition and shoddy workmanship from below. Its range of publications was stagnating, and especially in the field of classical literature, it was in some danger of becoming a forum for the mutual admiration or vituperation of the same group of scholars – few of whom showed any appreciation of its problems or its potential. Already, there was a sinister nostalgia for the vanished skills of Jenson. The press had in fact lost the sheen of novelty without acquiring the lustre of respectability.

Aldus struck at the heart of this problem by his concentration on the most challenging and prestigious subject of the time – Greek literature and philosophy. Whether the texts recovered by the Italian humanists of the previous century would have been lost again and irrevocably in the ashes of the Italian Wars if Aldus had not printed them is now, fortunately, a hypothetical question. Personally, I do not believe they would: printers like Callierges and Giunti waited only for the Aldine copyrights to lapse before embarking on their own programmes, the Marciana survived the Venetian senate's indifference and the Vatican library survived the Sack of Rome. But nothing can take from Aldus the credit for his Greek first editions, and he has received far less recognition than he deserves for the pains which they must have cost him. To publish successfully in Greek needed not only idealism, but patience and tact in assembling the means necessary to do so: and Aldus' company was a business concern, not a humanist cadre sponsored by Alberto Pio. The gaps in our information about the early 1490s mean that we cannot know what sort of difficulties Aldus had to face in finding capital backing and technical expertise: but the fact that he emerged with the doge's nephew and a highly successful publisher to underwrite his plans, and Francesco Griffo to cast his types, is sufficient proof of his determination. The patience with which Aldus calmed Torresani's fears about the slow sale of Greek texts and eventually made him a convert to his own ideals, must stand as one of the most remarkable achievements of his career. But it has passed completely unnoticed.

While he was selling scholarship to the printers with one hand, with the other Aldus was selling printing to the scholars. This is an aspect of his career which has been more fully investigated, but I think still not fully understood because of a failure to see the gulf which separates the equivocation of Sabellico and the portentous warnings of Filippo di Strata from the excited activity which centred on Aldus' workshop by the later 1490s. His carefully integrated campaign for support seems to date from the moment of his arrival in Venice. First, scholars like Leoniceno and Urceus were cultivated by personal assistance or deferential requests for advice. Next, when the work of publication had begun, they were placated by the appearance of texts which were needed for their own lectures, and whose types bore the closest possible resemblance to the most fashionable hand-written scripts: the wide margins of an expensive manuscript were indeed copied so faithfully that Urceus objected to the waste of paper.[7] Finally, when their interest had been thoroughly and widely aroused, the intellectuals of Italy and Europe were given a sense of collective identity and vocation by the dream of a New Academy. If the reality was unimpressive enough, then we saw in the final chapter how little reality mattered compared to a feeling of participation in the revival of the ancient world. And at every stage in his career, Aldus encouraged that feeling by his skilful use of dedications and prefaces. They could perform great personal services by putting the name of a comparatively unknown scholar like Daniele Clari before a large audience: at the other end of the social scale they could canvass the support of Matthew Lang or Lucrezia Borgia; and at all levels, they could subtly spread the printer's own ideals through the reading public. I sometimes think it has become too easy to attribute every liberal tendency in early sixteenth-century thought to "Erasmian influences", irrespective of the fact that Erasmus depended entirely on the means by which his ideas were communicated and that those ideas were not, in themselves, particularly original. The improvement of society through education, the printing and study of the Bible in all three ancient languages, the establishment of specialised colleges, were all schemes which Aldus had broadcast throughout Europe in his prefaces when Erasmus was still an almost unknown wanderer in Paris and Oxford.

It is certainly clear that Aldus gained an emotional hold over the scholars of his time which his predecessors had never tried to establish and which his successors, in a more difficult age, were unable to reproduce. His gift for friendship was remarkable. Only very occasionally do we hear a jarring note: when Apostolis is forced to return ten ducats which he feels he has earned honestly,[8] or when Griffo complains that the credit for Aldus' famous types is due to him. Both these men appear to have been prickly characters, and both may have suffered from the printer's snobbish assumption that they were social inferiors whose goodwill and services were equally dispensable. For the most part, we find Aldus cultivating the sympathy even of sworn rivals: in an age of vicious academic backbiting, his name is surrounded by an aura of astonishing calm. And through men like Reuchlin or Linacre, he could speak indirectly to the leading intellectual cadres of northern European countries and make friends whom he never even met. Certainly the use of the Marciana would have given better results than an unremitting but uncritical quest for material across the face of a continent: but if Aldus had been able to rely on a single source for his most important publications, his whole system of contacts and all the exchange of information that it involved might have remained unexplored and unnecessary.

Of his contribution to the social acceptance of the printed book many of the same points could be made. Aldus did not reduce book prices, at least not uniformly, and it is highly improbable that he was reaching towards a mass-market. What he did achieve was to raise the prestige of the mass-produced book by convincing a more exclusive market that it was reputable. Modish prejudices against ink-stained barbarians and the ready services of men like Vespasiano de' Bisticci left the aristocratic patrons of the fifteenth-century little affected by the arrival of print. Aldus changed this decisively. His own impeccable connections helped him to cut through the existing attitudes, and quickly gain the support of intellectual noblemen in Venice. Through them, he was soon accepted in the polished groups of contemporary Padua, and from Padua, it was only a short step to the intellectual and social élites of Italy and Europe. Excluding those to whom he dedicated editions in which they might or might not be interested, Aldus' personal correspondents included the Emperor Maximilian, the Elector of Saxony, Prince Cesare of Naples, the duke of Atri, the marquis of Mantua and his still more illustrious wife, Isabella d'Este, besides bishops, ambassadors, and royal councillors beyond counting. Illuminated copies offered a special bait to the aristocratic buyer, and we have only to glance at the libraries of Grolier or Pirckheimer to see how readily such people were tempted. This campaign for noble recognition played a crucial part in raising the status of the printed book towards that of the manuscript, which it was now ready to replace.

But as the manuscript disappeared, a great part of Aldus' world disappeared with it, and it is this very fact which has left him such a shadowy figure. Though he was, unquestionably, a powerful individual and a man of both vision and determination, more than half his life is almost completely unknown and even his letters were collected only by friends anxious to preserve his fast-fading memory. Much of his importance lies in the short, hectic period of his printing career: he spoke to the intellectual élite of Europe during the last two decades when it was possible for any one man to address a group bent on restoring a common tradition, and largely agreed on the most important features of that tradition. Within a few years of his death, Aldus' friends in Wittenberg had more to occupy their minds than the latest Greek texts. A few years more, and the linguistic traditions themselves were shifting as the vernacular and national literatures rose to challenge the dominance of cosmopolitan Latin and Greek. Aldus' own dreams of a world filled with good books had played some part in this process of fragmentation: his work meant that soon, scholars had no longer to look to the rich libraries of Italy for an intellectual lead, and that the future of scholarship itself lay with the individual in his study amongst his grammar-books and critical editions. The dedicated groups gathered round the manuscripts in those unforgettable exchanges of information and ideals, were now a thing of the past. They had been only an exhilarating incident in the grand process of transition. If Aldus died a melancholy man, it was not altogether without reason: for he had played a great part in destroying the world that had created him, and he could not yet foresee the veneration in which he would be held by the new world that he was calling into being.

NOTES

1 Codri Urcei *Opera,* Platonides, Bologna, 1502, f. D i r. D. Erasmi Roterdami *Opera Omnia,* Leyden, 1703–6, Vol. IX, col. 1137.
2 Bodleian Library, MS. Ashmole, No. 1142, Vol. II, ff. 1v–74r.
3 Bibliothèque Nationale, Paris, Imprimés Rés. Yb 782.
4 D. Manni, *Vita di Aldo Pio Manuzio insigne restauratore delle lettere greche e latine,* Venice, 1759: A. Zeno, *Notizie intorno ai Manuzii,* Venice, 1736. The Spencer collection now forms the nucleus of the John Rylands Library's Aldine holdings.
5 Schuck, No. XVI, p. 136.
6 CAM 25, 26, 29.
7 Dorez, "Alde Manuce et Ange Politien", pp. 323–4.
8 Geanakoplos, *Greek Scholars,* pp. 174–6.

BIBLIOGRAPHY

ARCHIVAL AND MANUSCRIPT SOURCES

Archivio di stato, Mantova, Carteggio estero, Carteggio ad inviati, Busta, 1440.
Archivio della curia patriarcale di Venezia, Professioni di fede richieste agli insegnanti, 1587.
Archivio di stato, Venezia.
    Consiglio di Dieci, Deliberazioni Misti.
    Marco Barbaro, Genealogie delle famiglie patrizie veneziane.
    Savii sopra le Decime in Rialto, Condizione della città, 1514.
    Senato, Deliberazioni Terra.
    Signori di Notte, Notizie di Crimini, 1472–1507.
Biblioteca Ambrosiana, Milan.
    Ms. Graecus C. 195 infra (= 881): Plutarch's *Moralia*.
    Ms. J. 100 infra: Index librorum Aldi Manutii.
Biblioteca Apostolica Vaticana.
    Ms. Graecus 1401: Grammar of Constantine Lascaris.
    Ms. Graecus 1413: Correspondence and book-indices of Janus Lascaris.
    Ms. Latinus 7121: various library indices.
    Incunabalum III, 16 (= 1135): Ovid's *Metamorphoses*, with extensive manuscript notes said to be those of Aldus.
Biblioteca Estense, Modena.
    Ms. Graecusa P, 5, 17 (= 115): Dioscurides, Theocritus and Sophocles.
    Ms. Graecusa W 9, 6 (= 131): Corpus Theognideum.
    Ms. Graecus N 7, 17: Pindar.
    Ms. Graecus V 5, 10 (= 127): Aristophanes.
Biblioteca Marciana, Venezia.
    Ms. Graecus 622 (851): Hesychius' *Lexicon*.

Ms. italiani Cl. I 72 (5054) ⎱ various writings of Filippo de
 II 133 (4846) ⎰ Strata.
Ms. italiano Cl. IX 203 (6757) Selection of early sixteenth-century poetry.
Ms. italiano Cl. XI 45 (7439) Day-book of Francesco da Madiis.
Bibliothèque Nationale, Paris.
 MS. Graecus 3064: indices of Greek texts and manuscripts.
 Supp. Graecum Ms. 212 ⎱ Tragedies of Euripides.
 Ms. 393 ⎰
 Supp. Graecum Ms. 924: Epistolographorum Graecorum Fragmenta.
Houghton Library, Harvard University.
 Ms. Graecus 17: Aristotelis et Theophrasti Fragmenta Naturalia.
Museo Correr, Venezia.
 Ms. Cicogna 949: Hironimi Bononii Promiscuorum libellus septimus.
Staatsbibliothek, Munich.
 Ms. Latinus 10801: commonplace book of Zuane Bembo.
Universitätsbibliothek, Basel.
 Ms. Graecus AN IV i ex B VI 25: Novum Testamentum Graece.
 Ms. Graecus F. VI 54: Grammatical writings.
 Ms. Latinus AN VI 36: Boniface Amerbach's Book of Hours, with manuscript notes.

PRINTED SOURCES

Aleander, Jerome, *Journal Autobiographique du Cardinal Jérôme Aléandre, 1480–1530*, ed. H. Omont, in *Notices et Extraits des Manuscrits de la Bibliothèque Nationale et Autres Bibliothèques*, Vol. XXXV, Paris, 1895.

Allen, P. S., ed., *Opus Epistolarum Desiderii Erasmi*, 12 vols., Oxford, 1906–53.

Barbaro, Ermolao, *Epistolae, Orationes et Carmina*, 2 vols., ed. V. Branca, Florence, 1943.

Baschet, A., ed., *Aldo Manuzio, Lettres et Documents, 1495–1515*, Venice, 1867.

Bossi, M., *Familiares et Secundae Epistolae*, Mantua, 1498.

Botfield, B., *Praefationes et Epistolae Editionibus Principibus Auctorum Veterum Praepositae*, Cambridge, 1861.

Brant, S., *Die Narrenschiff*, translated and edited as *The Ship of Fools*, E. Zeydel, New York, 1962.

Briefwechsel des Konrad Celtis, ed. H. Rupprich, Munich, 1934.
Briefwechsel des Mutianus Rufus, ed. C. Krause, Kassel, 1885.
Budaei Opera Omnia, Basel, 1557.
Castellani, C., *La stampa in Venezia dalla sua origine alla morte di Aldo Manuzio seniore*, new edition, 1973.
Castrifrancani, A., *Oratio habita in Funere Urbani Bellunensis*, Venice, 1524.
Codri Urcei Opera Omnia, Bologna, 1502.
Conway, W., ed., *The Writings of Albrecht Dürer*, London, 1958.
Fedelis, Cassandrae, *Epistolae et Orationes*, Padua, 1636.
Fulin, R., "Documenti per servire alla storia della tipografia veneziana", AV, XXIII, 1882, pp. 82–212, 390–405.
Hartfelder, K., *Fünf Bucher Epigramme von Konrad Celtis*, Berlin, 1881.
Hartmann, A., ed., *Die Amerbachkorrespondenz*, Vol. I, Basel, 1942.
Heiberg, J., "Beitrage zur Georg Vallas und seiner Bibliothek", ZBF, XVI, 1896, pp. 54–103.
Horawitz, A., ed., *Briefwechsel des Beatus Rhenanus*, Leipzig, 1886.
Joannis Pici Mirandulae Opera Omnia, Basel, 1557.
Lettere di Ludovico Ariosto, per cura di A. Capello, Milan, 1887.
Lettere volgari di Aldo Manuzio, Roma, 1592.
Malipiero, D., *Annali veneti*, in ASI, 7, pt. ii, 1844.
Navageri, A., *Opera Omnia*, Padua, 1718.
Noiret, H., *Lettres Inédites de Michel Apostolis, Bibliothèque des Écoles Françaises d'Athènes et de Rome*, Paris, 1889.
Nolhac, P. de, "Les Correspondants d'Alde Manuce: Matériaux Nouveaux d'Histoire Littéraire, 1483–1515", *Studi e documenti di storia e di diritto*, Anno VIII, 1887, and IX, 1888.
Orlandi, G., *Aldo Manuzio editore*, 2 vols., Milan, 1976.
Pastorello, E., *Inedita Manuziana*, Florence, 1960.
Politiani Opera Omnia, Aldus, Venice, 1498.
Poliziano, A., *Prose volgari inedite e poesie latine e greche edite e inedite*, a cura di I. del Lungo, Florence, 1867.
Priuli, Gerolamo, *Diarii*, ed. A. Segre, RIS, Tom XXIV, pt. iii, Città di Castello, 1912.
Rogers, E., ed., *St. Thomas More: Selected Letters*, Yale, 1961.
Sabellici Opera Omnia, 4 vols., Basel, 1560.
Sanudo, Marin, *Cronacetta*, Nozze Papadopoli-Hellenbach, Venice, 1880.
— *Diarii*, 58 vols., ed. R. Fulin, F. Stefani, N. Barozzi, G. Berchet, and M. Allegri, Venice, 1879–1903.

Valeriani, G. P., *De Litteratorum Infelicitate*, Padua, 1620.
— *Praeludia*, Venice, 1509.
Willibald Pirckheimers Briefwechsel, ed. E. Reicke, Munich, 1940.
Zambotti, B., *Diario ferrarese*, RIS, Tom. XXIV, pt. vii, Bologna, 1937.

SECONDARY WORKS

Adda, G. d', *Indagini storiche, artistiche e bibliografiche sulla libreria Viscontea-Sforzesca del Castello di Pavia*, Milan, 1875.
Allen, P. S., "Erasmus' Relations with his Printers", *The Library*, XIII, 1916, pp. 297–321.
— "Linacre and Latimer in Italy", *English Historical Review*, XVIII, 1903, pp. 314–17.
— "The Trilingual Colleges of the Early Sixteenth Century", in *Erasmus, Lectures and Wayfaring Sketches*, Oxford, 1934, pp. 138–63.
Amelung, P., "Bemerkungen zu zwei Italienischen Inkunabeln (Hain 4942 und Hain 13883)" in *Contribuiti all storia del libro italiano – Miscellanea in onore di Lamberto Donati*, Florence, 1969, pp. 1–9.
Armstrong, E., *Robert Estienne, Royal Printer*, Cambridge, 1954.
Arnauldet, P., "Graveurs de Caractères et Typographes de l'Italie du Nord", *Bulletin de la Société Nationale des Antiquaires de France*, 7e Ser., 4, 1903, pp. 288–95.
Astruc, C. and Concasty, M. L., *Bibliothèque Nationale, Catalogue des Manuscrits Grecs*, Tom. III, Paris, 1960.

Bandini, A. M., *Juntarum Typographicae Annales*, Lucca, 1791.
Bataillon, M., *Erasme et l'Espagne*, Paris, 1937.
Beaujon, P., "The Garamond Types: Sixteenth- and Seventeenth-Century Sources Considered", *The Fleuron*, 5, 1926, pp. 131–79.
Beloch, K. J., "La popolazione di Venezia nei secoli XVI e XVII", NAV, Nuova serie, III, 1902, pp. 5–49.
Bennett, J., "John Morer's Will: Thomas Linacre and Prior Sellyng's Greek Teaching", *Studies in the Renaissance*, XV, 1968, pp. 70–89.
Bergmann, J., *Corpus Scriptorum Ecclesiasticorum Latinorum*, Vol. 61, Vienna, 1926.
Bertanza, E. and Santa, G. della, *Maestri, scuole e scolari in Venezia fino al 1500, Reale Deputazione veneta di storia patria*, Serie I, 12, Venice, 1907.
Bertolotti, A., "Varietà archivistiche e bibliografiche", *Il Bibliofilo*, Anno VII, p. 181.

Bertoni, G., *La biblioteca Estense e la cultura ferrarese ai tempi del duca, Ercole I, 1471–1505*, Turin, 1903.
Biadego, G., "Intorno al Sogno di Polifilo", ARIV, LX, pt. ii, 1900–1, pp. 699–714.
Bica, L. and Marza, I., "Carti Aldine in Bibliotheca Batthyaneum din Alba Julia", *Apulum*, XI, 1973, pp. 311–50.
Bignami-Odier, J., *La Bibliothèque Vaticane de Sixte IV à Pie XI, Studi e testi*, No. 272, Città del Vaticano, 1973.
Billanovich, M., "Benedetto Bordon e Giulio Cesare Scaligero", IMU, XI, 1968, pp. 187–256.
— "Francesco Colonna, il *Polifilo*, e la famiglia Lelli", IMU, XIX, 1976, pp. 419–28.
Bolgar, R., *The Classical Heritage and its Beneficiaries*, New York/London, 1964.
Bologna, P., "La stamperia fiorentina del monastero di S. Jacopo di Ripoli e le sue edizioni", GSLI, XX, 1892, pp. 349–78.
Bónis, G., "Gli scholari ungheresi di Padova alla corte degli Iagelloni", in *Venezia e Ungheria nel Rinascimento*, ed. V. Branca, Florence, 1973, pp. 227–44.
Branca, V., "Ermolao Barbaro and Late Quattrocento Venetian Humanism", in *Renaissance Venice*, ed. J. R. Hale, London, 1973, pp. 218–43.
Braudel, F., *Le Méditerranée et le Monde Méditerranéen à l'Époque de Philippe II*, 2 vols., New Edition, Paris, 1966.
Brenzoni, R., *Fra Giovanni Giocondo veronese*, Florence, 1960.
— *La lettera autografa di fra Giocondo ad Aldo Manuzio*, Verona, 1962.
Brown, H., *Studies in Venetian History*, 2 vols., London, 1907.
— *The Venetian Printing Press*, London, 1891.
Brucker, G., "The Ciompi Revolution", in *Florentine Studies*, ed. N. Rubinstein, London, 1968, pp. 314–56.
Brunelli, B., "Shakespeare e lo studio di Padova", AV, Nuova serie, I, 1922, pp. 270–83.
Brunetti, M., "L'Accademia Aldina", *Rivista di Venezia*, VIII, 1929, pp. 417–31.
Buchwald, G., "Archivalische Mittheilungen über Bücherbezüge der Kurfürstlichen Bibliothek und Georg Spalatinus in Wittenberg", *Archiv für Geschichte des Deutschen Buchhandels*, 18, 1896, pp. 7–15.
Bühler, K., "Aldus Manutius and the Printing of Athenaeus", GJB, 1955, reprinted in *Early Books and Manuscripts*, Pierpont Morgan Library, 1973, pp. 220–2.

Bühler, K., "Aldus Manutius: the First Five Hundred Years", *Papers of the Bibliographical Society of America*, XLIV, 1950, pp. 205-15.
— "Aldus' Paraenesis to his Pupil, Lionello Pio", *The Library*, Fifth Series, XVII, 1962, pp. 240-2.
— "Some Documents Concerning the Torresani and the Aldine Press", *The Library*, Fourth Series, XXV, 1945, pp.111-21.
— *The Fifteenth-Century Book*, Philadelphia, 1960.
— "The First Aldine", *Papers of the Bibliographical Society of America*, XLII, 1948, pp. 3-14.
— *The University and the Press in Fifteenth-Century Bologna*, Indiana, 1958.
Burrows, M., "A Memoire of William Grocyn", *Oxford Historical Society Collectanea*, II, 1890, pp. 319-80.
Bustico, G., "Due umanisti veneti – Urbano Bolzanio e Piero Valeriani", *Civiltà Moderna*, IV, 1932, pp. 86-103.

Camerini, P., *Annali dei Giunti*, 2 vols., Florence, 1962.
— "In difesa di Lucantonio Giunta dall'accusa di contrafattore delle edizioni di Aldo Romano", *Atti e memorie della reale Accademia di scienze, lettere ed arti in Padova*, Anno CCCXCIII, 1933-4, pp. 165-94.
Cammelli, G., *Demetrio Calcondila*, Florence, 1954.
Carter, H., *A View of Early Typography to about 1600*, Oxford, 1969.
Case, A. E., "More about the Aldine Pliny of 1508", *The Library*, Fourth Series, XVI, 1935, pp. 173-87.
Casella, M. T. and Pozzi, G., *Francesco Colonna, biografia e opere*, 2 vols., Padua, 1959.
Cassamassima, E., "Litterae Gothicae: note per la storia della riforma grafica umanistica", *LBF*, LXII, 1960, pp. 109-43.
Castellani, C., *Early Venetian Printing Illustrated*, Venice/London/New York, 1895.
— "Il prestito dei codici manoscritti nella biblioteca di S. Marco a Venezia nei suoi primi tempi e le conseguenti perdite dei codici stessi", *ARIV*, Ser. VII, 8, 1896, pp. 311-77.
Castiglioni, C., "The School of Ferrara and the Controversy on Pliny", in *Science, Medicine and History: Essays on the Evolution of Scientific Thought and Medical Practice Written in Honour of Charles Singer*, ed. E. Underwood, Vol. 2, Oxford, 1953, pp. 269-79.
Cavazzana, C., "Cassandra Fedele, erudita veneziana del rinascimento", *Ateneo veneto*, Anno XXIX, ii, fasc. i, July-August 1906, pp. 73-91, 361-72.

Cecchetti, B., "Libri, scuole e maestri, sussidii allo studio in Venezia nei secoli XIV e XV", AV, XXXII, 1886, pp. 329–63.
— "Stampatori e libri stampati nel secolo XV: testamento di Niccolo Jenson e di altri tipografi in Venezia", AV, XXXIII, 1888, pp. 457–73.
— "Una libreria circolante a Venezia nel secolo XV", AV, XXXII, 1886, pp. 161–8.
Ceruti, A., "Lettere inedite dei Manuzi", AV, XXI, 1881, p. 269.
Chambers, D., "Studium Urbis and Gabella Urbis: the University of Rome in the Fifteenth Century", in *Cultural Aspects of the Italian Renaissance: Essays Presented to P. O. Kristeller*, ed. C. Clough, Manchester, 1976, pp. 65–87.
— *The Imperial Age of Venice*, London, 1970.
Chaytor, H. J., *From Script to Print: an Introduction to Medieval Literature*, Cambridge, 1945.
Chiti, A., *Scipione Fortiguerra, il Carteromacho: studio biografico con una raccolta di epigrammi, sonnetti, e lettere di lui e a lui dirette*, Florence, 1902.
Christie, R., "The Chronology of the Early Aldines", in *Bibliographica*, I, 1895, and *Selected Essays*, London, 1902, pp. 193–222.
Cian, C., *Un decennio della vita di Pietro Bembo*, Turin, 1885.
Cicogna, E., *Delle iscrizioni veneziane*, 6 vols., Venice, 1824–56.
Cittadella, L. N., *Documenti ed illustrazioni riguardanti la storia artistica ferrarese*, Ferrara, 1868.
Clough, C. H., "Pietro Bembo's Asolani of 1505", *Modern Language Notes*, 84, 1969, pp. 16–45.
— "Pietro Bembo's Library Represented in the British Museum", *British Museum Quarterly*, XXX, i, 1965, pp. 3–17.
— "Thomas Linacre, Cornelio Vitelli, and Humanistic Studies at Oxford", in *Linacre Studies: Essays on the Life and Work of Thomas Linacre, c. 1460–1524*, ed. F. Maddison, M. Pelling and C. Webster, Oxford, 1977, pp. 1–23.
Coggiola, G., "Il prestito di manoscritti della Marciana dal 1474 al 1527", ZFB, XXV, 1908, pp. 47–70.
Cohn, H. J., "The Early Renaissance Court at Heidelberg", *European Studies Review*, I, 1971, pp. 295–322.
Cotton, J., "Alessandro Sarti e il Poliziano", LBF, LXIV, 1962, pp. 225–246.
Coyecque, E., "Inventaire Sommaire d'un Minutier Parisien", *Bulletin de la Société de l'Histoire de Paris et de l'Île de France*, 21, 1894, p. 149.

Davis, J. C., "Shipping and Spying in the Career of a Venetian Doge, 1496–1502", *Studi veneziani*, XVI, 1974, pp. 97–108.
Davis, N. Z., "A Trades Union in Sixteenth Century France", *Ec. H.R.*, 19, 1966, pp. 48–69.
Dazzi, M., "Aldo Manuzio", LBF, LII, 1950, pp. 109–149. (This volume was reprinted separately as *Scritti sopra Aldo Manuzio*, Florence, 1955.)
— *Aldo Manuzio e il dialogo veneziano di Erasmo*, Vicenza, 1969.
Deacon, R., *A Biography of William Caxton*, London, 1976.
Delaruelle, L., *Guillaume Budé: les Origines, les Débuts, les Idées Maitrisses*, new edition, Geneva, 1970.
Dickens, A. G., *The German Nation and Martin Luther*, London, 1974.
Dionisotti, C., "Aldo Manuzio umanista", in *Umanesimo europeo e umanesimo veneziano*, Venice, 1963, pp. 213–43.
— *Gli umanisti e il volgare fra Quattrocento e Cinquecento*, Florence, 1968.
— "Calderini, Poliziano e altri", IMU, XI, 1968, pp. 151–85.
— "Questioni aperte su Aldo Manuzio editore", *Quinto congresso internazionale di bibliofili*, 1–7 Ottobre 1967, Verona, 1970, pp. 95–108.
Donati, L., "Bibliografia aldina", LBF, LII, ii, 1950, pp. 189–204.
— "Il mito di Francesco Colonna", LBF, LXIV, 1962, pp. 247–70.
— "La seconda Accademia Aldina e una lettera ad Aldo Manuzio trascurata da bibliografi", LBF, LIII, 1951, pp. 54–9.
— "Le marche tipografiche di Aldo Manuzio il Vecchio", GJB, 1974, pp. 129–32.
Dorez, L., "Alde Manuce et Ange Politien", *Revue des Bibliothèques*, VI, 1896, pp. 310–26.
— "Des Origines et de la Diffusion du *Songe de Polifile*", *Revue des Bibliothèques*, VI, 1896, pp. 239–83.
— "La Marque Typographique d'Alde Manuce", *Revue des Bibliothèques*, VI, 1896, pp. 143–60.
— "La Mort de Pic de Mirandole et l'Édition Aldine des Oeuvres d'Ange Politien, 1494–8", GSLI, XXXII, 1898, pp. 360–4.
Dukas, J., *Notes Bio-Bibliographiques sur un Recueil d'Opuscules très Rares Imprimés par Alde l'Ancien en 1497*, Paris, 1876.
Dunston, J., "Studies in Domizio Calderini", IMU, XI, 1968, pp. 71–150.

Eckert, W. and Imhoff, C. von, *Willibald Pirckheimer, Dürers Freund im Spiegel seines Lebens, seiner Werke, und seiner Umwelt*, Cologne, 1971.

Ehrenberg, R., *Capital and Finance in the Age of the Renaissance*, London, 1928.

Fainelli, V., "Aspetti della Roma cinquecentesca: le case e le raccolte archeologiche del Colocci", *Studi romani*, x, 1962, pp. 391–402.
— "Il ginnasio greco di Leone X a Roma", *Studi romani*, IX, 1961, pp. 379–93.
— ed., F. Ubaldini, *Vita di Mons. Angelo Colocci*, Studi e testi No. 256, Città del Vaticano, 1969.
Fava, D., *La biblioteca Estense nel suo sviluppo storico*, Modena, 1925.
— "Libri membranacei stampati in Italia nel Quattrocento", GJB, 1937, pp. 55–84.
— "L'introduzione del corsivo nella tipografia e l'opera di Benedetto Dolcibello", *Internationale Vereinigung für Dokumentation*, IX, fasc. i, 1942, pp. 2–7.
Febvre, L. and Martin, H./J., *L'Apparition du Livre*, Paris, 1958.
Ferrigni, M., *Aldo Manuzio*, Milan, 1925.
Firmin-Didot, A., *Alde Manuce et l'Hellénisme à Venise*, Paris, 1875.
Floriani, P., "La giovinezza umanistica di Pietro Bembo fino al periodo ferrarese", GSLI, CXLIII, 1966, pp. 25–71.
Foffano, F., "Marco Musuro, professore di Greco a Padova ed a Venezia", NAV, III, 1892, pp. 453–72.
Fonkich, B., "On the Manuscript tradition of the Aldine Edition of the Tragedies of Sophocles", *Vizantiskij Vremennik*, XXIV, 1964, pp. 109–21. (Original in Russian.)
Foster, K., "Vernacular Scriptures in Italy", in *The Cambridge History of the Bible*, Vol. II, Cambridge, 1969, pp. 453–65.
Franklin, A., *Précis de l'Histoire de la Bibliothèque du Roi, Aujourd'hui Bibliothèque Nationale*, Paris, 1875.
Friedensburg, W., *Urkendenbuch der Universität Wittenburg*, Magdeburg, 1926.
Fulin, R., "Una lettera di Alessandro VI", AV, I, 1871, p. 157.

Gabotto, F. and Badini-Confaloniere, A., *Vita di Giorgio Merula*, Alessandria, 1893.
Garin, E., *Il pensiero pedagogico dell' umanesimo*, Florence, 1958.
— "La cultura fiorentina nella seconda metà del '300 e i 'barbari Britanni'", *Rassegna della letteratura italiana*, Anno 64, 2, 1960, pp. 181–95.
— *L'educazione in Europa*, Bari, 1957.

Garin, E., *Portraits from the Quattrocento*, New York/London, 1972.
— "Richerche su Giovanni Pico della Mirandola – l'epistolario", in *La cultura filosofica del rinascimento italiano*, Florence, 1961, pp. 254–79.
Geanakoplos, D., *Greek Scholars in Venice*, Harvard, 1962.
— "The Discourse of Demetrius Chalcondylas on the Inauguration of Greek Studies at the University of Padua in 1463", *Studies in the Renaissance*, XXI, 1974, pp. 118–34.
Gerulaitis, L., *Printing and Publishing in Fifteenth-Century Venice*, London, 1976.
— "The Ancestry of Aldus Manutius", *Renaissance News*, XIX, i, 1966, pp. 1–12.
Gilbert, C., "When did a Man in the Renaissance Grow Old?" *Studies in the Renaissance*, XIV, 1967, pp. 7–32.
Gilbert, F., "Biondo, Sabellico and the Beginnings of Venetian Official Historiography", in *Florilegium Historicale: Essays Presented to Wallace Ferguson*, Toronto, 1971, pp. 276–93.
— "Cristianesimo, umanesimo, e la bolla 'Apostolici Regiminis' del 1512", RSI, Anno LXXIX, 1967, fasc. i, pp. 976–90.
— "Venice in the Crisis of the League of Cambrai", in J. R. Hale, ed., *Renaissance Venice*, London, 1973, pp. 274–92.
Gilmore, M., "Erasmus and Alberto Pio, Prince of Carpi", in *Action and Conviction in Early Modern Europe: Essays in Memory of E. H. Harbison*, ed. T. Rabb and J. Seigel, Princeton, 1967, pp. 299–318.
Gilson, E., "L'Affaire de l'Immortalité de l'Âme à Venise au Début du XVI siècle", in *Umanesimo europeo e umanesimo veneziano*, Venice, 1963, pp. 31–61.
Gnoli, D., "Il Sogno di Polifilo", LBF, I, 1900, pp. 189–212.
Goldschmidt, E. P., *Medieval Texts and Their First Appearance in Print*, London, 1943.
— *The Printed Book of the Renaissance*, Cambridge, 1950.
Goleniščev-Kutuzov, I. N., *Il rinascimento italiano e le lettere slave dei secoli XV e XVI*, Milan, 1973, from Russian original, Moscow, 1963.
Govi, E., "La biblioteca di Jacopo Zen", *Bolletino dell' istituto di patologia del libro*, Anno X, fasc. i–iv, 1951, pp. 34–118.
Gow, A. S. F., *Theocritus*, 2 vols., Cambridge, 1952.
— and Page, D. L., *The Greek Anthology*, 3 vols., Cambridge, 1969.
Grendler, P., *The Roman Inquisition and the Venetian Press*, Princeton, 1977.

Grossman, M., *Humanism in Wittenberg, 1485–1517*, Bibliotheca Humanistica et Reformatoria, Vol. XI, Nieuwkoop, 1975.
Guaitoli, P., "Memorie sulla vita d'Alberto Pio III", *Memorie storiche e documenti sulla città e sull'antico principato di Carpi*, I, 1877, pp. 135–41.
Gulyas, P., "Catalogue descriptif des Aldines de la Bibliothèque Szechenge du Musée Nationale Hongrois", *Magyar Könyvzemle*, Ser. 2, 15, 1907, pp. 17–33, 149–65, 241–56, 331–51; Vol. 16, 1908, pp. 51–72, 148–65.
Gundersheimer, W., *Ferrara: the Style of a Renaissance Despotism*, Princeton, 1973.
— *French Humanism, 1470–1600*, London, 1969.

Haebler, K., "Das Testament des Johann Manthen von Gerresheim", LBF, XXVI, 1924, pp. 1–9.
— "Schriftguss und Schriftenhandel in der Frühdruckzeit", ZBF, 41, 1924, pp. 81–104.
Heckthorn, G., *The Printers of Basle in the XV and XVI Centuries: Their Biographies, Printed Books and Devices*, London, 1897.
Hexter, J., "The Education of the Aristocracy during the Renaissance", *Journal of Modern History*, XXII, 1950, pp. 1–20.
Hildebrandt, E., "Die Kurfürstiche Schloss- und Universitätsbibliothek zu Wittenberg, 1512–1547", *Zeitschrift für Buchkunde*, 2, 1925, pp. 158–64.
Hillyard, B., "Girolamo Aleandro, editor of Plutarch's *Moralia*", *Bibliothèque d'Humanisme et Renaissance*, XXXVI, 1974, pp. 517–31.
Hirsch, R., "Pre-Reformation Censorship of Printed Books", *The Library Chronicle*, XXI, No. i, 1955, pp. 100–5.
— *Printing, Selling and Reading, 1450–1550*, Wiesbaden, 1967.
Hobson, G. D., *Notes on Grolier with a Eulogy of the Late Dr. Theodor Gottlieb*, London, 1929.
Hofer, P., "Variant Copies of the 1499 Poliphilus", *Bulletin of the New York Public Library*, XXXVI, 1932, pp. 475–86.
Hogrefe, P., *The Life and Times of Sir Thomas Elyot, Englishman*, Iowa, 1967.
Holmes, G., *The Florentine Enlightenment*, London, 1969.
Horawitz, A., *Die Bibliothek und Correspondenz des Beatus Rhenanus zu Schlettstadt*, Vienna, 1874.
Howe, E., "An Introduction to Hebrew Typography", *Signature*, 5, 1937, pp. 12–29.
Hraban, G., "Alde Manuce et ses amis Hongrois" (French résumé of Hungarian original), *Magyar Könyvzemle*, LXIX, 1945, pp. 38–98.

Jannelli, C., *De Vita et Scriptis Auli Jani Parrhasii Consentini, Philologi Saeculo XVI Celeberrimi, Commentarius*, Naples, 1844.
Jedin, H., "Contarini und Camaldoli", *Archivio italiano per la storia della pietà*, II, 1959, pp. 11-65.
Johnson, A. F., "Books Printed at Lyons in the Sixteenth Century", *The Library*, Fourth Series, III, 1922, pp. 145-74.
— "Geofroy Tory", *The Fleuron*, 6, 1928, pp. 51-66.
— *Type-Designs: Their History and Development*, London, 1934.
Joppi, V., "Dei libri liturgichi a stampa della Chiesa d'Aquileia", AV, XXXI, 1887, pp. 259-67.
Jovy, M., "François Tissard et Jérôme Aléandre: Contribution à l'Histoire des Origines des Études Grecques en France", *Mémoires de la Société des Sciences et des Arts de Vitry-le-François*, XIX, 1899, pp. 318-457.

Kagan, R., "Universities in Castile, 1500-1700", *Past and Present*, 49, 1970, pp. 44-71.
Kenney, E. J., "The Character of Humanist Philology", in *Classical Influences on European Culture*, ed. R. Bolgar, Cambridge, 1971, pp. 119-28.
— *The Classical Text*, Berkeley, 1974.
Kibre, P., "The Intellectual Interests Reflected in Libraries of the XIVth and XVth Centuries", *Journal of the History of Ideas*, VII, No. 3, 1946, pp. 257-97.
King, M. L., "The Patriciate and the Intellectuals: Power and Ideas in Quattrocento Venice", *Societas*, V, No. 4, 1975, pp. 295-312.
Kleehoven, M. von, "Aldus Manutius und der Plan einer Deutschen Ritterakademie", LBF, LII, 1950, pp. 169-77.
Knod, G., *Deutsche Studenten in Bologna, 1289-1562*, Strassbourg, 1899.
Knös, B., *Un Ambassadeur d'Hellénisme: Janus Lascaris*, Paris/Uppsala, 1945.
Kunert, S. de, "Un padovano ignoto e un suo memoriale dei primi anni del Cinquecento (1505-1511), con cenni su due codici miniati", *Bolletino del Museo Civico di Padova*, Anno X, 1907, No. 1, pp. 1-16.

Labowsky, L., "Il Cardinale Bessarione e gli inizi della Biblioteca Marciana", in *Venezia e l'Oriente fra tardo medievo e rinascimento*, ed. A. Pertusi, Florence, 1965, pp. 159-82.
— "Manuscripts from Bessarion's Library Found in Milan", *Medieval and Renaissance Studies*, V, 1961, pp. 117-26.

La Fontaine Verwey, H. de, "Les Débuts de la Protection des Caractères Typographiques du XVIe Siècle", GJB, 1965, pp. 24–34.
Lancellotti, G., *Poesie italiane e latine di Monsignor Angelo Colocci, con piu notizie intorno alla persona di lui e sua famiglia*, Iesi, 1772.
Lane, F. C., "Naval Actions and Fleet Organisation, 1499–1502", in *Renaissance Venice*, ed. J. R. Hale, London, 1973, pp. 146–73.
— *Venice, a Maritime Republic*, Johns Hopkins, 1973.
Laurent, M., "Alde Manuce l'Ancien, Éditeur de S. Catherine de Siene", *Traditio*, V, 1947, pp. 357–63.
Lazzarini, V., "Un maestro di scrittura nella cancelleria veneziana", in *Scritti di paleografia e diplomatica*, Venice, 1969, pp. 64–70.
Lefranc, A., *Histoire du Collège de France depuis ses Origines jusqu'à la Fin du Premier Empire*, Paris, 1893.
Legrand, E., *Bibliographie Hellénique où Description Raisonnée des Ouvrages Publiés en Grec par des Grecs au XV e XVI Siècles*, 5 vols., Paris, 1885–1906.
Leicht, P. S., "I prezzi delle edizioni aldine del '500", *Il libro e la stampa*, Anno VI, fasc. iii, 1912, pp. 74–84.
Lempicki, S., *Renesans i humanizm w Polsce: materiaty do Studiow*, Cracow, 1952.
Lenhart, J., *Pre-Reformation Printed Books*, New York, 1935.
Le Roux de Lincy, M., *Recherches sur Jean Grolier, sur sa Vie, et sur sa Bibliothèque*, Paris, 1866.
Levi d'Ancona, M., "Benedetto Padovano e Benedetto Bordone: prime tentative per un corpus di Benedetto Padovano", *Commentari*, XVIII, 1967, pp. 31–43.
Liddell, J. R., "The Library of Corpus Christi, Oxford, in the Sixteenth Century", Oxford B.Litt. thesis, 1938, summarised in *Transactions of the Oxford Bibliographical Society*, XVIII, 1938, pp. 385–416.
Logan, O. M. T., *Culture and Society in Venice, 1470–1790*, London, 1972.
Lorenzetti, G., *Venice and its Lagoon*, Rome, 1961.
Lowe, E. A. and Rand, E. K., *A Sixth-Century Fragment of the Letters of Pliny the Younger: a Study of Six Leaves of an Uncial Manuscript Preserved in the Pierpont Morgan Library, New York*, Washington, 1922.
Lowry, M. J. C., "The New Academy of Aldus Manutius a Renaissance Dream", BJRL, 58, No. 2, 1976, pp. 378–420.

Lowry, M. J. C., "Two Great Venetian Libraries in the Age of Aldus Manutius", BJRL, 57, No. 1, 1974, pp. 128–66.

Ludwig, G., "Contratti fra lo stampador Zuan di Colonia ed i suoi soci e inventario di una parte del loro magazzino", *Miscellanea di storia veneta, Reale deputazione veneta di storia patria*, Seconda serie, Tom. VIII, 1902, pp. 57–88.

Lupton, J. H., *A Life of John Colet, D.D.*, new edition, New York, 1974.

McLuhan, M., *The Gutenberg Galaxy: the Making of Typographic Man*, London/Toronto, 1962.

McNeil, D., *Guillaume Budé and Humanism in the Reign of Francis I*, Travaux d'Humanisme et Renaissance, No. CXLII, Geneva, 1975.

Malagola, C., *Della vita e delle opere di Antonio Urceo, detto Codro*, Bologna, 1878.

Malagola, C. and Friedlander, E., *Acta Nationis Germanicae Universitatis Bononiensis ex Archetypis Tabularii Malvessiani*, Berlin, 1887.

Mallett, M. E., *Mercenaries and Their Masters*, London, 1974.

— *The Borgias*, London, 1971.

Manacorda, G., "Notizie intorno alle fonti di alcuni motivi satirici", *Romische Forschungen*, XXII, 1908, pp. 733–60.

Manzoni, G., *Annali tipografi dei Soncino*, Bologna, 1886.

Marcel, R., "Pic et la France", in *L'opera e il pensiero di Giovanni Pico della Mirandola*, Florence, 1963, pp. 205–30.

Mardersteig, G., "Aldo Manuzio e i caratteri di Francesco Griffo da Bologna", in *Studi di bibliografia e storia in onore di Tamaro di Marinis*, Vol. III, Verona, 1964, pp. 105–47.

— "La singolare cronaca della nascita di un incunabolo", IMU, VIII, 1965, pp. 249–65.

Mariani-Canova, G., *La miniatura veneta del rinascimento*, Venice/Milan, 1969.

— "Profilo di Benedetto Bordone miniatore padovano", ARIV, CX–CXVII, 1968–9, pp. 99–121.

Martellozzo Forin, E., *Acta Graduum Academicorum ab Anno 1501 ad Annum 1525*, Istituto per la storia dell'università di Padova, 1969.

— "Note d'archivio sul soggiorno padovano di studenti ungharesi, 1493–1563", in *Venezia e Ungheria nel Rinascimento*, ed. V. Branca, Florence, 1973, pp. 245–60.

Martini, A. and Bassi, D., *Catalogus Codicum Graecorum Bibliothecae Ambrosianae*, Vol. II, Milan, 1906.

Martini, G., "La bottega di un cartolaio fiorentino della seconda metà del Quattrocento", LBF, LVIII (supp.), 1956, pp. 1–22.

Marx, A., "Aldus and the First Use of Hebrew Type in Venice", *Papers of the Bibliographical Society of America*, 13, 1919, No. 1, pp. 64–7.

Marzi, D., "I tipografi tedeschi in Italia durante il secolo XV", *Festschrift der Stadt Mainz zur Gutenberg feier im Jahre 1900*, pp. 408–53.

— "Una questione libraria fra i Giunti e Aldo Manuzio il Vecchio", Nozze Malpurgo-Franchetti, 1895, and *Giornale della Libreria*, IX, 1896.

Mauro, A., "Le prime edizioni dell'*Arcadia* di Sannazaro", *Giornale italiano di filologia*, IV, 1949, pp. 341–51.

— ed., Sannazaro, *Opere volgari*, Bari, 1961.

Mazzuchelli, Io.-M., *Gli scrittori d'Italia*, Brescia, 1753–63.

Meiss, M., *Andrea Mantegna as Illuminator: an Episode in Renaissance Art, Humanism, and Diplomacy*, Columbia, 1957.

— "Towards a More Comprehensive Renaissance Palaeography", *The Art Bulletin*, XLII, 1960, pp. 97–112.

Mercati, Cardinal G., *Codici latini Pico, Grimani, Pio e di altra biblioteca ignota del secolo XVI essistenti nell'ottoboniana, e codici greci Pio di Modena*, Studi e testi No. 75, Città del Vaticano, 1938.

Merrill, E., "The Morgan Fragment of Pliny's Letters", *Classical Philology*, XVIII, 1923, pp. 97–119.

Mestica, G., "Il canzoniere del Petrarca nel codice originale a riscontro col manoscritto del Bembo e con l'edizione aldina del 1501", GSLI, XXI, 1893, pp. 300–34.

Minio-Paluello, L., "Attività filosofica-editoriale dell'umanesimo", in *Umanesimo europeo e umanesimo veneziano*, ed. V. Branca, Venice, 1963, pp. 245–63.

Mioni, E., "La biblioteca greca di Marco Musuro", AV, Ser. V, XCIII, 1971, pp. 5–28.

Mitchell, R. J., "Thomas Linacre in Italy", *English Historical Review*, L, 1935, pp. 696–8.

Mommsen, T., "Autobiographie des Venezianers Giovanni Bembo", *Sitzungsberichte der Bayerischen Akademie der Wissenschaften*, I, 1861, pp. 584–609.

Monfasani, J., *George of Trebizond, a Biography and a Study of his Rhetoric and Logic*, Leiden, 1976.

Moran, J., *Printing Presses*, London, 1973.

Morawski, C., *Histoire de l'université de Cracovie*, transl. P. Rongier, Vol. III, Paris/Cracow, 1905.
Morelli, G., *Aldi Manutii Scripta Tria Longe Rarissima*, Bassani, 1806.
— *Dissertazioni intorno ad alcuni viaggiatori eruditi veneziani poco noti*, Venice, 1803.
Morison, S., "Early Humanistic Script and the First Roman Type", *The Library*, Fourth Series, XXIV, 1944, pp. 1-29.
— *Politics and Script*, Oxford, 1972.
— "The Type of the *Hypnerotomachia Polifili*", *Gutenberg Festschrift*, Mainz, 1925, pp. 254-8.
— *The Typographic Book*, London, 1963.
— "Towards an Ideal Type", *The Fleuron*, 2, 1924, pp. 57-75.
— and Johnson, A. F., "The Chancery Types of Italy and France", *The Fleuron*, 3, 1924, pp. 23-51.
Morselli, A., "Alberto e la corte di Carpi", *Memorie storiche e documenti sulla città e sull'antico principato di Carpi*, XI, 1931, pp. 153-83.
— "Notizie e documenti sulla vita di Alberto Pio", *ib.*, pp. 135-52.
Motta, E., "Demetrio Calcondila, editore", ASL, 20, 1893, pp. 144-166.
— "Pamfilo Castaldi, Antonio Planella, Pietro Ugleimer, ed il vescovo d'Aleria", RSI, I, 1884, pp. 252-72.
Müller, K., "Neue Mittheilungen über Janos Lascaris und die Mediceische Bibliothek", ZFB, I, 1884, pp. 333-413.
Munroe, P., *Thomas Platter and the Educational Renaissance of the Sixteenth Century*, New York, 1904.
Mutinelli, F., *Annali urbani di Venezia*, Venice, 1841.

Nardi, B., "Letteratura e cultura veneziana del Quattrocento", in *Civiltà veneziana del Quattrocento*, Fondazione Cini, 1956, pp. 99-145.
Niero, A., "Decreti pretridentini di due patriarchi di Venezia su stampa di libri", *Rivista di storia della Chiesa in Italia*, XIV, 1960, pp. 450-2.
Nixon, H. M., *Bookbindings from the Library of Jean Grolier: a Loan Exhibition, 23rd September-31st October, 1965*. (British Museum Publications.)
Nolhac, P. de, *La Bibliothèque de Fulvio Orsini*, Paris, 1887.
— *Le canzioniere autographe de Petrarque*, Communication faite à l'Academie des Inscriptions et Belles-Lettres, Paris, 1886.

Novati, F., "Ancora di Fra Filippo di Strata: un domenico nemico degli stampatori", *Il libro e la stampa*, 5, N.S. fasc. iv, 1911, pp. 117-28.

Offenbacher, E., "La Bibliothèque de Willibald Pirckheimer", LBF, XL, 1938, pp. 241-63.
Omont, H., *Catalogue des Manuscrits Grecs des Bibliothèques de Suisse*, Leipzig, 1886.
— "Essai sur les Débuts de la Typographie Grecque à Paris, 1507-1515", *Mémoires de la Société de l'Histoire de Paris de l'Île de France*, XVIII, 1891, pp. 1-14.
— *Inventaire des Manuscrits Grecs et Latins donnés à Saint Marc de Venise par le Cardinal Bessarion en 1468*, Paris, 1894.
Orme, N., *English Schools in the Middle Ages*, London, 1973.
Overfield, J. H., "A New Look at the Reuchlin Affair", *Studies in Medieval and Renaissance History*, VIII, 1971, pp. 167-207.

Painter, G., "The *Hypnerotomachia Polifili* of 1499: an Introduction to the Dream, the Dreamer, the Artist, and the Printer", introduction to Eugrammia Press edition, London, 1963.
Panizzi, A., *Chi era Francesco da Bologna?*, London, 1858.
Panofsky, E., "The Neoplatonic Movement in Florence and Northern Italy", in *Studies in Iconology*, New York, 1967, pp. 129-69.
Papinio, P., "Nuove notizie intorno ad Andrea Navagero e Daniele Barbaro", AV, III, 1872, pp. 255-61.
Paquier, J., *Jèrôme Aléandre de sa Naissance à la Fin de son Sejour à Brindes, 1480-1529*, Paris, 1900.
Parks, G., *The English Traveller in Italy*, Rome, 1954.
Pascal, C., "Una lettera pontoniana del Summonte ed un autografo inedito del Pontano", *Atti del Reale Accademia Pontoniana*, LVI, 1926, pp. 178-86.
Pastor, L. von, *History of the Popes*, 40 vols., London, 1898-1953.
Pastorello, E., "Di Aldo Pio Manuzio: testimonianze e documenti", LBF, LXVII, 1965, pp. 163-220.
— *L'Epistolario Manuziano: inventario cronologico-analitico, 1483-1597*, Florence, 1957.
Percopo, E., "La vita di Giovanni Pontano", *Archivio storico per le provincie napoletane*, Nuova serie Anno XXII, 1936, pp. 116-250.
Pertusi, A., "Gli inizi della storiografia umanistica del Quattrocento", in *La storiografia veneziana fino al secolo XVI*, Florence, 1970, pp. 269-332.

Pesenti, G., "Diario odeporico-bibliografico del Poliziano", *Memorie del Reale istituto lombardo di scienze e lettere*, Classe di lettere, scienze morali e storiche, XXIII–XXIV, Ser. III, fasc. vii, Milan, 1916, pp. 229–39.

Pettas, W., "Niklaos Sophianos and Greek Printing in Rome", *The Library*, Fifth Series, XXIX, No. 2, June, 1974, pp. 206–13.

— "The Cost of Printing a Florentine Incunable", LBF, LXXV, 1973, pp. 67–85.

Philips, M. M., *The Adages of Erasmus – a Study with Translations*, Cambridge, 1964.

Piana, C., *Ricerche sulle università di Bologna e di Parma nel secolo* XV, Florence, 1963.

Piccolomini, E., "Delle condizioni e delle vicende della libreria Medicea privata dal 1494 al 1508", ASI, ser. iii, XIX, 1873, pp. 101–29.

Pieri, P., *Il rinascimento e la crisi militare italiana*, Turin, 1970.

Pignatti, T., "German and Venetian Painting", in *Renaissance Venice*, ed. J. R. Hale, London, 1973, pp. 244–73.

Post, R. R., *The Modern Devotion – Confrontation with Reformation and Humanism*, Leyden, 1967.

Pozzi, G., "Da Padova a Firenze nel 1493", IMU, IX, 1966, pp. 192–201.

Preisdanz, K., "Die Bibliothek Johannes Reuchlin", in *Festgabe Johannes Reuchlin*, ed. M. Krebs, Pforzheim, 1955, pp. 80–2.

Proctor, R., *The Printing of Greek in the Fifteenth Century*, Oxford, 1900.

Pullan, B. S., *Rich and Poor in Renaissance Venice*, Oxford, 1971.

Putnam, C., *The Censorship of the Church of Rome and its Influence on the Production and Distribution of Literature*, 2 vols., London, 1906.

Quaranta, E., "Osservazioni intorno ai caratteri greci di Aldo Manuzio", LBF, LV, 1953, pp. 123–30.

Reed, A., "John Clement and his Books", *The Library*, Fourth Series, VI, 1925–6, pp. 329–39.

Relazioni tra Padova e la Polonia, Padova, 1964.

Renaudet, A., *Erasme et l'Italie*, Geneva, 1954.

— *Préréforme et Humanisme à Paris pendant les Premières Guerres en Italie*, Paris, 1916.

Renouard, A., *Annales de l'Imprimerie des Alde*, 3 vols., Paris, 1825.

Reynolds, L. and Wilson, N. G., *Scribes and Scholars*, Oxford, 1968.

Rhodes, D. E., ed., *V. Scholderer: fifty Essays in Fifteenth- and Sixteenth-Century Bibliography*, Amsterdam, 1966.

Rice, E., "The Patrons of French Humanism, 1490-1520", in *Renaissance Studies in Honor of Hans Baron*, ed. A. Molho and J. Tedeschi, Florence, 1971, pp. 689-702.

Ridolfi, R., *La stampa in Firenze nel secolo XV*, Florence, 1957.

Robathan, D., "Libraries of the Italian Renaissance", in *The Medieval Library*, ed. J. W. Thompson, Chicago, 1939, pp. 509-89.

Robertson, E., "Aldus Manutius, the Scholar-Printer, 1450-1515", BJRL, XXXIII, 1950-1, pp. 57-73.

Romanin, S., *Storia documentata di Venezia*, new edition, 10 vols., Venice, 1973-5.

Roover, E. de, "Per la storia dell'arte della stampa in Italia: come furono stampati a Venezia tre dei primi libri in volgare", LBF, LV, 1953, pp. 107-15.

Roover, R. de, *The Rise and Decline of the Medici Bank, 1397-1494*, New York, 1966.

Rose, P., "Bartolomeo Zamberti's Funeral Oration for the Humanist Encyclopedist Giorgio Valla", in *Cultural Aspects of the Italian Renaissance: Essays Presented to P. O. Kristeller*, ed. C. Clough, Manchester, 1976, pp. 299-310.

Ross, J. B., "Venetian Schools and Teachers, Fourteenth to Early Sixteenth Century – a Survey and a Study of Giovanni Battista Egnazio", *Renaissance Quarterly*, XXXIX, No. 4, 1976, pp. 521-60.

Rossi, V., "Maestri e scuole a Venezia verso la fine del medioevo", *Rendiconti del reale istituto lombardo di scienze e lettere*, Ser. ii, XL, 1907, pp. 765-81.

Rupprich, H., "Willibald Pirckheimer: a Study of his Personality as a Scholar", in G. Strauss, ed., *Pre-Reformation Germany*, London, 1972, pp. 380-435.

Ruysschaert, J., "Trois Recherches sur le XVIe Siècle Romain", *Archivio della societa romana di storia patria*, Ser. III, XXV, fasc. i, 1971, pp. 11-29.

Sabbadini, R., *La scuola e gli studi di Guarino Veronese*, Catania, 1896.
— *Le scoperte dei codici latini e greci nei secoli XIV e XV*, new edition, 2 vols., Florence, 1967.

Saffrey, H. D., "Un Humaniste Dominicain, Jean Cuno de Nuremberg, Precurseur d'Erasme à Bâle", *Bibliothèque d'Humanisme e Renaissance*, XXXIII, 1971, pp. 19-62.

Salvo Cozzo, G., *Codice Vaticano 3195 e l'edizione aldina del 1501*, Rome, 1893.
— "Le rime sparse di Francesco Petrarca nei codici Vaticani latini 3195 e 3196", GSLI, xxx, 1897, pp. 375–80.
Sandre, G. de, "Dottori, università, commune a Padova nel Quattrocento", *Quaderni per la storia dell'università di Padova*, I, 1968, pp. 154–47.
Santa, G. della, "Il tipografo dalmata Bonino de Boninis, confidente della Republica di Venezia, decano della cattedrale di Treviso", NAV, xxx, 1915, pp. 174–206.
— "Nuovi appunti sul processo di Giorgio Valla e di Placidio Amerino in Venezia nel 1496", NAV, x, 1895, pp. 13–23.
Scaccia Scarafoni, C., "La più antica edizione della grammatica latina di Aldo Manuzio finora sconsciuta ai bibliografi", in *Miscellanea bibliografica in memoria di Don Tommaso Accurti*, Rome, 1947, pp. 193–203.
Scholderer, V., "A Fleming in Venetia: Gerardus of Lisa, Printer, Bookseller, Schoolmaster and Musician", *The Library*, Fourth Series, x, 1930, pp. 253–73, and *Fifty Essays*..., pp. 113–25.
— *Greek Printing Types, 1465–1927*, London, 1927.
— "Printers and Readers in Italy in the Fifteenth Century", *Proceedings of the British Academy*, xxxv, 1949, pp. 25–47, and *Fifty Essays*..., pp. 202–15.
— "Printing at Ferrara in the Fifteenth Century", in *Gutenberg-Festschrift, zur Feier des 25jährigen Bestehens des Gutenberg-Museums in Mainz*, 1925, pp. 73–8, and *Fifty Essays*..., pp. 91–5.
— "Printing at Venice to the End of 1481", *The Library*, Fourth Series, v, pp. 129–52, and *Fifty Essays*..., pp. 74–89.
— "The Petition of Sweyheim and Pannartz to Sixtus IV", *The Library*, Third Series, vi, 1915, pp. 186–90, and *Fifty Essays*..., pp. 72–3.
Segarizzi, A., "Cenni sulle scuole pubbliche a Venezia nel secolo XV e sul primo maestro di esse", ARIV, LXXV, pt. ii, 1915–6, pp. 637–67.
— "Un calligrafo milanese", *Ateneo veneto*, xxxii, 1908, pp. 63–77.
Sella, D., "The Rise and Fall of the Venetian Woollen Industry", in Pullan, B.S., ed., *Crisis and Change in the Venetian Economy in the Sixteenth Century*, London, 1968, pp. 106–26.
Serena, A., *La cultura umanistica a Treviso nel secolo decimoquinto*, Miscellanea di storia veneta, Ser. iii, iii, Venice, 1912.

Seward, D., *Prince of the Renaissance*, London, 1973.
Shepherd, L. A., "A Fifteenth-Century Humanist, Francesco Filelfo", *The Library*, Fourth Series, XVI, 1936, pp. 1-26.
Sherwin-White, A. N., *The Letters of Pliny*, Oxford, 1966.
Sicherl, M., *Handschriftliche Vorlagen der Editio Princeps des Aristoteles*, Mainz, 1976.
— "Die Editio Princeps Aldina des Euripides und ihre Vorlagen", *Rhein Museum*, 118, 1975, pp. 205-25.
Simone, F., *The French Renaissance*, trans. G. Hall, London, 1969.
Sorbelli, A., "Il mago che scolpì i caratteri di Aldo Manuzio – Francesco Griffo da Bologna", GJB, 1933, pp. 117-23.
Spitz, L., *Conrad Celtis, the German Arch-Humanist*, Harvard, 1957.
— *The Religious Renaissance of the German Humanists*, Harvard, 1963.
Stella, A., *Chiesa e stato nelle relazioni dei nunzi pontifici a Venezia*, Studi e testi, No. 239, Città del Vaticano, 1964.
Stone, L., "The Educational Revolution in England", *Past and Present*, 28, 1964, pp. 41-80.
Sturge, G., *Cuthbert Tunstall – Churchman, Scholar, Statesman, Administrator*, London, 1938.

Thomas, D., "What is the Origin of the 'Scrittura Humanistica'?" LBF, LIII, 1951, pp. 1-10.
Thompson, C. R., trans. and ed., *The Colloquies of Erasmus*, Chicago, 1965.
Tinto, A., *Il corsivo nella tipografia del Cinquecento: dai caratteri italiani ai modelli germanici e francesi*, Verona, 1972.
— and Balsamo, L., *Origini del corsivo nella tipografia italiana del '500*, Milan, 1967.
— "The History of a Sixteenth-Century Greek Type", *The Library*, Fifth Series, XXV, 1970, pp. 285-93.
Turyn, A., *Studies in the Manuscript Tradition of the Tragedies of Sophocles*, Illinois Studies in Language and Literature, XXXVI, 1952.

Ullman, B., *The Origin and Development of Humanistic Script*, Rome, 1960.

Vaccari, P., *Storia dell' università di Ferrara, 1391-1950*, Bologna, 1950.
Venturi, L., "Le compagnie della Calza, secoli XV-XVI", NAV, Nuova Serie, XVI, 1908, pp. 161-221.
Veress, A., *Matricula et Acta Hungarorum in Universitate Patavina Studentium, 1264-1864*, Budapest, 1915.

Vian, F., *Histoire de la Tradition-Manuscrite de Quintus de Smyrne*, Paris, 1957.
Villari, P., *The Life and Times of Gerolamo Savonarola*, 2 vols., Florence, 1888.
Vitaliani, D., *Della vita e delle opere di Niccolo Leoniceno vicentino*, Verona, 1892.
Vocht, H. de, *History of the Foundation and Rise of the Collegium Trilingue Lovaniense, 1517-1550*, 4 vols, Louvain, 1951-5.
Volpati, C., "Gli Scotti di Monza, tipografi-editori in Venezia", ASL, 59, 1932, pp. 365-82.

Wagner, K., "Aldo Manuzio e i prezzi dei suoi libri", LBF, LXXVII, 1975, pp. 77-82.
— "Sulla sorte di alcuni manoscritti appartenuti a Marin Sanudo", LBF, LXXIII, 1971, pp. 247-62.
— "Altre notizie sulla sorte dei libri di Marin Sanudo", LBF, LXXIV, 1972, pp. 185-90.
Wardrop, J., *The Script of Humanism*, Oxford, 1963.
Wegg, J., *Richard Pace, a Tudor Diplomatist*, London, 1932.
Weiss, R., "Notes on Thomas Linacre", in *Miscellanea Giovanni Mercati*, Vol. IV, Città del Vaticano, 1956, pp. 373-80.
— "In memoriam Domitii Calderini", IMU, III, 1960, pp. 309-320.
— *The Renaissance Discovery of Classical Antiquity*, Oxford, 1969.
Wilson, N. G., "The Book-Trade in Venice, ca. 1400-1515", in *Venezia, centro di mediazione tra oriente e occidente (secoli XV-XVI): aspetti e problemi*, Florence, 1977, pp. 381-97.
— "The Triclinian Edition of Aristophanes", *Classical Quarterly*, LVI, 1962, pp. 32-47.
Winship, G. P., "The Aldine Pliny of 1508", *The Library*, Fourth Series, VI, 1925, pp. 358-69.
Woody, K., "A Note on the Greek Founts of the Complutensian Polyglot", *Papers of the Bibliographical Society of America*, 65, 1971, pp. 143-9.

Yates, F., *The Art of Memory*, London, 1969.

Zeno, A., *Dissertazioni vossiane*, 2. vols., Venice, 1753.
— *Notizie intorno ai Manuzii*, Venice, 1736.

Zeno, A. and Manni, D. M., *Vita di Aldo Manuzio insigne estauratore delle lettere greche e latine*, Venice, 1759.

Zippel, G., *Le vite di Paolo II di Gaspare di Verona e Michele Canensi*, RIS, Tom. III pars xvi, Città di Castello, 1904. (Introduction.)

Zotta, C. and Brotto, I., *Acta Graduum Academicorum Gymnasii Patavini ab Anno 1406 ad Annum 1450*, Padua, 1922.

INDEX

Accursius, Bonus, early Milanese Greek editions of, 81, 87: price of, 116; Aldus follows texts of, 225, 233: 274
Adramyttenus, Manuel: teaches Aldus Greek, 53–4, 55; script of, 134
Aeschylus, 166, 258
Aesop, 81, 127, 273, 274
Agostini, Mafio, 98, 129
Alantsee, Leonard, 267
Alberti, Leon Battista, 136
Alcala, University of, 201, 262, 286
Aleander, Gerolamo, 161: teaches privately in Venice, 186, and Padua, 190–1; edits Plutarch's *Moralia*, 240; contribution to early French Hellenism, 259, 283–4; quarrel with Erasmus, 300
Alexander the Great, 34, 57
Alexander of Aphrodisias, 162, 163
Alexandros, Cretan typographer in Venice, 81, 87
Alopa, Lorenzo, early Florentine Greek typographer, 74, 81: collapse of his press, 126, 127; uncial Greek type, 134–5: 274
Amaseo, Gerolamo, 73, 78, 79, 82: *Vaticinium*, 113, 117, 279
— Gregorio, 194
Amatus, Sylvius, 289
Amerbach, Basilius, 270–1
— Boniface, 270–1, 280
— Bruno, 270–1
— Johan, father of the above, 242, 264: Aldus' influence on him, 269–73
Ambrose, 54
Antenori, Carlo, 73
Antiquario, Jacopo, 184, 189, 202, 280

Apollonius Rhodius, 81, 274
Apostolis, Arsenios: scribe of Aldus' manuscript of Lycophron, 61; studies in Florence, 74; script of, 134, 195, 301; quarrel with Aldus, 305
Arator, 148
Aratus (in *Astronomici Veteres*), 111, 112, 190
Archimedes, 183, 184, 188, 190
Ares and Aphrodite, loves of, 124
Ariosto, Ludovico: buys Aldine texts, 115, 116
Aristophanes: Urceus lectures on, 79; Aldine edition of, 112, 114; price of, 115; Gregoropoulos lectures on, 198; "Venetus A" manuscript of, 230; Barbaro manuscript of, 232; copy in New College library, 261, 262
Aristotle, 34: Aldine edition of, 75; lectures of Leonicus Tomaeus, 79, and Ermolao Barbaro, 80: 111, 112; cost of Aldine text, 115–16; 'Aristotle' fount, 131, 135, 183, 191, 192; editorship of Aldine text, 234–7; Urceus comments on, 240: 246, 258; Linacre editor, 260; copies of Linacre and Grocyn, 261: 262, 263; Pirckheimer's copy, 275; copy in Wittenberg, 278
Arrighi, Ludovico degli, 140, 284
Arrivabene, Zorzi, 16, 22, 85
Asconius, 49
Asola, 77, 159
Athenaeus, 162, 163, 165, 230, 232, 242
Atri, duke, of, 202, 306
Augsburg, missals printed in, 21
— Rynman of, 11

Augustine, 32, 50, 143, 241
Aulus Gellius, 32, 80
Augurelli, Aurelio, 223
Ausonius, 248
Avanzio, Gerolamo: on size of Aldine press-run, 174 n. 96; editor of Pliny, 245, 257
Averroes, 111
Avogadori del Commun, 155

Bade, Josse, 158
Badoer, Andrea, 9
Badoer, Jacobo, 20
Bandello, Matteo, 122: plans for Academy in Milan, 202-3; sends short-story to Aldus, 228-9
Baptista Mantuanus, 28
Barbarigo, Venetian noble family, 84, 85, 160
— Agostino, doge, 1486-1501, 84, 189
— Marco, brother of Agostino, doge 1485-6, 83, 84
— Pierfrancesco, son of Marco: partnership with Aldus and Torresani, 83-5; mentioned, 91, 98, 100, 258, 304
Barbarigo, Santo, natural son of Pierfrancesco, pupil of Aldus, 83, 180, 192
Barbaro, Venetian noble family, 118, 282
Barbaro, Alvise, 191, 233
Barbaro, Ermolao, 48, 56: views on censorship, 57-8: 66: informal teaching in Venice, 79-80: 183, 186, 190; description of life at university of Padua, 191; death of, 193, 233, 243
Barbaro, Francesco, 232
Bardellone, Giangiacomo: his manuscript of Hesychius, 246, 302
Barozzi, Pietro: bishop of Padua, 56, 57; patron of Giorgio Valla, 188
Bartolomeo da Alzano, 125
Barzizza, Gasparino da, 37
Basel, city of, 227, 237, 246, 265: humanist circle in, 268-73
Basel, Leonardus of, 81
Bassiano, 48
Batrachomyomachia, 80, 81

Beatus Rhenanus, 237, 269, 271
Becichemo, Marin, 164
Bembo, Venetian noble family, 141
— Bernardo, father of Carlo and Pietro, 188, 232
— Carlo, co-editor of Petrarch's *Cose volgari*, 148, 226
— Pietro, 60, 167, 191, 193, 199, 205, 206: brings manuscript of Lascaris' Grammar to Aldus, 219, 224; co-editor of Petrarch, 225-7; librarian of Marciana, 231: 241
— *Gli Asolani*, 109, 152, 154: Giuntine edition, 158: 223
— *De Aetna*, 112, 116, 135, 223
— *Prose della volgar lingua*, 190
Bembo, Torquato, natural son of Pietro, 224
Bembo, Zuane: on Aldus' partnership, 83-4: 182, 185, 189
Benalius, Bernardus, 22, 23, 28, 31
Benedetti, Alessandro: *Diaria de bello Carolino*, 112, 116-17, 219
— friend of Francesco Colonna, 121: friend of Giorgio Valla, 193, 223; lost library, 233
Benedetti, Platon, 118
Benzoni, Piero, 97
Bernardino da Tridino, 111
Bernardo, Venetian noble family, neighbours of Aldus, 94
Bernardo, Nicolò, 98
Beroaldo, Filippo, 72, 223, 288
Bertochus, Dionysius, 81
Bessarion: papal legate in France, 48; endows chair of Greek at Padua, 79: 80, 235, 239; *In Calumniatorem Platonis*, 50, 145, 148, 232, 277, 279
— His library, later the Biblioteca Marciana: bequeathed to the Republic, 72-3; neglected, 74, 79; manuscripts of Musurus in, 165; Navagero as librarian, 204-5; unused by Aldus, 229-32, 244: 246, 248, 258, 301, 304, 305
Bevilaqua, Simon, 21, 32
Bible, trilingual version of, 109, 267, 275, 305

Biblioteca Ambrosiana, Milan, 240
Bibliothèque Nationale, Paris, 117, 234, 237, 239, 280
Bissolo, Giovanni, 127
Bitzimanos, Thomas, 237
Blois, site of French Royal Library, 193, 244, 281
Bologna, 22, 52, 54, 73, 79, 88, 160, 263, 287, 288, 289
— Francesco da, 11
Bologni, Gerolamo, Trevisan humanist: tribute to Aldus, 41, 47 n. 105, 217; Aldus refuses to publish his work, 303
Bombasio, Paolo, 96, 206
Bonapace, Vettore, 185
Bordone, Benedetto, engraver and illuminator: possibly engaged by Aldus, 99; possible illustrator of Polifilo, 122, 170–1 n. 47; Aldine vellum copies in his style, 146, 174 nn. 104–5, 275; resemblance of Grolier's copies, 280, 297 n. 93
Borgia, Cesare, 193
— Lucrezia, duchess of Ferrara, executor of Aldus' will, 53: offers to sponsor Aldine Academy, 202, 207; sponsors edition of *Strozzorum poemata*, 223: 305
Borgia, Roderigo, later Pope Alexander VI, 49: releases Aldus from vow, 119: 126
Bossi, Matteo, 248
Bragadin, Giovanni, 84
Brant, Sebastian, 27, 269
Brasichella, Gabriel of, early Greek typographer in Venice, 91, 126; lawsuit with Aldus over edition of *Brutus and Phalaris*, 126–7: 129, 131, 154
Brescia, 155, 164, 303
Brethren of the Common Life, 25, 276
Brodarich, Stefan, 287–8
Brugnolo, Benedetto, head of School of San Marco, 20, 36; influence on Venetian education, 181–3: 185; dies 1502, 195: 198
Brunetti, Mario, 83
Bruni, Leonardo, 32, 37, 263; *Florentine History*, 14

Bruno, Giordano, 121
Budé, Guillaume, classicist in French Chancellery, 245, 259: visits Venice, 282; advises Aleander, 283; royal librarian, 285; *On the Ass*, 280
Bühler, Curt, criticises Aldine types, 130
Buonaccorsi, Filippo, Italian humanist exile in Poland, 288–9
Burkhard, Georg (Spalatinus), advises on Wittenberg library, 276–8, 303
Busleyden, Jerome, 201, 271

Caballi, Francesco, 114
Caesar, Julius, 57, 64: Aldine edition of, 162, 164: work of Fra Giocondo on text of, 204, 282
Caesarea, St Basil of, 32, 66
Cafa, Pietro of, 95
Calbero, Gerolamo, 194–5
Calderini, Domizio, 20: philological studies and lectures in Rome, 48–9: only slight influence on Aldus, 51: 143; at School of San Marco, 182
Calfurnio, Giovanni, 60: at School of San Marco, 182: 274
Callierges, Zacharias, Cretan scribe and printer, 13, 72, 91: five years of experiment with Greek type, 103 n. 44; cooperates with Aldus, 126; involved in Lippomano bankruptcy, 127–9, 149; invited to Rome, 161: 184, 195, 204; Greek editions in Rome, 206; editions in Pirckheimer's library, 274: 304
Callimachus, 81
Cambrai, League of, 110, 159, 203, 269
Camerte, Varino, 73
Campagnolo, Julio, commissioned to cast cursive capitals for Aldus, 91, 141
Cantalycius, 46 n. 95, 49
Cantiuncula, Claudius, 271
Capello, Alvise, 116
Capello, Zuane, 27, 45 n. 77
Capodistria, Marco da, 95
Carbone, Ludovico, 36, 42 n. 15
Carlstadt, Andreas, 278

Carpi, Aldus' residence in, 52, 54, 55: artistic patronage of Alberto Pio, 58–9; birthplace of Bissolo and de Manzi, 127: 195, 302

Casa Romana, 81

Castellesi, Adriano, author of *Venatio*, 223

Cato, Marcus, 162, 164: Fra Giocondo's research on text of, 282

Cattus, Lydus, 190

Catullus, Aldine edition of, 142: predecessors, 143: 145; Giuntine copy, 158; as evidence on size of Aldine press-runs, 257; early French italic edition, 284

Caxton, William, 2, 90

Celtis, Conrad, 120: contacts Aldus, 195; plans to bring Aldus to Empire, 199, 201: 259; influence on German humanist circles, 264–8: 271, 273, 274, 275, 302

Ceresara, Federigo da, causes Aldus' arrest, 96–7: own arrest, 200: documents on, 106 n. 91, 214 n. 92

Cervini, Marcello, later Pope Marcellus II, 87

Chalcondylas, Demetrius, 73: teaching in Florence, 74; teaching in Padua and Milan, 79; part in early Greek editions, 81, 91, 99, 127; possible successor to Giorgio Valla, 194; tutors Linacre and Grocyn in Greek, 259, 274

Charles VIII, King of France, 258

Charles, Jeffroy, rescues Aldus from prison, 107 n. 93, 202, 280

Chrysoloras, Manuel, 80: early editions of his Greek Grammar, 80–1; French edition, 283

Cicero, Marcus Tullius, 20, 29: first Italian editions, 50: 57, 78, 146, 183; Aldine octavo editions, 142, 144, 162, 164, 204, 247, 287

Ciotek, Erasmius, 289

Ciriaco d'Ancona, 140

Claretti, Constanzo, 289

Clari, Daniele: receives dedication of Aldine Aristophanes, 114; directs Genoese author to Aldus, 148: 305

Clement, John, 262, 268

Colet, John, 182

Collauer, John, sponsors scheme to bring Aldus to Empire, 199–200: 268

Colocci, Angelo: and Roman Academy, 195, 197; promises to Aldus, 204; and Greek Academy in Rome, 204–5: 212 n. 70

Cologne, John of: partnership with Jenson, 18–19, 20: legal texts, 22; Merula edits classical texts for, 28, 29: 38, 78, 97, 153

Cologne, university of, 35

Colonna, Francesco, probable author of *Hypnerotomachia Polifili*, 121–2

Common Life, Brethren of, 25, 276

Commynes, Philippe de, 101 n. 16

Contarini, Antonio, 35

Contarini, Gasparo, 246

Contarini, Tadio, 97

Conti, Sigismondo, 204

Corner, Venetian noble family, 84, 185, 189

— Caterina, 185

— Marco, 186

— Zorzi, father of Marco, brother of Caterina, 185

Corvinus, Matthias, library of, 287

Cosmas, 148

Council of Ten, 27: and Francesco Colonna, 122; and protection of Aldine italic, 155; and Filippo Giunti, 156; arrests Giorgio Valla, 194

Cracow, university of, classical studies in, 288–9

Crasso, Francesco, 121

Crasso, Leonardo, editor of *Polifilo*, 119, 125, 301

Craston, Giovanni, Greek, Lexicon of, early editions, 81: Aldine edition, 112, 114; price of, 115; Latin translation of Lascaris' Grammar, 225; Lexicon purchased for Wittenberg library, 278; French edition of, 283

Crates, letters of, 231

Cremona, 21

Crinitus – see Ricci

INDEX 337

Csulai, Philip, Hungarian ambassador in Venice, 287: death at Mohacz, 288

Cues, Nicholas of, 25

Cuno, John: reports Torresani's opposition to Greek editions, 86; pupil of Aldus, 94; comments on *Gli Asolani*, 152: 153; reports on progress of editions, 158; negotiates for Aldine Academy in Empire, 198–201; collects press-copy of Aristotle and Theophrastus, 235; and *Epistolographi Graeci*, 237; and Euripides, 239: 240; early Greek studies in Heidelberg, 265; teaching and editorship in Basel, 268–71; agent for Pirckheimer, 275: 279

Curtius, Quintus, 189

Czepiel, Nicolai, 289

Dalberg, Johan von, 264, 265

D'Alviano, Bartolomeo, 159

Da Aquila, Sebastiano, 115

Da Canal, Paolo, Italian poet, 175 n. 111, 190: and statute of Aldine Academy, 196

Da Madiis, Francesco: sales reveal uneven market, 16; sale of classical texts, 20; of religious books, 21; of legal texts, 22; prices compared with Aldine catalogues, 115–16: 303

Damascus, John of, 148

Da Molin, Venetian noble family, neighbours of Aldus, 94, 146

Da Molin, Gerolamo, 233

Dante, 65, 144, 147, 223

De'Bisticci, Vespasiano, 36, 285, 306

De Busca, Ercole, 77

De Bussi, Gianandrea, bishop of Aleria: editor for Sweynheim and Pannartz, 14; views on editing, 24–5, 29, 30, 36, 38; possible influence on Aldus, 50; rapid editorship, 233: 242

Decembrio, Piercandido: contribution to *Poetae Christiani Veteres*, 149; checks Florentine manuscripts for Aldus, 249

De Colines, Simon, 136, 284–5

Dee, John, 300

De Foix, Anne, 287

De Gabiano, Balthazar, 156

De Gourmont, Gilles, 282–3

De Gregoriis, Joannes and Gregorius: graduate from classical to legal texts, 22; Roman types, 88; editions of Aristotelian translations, 111; success during 1490s, 126 and 171 n. 59: 129

De Manzi, Benedetto, printer in Carpi, 59: sued by Aldus, 127

Demosthenes, 115: Aldine edition of, 150, 151; demanded by Angelo Gabriel, 152; Fortiguerra's lectures on, 198; small press-run, 257: 258

De Nevo, Alessandro, 23

D'Este, ruling family of Ferrara: and university, 52

— Alfonso, 37

— Isabella: returns Aldine vellum copies, 86; interest in Petrarch, 148, 225: 306

De'Tagliente, Antonio, and the italic, 140–1, 284, 301

De Tortis, Baptista and Silvestro: partnership with Arrivabene, Scotto, and Giunti, 16–17, 85; success during 1490s, 126 and 171 n. 59

Dinslaken, Gaspar von, 19, 97

— Hironima von, 19, 32, 37, 97

— Jordan von: trades in Aldine and later Lutheran texts, 97–8, 257, 264

Diogenes Laertius, 20, 32

Dionysius Periegetes, 268

Dioscurides, 57, 65: Aldine edition of, 112, 114, 115, 131; Valla's manuscript of, 183; and botanical studies, 191: 268, 278

Di Rolandello, Francesco, 186–7

Di Soardis, Lazzaro, 142

Di Strata, Filippo, critic of the press and Aldus, 26–7: ideas widespread, 29; fear of vulgarisation, 31–2; moral anxieties and religious prejudice, 33–6: 189, 303, 304

Dominici, Giovanni, 32

Donatello, 136

Donà, Venetian noble family, neighbours of Aldus, 94

Donà, Tomaso, 33, 119, 124
Donato, Gerolamo, 36, 186, 187, 195
Donato, Nicolo, 21, 36
Donatus, Latin Grammar of, 63
Drach, Joannes, 265
Ducas, Demetrius, 161: editor of Aldine Plutarch, 240: influence on Complutensian Polyglot, 286
Du Pins, Jean, 285
Dürer, Albrecht: and *Hypnerotomachia Polifili*, 124: agent and illuminator for Pirckheimer, 275–6

Egnazio, Giambattista: rivalry with Sabellico, 51, 60; criticism of Andrea Torresani, 77; attends Pacioli's lectures, 137: 167; reconciliation with Sabellico, 183, 184–5; signs statute of Aldine Academy, 196; named tutor to Aldus' son, 203; in Venetian public life, 205; tribute of Erasmus, 228; friend of Jean Grolier, 281
England: cultural links with Ferrara, 53; participation in Holy League, 161; Aldine influence in, 259–63
Epicurus, 111
Epiphanius, 148
Erasmus, Desiderius: 8, 28, 29, 36, 50; quarrel with Alberto Pio, 58; on Aldus' library, 60; jokes about Aldus' Grammars in *Praise of Folly*, 62: 97; account of the Torresani household, 98–9, 110; praise of Aldine italic, 130: 167, 186, 201, 204, 205, 233; editorial work on Terence, 242: 246, 247, 258, 259; English friends of, 260, 262; editorial activity in Basel, 270–1, 273; recommends Aleander to go to Paris, 283: 290, 300, 301, 302, 305; translations of Euripides' *Hecuba* and *Iphigenia*, 158, 220, 223, 227, 260; *Adagia*, 84, 86, 109, 151, 159, 228, 241, 263, 278, 283; *Opulentia Sordida*, and attack on Andrea Torresani, 76–7, 78, 86; *Apologia adversus rhapsodias...Alberti Pii*, 92–5, 98, 106 n. 83

Erfurt, 198, 276
Estienne, Robert, 91, 284
Euclid, 137, 190
Eugenius IV, Pope, 136
Euripides: Alopa edition of, 81; Aldine edition, 142, 145, 151; manuscript copies of, 238–9; mentioned by Thomas More, 262
Eustathius, 64

Fedele, Cassandra, 189
Feliciano, Felice, 136, 140
Feltre, Vittorino da, 24, 201
Ferrando, Tommaso, 80
Ferrara: university of, 22; development during fifteenth century, 52–3; Aldus studies in, 55, 58: 73; effect on Aldine editorial programme, 114; as a market for Aldine texts, 115, 134; Hungarian students at, 287; court of, 91; Aldus flees to, 159–60; possible centre for Aldine Academy, 203: 302
Ficino, Marsiglio, 74: editorial help for Aldus, 111, 115; and Alopa press, 127; death of, 193: 195, 205, 220–1, 227, 263
Filelfo, Francesco, 45 n. 85
— Gianmario, and School of San Marco, 181–2
Firmicus, in *Astronomici Veteres*, 278
Florence: slow expansion of printing in, 15: 54, 55, 58; vitality of Greek studies in, 74, 79; early Greek typography in, 81, 82: 126–7, 134; French invaders in, 193, 258; Linacre and Grocyn study in, 259–60; German students in, 263: 264
Fontainebleau, French Royal library at, 285
Foresti, Jacopo Filippo, *Supplementum Chronicarum*, 31, 32, 36
Fornovo, Battle of, 193, 219
Fortiguerra, Scipio: Pistoiese humanist, studying at Padua, 73; follows Aldus' fortunes from Rome, 152, 153; editorial work in Rome, 163; teaching in Venice, 186; and the Aldine Academy in Venice, 195–6; lectures in Venice,

Fortiguerra, Scipio *(cont.)*
  198: 199; negotiates on Aldus' behalf in Rome, 203–4: 223; editorial work on Virgilian *Catalepton*, 242; *Oratio de Laudibus Literarum Graecarum*, 198, 273
Foscari, Francesco, proprietor of Aldus' book-store, 97
Foscarini, Ludovico, 29
Fossano, Pietro, 23
Fox, Richard: founder of Corpus Christi College, Oxford, 201; books donated by, 262
Francis I, King of France: Aldine texts collected for, 285
Franco, Nicolo, 35, 36
Frank, Hans, 11
Frankfurt, book-fairs of, 14, 264
— Nicholas of, 17
Fries, Wolf: purchases Aldine texts for Wittenberg library, 278
Froben, Johan: edits New Testament with Erasmus, 246; partner of Johan Amerbach, 269–71; follows Aldine style of printing, 273: 284
Fruticenus, Joannes, 268
Fugger, Augsburg bankers, trade in Aldine texts, 98

Gabriel, Venetian noble family, library of, 233
— Angelo: and Aldine edition of Demosthenes, 152; in cloth-trade, 164; studies Greek under Constantine Lascaris, 191; pupil of Giorgio Valla, 193; and manuscript of Lascaris' Greek Grammar, 224
Galaeomyomachia, Aldine edition of, 82, 112, 131
Galen, 109, 166
Gallus, Jodocus, 264, 265
Garamond, Claude, 11, 90, 91, 136, 285
Garzoni, Andrea, 128
Gaza, Theodorus: Greek Grammar of, 112; cost, 115: 131, 135, 262, 265, 266, 273, 284; Aristotelian translations of, 149, 150; dedication to Matthew Lang, 199
Ghiberti, Lorenzo, 136
Giocondo, Fra Giovanni: fee for editorial help, 99; "sfratato", 121; attends Pacioli's lectures, 137; handwriting of, 140–1; goes to Rome, 167; and intellectual life in Venice, 204; and the Paris manuscript of Pliny, 244–5; and French intellectual life, 281–2, 284
Giorgione, 101
Giunti family, 89, 156, 300
— Bernardo: son of Filippo, 156, 161
— Filippo, 140: lawsuit with Aldus over use of italic type, 156–8, 273: 304
— Lucantonio, brother of Filippo: contract with Scotto, Arrivabene and de Tortis, 16–17, 85: success, 17–18, 19; illustrated edition of Ovid's *Metamorphoses*, 33; Italian Bibles, 34
Giustiniani, Marcantonio, 84
Gonzaga, Federigo: releases Aldus from prison, 96; letter from Emperor to, 160: 242, 306
Gonzaga, Gianfrancesco, 25
Gotha, 276
Greek typography: general problems of, 72, 87; early solutions, 80–1; Aldine solution, 89–90; criticism of Aldine Greek types, 130; the cursive style and its development, 131–4; Alopa's uncial, 135; spread of the cursive style, 273, 286
Gregoropoulos, Greek scribal family, 239
— John, 134: possible signatory of Aldine statute, 196; lectures on Aristophanes, 198
Gregory Nazanzenus, in *Poetae Christiani Veteres*, 149, 150, 220
Griffo, Francesco: relations with Aldus and their quarrel, 87–91: 99, 134, 135, 140, 143, 241, 301, 304, 305
Grimani, Antonio, 107, 124, 129
Grimani, Domenico, cardinal, son of the above, 8, 186, 191
Grimani, Marin, 186
Gritti, Andrea, 187

Grocyn, William: writes to Aldus, 195; and Erasmus, 223: 259; library and teaching of, 261–2: 268

Grolier, Estienne, 280

— Jean: library of, 147; in French administration in Milan, 202; relations with Aldine circle, 280–1: 285, 302, 306

Gryphius, Sebastianus, 284

Guarino, Battista: views on press relayed by Sabellico, 36–7; teaching in Ferrara, 51–3; influence on Aldus, 66; dedication of Aldine Theocritus to, 114; Hungarian students of, 287; *De Ordine Docendi et Studenti*, 53

Guarino veronese, father of the above, 49, 52, 80

Gutenberg, Johan, 10, 11, 90, 131

Haller, John, 289

Harlem, Nicholas of, 9

Heidelberg, early Greek studies in, 264–6, 267, 268, 269, 273, 282

Henry II, King of France, 285

Hermogenes, 115

Hermonymus, George, 282

Herod, 34

Herodotus, 32, 88: Aldine edition of, 142, 144, 151, 258, 262, 275

Heron, 184, 232

Hervagius, Joannes, 8

Hesiod, dedicated to Battista Guarino by Aldus, 53: 79: early Milanese edition of, 81; Aldine edition, 114; French edition on pattern of Aldine, 283

Hesychius, Lexicon of, Aldine edition, 162, 164, 234, 244: Bardellone's manuscript of, 245–7: 262, 302

Hippocrates, 268

Holt, John, Latin Grammar of, 63

Homer, 65, 79, 80: Florentine first edition, 81; Aldine edition, 149, 150; Bessarion's manuscript of 229; Valeriani's manuscript of, 232: 262, 267, 274; in Wittenberg library, 278

Horace, 20, 57, 64, 65: Aldine edition, 142; popularity of, 143: 144; Thurz praises octavo format, 147; plagiarised versions, 155; copies sent to Celtis, 267: 278; Giuntine copy, 158

Hummelberg, Michael, 240–1

Hungary, 194: Aldus' influence in, 287–8

Hypnerotomachia Polifili, 109, 118–25, 126: types of, 135–6: 280, 284, 301

Iamblichus, 111, 112: copy owned by Felino Sandeis, 119: 221

Interiano, Giorgio, *Vita de' Zichi*, 144: directed to Aldus by Daniele Clari, 148: 221, 227

Isocrates, 81

Jacomo Ungaro, type-designer, associate of Aldus, 90–1

Jenson, Nicholas: commercial success, 8–9; technical skills, 10–11; commission from Gerolamo Strozzi, 15–16; as bookseller, 17–18; partnership with John of Cologne, 18–19: 20; legal texts, 22; comments of Merula, 28, 29: 34; followers of, 38: 76; possible link with Torresani, 77: 78; Greek types, 80; possible connection with Francesco Griffo, 87; Roman type designs, 90: 97, 125, 136, 141, 142, 153, 192, 300, 303

Jerome, 25, 32, 67, n. 7, 143, 270

Johannes Grammaticus, 54, 149, 150

Julius II, Pope, 203, 205

Juvenal, Calderini's commentary on, 49: 51: plagiarised versions of Aldine edition, 155; Valla's commentary on, 183: 278, 280

Juvencus, 148

Ketham, Joannes de, *Fasciculus Medicinae*, 88

Koberger, Anton, 269

Kress, Anton, 275

Lactantius, edited by Sweynheim and Pannartz, 49

INDEX

Lang, Matthew, cardinal of Gurk, approached by Aldus in dedication of Theodorus Gaza, 160, 199–200, 305
Lang, Vincent, 267
Laonicus, Cretan typographer in Venice, 81, 87: see also Alexandros
Lascaris, Constantine, Greek Grammar of, 63, 66: first edition printed by Demetrius, 80, 81; Aldine edition, 82, second printing, 109: 112; price of, 115: 116, 131, 135, 152; Lascaris teaches in Milan, 183; friend of Giorgio Valla, 183–4; named as possible successor to Valla, 194; teaches in Messina, 219; manuscript of his Greek Grammar brought to Aldus, 223–5, 227, 229: 234, 262; copied onto manuscript in Basel, 265: 266, 269–70, 278, 283, 289
Lascaris, Janus, Greek exile teaching in Florence, 73–4, 78: works for Alopa press, 81; reproaches Aldus for printing in Italian, 86; experiment with Greek types, 87; leaves Florence for France, 127; uncial edition of Greek Anthology, 134–5; in French diplomatic service, 146, 147: 152; supplies Aldus with manuscript of Sallust, 159, and Greek orators, 163; goes to Rome, 167; visit to Giorgio Valla's library, 184; impact on Greek studies in Venice, 199, 228: 233; search for manuscripts in Greece sponsored by Lorenzo de'Medici, 244: 245, 258, 281–2, 284
Latimer, William, English student in Padua and friend of Aldus and Erasmus, 94, 193, 223, 259, 260
Lefèvre d'Étaples, Jacques, 259: in Florence, 282; helps Aleander in Paris, 283
Lelli, Trevisan noble family: and *Hypnerotomachia Polifili*, 120, 122
— Lucrezia, ("Polia"), 122
— Teodoro, bishop of Treviso, 122
Leo X (Giovanni de'Medici), 156, 205–6, 271
Leonardo da Vinci, 91
Leone, Ambrogio, 137

Leoniceno, Niccolo, lectures in Ferrara, 52–3: invited to Mirandola by Pico, 54–5; correspondence with Poliziano, 57; editorial assistant with Aldine text of Aristotle, 114; and Giorgio Valla, 184, 191–3, 233; manuscript of Theophrastus copied for Aldus, 235–6: 304; *De Morbo Gallico*, published by Aldus, 112, 116, 135, 223; *De Tiro seu Vipera*, published by Aldus, 112, 116, 223
Leonicus Tomaeus, 73, 79; appointed lecturer on Greek texts of Aristotle in Padua, 111; Greek lecturer in Venice, 195, 198; borrows manuscript from Marciana, 231
Lepanto, Gulf of, 124
Le Rouge, Jacques, 15, 16
Leto, Pomponio, and the Latin classics, 51: teaches Sabellico, 183; death of, 193; villa bought by Colocci, 195; Roman Academy of, 196: 288
Linacre, Thomas: editorial assistant with Aldine text of Aristotle, 114, 195; contact with Erasmus, 223; and Greek studies in England, 259–63: 302, 305
Lippomano, Tomaso, 128
Lisa, Gerard of, 9
Livy, popularity of, 20, 42, 78
Locatellus, Bonetus, 23, 119, 126 and 171 n. 59
London, early humanism in, 261–2, 279, 290
Loredan, Leonardo: hires tutor, 186; helps Poliziano's research in Venice, 191; grants privileges to Aldus, 196, 217
Loredan, Lorenzo, son of Leonardo, 187
Loschi, Bernardino, 59
Louis XII, King of France: special copy of Amaseo's *Vaticinium*, 95: 214
Louvain, trilingual college of, 201
Lubranski, John: Aldus dedicates Valerius Maximus to, 146, 197; travels in Italy and effect on Polish scholarship, 288–9; influence, 302
Lucan, Aldine edition of, 142, 144: plagiarised version, 155
Lucca, Giampietro of, 182

Lucian: Alopa edition of, 81; Aldine edition, 145, 261, 262; Pirckheimer owns Alopa text, 274: 278, 283, 284

Lucretius, Aldine edition of, 111, 113: price of, 146; second edition, 163, edited by Andrea Navagero, 204, 247

Luther, Martin, 276, 278

Lycophron, Aldus' manuscript of, 61

Lyons, book fairs of, 14

— centre for production of counterfeit Aldine editions, 155–6, 273, 284, 303

Macarius Mutius, *De Triumpho Christi*, 33

Mainz, archbishop of, (Berthold von Hennenberg), 35

Maioli, Lorenzo: editorial assistant with Aldine text of Aristotle, 114, 120; *De Gradibus Medicinarum*, published by Aldus, 112, 116; *Epiphyllides in Dialectis*, published by Aldus, 112, 116, 220, 223

Malermi, Nicolo, Venetian abbot, translator of Bible, 34, 36

Malipiero, Domenico, Venetian noble and diarist, 76, 230

Mantegna, Andrea, and Roman inscriptional capitals, 137

Manthen, John, partner of John of Cologne, 18

Mantua, 24, 77, 91, 160

Mantuanus, Baptista, 32–3

Manutia, Alda, daughter of Aldus, 160

— Letitia, daughter of Aldus, 160

Manutius, Aldus junior, son of Paulus, grandson of Aldus senior; on date of grandfather's birth, 48, 66 n. 1; tries to sell family library, 60–1; on invitation of his grandfather to Naples, 202

Manutius, Aldus senior: 13, 18, 24; Venetian background of, 36–41; family and early life, 48; education in Rome and possible influence of de Bussi, 49–51; studies in Ferrara, 51–3; influence of Pico, 53–6; *Musarum Panegyris*, 56–7; tutor to Alberto Pio, 58, 59; Latin Grammar, 62–3, and general outlook on the ancient world, 59–66; search for financial support, 72, 74; later relations with Alberto Pio, 75, and Andrea Torresani, 76–82; partnership with Barbarigo and Torresani, 83–6; relations with Francesco Griffo, 87–91; marries Maria Torresani, 92; print shop near S. Agostin, 92–4; attitude to workers, 95–6; arrest, 96–7; criticism of a bookseller, 97; expenses, 98–9, 100; review of his output, 109–10; Greek editions up to 1500, 111; cost of Greek editions, 115–16; Latin editions before 1500, 116–18; catches the plague, 119; attitude to *Polifilo*, 120–1; illustration of *Polifilo*, 122; atones for *Polifilo*, 125–6; position in Venetian typography c. 1500, 126; lawsuit with Gabriel of Brasichella, 127; outstrips competitors, 129; conflicting opinions of his types, 130; Greek founts, 131–5; Roman, 135–7; italic, 137–41; experiments with Hebrew type, 142; aims of the Aldine literary octavo, 142–7; difficulties around 1503, 148–9; the "Dolphin and Anchor", 149; closer alliance with Torresani family, 152–4; action against Lyons plagiarists and Giunti, 154–8; Erasmus' approach to, 158; flees to Ferrara, 159–60; returns to Venice, 161; disappointment in later life, 165–7; as a teacher, 180; and Giorgio Valla's circle, 184, 191–2; and Bembo's library, 188; development of own intellectual circle, 193–9; the Venetian "New Academy", 196–9; plans for Aldine Academy in Empire, 199–201, in Milan, 201–2, in Ferrara, 203, in Rome, 203–6; attitude to the classical texts, 217; and to contemporary writers, 219–24; editorial technique as reflected in Lascaris' Grammar, 224–5; and in Petrarch's *Cose vulgari*, 225–7; personal treatment of authors, 228–9; does not use capital manuscripts of Marciana, 229–32; press copies of Aristotle and Theophrastus, 234–7; of

Manutius, Aldus senior *(cont.)*
　Epistolographi Graeci, 237-8; of Euripides and Sophocles, 239; of Plutarch's *Moralia*, 239-40; criticism of his editorship, 240-1; evidence against such criticism, 242-3; tribute to Lascaris, 244; edition of Pliny's Letters, 244-5; reputation as a textual critic, 247-9; overall number of copies produced, 257; English friends, 259-63; influence on early Greek studies in Heidelberg, 264-6; on Viennese humanism, 266-8; on humanism in Basel, 269-71; Froben follows Aldus' example, 273; Pirckheimer buys Aldine texts, 273-6; Frederick the Wise buys Aldine texts, 276-8; friends in France, 279; Grolier's Aldine texts, 280; early influence of Aldine texts in Paris, copied by French typographers, 284; Aldine texts in French Royal Library, 285; influence in Spain uncertain, 286-7; Hungarian friends of, 287-8; Polish friends, 288-90; continuing reputation and justification for it, 300-7
Manutius, Antonius, son of Aldus senior, 160
— Marcus, son of Aldus senior, 160
— Paulus, son of Aldus senior: on father's birth, 48, 66 n. 1, 289
Marcelli, Adriano, 86
Marcello, Nicolo, doge, 26
Marcellus, Nonius, 282
Marignano, Battle of, 161
Marius Rusticus, 49
Marschalk, Nickolaus, 277
Martial, 20, 49, 51; Aldine edition of, 142, 144, 280; plagiarised version, 155
Maufer, Peter, 17, 70, 85
Mayner, Accursius, French ambassador in Venice, 117; Aldus dedicates *In Calumniatorem Platonis* to, 279; Budé in retinue of, 282
Maximilian I: Aldus' friends negotiate with, 153; writes to Marquis of Mantua on Aldus' behalf, 160; and plans for Academy in the Empire, 199-201;

patron of Celtis, 267; relations with Venice deteriorate, 268; lost personal letter to Aldus, 306
Mayno, Jason de, 23
Medici, ruling family of Florence, 73, 193, 258
— Lorenzo de', 74, 205, 244
— Piero de', 74, 205, 244
Melanchthon, Philip, 277, 278
Menochio, Hironimo, and statute of Aldine Academy, 196
Merceria, centre of Venetian book-trade, 8, 37, 231, 275
Merula, Bartolomeo, 186
— Giorgio, 20, 24: uncertain attitude to the press, 28, 29, 32, 36; lecturer in Venice, 181, 192, 217
Messina, Antonello da, 18: teaching of Constantine Lascaris in, 219, 224
Mestre, 98
Milan: Chalcondylas teaches in, 73, 74, 79; Demetrius of, early Greek typographer, 80-1; growth of Greek typography in, 81, 82; invaded by French and Venetians, 117; Aldine agent in, 160; Merula teaches in, 181; Lascaris teaches in, 183, 193, 194; plans for Aldine Academy in, 202-3, 244; French administration of, 279-80
Mithridates, King of Pontus, 189
Mocenigo, Alvise, 245
— Andrea, 182
Modon, loss of, 124
Mohacs, Battle of, 287-8
Monopoli, Hironimo da, 164
Montefeltro, family of, 193
— Federigo da, 57
More, Thomas, 258: early Greek studies, 261-2: 268
Moreto, Antonio, 146
Morison, Stanley, praises Aldus' Roman types, 130, 301
Morosini, Antonio, 146
— Marcantonio, 20
Musaeus, Aldine edition of, 82, 112, 131, 266, 267
Musurus, Marcus: and Alberto Pio, 29;

Musurus, Marcus *(cont.)*
edits Aldus' Greek Grammar, 62; early career in Florence, 74; edits Aldine text of Aristophanes, 114; his Greek script, 134; work on Alexander of Aphrodisias, 163; seeks refuge in Venice, 164, and becomes public lecturer in Greek, 165; goes to Rome, 167; member of Aldine circle in Venice, 195, 204; elegiac address to Leo X in Aldine Plato, 205; and Greek college in Rome, 206; tribute of Erasmus, 228: 231, 232; edits Athenaeus, 242, and Hesychius, 246, 247; Cuno hears his lectures, 269; dedicates Aldus' Greek Grammar to Grolier, 280; Aleander studies with, 283, 301, 302

Mutian (Conrad Muth): studies in Italy, and advice on Wittenberg library, 276-7

Naples, Kingdom of, 193: Pontano's Academy in, 195: 202-3: 222, 281; Prince Cesare of, 306

Navagero, Andrea: receives dedication of Pindar, 161; and *Ad Herennium*, 165; interest in botany, 190; edits Latin classics, 204; librarian of Marciana, 205, 230-1; works on Quintilian, 233: 242, 243, 246, 247

Nesen, Wilhelm, 271

Nevo, Alessandro de, 17

Nicander, 86, 114, 131

Niccoli, Niccolo: development of Roman script, 140; and italic, 146

Nicholas V, Pope, 49

Nicholas of Lyra, Biblical commentary of, 13, 116, 241

Nijmegen, Rinaldus of, 19

Nonnus, unpublished fourth volume of *Poetae Christiani Veteres*, 149; Froben secures copy of, 270

Novara, Battle of, 161

Ockham, William of, 259

O'Fihely, Maurice, 164

Ognibene da Lonigo, 181

Orsini, Fulvio, 61 and 70, n. 53: 226

Ottomans, 7, 124, 128

Ovid, 32, 51, 63, 64: Aldine edition, 142, 143, 145, 146, 147, 204, 247, 278

— *Metamorphoses*: popularity of, 32; Rubeo's illustrated translation of, 33; Aldus' copy of 61: 65: 124, 125

— *Sappho and Ibis*, Calderini's commentaries on, 49

— *Fasti*, Celtis promises manuscripts of later books, 267

Oxford, early humanism in, 261, 305

— Corpus Christi College, 201: library of, 262

Pace, Richard, 260-1

Pacioli, Luca: *On the Divine Proportion*, 137

— *On Euclid's Elements*, 137

Padua, Marsiglius of, 283

— Peter of, 10

— University of, 9, 12: Law School and Venetian press, 22-3: 52, 78; development of Greek studies in, 79: 84, 85, 94, 114, 122, 134, 147; migration of scholars from, 164: 188; student life in, 190-1, 192; literary and poetic experiment in, 197-8, 199, 228; Cuno collects manuscripts in, 237; Linacre takes doctorate, 260; German students in, 263: 269, 271; Pirckheimer studies in, 274-5; Hungarian students in, 287: 289, 290, 306

Paganino de Paganinis, 13, 116, 241

Palladius (in *Scriptores Rerum Rusticarum*), 64

Pannartz Conrad: early editions in Rome, 13-14; and de Bussi, 24, 36, 50; and Roman style of printing, 136

Pannonius, John, 287-8

Paola, widow of John of Speyer, 18

Paris: and early printing, 7; visit of Pico to, 55; Aleander re-edits Plutarch in, 240; Amerbachs study in, 241, 269, 270: 279; Aleander and Fra Giocondo in, 281-3: 284, 290, 305

INDEX

Parma, Hilarius of, 96
Parrhasius, Janus: emendations to Virgilian *Catalepton*, 242-3: 248: 301
Paul II, Pope, 25, 49
Pausanias, 166, 242
Pavia, Battle of, 280
— Matteo of, 29
— Lorenzo da: on Aldine edition of Petrarch, 225-7
— university and city of, 15, 22, 54, 55, 274, 275, 287
Pellicier, Guillaume, and French Royal Library, 134, 285
Perotti, Niccolo, 97
Petrarch: 38; Aldus defends his text of, 65; Griffo edits, 88; influence on style of script, 136; Aldine edition, illuminated copies of, 146: 147; Bembo's editorship of, 158; Giuntine edition of, 158; a founder of Rialto School, 181; Aldus' access to autograph copy of, 218, 223, 225-7, 229, 240; criticism of his edition, 241, 248, 286, 302
Philostratus, 127, 144, 148, 237
Pia, Catherina, mother of Alberto Pio: Aldus' open letter to, 56-7, 58, 76, 192
Piccolomini, Francesco, later Pope Pius III: receives dedication of Letters of St. Catherine of Siena, 126
Pico della Mirandola, Gianfrancesco: and collection of Poliziano's works, 118; *Liber de Imaginatione*, 144, 223
Pico della Mirandola, Giovanni: early relationship with Aldus, and recommendation of him as tutor, 52, 53-6: Aldus' admiration for, 56: 58, 66, 74, 76, 141; and library of Giorgio Valla, 184; library of, 191; death of, 193; interest in Hebrew, 201: 223, 258; influence on Reuchlin, 264; studies in Paris, 282
Piero della Francesca, 137
Pierpoint Morgan Library: fragment of Aldine Athanaeus, 242; "Morgan Fragment" of Pliny's Letters, 245
Pincius, Philippus, 20, 28, 38
Pindar, Aldine edition of, 161, 162: Lorenzo Loredan's manuscript of, 187:

205; Roman edition of Callierges, 206; Bembo's manuscript of, 232; Aldine edition in Wittenberg library, 278
Piner, Peter, 97
Pio, Alberto: Aldus tutor to, 52, 56; artistic and intellectual patronage of, 58-9; and Aldine edition of Aristotle, 75; not directly involved in Aldine company, 75, 82; dedication of Lucretius, 111; at university of Ferrara, 115, 116: 127; buys Giorgio Valla's library, 134; advises Aldus on arrangements in 1509, 159; imperial ambassador in Venice, 164: 184; plans for an Academy, 195-6, 223; friendship with Linacre, 260; quarrel with Eramus, 300: 304
Pio, Giberto, cousin and rival of Alberto, 59
Pio, Lionello, brother of Alberto, 52, 55
Pirckheimer, Willibald: Cuno reports to, 86, and 102, n. 22; library of, 273-6; 280, 281, 306
Pisa, 106, 128
Pisani, Venetian noble family, neighbours of Aldus, 146
Pizzamano, Antonio, 191
Placidio Amerino, 194
Plantin, Christopher, 90
Planudes, Greek Anthology of: Alopa edition, 81, 134-5; autograph in Marciana, 230, 274
Plato: views on censorship, 32, 58, 66; Aldine edition of, 109, 111: 124, 158, 162, 163, 198; educational theories of *The Republic*, 201; dedication of Aldine edition to Leo X, 205: 242, 258, 262, 275, 278
Platter, Thomas, 8
Pliny the Elder: *Natural Histories* of, Italian translation, 15: 32; Sabellico comments on, 37, 50; Leoniceno's research on, 52, 57: 64, 95, 114, 183, 188, 189
Pliny the Younger: Aldine edition of, 151; and Paris manuscript, 244-5; 290, 302
Plutarch, 32, 115, 151, 158: Aldine edition and Ambrosian manuscript,

Plutarch *(cont.)*
239–40, 246: 262, 275; in Wittenberg library, 278; new edition of Aleander, 283: 286
Poggio, Florentine Histories of, 14: 38; and humanistic script, 136
Poitiers, Diane de, 285
Pole, Reginald, 260
Poliziano, Angelo: *Miscellanea*, 30; letter of Aldus to, 53–4; *Silvae*, 54; *Enchiridion Epicteti*, 55: 56, 57; views on printing, 58: 60, 66, 73; unable to visit Marciana, 74: 76; Aldine edition of *Opera Omnia*, 113, 118, 135; respects Brugnolo, 182; visits Valla's library, 184: 187; visits Bembo's library, 188; and Cassandra Fedele, 189: 191; death of, 193: 202, 205, 217, 220, 231, 232, 233, 243; interest in palaeography, 248: 258; English students of, 259; sale of *Opera* by Amerbach, 270; *Opera* purchased for Wittenberg library, 278: 281, 302
Pollux, 127, 277
Pomponazzi, Piero, 23, 274
Poncher, Etienne, 284
Pontano, Giangiovano, 162, 163: Academy of, 195, 196, 197; *Urania*, 200: 201; Aldine edition of his poems, 221–2: 248, 278
Porcari, Roman noble family, 37
Pordenone, 159
Porphyrius, 237
Poznań, 197, 289–90
Priapus, 123
Priscian, 64
Proclus, 167: n. 4
Proctor, Robert, 81: on Aldine types, 130–1
Procuratori di San Marco, 68, 69
Propertius, 49, 158
Proveditori sopra la sanità, 119
Prudentius (in *Poetae Christiani Veteres*), 64, 148: manuscripts of, 243, 263
Ptolemy, 183, 184

Querini, Vicenzo, 137, 190, 205
— Zuane, 182

Quintilian: edition of Calderini, 49: 50, 57; Navagero edits, 204, 233, 247

Rabelais, François, 120
Racine, Jean, 300
Raibolini, Francesco, 87
Ratisbon, Leonardus of, 17
Rauchfass, Johan, 11: partnership with Jenson, 17, 18: 87
Ravenna, Aldus visits, 160
— Battle of, 161, 203, 204, 277
Regius, Raphael: quarrel with Calfurnio, 60; leaves Padua for Venice, 164; at School of San Marco, 182; on spread of books, 188: 192; possible successor to Valla as lecturer in Venice, 194; friend of Lubranski at Padua, 197, 287
Renier, Daniel: interlocutor in *De Latinae Linguæ Reparatione*, 36; at School of San Marco, 182: 192; lost library, 233
Renouard, Augustin, 155, 231, 300
Reuchlin, Johan, 97: oration published by Aldus, 113, 117; visit to Aldus, 195; plans to bring Aldus to Empire, 199, 223: 259; teaches in Heidelberg, 264: 266: 267, 269, 273, 274, 279, 302, 305
Rhetorica ad Herennium, Aldine edition of, 162, 165–6, 206
Rhosos, John, 187, 196
Ricci, Pietro (Crinitus): editorial work on Poliziano's *Opera*, 118; *Lives of the Poets*, 158; emendations to Virgil, 243, 245: 301
Ripoli, San Jacopo di, 15
Rome: Aldus' early education in, 48–51, 53, 55, 57; mission of Reuchlin to, 117; intellectual life in, 193, 195: 244
Rosetto, Francesco, 196
Rubeo, Giovanni, and Ovid's *Metamorphoses*, 32, 124, 125

Sabellico, Marcantonio, 24: Latin lecturer and historian in Venice, 28–9, 30; *De Latinae Linguae Reparatione*, 36–7, 38: 49, 51, 60; Torresani edits, 78; teaching in

Sabellico, Marcantonio *(cont.)*
Venice, 181–3; quarrel with Egnazio, 185: 187, 188–9, 192; promoted after Valla's death, 194; illness and death, 195: 219, 220; librarian of Marciana, 230: 269, 304
St. Paul's School, 182, 262
Sallust, 146, 159, 282
Salutati, Coluccio, 32
San Cipriano, monastery of, 26
Sandeis, Felino, 119
San Giovanni e Paolo, Dominican house of, 121, 122: modern Civic Hospital, 76
San Marco, School of, 20, 36, 181, 187, 198, 204; Scuola grande di, 75–6
Sannazaro, Jacopo, 65, 148, 163, 164: hesitation on publication of his works, 221, 227, 229, 248
San Paternian, Venetian parish, centre of printing industry, 8, 92, 153
San Polo, sestiere of Venice, 92
Sansovino, Jacopo, 231
Sant' Agostino, site of Aldus' first print-shop, 92–4, 98; Aldus leaves, 153: 193, 195, 198, 200
Sanudo, Marin the Younger, diarist and bibliophile; his library, 8; neighbour of Aldus, 95; customer of Jordan von Dinslaken, 97; Aldus' dedications to, 146, 147; on Venetian cultural life during wars of League of Cambrai, 164; on education in Venice, 180, 185; on university of Padua, 190: 195
San Vito, Bartolomeo di, probable designer of Aldine italic fount, 141
San Zulian, Venetian parish, centre of printing industry, 8: Benedetto Bordone has workshop in, 122
Sapienza, University of Rome, 49
Sarti, Alessandro, and edition of Poliziano's *Opera*, 118, 220
Savonarola, Gerolamo, 218
Saxony, Elector Frederick the Wise of: writes to Aldus, 276, 306
Schenk, Burkhard, 278
Schlettstadt, 269
Scholderer, Victor, 18, 20, 87

Scita, Giambattista: early colleague of Aldus, 55; briefly public lecturer in Venice, 194
Scotto, Amadeo, 16, 17, 85
Scotus, Duns, 259
Sedulius, in *Poetae Christiani Veteres*, 148
Sellyng, William, 259
Sicherl, Martin, 234, 236, 237
Sidney, Sir Philip, 120
Siena, 160, 204
— St. Catherine of, Works of: Aldus pays deposit on manuscripts of, 99; as atonement for *Polifilo*, 113, 125: 135; first use of italic type, 137: 154
Signori di Notte, 12; and the press, 155; case against Filippo Giunti, 156
Silius Italicus, 233
Smyrna, Quintus of, 231, 233
Soardis, Lazzaro di, 142
Socrates, 34
Soncino, Gerolamo, and Francesco Griffo, 88–90, 241
Sophocles, 65: last distinct Aldine fount, 89, 131: 142, 151; Valla's manuscript of, 183; colophon of, 196; press-copies of, 238–9: 262; Racine's copy of, 300
Spain, participation of in Holy League, 160: early Greek typography in, 161; Aldus' influence in, 286–7
Speigel, Jacob, 200
Spieshammer, Johan, 199, 201: and Aldine Valerius Maximus, 267–8; 274
Speyer, John of, first printer in Venice, 7, 18, 38
— Windelin of, brother and successor of the above, 7, 18: and Merula, 28: 38; Roman types of, 136
Spinelli, Giambattista, 286
Squarciafico, Hironimo: comments on press, 29, 31, 36, 37, 192, 219
Stagnino, Bernardino, 16
Statius, 48, 49, 51, 142, 144, 222
Stephanus, 115, 249
Strabo, 32
Strozzi, Tito and Ercole, Latin poets, Florentine exiles in Ferrara, 162, 164, 223

Strozzi, Gerolamo, 14–15, 16
— Palla, 235
Suardo, Suardino, 222
Subiaco, first press-centre in Italy, 41 n. 7, 50
Suda, the (Suidas), 115: Milanese edition, 127: 242
Suetonius, 32, 37, 64, 183
Suleiman the Magnificent, 288
Suliardes, Michael, 184
Summonte, Pietro: and edition of Sannazaro, 221–2, 228, 248
Sweynheim, Arnold, early editions in Rome, 13–14: and de Bussi, 24, 36, 50; and Roman style of printing, 136
Symmachus, 64
Szatmari, Gyorgy, 287

Tacuinus, Johannes, 20, 22, 38: success during 1490s, 124, and 171, n. 59: 129, 186
Talenti, Tomaso: and Rialto School, 181
Tanai, Bernardo and Neri di: sponsor first edition of Homer, 81
Tartagni, Alessandro, 23
Terence, 64: Bembo's manuscript of, 232: Erasmus works on Aldine text of, 242; 247; 1521 edition dedicated to Grolier, 280: 281
Theocritus, 48, 50, 51: edition dedicated to Battista Guarino, 53; Urceus lectures on, 79; Milanese first edition of, 81; Aldine edition of, 112, 114, 131, 135; Valla's manuscript of, 183; Urceus advises Aldus on text of, 192; two issues of Aldine text, 233–4; Trithemius buys Aldine text, 266; Pirckheimer's copy illuminated by Dürer, 275; early Parisian edition of, 284
Theognis, 184
Theon, (in *Astronomici Veteres*), 111
Theophrastus: Aldus' problems with manuscript of, 231, 233; Paris and Harvard manuscripts of, 235–8; More's joke about, 262: 266, 268

Thesaurus Cornucopiae, Aldine edition of *Grammatici Veteres*, 72, 112, 114
Thucydides, Aldine edition of, 142, 151, 258, 262, 275, 278
Thurz, Sigismund: on Aldine octavos, 146, 147; studies at Padua, 287; and Polish humanism, 288: 302
Tibullus, 32, 158
Tiepolo, Nicolo, 190
Tissard, François: and Greek lectures in Paris, 270; and early Greek typography in Paris, 282–3
Tiziano (Titian), and *Hypnerotomachia Polifili*, 124
Torresani, Andrea, 8: and Jenson's types, 10: 17; legal and philosophical texts, 22–3: 28, 38; Aldus' meeting with, 76; character as described by Erasmus, 76–8; supporting Aldus, 78–82; partnership with Aldus and Barbarigo, 82–6, 91; shop near Rialto, 92, 97; edition of Averroes, 111; growing interference after 1503, 152–3; plans to save property during war, 159, 160; successor to Aldus, 166–7, 192, 200; edition of Terence, 242, 258, 269; completes order for Wittenberg library, 278: 280, 304
Torresani, Federigo, son of Andrea, 77
— Gianfrancesco, son of Andrea, 111, 135, 236
— Maria, daughter of Andrea, wife of Aldus, 92, 153
Tory, Geoffroy, *Le Champ Fleury*, 284–5
Tose, William, 15
Traversari, Ambrogio, 49
Trebizond, George of, 181, 185–6
Treviso, 120, 122
Trithemius, Johannes, abbot of Sponheim, 264: library of, 266
Troth, Barthélemy, 156
Tudor, Arthur, Prince of Wales, 261
Tunstall, Cuthbert, 223, 260–1

Uglheimer, Margherita, widow of Peter, 125
— Peter, 18

Urbanus, Henry, 198, 277
Urbino, 193, 243
Urceus, Antonius Codrus, lecturer in classical literature at Bologna, 30: period of study at Ferrara, 53: 63, 74, 79; on price of Aldine Greek texts, 116 and 168, n. 21; correspondence with Aldus, 191-2: 219; mistrusts Aldus' textual accuracy, 240; teacher of Constanzo Claretti, 289: 300, 304

Valdezocco, Bartolomeo, 17, 77, 85
Valeriani, Giampietro, 186, 190-1, 197
— Fra Urbano, Franciscan, teacher of Greek in Venice, 79-80, 82; status in Franciscan Order, 121: 184: 186; secretary to Andrea Gritti, 187; tutor to future Pope Leo X, 205; Erasmus' tribute to, 228; lost manuscript of Homer, 232
— *Institutiones Grammaticae Graecae*, 112, 114: cost of, 115; commissioned by Aldus, 220, who sends a copy to Celtis as a gift, 265, 267; copy owned by Froben and the Amerbachs, 270; reprinted in Paris, 284
Valerius Maximus, 20, 32, 37, 143, 145, 148, 183; Aldine edition dedicated to John Lubranski, 197; Spiesshammer sends new sections of, 268: 288
Valla, Gianpietro, 220
Valla, Giorgio: lecturer in Venice, 30; possible study in Ferrara, 53; library purchased by Alberto Pio, 59: 79, 82; friend of Benedetti, 117, 121: 134; teaching and scribal circle, 181-4, 187, 188-9; and Aldus, 191-3; arrest and death, 194-5, 198: 202, 204, 218, 219-20, 223-4, 232, 233, 236
— *De Expetendis et Fugiendis Rebus*, 144, 183, 219-20, 278
Valla, Lorenzo, 37, 38
Varano, Fabrizio, 242
Vatican, Library of, 26, 61, 87, 224, 304

Vellutello, Alessandro, 241
Vendramin, Venetian noble family, 186
Venice: expansion of printing in, 7-8: Corvus of, 11; galley fleets of, 15; demand for books in, 15-16; reading habits in, 20-3; production of Bibles in, 34; war with Ferrara, 52, 53; Aldus in, 58, 72 f; cultural life in c. 1490, 72-3; prosperity of, 75-6; early Greek studies in, 79-80; war with League of Cambrai, 110; alliance with France, 117; war with Turks, 124-5; economic crisis, 1499, 127-8, and consequent depression in printing, 129; visit of Luca Pacioli, 137; Aldus leaves, 153, 159; joins Holy League, 160-1; misfortunes in 1513, 161; cultural life during wars, 164; public education in, 180-4; intellectual life c. 1500, 194-5, 228, 237; English scholars in, 260; German merchants in, 263, 274; trade with Basel, 269; and Wittenberg library, 278: 302, 303, 304
Vercelli, Bernardino da, 221
Vernia, Niccoletto, 111
Verona, Gaspare da, teacher in Rome: possible influence on Aldus, 48-9, 50, 51
Vettori, Francesco, 156
Viaro, Francesco, 9
Vicenza, city of, 81
— Reno da, 80
Vienna, 201: early Greek studies in, 266-7: 279, 289, 290, 302
Villedieu, Alexander of, *Doctrinale*, 62-3
Virgil, 20, 32, 62, 64, 88: first of the Aldine octavos, 137, 142, 144; praised by Thurz, 147; new edition, 152: 155; Giuntine edition, 158; Navagero's work on, 204; *Catalepton*, 242; "Codex Mediceus", 243: 248, 267, 278
Viterbo, 37
Vitruvius, 183, 189, 282
Vlastos, Nicholas: underwriter of Callierges press, 128; copies manuscript, 184: 195
Voragine, Jacopo de', 117
Vyrthesi, Janus, 165

Wacker, Johan, 264
Wimpfeling, Jakob, 269
Wissemburg, Abbey of, 95
Wittenberg, University of, 276–8, 306

Xenophon, 142, 151, 258, 277
Ximenes de Cisneros, 201, 262, 286

Zanoti, Antonio di, 143
Zorzi, Bernardo, 198
Zebrzydowski, Andrej, 289
Zen, Jacopo, 23
Zeno, Apostolo, 300
Zorzi, Lorenzo, 20